AF608253

The Excavations at Ancient Halieis

Volume 2

The Excavations at Ancient Halieis

Conducted by the University of Pennsylvania and Indiana University
Porto Kheli, Greece

– Volume 2 –

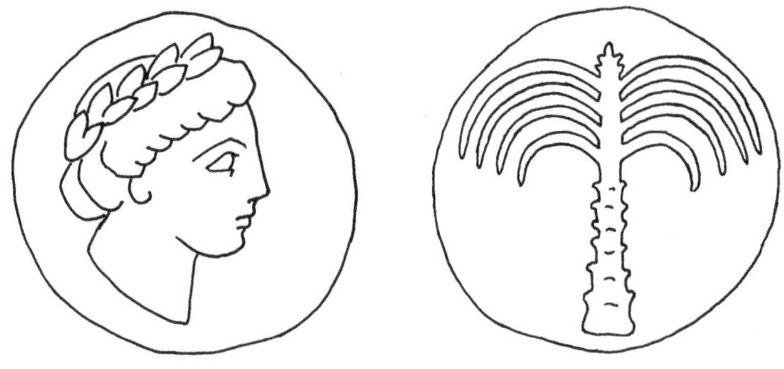

Halieis Publication Committee
Michael H. Jameson
Marian H. McAllister
Wolf W. Rudolph
James A. Dengate

Coordinating Editor, Christina F. Dengate

The Houses

The Organization and Use of Domestic Space

Bradley A. Ault

Indiana University Press
Bloomington & Indianapolis

The publication of this book has been supported
by the E. A. Schrader Fund,
Indiana University Foundation.

This book is a publication of

Indiana University Press
601 North Morton Street
Bloomington, IN 47404-3797 USA

http://iupress.indiana.edu

Telephone orders 800-842-6796
Fax orders 812-855-7931
Orders by e-mail iuporder@indiana.edu

The paper used in this publication meets the minimum requirements of American National Standard for Information Sciences—Permanence of Paper for Printed Library Materials, ANSI Z39.48-1984.

Manufactured in the United States of America

Library of Congress Cataloging-in-Publication Data

Excavations at ancient Halieis.
v. cm.
Includes bibliographical references and indexes.
Contents: v. 1. The fortifications and adjacent structures / Marian H. McAllister ; with contributions by Michael H. Jameson, James A. Dengate, and Frederick A. Cooper — v. 2. The houses : the organization and use of domestic space / Bradley A. Ault.
ISBN 0-253-34710-6 (cloth : v. 1 : alk. paper) — ISBN 0-253-34709-2 (cloth : v. 2 : alk. paper)
1. Halieis (Extinct city)—Buildings, structures, etc. 2. Excavations (Archaeology)—Greece—Portokhélion. 3. Portokhélion (Greece) —Antiquities. I. McAllister, Marian Holland.
DF261.H25E93 2005
623'.19388—dc22

2005018886

1 2 3 4 5 10 09 08 07 06 05

Designed and set by Anne & Christopher Chippindale,
Cambridge, England

For Christian William Ault
and Lizabeth to Whom I Owe So Much

Contents

Tables

Illustrations

Figures

Plates

Foreword

WOLF W. RUDOLPH

This book presents a view of the complexity of households and housing structures at a small polis in the Southern Argolid in the 4th century B.C.E.[1] Halieis was a common enough community of those days without much weight in the politics of the times, located between two Classical superpowers. But the archaeological discoveries made there, accompanied by auspicious circumstances of preservation, have made it possible to approach the topic on an unusually broad basis. What is shown here is the reading of as complete a context as possible, accomplished through a particular methodology.

To understand the research outlook that created this volume, one has to remember that not just the reading of a context uncovered has undergone many changes since the beginning of field archaeology in Classical lands, especially during the last two generations. It also has to be recalled that it took a long time to arrive at even the recognition of the existence of the phenomenon "context" as understood in modern scholarship. The most convenient and easiest road to an archaeological interpretation has long been via individual types of materials. These, be it Classical pottery for one or sculpture for another and likewise architecture and to a lesser extent the miniature world of gems, coins, and so forth, carried a hierarchic ranking in the world of Classical archaeology/art history. And additionally, such "nice" artifacts always have represented something simple, understandable, and tangible; they have been the catalysts for building connections between the viewers present and the distant past. This narrow view has been strictly abandoned in the present volume.

One of the first to see beyond such individual strands of typologically grouped artifacts, especially members of the "high arts," was Heinrich Schliemann who for his excavations in Troy assembled specialists from many disciplines in order to arrive at the broadest possible base for interpretation. He was, in a way, the forerunner of modern field archaeology, since his interest was fueled by everything reflecting human activities. He was also keen on adding to the repertoire of the historian, fixated on written records, the *archaeological* record that, although silent at first, could answer questions if made legible and interrogated from the right perspective.

His approach was the appropriate one because, when putting spade to Troy, Schliemann was setting out to unveil a historical event that was the final result of numerous processes executed by humans. Confirmation of the right choice of place—Ilios or Troy—came for him early on in the top levels of excavations with inscriptions and other tokens of the Hellenistic period. But Ilios, this top-level Trojan city, was but a layer for him to pass on the road to prehistory—his real goal lay deep down in the "City of Priam," a place he thought would yield an explanation to the riddles told by Homer.

Since Schliemann's time excavations of towns in the Classical world have been relatively few, especially in Greece.[2] But with the advent of

[1] Because this is the first volume of the Lower Town excavations, it is only fitting to stress the contributions of two longtime collaborators of the Halieis staff and to evoke the memories of Jane Hackbarth Leslie (d. 1999) and Birgitte Rafn (d. 1997). Their work will be outlined in detail in the appropriate volumes.

[2] For a survey, see Wolfram Hoepfner and Ernst-Ludwig Schwandner, *Haus und Stadt im klassischen Griechenland.* Wohnen in der klassischen Polis, 1 (Munich, 1986), 11. (Note: This author does not share the view that the foundation of Halieis took place in the 6th century B.C.E. It happened earlier.)

surveys in particular regions during the 1970s greater attention has been paid not only to the existence and recording of settlements large and small. More important, one began to understand them as human-made organisms, interacting with their surroundings and as parts of larger, complex systems that in and of themselves deserved attention to understand the sequences of events as well as the human habits and rituals that might once have created and governed them.

This required a different set of attitudes concerning the nature of archaeology and the classical idea. It demanded going further in evaluating materials than previous excavations such as at the Athenian Agora (since 1930) or at Olynthos (1928–1938) had done. Therefore it turned out to be a fortuitous circumstance that, unlike Olynthos and the Athenian Agora, the site of Halieis at Porto Cheli was archaeologically a virtual nonentity without any history to speak of since its abandonment. Remains were to be seen and had been visited as early as 1838 by the British Royal Navy. And while, as for the Agora and Olynthos, historical records existed, they were feeble and ambiguous.

The finding of an inscription in Athens served as catalyst for the ensuing major exploration at Halieis.[3] But once begun, the historian's point of view and dedicated interest had to address the realities of the archaeological site. Consequently, a different research perspective began to be developed from the late 1960s in collaboration with excavations at Franchthi Cave. When it was decided that the fortified town of Halieis was to be considered as but one part in exploring the puzzle of the entire Southern Argolid, a new investigative outlook was set in motion. It served the situation better, since no more than a faint echo of Halieis's existence had come into the history books and the polis had left no recorded primary voice from within her chora. A narrative history in the traditional sense could not be written and had to be reconstructed by changing classes of evidence and by relying fully on the archaeological context. Because, to arrive at a narrative at all, one had to concede that this polis's historic position and source materials required that alternative, that is, archaeological, sources must therefore be decoded for this purpose.

What made the methodological approach, demonstrated in the current volume, possible was the particular nature of the site. Founded ca. 700/680 B.C.E., Halieis existed as a polis into the early 3d century and then lay abandoned for some seven hundred years. The ensuing Late Roman, early Byzantine reuse of the site was slight, leaving the remains of the principal *floruit* period of the 4th century B.C. more or less intact. Deep plowing had not disturbed the layers located close to the surface, and practically no houses had been constructed over the site. The recovery process was based upon a detailed approach to information retrieval, producing as exact as possible a reflection of what was in the ground and of its interconnections. As a consequence, it became possible to pursue the creation of a more accurate picture of the city's diachronic life, incorporating cultural, economic, and environmental questions as well as methods to try to gain insights into sociological complexities that might have governed such an ancient town.

To interpret the site's life, the combination of finds, the traces and artifacts in their associations and assemblages in the ground were translated into clusters and numbers. This created understandable larger patterns that were formed into the foundation upon which the analysis was built. The reading of any single find's information was granted only a relative value in comparison to others. The procedure itself required a detailed study of the individual artifactual assemblages by location. This is possible, because every item was noted, nothing was discarded before being recorded. If discard took place, it happened only after a second in-depth check for joins and any other traces of information possibly overlooked. This method allows us to contemplate the mechanics—intentional or unintentional, human or natural as they might have been—of the "team work" that produced the patterns of finds in the ground.

This combinatory approach is fitting, because the archaeological record supports only one interpretation: the polis of Halieis was built on a foundation of mutual, internal understanding and agreement of its citizens. Otherwise the walls, the streets, the houses, the mint, the sanctuaries, and the cemetery would not have been built. From the silent archaeological record, the knowledge

[3] Treaty with Athens 424/23 B.C.E. *IG* I², 87+(= I³, 75). See M. H. Jameson, "Excavations at Porto Cheli and Vicinity, Preliminary Report I: Halieis, 1962–1968," *Hesperia* 38 (1969): 314, n. 10.

can be gleaned that in an Early Archaic society a political organism created its physical environment by relying on the interaction of all participants for their own good and for that of their city. Therefore, taking the finds as tokens of human activities, it becomes possible to question aspects of the daily life of the anonymous human populus in a small Greek country town of the Classical period.

Publication of artifactual documentation normally comes first in an excavation's publications efforts. But the enthusiasm of the author and his long commitment to topics domestic in general[4] and to Halieis in particular made it possible to present this volume now. His free access to the data structures that have been at the heart of the work in the Lower Town of Halieis has paid off, in that Bradley Ault has drawn attention as to how the body of material evidence can be read as a shadow picture of the existence of the "koinotis Halieon" within her city. The study on the "Organization and Use of Domestic Space" at Halieis represents an effort at bringing together the two adamantly opposing poles of any archaeological endeavor: the static nature of the finds, often poured into the molds of equally static catalogs, and the fluid, multitudinous flow of a past daily life. Fine-tuning one's modern sensibilities and looking beyond the mere statistics of the Halieis record presented here, it emerges that human behaviors now and then liked to oscillate between established routines and exceptions from the same. At the same time, this study represents a first necessary step toward the creation of metadata[5] that is intended to make the work at the Lower Town of Halieis available for broader, comparative studies that deal with the development of town and country in the ancient world.

[4] See, for instance, Bradley A. Ault, "*Koprones* and Oil Presses at Halieis: Interactions of Town and Country and the Integration of Domestic and Regional Economies," *Hesperia* 68 (1999): 549–73.

[5] On this topic and its impact, see Kim H. Veltman, "New Media and Transformation in Knowledge I and II," in C. Gemmer, H. John, and H. Krämer, eds., *Euphorie digital? Aspekte der Wissensvermittlung in Kunst, Kultur und Technologie,* Publication der Abteilung Museumsberatung, 10 (Bielefeld: Landschaftsverband Rheinland, Heinz Nixdorf MuseumsForum, 2001), 35–68, 131–66. On metadata, see ibid., 155, n. 5: <http://204.254.77.2/bulletinsuk/212e-1a6.htm> and others.

Acknowledgments

Many individuals have contributed in a multitude of ways to the furthering and completion of this work. I would like to thank them here, while at the same time absolving them of any responsibility for the inevitable shortcomings that remain. Michael Jameson and Virginia Jameson take pride of place for what amounts to their "rediscovery" of Halieis and for all they have done to foster its discovery by others, myself included. Christina Dengate has provided outstanding editorial guidance at every step of the way, assisting me to transform a doctoral dissertation into a monograph. James Dengate and Marian McAllister have also been extremely helpful in many matters of content and presentation. In Wolf Rudolph I have had a mentor, a Doktorvatter, a friend, and a colleague. To the Program in Classical Archaeology at Indiana University, which provided my home base for a number of years, my fellow students and the faculty there, I am truly grateful. The successive directors, Thomas W. Jacobsen and Karen D. Vitelli, provided a constant source of support and inspiration. Currently, at Indiana University, Bradley Cook of the Indiana University Archives has been unflagging in his concern for the well being of the Halieis archive and making it accessible for consultation. The American School of Classical Studies at Athens has been most supportive of my past and ongoing interests in Halieis. In Germany, I have also repeatedly benefited from the good will and kindnesses offered to me by Wolfram Hoepfner and Ernst-Ludwig Schwandner. I am extremely grateful to Nicholas Cahill for reading my manuscript and for his extensive comments about it. Lisa Nevett has also given freely of her expertise in matters of ancient housing and households over the course of our long and ongoing friendship. At the University at Buffalo I have benefited from a number of outstanding colleagues and many fine students. Stephen L. Dyson, Park Professor of the Humanities, has been critical to so many phases of my career, and funds provided by the Park Professorship have facilitated the production of this work, especially its illustrations. These are the result of many hours of labor by a number of individuals. The original field photographs reproduced here are the work of Reg Heron. Balloon photography in Areas 6 and 7 was conducted by Wil Myers and Elly Myers. The house plans, upon which my own are based, were drawn by Thomas Boyd. The site plan (Fig. 1) has been revised by Marian McAllister, from the original done by herself, Frederick Cooper, Nancy Kelly, and Thomas Boyd. More recently, in the process of transferring all images to digital format, Gerry Shiela, Gary Devore, Danya Diab, Cindi Tysick, and Sandra Boero-Imwinkelreid, have all made important contributions. Margie Towery prepared the index. I would especially like to thank Marian McAllister for her reconstruction drawings of Houses 7, A, D, and E.

Finally, I would like to acknowledge the trench supervisors who oversaw the excavation of the domestic architecture in the Lower Town from 1974 through 1976. These include James Bennett, Janice Bennett, Thomas Boyd, Loreen Boyle, Diana Bowler, Philippa Buhayar, Irme Cuadros, Tracey Cullen, Clarissa Culling, Jeff Danielson, Gregory Elftman, John Elliott, Michalis Fotiades, Stockton Garver, Katherine Gay, Jane Graham, Pat Gyenes, Debbie Hester, Louis Jerkich, Else Jones, Donald Keller, Susan Langdon, Dianne Frost-Larsen, Jane Leslie, Brian MacDonald, Rita Michael, Priscilla Murray, Douglas Orr, Jan Østergaard, Helen Papoulias, Karl Petruso, Nancy Petruso, Diane Price, Birgitte Rafn, Curtis Runnels, David Rupp, Helmut Shade, Leslie Simon, Lone Wriedt Sørensen. Omission of some names here is inevitable, as well as regrettable.

The Excavations at Ancient Halieis

Volume 2

– CHAPTER ONE –

Introduction to the Site and Methodology

> Dead archaeology is the driest dust that blows.
>
> —Mortimer Wheeler

This volume in the series *The Excavations at Ancient Halieis* is devoted primarily to the houses and associated artifact assemblages recovered in the eastern half of the lower town in 1974, 1975, and 1976 (Fig. 1).[1] These houses, as well as their excavated contents, date in the main to the latest phase of occupation at Halieis, during the 4th century (Level A–Level B).[2] This material is, in addition, directed at a more general exploration of the ancient Greek house, household, and the domestic economy. Although grounded in the archaeology of the household and its contents, this study includes supporting evidence ranging from the primary textual sources to artistic and ethnographic comparanda.

The history of the site and the excavations are discussed in the third Halieis volume (C. Dengate et al., n.d.). The fortifications are the subject of volume 1 (McAllister 2005), which includes a study of the city mint and coinage (J. A. Dengate in McAllister 2005). The principle pottery study is being undertaken by Rudolph (forthcoming). Other aspects of Halieis's topography, architecture, and specialized treatments of classes of artifacts recovered there will be the subject of additional volumes in this series.[3]

This work aims not only to describe the remains but also to provide a synthesis of the primary archaeological data. It is not intended to be a detailed architectural study but an analysis of the use of domestic space in a few well-excavated houses that seem to be typical of Classical dwellings at Halieis and elsewhere. Similarly, the findings presented here are made in advance of the main publication of the pottery. This can be done since preliminary study has shown that the pottery from 4th-century Halieis is consistent with and compares closely to established sequences for Attic and other wares. Ultimately, the intent of this work is to serve as social-historical as well as archaeological documentation. In keeping with this goal, I attempt here to place it within the intellectual milieu of the discipline and within the more specialized area of studies of Greek domestic architecture and household organization.

Studia Domestica: Background and Foreground

Many of the earliest monumental scholarly undertakings of archaeology in general and classical archaeology in particular were at least in part dedicated to examining domestic themes

[1] Only the most completely recovered houses and their assemblages are treated in detail. Although Area 6 and the partially excavated houses in Area 7 are described briefly, owing to limited horizontal exposure of these houses no attempt has been made to analyze the associated artifact assemblages.

[2] For the chronological scheme employed during the excavations of the lower town at Halieis, as well as the areal designations of the site, see Boyd and Rudolph 1978, 333–37. Rudolph (1984, 136–45) presents some revision to the chronology. For the chronology of the Halieis acropolis, see C. Dengate et al., n.d., chap. 1.

[3] For general surveys of the history and archaeology of Halieis and the southern Argolid, see van Andel and Runnels 1987; Ault 1994, 23–59; Bölte 1912; Boyd and Jameson 1981; Boyd and Rudolph 1978; Jameson 1969; and Jameson, Runnels, and van Andel 1994, esp. 57–148. Bibliographies listing preliminary reports for the Halieis excavations may be found in Foley 1988, 194; Jameson 1969, 313, n. 3; Rudolph 1984, 123, n. 1, and C. Dengate et al., n.d.

under the guise of daily or private life (the *Alltagsleben, vie privée* or *quotidienne* of Continental Altertumswissenschaft).[4] These collections culled a great deal of information. While comprising primarily literary and artistic sources, some actual archaeological evidence (mainly artifacts and materials illustrating iconography) was incorporated. Such corpora continue to constitute major resources in the discipline. But we now have access to recent developments in the social sciences and humanities, especially those in archaeological methodology, upon which this study relies heavily.

In the meantime, numerous popular and semipopular accounts have appeared that are cast generally as explorations of "daily life in ancient times."[5] And while these recurrent variations on old themes have, in turn, succeeded in abridging and updating (and thereby making more accessible) their distinguished forebears, they have not often gone much beyond them. Frequently, too, they perpetuate antiquated approaches to the subject or restate demonstrable fallacies.[6]

This is not surprising. For despite broad advances made generally in the field of archaeology, classical archaeology is still seen as a bastion of conservative scholarship, caring little for what its kindred practitioners working in prehistoric, or even in other historical periods, have accomplished. This gulf, or "great divide," as it has come to be called, between the "great tradition" of classical archaeology and all other archaeologies has received much attention. In 1967 S. C. Humphreys issued an unprecedented manifesto, lauding the contribution that archaeology could make to classical scholarship. Since then a number of scholars have acted as proverbial gadflies, stinging classical archaeology for its insular behavior, while also singling out for praise those among its ranks (not a few in number) who have increasingly opted for more ambitious research designs and results.[7] Humphreys's article appeared at the height of the tumult created by the "new" anthropological approach to prehistoric archaeology in the United States and Britain. Also known as "processual archaeology," this approach emphasized rigorous methodology and lawlike proclamations as interpretation. But what Humphreys and others have advocated is something more fluid and less particular, open to interpretation on multiple levels. This newer archaeology has come to be known as "post-processual."[8] While I have tried to eschew the jargon of theory in what follows, given the concerns of this work with the relationship between architecture, artifacts, behavior, and ideology, it is decidedly post-processual.[9]

Much of the current research and publication in classical archaeology goes beyond the positivist tendency of excavating monuments simply because they are monumental or believed to have connections with historical persons or events. Especially productive work is being carried out in the areas of Aegean prehistory, provincial Roman studies, and regional survey projects all over the Mediterranean.[10] Nevertheless, the study of Classical Greek houses and households until recently occupied a lacuna in the coverage of the discipline, a subject more neglected than anything else.[11] And while, taken all together, there have been many houses excavated at numerous sites, relatively few have been

[4] E.g., Baumeister 1885–1889, Daremberg and Saglio 1877–1919, and Wissowa and Kroll 1893–.

[5] E.g., Pope 1976; Quennell and Quennell 1931a, 1931b; Webster 1969.

[6] A superior recent contribution is provided by Garland 1998.

[7] Humphreys 1967. Cf. Dyson 1981, 1989a, 1989b, 1993, 1998, 1999; Grant 1990 (esp. 172–75); Morris 1994a; Renfrew 1980; Shanks 1996; Snodgrass 1985, 1988 (esp. 1–35). Spencer (1995) offers commentary upon and case studies that aim to span this divide.

[8] Although the term "post-processualist" and its attendant doctrine are associated with Hodder (e.g., 1991), Humphreys's work (1967) presaged Hodder's by nearly twenty years. In this regard, she could be considered "pre"-post-processualist. In addition to and as part of Hodder's affiliation with post-processualism, a portion of his work has been devoted to the archaeology of domesticity. In *The Domestication of Europe* (Hodder 1990), the rise of the "domus concept" in the Neolithic is seen as a crystallizing moment on the road to civilized society. In this study I advocate a similarly central role for the Greek household.

[9] The oft-cited battle cry (or mantra) for the new archaeology was "archaeology as anthropology." Taken from the title of a seminal article by Binford (1962), high priest of processual archaeology, it in turn originated in Willey and Phillips's statement that "American archaeology is anthropology or it is nothing" (1958, 2). It is worth comparing this with Flannery's rejoinder, "Fellows, if it is evolution you are interested in, anthropology is archaeology or it is nothing" (cited in Renfrew 1980, 295). Indeed, a paraphrase of the latter is appropriate vis-à-vis the discipline of classics and archaeology as well.

[10] Additional interconnections (see note 7 above) are the association of Renfrew with Aegean prehistory, of Dyson with the Roman provinces, and that, along with Snodgrass, all three are major proponents and practitioners of archaeological survey work.

[11] Among the most prominent surveys and synthetic works to appear recently are: Barr-Sharrar 1988; D'Andria and Mannino 1996; Dvorsky-Rohner 1995; Hoepfner 1999c; Hoepfner and Schwandner 1994; Isler and Käch 1997; Jameson 1990a, 1990b, 1996; Kiderlen 1995, 1996; F. Lang 1996; McKay 1988; Morris 1998a; Nevett 1992, 1995b, 1999; Pesando 1987, 1989; Tsakirgis 1996; Walter-Karydi 1994, 1996, 1998.

analyzed in great detail.[12] Even fewer have received any systematic treatment of artifact assemblages that were recovered in the course of excavation.[13] There has been little discussion of household organization, that is, the domestic economy (or economies), and almost no employment whatsoever of excavated remains in any discourse.[14] Finally, while our museums and libraries are filled with objects of and publications devoted to classes of material best defined as "popular art," there is little treatment of them in terms of the domestic context for which they were created and in which they once functioned.[15]

In short, the traditional approach of classical archaeology to the Greek house has concentrated on the recovery of ground plans, often as a by-product of the search for intrinsically and aesthetically interesting finds, with other artifacts used primarily for dating purposes. And while domestic architecture could illustrate select literary sources on any number of points, there was little else thought to be gained from its study. Indicative of the situation is the fact that eighty-four years elapsed between the appearance of the only two English-language monographs to explicitly provide synthetic discussion of the Greek house, B. C. Rider's *The Greek House* (1915) and L. C. Nevett's *House and Society in the Ancient Greek World* (1999).[16] Happily, a comparison of the two demonstrates both quantitative and qualitative progress in the field. For example, thirteen of Rider's sixteen chapters were dedicated to Neolithic, Bronze Age, and Homeric housing. Although surely resulting from the flurry of activity in the new field of Aegean prehistory, it reflected poorly on the state of affairs for historical Greece. In addition to considering the literary sources (the same ones that continue to constitute text-based discussions of the Greek house), Rider was able to illustrate only very few plans of "Greek" houses from the Classical and later periods. Examples from Delos, Peiraeus, Pompeii, and Priene had to suffice because so few other houses were known at the time. But Nevett is able to include numerous houses at more than two dozen sites from all over the Greek world, including Magna Graecia and Sicily. Moreover, her work is embedded within a post-processual theoretical and methodological framework that allows real hypotheses to be generated and tested. Most prominent among these are her specification of an "oikos concept"[17] and the identification of the "single entrance courtyard house" type. Both of these are tied to her elucidation of the gendering of domestic space and in the geographical and chronological variability of household organization that she traces.

In the interim, and uncontested as the most significant contribution to the study of Greek

[12] The following constitutes a representative, but not exhaustive, listing of major sites other than Halieis where Classical houses have been studied or excavated and published, at least in preliminary fashion. Hellenistic examples are included where they have direct bearing on their Classical forebears. The citations include the most current literature, in which may be found references to earlier works, as well as the most comprehensive reports: Abdera (Hoepfner and Schwandner 1994, 180–87); Ammotopos (Dakaris 1986; Hoepfner et al. 1999b); Athens and Attica in general (Hoepfner 1999a; J. W. Graham 1974; J. E. Jones 1975; Travlos 1971, 392–401; Tsakirgis 1997); Colophon (Hoepfner and Osthues 1999; Holland 1944); Delos (Hoepfner 1999b; Trümper 1998); Dema House, Attica (J. E. Jones et al. 1962); Dystos (Hoepfner and Schwandner 1999); Eretria (Ducrey, Metzger, and Reber 1993; Reber 1998); Halos (Haagsma 1990, 1991, 1994; Reinders 1988); Himera (Adriani et al. 1970; Allegro et al. 1976; Boncasa 1976; Hoepfner and Schwandner 1994, 13–16); Ilion (Aylward 1999); Kallipolis (Themelis 1999); Kassope (Dakaris 1989; Hoepfner and Schwandner 1994, 114–58); Leukas (Fiedler 1999); Lokroi Epizephyrioi (Bagnasco 1992); Monte Iato (Dalcher 1994); Morgantina (Tsakirgis 1984, 1995, and forthcoming, a); Mycenae (Bowkett 1995; cf. Anderson-Stojanović 1997); Olynthos (Cahill 1991, 2002; Hoepfner and Schwandner 1994, 68–113; Nevett 1999, 53–79; D. M. Robinson 1946; D. M. Robinson and J. W. Graham 1938); Pergamon (Wulf 1999; Wulf-Rheidt 1998); Peiraeus (von Eickstedt 1991, 97–112; Hoepfner and Schwandner 1994, 22–50); Priene (Hoepfner and Schwandner 1994, 188–225); Stymphalos (H. Williams et al. 1997); Tauric Chersonesos, Crimea (Dufkova and Pećirka 1970; Saprykin 1994); Thasos (Grandjean 1988); Thorikos (Mussche 1990); Vari House, Attica (J. E. Jones et al., 1973).

[13] We have attempted to address this in Ault and Nevett 1999.

[14] Gallant (1991) provides a useful exception. Cahill (1991, 2002) has also made significant contributions, not only for Olynthos, but to the topic generally. Ault 1999b is explicitly a treatment of archaeological evidence for the domestic economy at Halieis, and many of its arguments are reintroduced in the course of this study. While not archaeologically oriented, Pomeroy's new translation of and commentary on Xenophon's *Oeconomicus* (1994) is a milestone. Other works represent the rise in domestic studies focusing on Classical Greece (not to mention the Roman world, which has also seen a marked increase in offerings within this type of social history). These include Booth 1993, Cox 1998, and Pomeroy 1997, and show the primacy of the household for a whole range of inquiry.

[15] By "popular art" I am referring primarily to fine-ware and painted pottery, terracottas, and metalwork, but the definition also extends to the virtually invisible inventory of textiles and other perishable material. Kiderlen makes the useful observation that it is in the private and semipublic realm of the household, rather than in the public arena, that artistic styles develop and are codified (1995, 1). Also, I refer to the domestic context in order to stress its distinction from the funerary one (the most common source for museum quality objects), where the recovery and publication of grave inventories is standard practice.

[16] Rider 1915, Nevett 1999. I exclude D. M. Robinson 1946, and D. M. Robinson and J. W. Graham 1938, since both are part of the series of final publications from the Olynthos excavations.

[17] Cf. Hodder's "domus concept" cited above, note 8.

houses, *Wohnen in der klassischen Polis* has appeared. This project was begun in 1974 by Wolfram Hoepfner and E.-L. Schwandner. Three fascicles of the multivolume series have now appeared, and the most important of these, *Haus und Stadt im klassischen Griechenland*, has been reissued in a second, revised and expanded edition.[18] In its scope, *Wohnen in der klassischen Polis* is a truly interdisciplinary effort, ranging from studies of urban planning and housing to gardens, to kitchens and cooking, to a compendium of textual sources on domestic affairs.[19] *Haus und Stadt im klassischen Griechenland* provides a synthesis of urban planning and domestic architecture from more than twenty sites ranging in date from the Archaic through the Hellenistic periods and from the western Greek colonies to the homeland and as far afield as Mesopotamia. At Miletos, Peiraeus, Rhodes, Priene, Abdera, and Dura Europos standard house types have been identified within a grid based on Pythagorean number theory as codified by Hippodamos of Miletos. This makes a strong case for the principle of isonomia (literally, "equality under the law") as a guiding principle for city planning. Although not without its critics, isonomia is seen by Hoepfner and Schwandner as an overarching principle in the Greeks' ordering of their world view, finding a place in government and philosophy, as well as the performing and applied arts.[20]

While I do not advocate the degree of conformity that Hoepfner and Schwandner's uniformitarian tendencies have imposed upon many Greek cities, I do sense in their arguments certain underlying truths about practices of ancient land apportionment generally, in both urban and rural settings.[21] At some level this must also reflect aspects of organization within the body politic and even the household.[22] In case after case I think we can find examples where egalitarian principles of allotment were used, at least initially at the time of foundation (as in the colonies) or reorganization (as at Halieis), even when these were quick to break down and be superceded by more hierarchical impulses. I will argue that similar tendencies are present at the domestic level. The domestic architecture of Halieis, along with the artifact residues of household inventories and activities, comprise the objective traces of this organization, of oikonomia. Interpreting these remains a subjective enterprise, but it is one that must be engaged. In what follows I undertake the presentation of the data and its possible interpretations.

Methodology

> Data, however, even if very good, do not speak for themselves. They may give answers, but it is the historian who must ask the right questions. And he must develop theories and rules before the data can provide answers to those questions. Wrong answers to interesting questions are of no value, but right answers to unimportant questions are boring.
>
> —Willem Jongman

The remains discussed in what follows are located in the two largest tracts of excavation in the lower town at Halieis. Lying in the eastern half of the city, these are known as Areas 6 and 7 (Pl. 1, Fig. 2). Taken together and including the unexcavated land between them, they extend more than 140 m north to south. The terrain here is the broadest flat expanse within the city. It lies approximately five meters above sea level (hereafter "masl") and falls off gently northeast toward the present shoreline. These areas of excavation cut across portions of the city walls and several streets (Streets 1–5) and avenues (Avenues A, B, and C), in addition to blocks of insular housing.

Several aspects of the site and, in particular, its excavation, make the houses at Halieis ideally suited to detailed analysis. First is the relatively shallow deposition of the archaeological remains

[18] Carroll-Spillecke 1989; Hoepfner and Schwandner 1994; Schuller, Hoepfner, and Schwandner 1989.

[19] A list of the in-progress contributions by numerous authors was given in the first edition of Hoepfner and Schwandner 1994 (1986, 293). It is unclear how much of this ambitious undertaking is still planned, but see Hoepfner 1999c for a recent complementary project. For literary testimony, the only collection now available is that in D. M. Robinson 1946, 399–452 ("Testimonia Selecta") and 453–71 ("Greek Words Concerned with the House"). Cf. also Hellman 1994, which, while concerned exclusively with epigraphic evidence, adds considerably to D. M. Robinson 1946.

[20] For their position, see Hoepfner 1986, 1989, 1999c (201–440, esp. 201–6); and Hoepfner and Schwandner 1994, esp. 299–330. For critiques, see Bommelaer 1988; Cahill 1991, 2002; Étienne 1991; Nevett 1999, 27.

[21] See the fundamental study relating urban and rural land division by Boyd and Jameson (1981). Cf. also Cahill's work on the subject, especially with the decree from Korkyra Melaina (1991, 81–92; 2002, 219–21).

[22] For the developmental trajectory of Greek democracy long before its galvanizing expression in late 6th-century Athens, see E. W. Robinson 1997. Cf. Morris 1998a, on the development of what he terms the "middling ideology" in Archaic Greece; at this time, he notes, the household "was a basic metaphor for the social order" (1998a, 10).

themselves. The houses all lay within a meter of the present ground surface and are buried largely in their own collapse debris, primarily decomposed mud brick. There has been little alluvion, erosion, or soil formation to expose the buildings or bury them deeply. Even more fortunate, to an archaeologist, is the thorough abandonment of Halieis. Periods of subsequent activity are largely negligible, and so the site is unencumbered by later constructions.[23] There has been relatively limited scavenging for building materials and almost no subsequent occupation to disturb the archaeological remains. Even the impact of agriculture has been minimal (the site of Halieis has for many years been home to olive groves). Finally, the excavation strategy meant that in general the houses were cleared down to their latest occupation levels and work ceased. Thus, for the most part, we can be confident that the buildings and their artifact assemblages are chronologically in phase and relatively synchronous.[24] This combination of shallow burial, good preservation, and comparatively broad horizontal exposure within a bracketed chronological period gives us an almost unparalleled sample of 4th-century domestic remains.

Excavations in the Lower Town

The following is a summary of the recovery and recording procedures employed in the excavations of the lower town at Halieis from 1972 on. These formed the methodological platform on which this study has been based.[25] The areas for excavation were defined by the purchase of available land and controlled through five-by-five-meter grid squares, the coordinates of which were based on those established by the Greek Geographical Survey. For convenience, the excavators used the last three digits of the north and east coordinates (i.e., 000/000), with decimal increments added when needed for precise location. This six-digit number designates a five-by-five-meter trench and is read from the northeast corner of each grid square. Following a strategy generally associated with Mortimer Wheeler, each grid square was excavated as an independent trench, initially as a four-by-four-meter area in which one-by-five-meter balks were left along the north and east sides. Later, when the balks were removed, the area was expanded to five-by-five meters (cf. Pls. 21 and 22; and Pl. 37).

The excavation technique was a combination of arbitrary and actual stratigraphic passes across each trench. Each pass is termed a "unit" in the recording system. These units were numbered from one to infinity, depending on the order in which they were recognized. (The numbering does not necessarily reflect the stratigraphic sequence proper.) Trench masters described their work on preprinted forms that were assembled into trench notebooks. Each unit has at least one page for its verbal description and a second showing a plan of its area after excavation. Elevations were taken at the top and bottom (i.e., before and after excavation) of the four corners of each unit, with as many more final elevations being added as deemed necessary to convey its contours. All these elevations appear on the unit plan. The unit page also bears headings for the inclusion of Munsell color readings for soils, the relationship of that unit with units above and below (i.e., unit "y" lay below unit "x" and above unit "z"), and an area for noting which artifacts recovered were likely candidates for inventorying. The latter, noted by the trench master during excavation, were termed "pick-ups." The number of artifacts that were eventually inventoried was often greater or less than those originally noted in the pick-up category. Each trench notebook closes with section (or "scarp") drawings of the four vertical faces of the four-by-four-meter trench, a final horizontal or state plan of the trench, and a final report on the season's work in that area. Additional pages describe in detail the construction of walls in the trench and list all "pick-ups." A list of all record photographs taken of the trench and contact prints of these photos is included as well.[26]

Processing the finds paralleled the actual excavation. All artifacts from each unit were kept together. After a unit was closed, the artifacts were washed if necessary, recorded, and stored. All pottery from a given unit was laid out, joins were

[23] The only large post-Classical, premodern building at Halieis is a late Roman bath built over the Hermione Gate. For evidence of late Roman and early Byzantine activity, see Jameson in McAllister 2004; Jameson 1969, 338–40; and Rudolph 1979a.

[24] The disadvantage of this strategy is that, except in a few instances, earlier phases of the site have not been explored. (Deep soundings in the houses are referred to as appropriate and are reported on in Rudolph 1984.)

[25] A more detailed account of excavation procedure, including information on the processing of finds, was provided in a pamphlet created for the excavation team by W. W. Rudolph, "Excavations at Halieis: Scheme of Operations" (n.d.).

[26] A separate series of notebooks was created for trench photography. Complementing the graphic recording, these include photographs of each of the four scarps and an end-of-season overhead view.

sought (generally with adjacent units as well), a list of finds was made, and selected items were inventoried. For the organization of the inventoried listing by unit, pottery was classified by ware, shape, and anatomical variable represented, ranging from "whole" vessel to "unidentified body" sherd. Although pottery provided the bulk of portable artifact material recovered, a similar procedure was applied to recording all other classes of artifacts.[27] The whole process is reflected in the finds notebooks, which like the trench notebooks are organized by each five-by-five-meter trench and the sequence of units within that trench.[28]

Subsequent stages of treatment, inventorying, and analysis in preparation for the final publication have included conservation and restoration, photography, and drawing. In addition, because of limited storage space some material, mainly nondiagnostic pottery and roof tiles, was discarded. Nothing was thrown, however, before being recorded as part of the full inventory of material from a given unit.

Study of Houses 7, A, C, D, and E

All five houses and their contents that are considered here were excavated and recorded according to the system outlined above. For this study, they were also analyzed using several additional steps.[29] This analysis began with two 1:50 scale plans of each house, the first a blueprint of the actual-state plan (see Figs. 7, 10, 13, 15, and 19), the second a redrawn schematic of the actual-state plan showing the outline of walls and other significant built features.[30] (Both plans are overlaid by the five-by-five-meter grid used in excavation.) Using the notebook for each trench that lay over the perimeter of the houses, all or part of fifty-five, five-by-five-meter trenches were studied, encompassing an area of some 834 m^2 for the five houses proper. For each trench all absolute elevations, that is, those taken on built features and the final depths to which the trench was excavated, were transferred onto the actual-state plan. This imposed the third dimension onto the graphic record that was thereafter available at a glance. The written record for each trench was condensed into a series of unit summaries, including the top and bottom elevations of units in order to estimate their average depth.[31]

This detailed analysis was used to create a stratigraphic matrix, also known as a "Harris Matrix," for each trench.[32] The matrix is a schematic diagram showing the position of all strata relative to one another, be they arbitrary or absolute, within an excavated area. By combining written descriptions, elevations, plans, photographs, and concentrations of artifacts, it was possible to ascertain which units were significant representatives of the latest habitation levels of the trench and, by extension, the house in question. These latest habitation levels (Level A, ca. 350–300) averaged 0.20 m in depth and lay just above, rested on, or comprised the latest floor surfaces. They were bracketed in descending order by topsoil, building collapse (primarily the decayed mud-brick house walls and roof tiles), and earlier deposits (Level B, ca. 400–350, and Level C, ca. 600–460).[33] With the matrices it was possible to

[27] Unfortunately the collection of organic remains was never systematically implemented. Little dry sieving and no water separation techniques were employed to recover floral or faunal data despite their presence at the site (and high degree of preservation in the water-logged conditions of the wells). The bones that were recovered from the houses themselves remain unstudied, although shells collected have been identified. This situation is reflected in the tables of artifact inventories from the houses. (For organic remains, see Tables 1, 4, 7, 10, 13, and 14.)

[28] Original copies of both the trench and finds notebooks, along with all other documentary materials from the excavations in the lower town, are now housed in the Indiana University Archives in Bloomington, Indiana (Accession Number 99/035).

[29] Other remains of domestic architecture in Areas 6 and 7 are presented in summary fashion by groupings of rooms that probably belonged to individual houses (see below, 12–13, 21–25). But they have not as yet been subject to the same degree of stratigraphic and artifact analysis as Houses 7, A, C, D, and E.

[30] Such features include wells, oil press installations, pits, and the like.

[31] A volumetric estimate of cubic meters of earth represented by each unit, which might prove useful, has not been carried out owing simply to the enormity of the task.

[32] See Harris 1989 for the fundamentals and Harris, Brown, and Brown 1993 for a series of related essays. Paice (1991) offers useful graphic elaborations on the system developed by Harris, especially with regard to incorporating architectural remains into the sequence. Having employed Harris matrices on excavations in England and Italy during eight field seasons, I am convinced that they are indispensable for interpreting the stratigraphic record, as well as facilitating its legibility for others. They are best suited to open-area excavation and the creation of a cumulative matrix for each of the five houses studied here would be quite impractical and unnecessarily cumbersome. But they have worked well within the limits set here. For published examples of matrices of the fills of the koprones in Houses 7 and D, see Ault 1999b, 569–70.

[33] The chronological framework used here is that adopted for the excavations of the lower town, outlined in Boyd and Rudolph 1978, 334–35. It reflects the poorly understood lacuna in the second half of the 5th century. It should be pointed out that the distinction between Levels A and B is not precise. Artifacts from both levels were intermixed in the earthen floors of the rooms at the time of occupation. Therefore, during excavation it was often difficult to distinguish levels A and B from each other so that they were frequently excavated together.

attempt a graphic link between units occurring in the same stratigraphic level, both within a single trench and across different five-by-five-meter grid squares. In some cases this could have been done without the aid of a matrix, such as a trench where only three units were recognized and excavation terminated at the level of a plaster floor. But such simple sequences are extremely rare. Rather, trenches contained an average of fourteen units apiece and could have been excavated over more than fifty such passes spread over several rooms and multiple periods of occupation. Overall, for the five houses considered below, nearly eight hundred excavation units were analyzed (and correspond to those recognized by the excavators themselves). Among these, 325 units were identified as belonging to the Level A–Level A/B strata.[34]

The final step was to link up these (re)-emerging strata across all trenches and the house as a whole using the second 1:50 plan. Like inserting pieces into a puzzle, the units that represented the Level A–Level A/B strata were plotted onto the schematic house plan. This mapping included the top and bottom elevations in order to allow for checking and comparison of how the same strata were recognized in adjacent trenches. The completed plan for all trenches of a house amounts to a reconstruction of its latest occupation level.

Study of the Finds

Loci. Following the analysis of all units associated with a house and after linking the significant units to determine the latest occupation level, the next step was to approach the distribution of finds and their quantification. It seems simple to equate the trench units that lie within a particular room to that room and to quantify the artifacts accordingly. But the area of a unit, and consequently the discrete collection of finds from that unit, does not invariably correspond to a single room. In many cases the area excavated as a single unit, and which lies within the latest occupation level, spans more than one room. The consequent splitting of artifact material between rooms, even if only a small portion of another room is represented, is a source of bias. Therefore, we need to introduce a concept or level of classification independent of the designation "room." For the purposes of studying artifact distributions within houses, rooms, while retained as an architectural entity, must be coupled with the notion of "loci."

A locus may represent only a portion of a room, correspond to its entire area, or span multiple rooms. Often several loci, each with distinct properties, considered together account for the area of a room. Loci need not be constrained to five-by-five-meter grid squares as are units and are more flexible than specific rooms. They form the bridge between units and rooms and allow for the grouping of units in a way that is just as significant as rooms for elucidating spatial distributions of artifacts, without being constrained by that purely architectural classification. "Locus" can also be used in a stratigraphic sense when it designates a large unit that reaches the floor deposit in one room and extends into another room where the floor was not reached. If the floor level was encountered in a subsequent unit limited to the latter room, a portion or all of this locus will underlie the prior example.[35] Such a concept enables the retention of significant finds with a spatial designation that would otherwise be dismissed as ambiguous or biased because, owing to excavation, they were collected from more than one room.[36] The locus plan for each house (included here as Figs. 8, 11, 14, 17, and 20) represents a culmination of the unit plans discussed above as they reflect all units significant for the latest habitation levels, combined into loci and partitioned into the principle areas of the house.

Quantification. No sophisticated techniques were used in this study (such as chi-squared or regression analyses).[37] Rather, the artifacts have simply been quantified according to their category. So typologically various and numerically rich are these assemblages that subjecting them to rigorous statistical analysis would be extremely cumbersome, if not actually counterproductive in terms of homogenizing an extremely diverse body of

[34] See Appendix I for a concordance between trenches, units, rooms, and loci that comprise the Level A–Level A/B strata for each of the five houses. This includes 67 units for House 7, 49 units for House A, 67 units for House C, 74 units for House D, and 68 units for House E.

[35] For example, in House 7 (Fig. 8), between Rooms 7-7 and 7-10, Locus X spans Rooms 7-10, where a floor level was reached, and 7-7, where the floor level was only encountered with a subsequent pass in Locus IV.

[36] In only one instance is an argument about the presence of material from a locus hampered by the fact that it is split over two rooms, and there it is noted in the course of discussion. See below, 38–39.

[37] On various analytical techniques in archaeology, see Orton 1980. Cf. Nevett's employment of an SPSS program for studying artifacts from Olynthos and Himera (1999, especially 61–68, 132–33, appendixes 1, 3–4).

material. Therefore, the assemblages have been considered within their stratigraphic, architectural, and social settings and not reduced to a disembodied set of figures.

For the purpose of expediting both analysis and presentation, all units that were determined by their relationship to a room or rooms to make up a spatially discrete locus or loci have had their artifacts lumped together.[38] The corresponding inventories of finds have also been streamlined by reducing the pottery data to lowest common denominators. Nearly 24,000 ceramic items (not including roof tiles, loom weights, lamps, miniature vessels, terracotta figurines, and glass) were recorded from the Level A–Level A/B strata of the five houses. Owing to the large numerical quantity, as well as physical bulk of the pottery alone, variables yielding the least amount of information with regard to determining activity areas have been absorbed into several overarching, more general categories.

The first variable to be sorted out of the pottery data (as presented in Tables 1, 4, 7, 10, 13, and 14) was the frequency of individual vessel shapes. From the five houses most completely excavated, more than seventy different vessel types in fine, plain, and coarse wares are represented. In order to offset the omission of shape data from the individual household inventories, Table 19 contains a summary of the occurrence of individual vessel types within and between houses. (It will be cited where appropriate.) A full listing of all pottery data by shape in the setting of each house would have considerably increased the already lengthy tables detailing household inventories. In its place has been substituted a breakdown of the categories by function.

Fortunately, there is a strong correlation between form and function in the exceptionally rich repertoire of Classical Greek pottery.[39] Function is, in its turn, an indicator of activities. The three primary functions to which pottery vessels in virtually all cultures have been put, whether so shape specific as the Greek or not, are the consumption and serving, the preparation, and the storage of food and drink. So here, for example, fine-ware vessels have been divided according to functions associated with food, drink, and "other." More precise divisions are applied to forms associated with drink: whether they were used for drink consumption (e.g., cups), serving and pouring (e.g., jugs), or serving and containing (e.g., larger containment vessels). Similar criteria are applied to the remaining array of vessels in other fabrics and devoted to other functions. From the analysis of pottery from each of the five houses, various scenarios develop that indicate certain spatial preferences for the overlapping and interpenetrating activities of food and drink consumption, preparation, and storage.

Quantifying the pottery was the next challenge. One significant measurement obtained from sherd quantities is the estimate of the minimum number of vessels they represent (hereafter abbreviated MNV).[40] This is found by counting sherds or weighing them.[41] For a variety of reasons, the Halieis sherds were not weighed and counts alone have been employed. The entries in the finds notebooks recorded the anatomical variables represented by sherds in addition to the vessel types from which the sherds originated. To estimate the MNV represented by these sherds, I used the standard features of rim and base/foot (possessed by virtually all classes of the Halieis pottery).[42] The total of rim and base sherds is combined with vessels that survived whole or as profiles (and are listed individually as such in Tables 1, 4, 7, 10, 13, and 14).[43] This sum is taken

[38] For a listing of all the relevant units that have contributed to locus designations, as well as their correspondence to trenches and rooms, see Appendix I.

[39] For discussions on the variety of Classical Greek vessel forms ranging from overviews to comprehensive studies, see G. R. Edwards 1975; Kanowski 1984; Richter and Milne 1935; and Sparkes and Talcott 1951, 1970 (which provides the most complete "shape histories" available). While the use of whole vessels for other than their original purposes and the reuse of worn-out or broken vessels must always be kept in mind, these do not affect generalizations about the functional specificity of original design (see Schiffer 1996, 27–46, on "reuse processes," and Rice 1987, table 9.3, for a comprehensive listing of attested secondary purposes served by pots). Vessel function is determined by cultural convention, implemented by a host of potters, and sustained by the pottery-consuming public.

[40] I have chosen to use MNV for "minimum number of vessels represented" over other abbreviations in use: e.g., NIV for "number of inferred vessels," EVREP for "estimated vessels represented," or EVE for "estimated vessel equivalent" (see the discussions in Orton 1980, 162–67; Orton 1989, 94–95; and Rice 1987, 290–93).

[41] For brief discussions of sherd weights versus counts, see the sources cited in note 40, especially for references therein to more thorough treatments and case studies.

[42] The two most common cooking vessels, the chytra and the lopas, possess rounded bottoms and therefore do not have bases per se. A glance at the tables, however, shows that they have not been undercounted.

[43] The mending of pottery was not systematically undertaken, but where groups of sherds were identified as coming from a single vessel, they are counted only once.

as the best quantifiable indicator of vessel frequency. The cumulative MNVs for each house appear in Tables 2, 5, 8, 11, 15, and 16.

Other anatomical variables, represented primarily by handles and body fragments, have been lumped into an "other" category. These do not contribute to the MNV because, in the case of handles, not all vessels possess them (e.g., bowls) while some possess more than one (e.g., skyphoi, hydriae). The body fragments were in many instances likely to be those that belonged to the same vessels as the rims and feet already counted. They might even join among themselves. Although joins were sought during the processing of finds and many joins were made and duly noted in the finds notebooks, it is among the body fragments that most would have been missed. Thus consideration of them could be a source of considerable bias in terms of overestimating the MNV. The strategy adopted here, counting elements present on all vessels, is widely accepted as valid and is used not only by archaeologists for estimating the size of pottery assemblages but also by zooarchaeologists for reconstructing animal populations where a recurring type of bone recovered (e.g., second pig phalanges) is counted.[44]

All other artifacts, from stone and metal objects to shells, were quantified by a simple count. But while counts from individual stratigraphic units were assiduously made for each kind of material, the vast numbers of roof tiles present tend to be estimates. This is because entries in the finds notebooks frequently specify "one small box" or "one-half" or "one-quarter small box pan tile body fragments." The estimated equivalencies I have adopted in order to reconstitute roof-tile quantities are as follows: one small box equals two hundred fragments, one-half small box equals one hundred fragments, and so on. Even more difficult to quantify are the designations "stack" and "zembili" (basket), which also appear in the finds notebooks. As with sherd counts converted to MNVs, but even more so, the numbers estimated for roof tiles should be considered as relative indexes of overall quantities. Only occasionally were roof-tile fragments analyzed in greater detail (i.e., Laconian or Corinthian, cover or pan).

Finds Quantification and Archaeological Formation Processes

Finally we have to account for what the MNV actually represents.[45] The figures derived from MNV estimates do not stand for a synchronic or contemporaneous representation of ceramic assemblages but rather for the diachronic history of such assemblages. Nor does a MNV figure indicate an entire assemblage. It is made up primarily of sherds, not whole vessels, and not the total number of sherds, but systematically selected ones at that. It reflects only a portion of any contemporaneous assemblage: those vessels that were broken and thus entered the fraction of the archaeological record recovered. The breakage of whole vessels into sherds, or one sherd into several more, occurred in a variety of circumstances. The transferal of a portion of a broken vessel from what was once a living context into an archaeological one results primarily from its status as refuse.[46] This is refuse that has accumulated over a span of time, ideally, of the two to three generations represented by Level A–Level A/B habitation at Halieis (ca. 400–300 within its widest bounds).

This raises questions about the nature of refuse, how it was treated, how households were maintained, and what processes account for its accumulation. Most important, can this refuse be taken as an indicator of activity areas? Archaeologists concerned with the spatial-functional dimension of refuse define two types.[47] Primary refuse is that deposited in the place it was created, while secondary refuse has been moved, principally by maintenance or cleaning activities, to another location. Distinction between the two types of refuse hinges in part upon its physical properties, where size and material are paramount. Large pieces of debris are more likely to be moved further away from an area of primary activity than small because they impede the ongoing use of that space. Their movement may be to the periphery of a room, to a central refuse pile in another room, or out of the house alto-

[44] Cf. the discussion of "number of identified specimens" (NISP) versus "minimum number of individuals" (MNI) in Payne 1985, 219–23.

[45] The work of M. B. Schiffer must loom large in any consideration of archaeological formation processes. In a recent lengthy treatise he summarizes previous contributions and includes citations to a plethora of literature for virtually all scenarios (Schiffer 1996). I have also offered a summary of the situation at Halieis, with examples, in Ault and Nevett 1999, 46–52.

[46] Loss, abandonment, disposal of the dead, and caching are additional processes of "cultural deposition" that account for this transferal (Schiffer 1996, 47; see the following pages there for a separate discussion of each process). Of these, loss and abandonment, as well as refuse disposal, have created the artifact assemblages recovered from the houses at Halieis.

[47] For a good discussion citing numerous case studies, see Schiffer 1996, 58–64.

gether, with the former locations serving as way stations en route to the latter.[48] Waste products that presented a danger, primarily sharp items such as glass, debitage from knapping, and the like will have been scrupulously removed from a living area. Also, organic refuse (e.g., kitchen scraps) may call for different treatment than inorganic, especially where it may become offensive or be collected as fertilizer, as appears to have been the case at Halieis. Areas of primary activity will be differentially maintained according to the intensity of that activity and the extent of space utilized.[49]

The MNV figures arrived at in this study are based on both primary and secondary refuse. Where they indicate refuse that has accumulated in a primary context, this is made clear by comparison with MNV figures for different vessel and function categories and by consideration of the architectural space within which they occur. The same is true for the recognition of secondary refuse that is distinguished by the mixed character of the assemblage and its circumstances of deposition.[50] Much of the debris making up the MNV figures has entered the archaeological record by integration into the floor matrix. Pieces of a broken vessel may have been swept up, but on earthen floors smaller, unobtrusive fragments were probably overlooked, especially in the dimly lit interior rooms and if there were textiles or seasonal coverings of rushes on the floors.[51] These "lost" fragments, be they in a primary or secondary context of deposition, will easily have become a part of the floor matrix itself and have consequently entered the archaeological record.[52] The periodic resurfacing of earthen floors with a new coat of mud is attested by ethnographic observation as well as in primary epigraphic sources from the classical world and accounts for the sealing of some debris.[53]

It could be argued that the pottery fragments represent a reintroduction of debris from elsewhere into the household, having been brought in with or intentionally added to the resurfacing material.[54] Likewise, the objection could be made that such debris was originally temper within the decomposed mud bricks that formed the primary soil matrix burying the house or that it served the function of chinking cracks in the walls. These scenarios might explain the origin of some of this material, but I do not think that they were the primary processes accounting for pottery remains in the houses at Halieis.[55] Agricultural land was a precious commodity. It is unlikely that earth for

[48] Cf. the discussion by Schiffer of "maintenance processes and waste streams" (1996, 64–72).

[49] Cf. Schiffer 1996, 62; and Arnold 1990, where it is documented that "waste management activities are in part conditioned by the size of the residential compound and the household population" (915). It should be noted, however, that Arnold's study is confined to the patio and peripheral areas of "houselots" and lacks comparative data for interior spaces.

[50] Although not systematically observed at Halieis, the dip or orientation of artifacts as they were recovered (e.g., whether they lay flat, on edge, or at an angle) has been inferred from descriptions in the trench notebooks and has helped to determine primary versus secondary deposition (cf. Schiffer 1996, 270–71).

[51] For the sale of several possible floor coverings in the Attic stelai, see Pritchett 1956, 244–54. In addition to textile rugs ("dapis" or "tapis"), these include mats of reeds ("kanna") and rushes ("psiathos"). Typically the latter are associated with sleeping (see lexicon entries for "matta," Hug 1930 and Pottier 1904). Although I have not found specific references to straw or rushes laid down as floor coverings in antiquity, the practice is standard in other times and settings. Cf., especially with regard to formation processes, Erasmus's disgust that beneath herb-strewn rush floor coverings lay "an ancient collection of beer, grease, fragments, bones, spittle, excrement of dogs and cats and everything that is nasty" (cited in Gies 1979, 60).

[52] Where it represents primary deposition, Schiffer has termed this "residual primary refuse" (1996, 62). The significance of such refuse trapped in floors, be it residual primary or residual secondary, has been taken up in a number of ethnoarchaeological and archaeological studies cited there.

[53] Unfortunately, ethnographers have not concerned themselves with the maintenance of earthen floors. Even Schiffer does not give this aspect due weight in formation processes. For the classical world proper, however, cf. *IG* XI 2, 199A,108, from Delos (dated ca. 275), which records a payment of 680 drachmas to one Kallikrates for stuccoing columns and coating a peristyle with earth (trans. D. M. Robinson 1946, 451, no. 154). The high price for the work suggests that the building in question was probably a large public one rather than a private residence. Hoepfner and Schwandner (1994, 104), referring to earthen floors at Olynthos, note that they would have been periodically resurfaced with a 0.02–0.05 m coating of earth (cf. Reber 1998, 113; and Schwandner 1999a). Both the Astynomic inscription from Pergamon (Klaffenbach 1953) and the Agoranomic Law from Athens (*SIG*[3] 313, 25–28 = *IG* II[2] 380, 25–28) forbade the piling up of earth that lay before houses or mixing it with water in the street. Presumably these latter testimonia refer at least in part to the major constituent used in such periodic resurfacings.

[54] Schiffer's "reclaimed" or "displaced refuse" (1996, 111–14). E.-L. Schwandner has remarked that the presence of pot sherds in an earthen floor would have helped prevent its cracking, but that straw would have been a better additive (personal communication, 1991).

[55] It is true, however, that ceramic inclusions are frequently observed in traditional mud-brick architecture. E.g., Rice 1987, 294, table 9.3 (citing Deal 1983, 176–79); Schiffer 1996, 111, with 112, fig. 5.4 (citing Deal 1985, 266; and Watson 1979, 119). In both ancient and modern mud-brick constructions I have examined, the presence of built-in ceramic material as inclusions or chinking is less frequent than its absence. There were also alternatives for chinking. As part of the strategy for keeping the litigious Philokleon confined to his house, the slave Xanthias tells Bdelykleon, "We caulked every chink with rags [ῥακίοισι] (Aristophanes *Wasps* 127–28, trans. Hadas 1962). Sherds were extremely rare (and mainly prehistoric) in the mud-brick fortification walls from all periods on the Halieis acropolis (C. Dengate et al., n.d., chap. 2).

surfacing was collected from fields (where sherds were deposited in the household manure and garbage used as fertilizer).[56] In addition, digging in a dump for clean surfacing material (on the order of the Monte Testaccio in Rome, for example) seems too time consuming.[57] As for the second scenario, at Olynthos, Thasos, and Halieis, where mud bricks occasionally survived in situ, were measured, and had their composition examined, no ceramic tempering was noted.[58] Finally, the very fact that such distinct patterns have emerged from the pottery data and the MNV estimates suggests deliberate activity rather than a secondary introduction of debris via building materials.

The Halieis domestic assemblages do not provide a synchronic view of household inventories, consumption, or discard patterns that approximate ethnographic "moments in time." Instead, they offer a select and diachronic sample of debris reflecting patterns of use and behavior over perhaps a century of several households' operations. The household "cycles" or "series" that produced this material must be recognized for what they are: glimpses, rather than a complete view, but ones that take into account the wax and wane of families and their fortunes.[59] As such they represent absolutely necessary steps in bridging the oft-perceived impasse between artifacts and society, as well as between archaeology and history.

Presentation

The following discussion of House 7, and the other four houses to be examined in detail, begins with a room-by-room analysis of the principal architectural remains. This incorporates some discussion of the stratigraphy encountered, primarily as it bears on determining the latest phases of occupation, Levels A and B, second and first halves of the 4th century, respectively.[60] References made to grid locations are the five-by-five-meter trenches (hereafter TR combined with the abbreviated coordinates), to units (hereafter u.), and to the stratigraphic levels excavated within each trench (i.e., TR 000/000: u. x).[61] This does not include a detailed description of wall construction or preservation, which can be seen on the actual-state plan, unless these bear on specific points of presentation.[62] When the term "stone" is used in the following descriptions, it refers to the local Halieis bedrock of conglomerate limestone. Finer quality limestone, poros, sandstone, and so forth are specified where they occur. The analysis of each house concludes with a discussion of the finds from the latest occupation levels as isolated stratigraphically. This focuses on the quantification of finds from each house (as presented in Tables 1–19) and describes meaningful distributions of artifacts as they relate to the architecture and identification of activity areas within it.

[56] See Wilkinson 1982, and Bintliff and Snodgrass 1985, for the relationship between sherd scatters in nonsettlement areas, as encountered by survey teams, to manuring practices for ancient field systems (as well as a critique of the "manuring hypothesis" by Alcock, Cherry, and Davis 1994). Cf. also the discussion of koprones below (63–65) and in Ault 1999b.

[57] Watson (1979, 119) notes that while one village in western Iran did indiscriminately build with earth containing domestic debris, others sought clean deposits.

[58] Mud brick at Olynthos was described as consisting "of coarse red clay . . . with a considerable admixture of gravel and small stones. . . . Traces of straw . . . were abundant" (D. M. Robinson and J. W. Graham 1938, 226). For Thasos, see Grandjean 1988, 383. At Halieis roof-tile fragments were occasionally used to create a leveling course between the rubble socle and mud-brick superstructure. Such an arrangement may be depicted in the tondo of a red-figured kylix at Yale by the Paris Painter (ca. 408; *ARV*^{2} 396.16; illustrated in Bérard et al. 1989, 29, fig. 36) where a house wall is shown with narrow, segmented, horizontal bands at regular intervals of its elevation.

[59] For an overview of positions regarding the household as representative of a "series," see Smith 1992. Gallant employs a variety of evidence to formulate hypothetical life cycles for Classical Greek households (1991, 11–33).

[60] See note 2 above for references to the chronological scheme used at Halieis.

[61] Both the excavation and finds notebooks, now curated by the Indiana University Archives, are organized according to this system.

[62] For brief discussions of wall construction, see Rudolph 1979b, 266 and 1983, 70. In general, the house walls at Halieis consist of a trench-laid, wide foundation course of conglomerate or poros blocks, on top of which was set a narrower orthostate course of conglomerate or poros blocks, which in turn bore the now decomposed elevation in mud brick. The orthostates were often used quite deliberately and impressively along the frontage of houses, where they would have been the most visible. In the case of internal and rear house walls, the orthostates were usually replaced by irregular mud-mortared rubblework.

– CHAPTER TWO –

House and Assemblage

Area 7

(Figures 2, 6–9; Plates 1–13)

Area 7, also known as Field 27, is an irregular trapezoid (Pls. 2, 3). The longest, northwestern, side spans twenty-nine meters. Area 7 contains portions of as many as three separate houses (Rooms 7-2 through 7-5, Rooms 7-20 through 7-23, and Rooms 7-24 through 7-27, respectively), all of a fourth (Rooms 7-6 through 7-17, hereafter referred to as House 7), the intersection of Avenue C with Street 1, and more than twenty meters of city wall that includes both the Southeast Gate and Tower 9. It should be noted here that the houses follow the orientation established by the orthogonal grid of streets in the eastern half of the lower town, where the major avenues run northwest to southeast. This layout, like the different orientation of the grid in the northwest portion of the city, is determined by the contours of the slope coming down from the acropolis.[1] House 7 is the primary subject of this section. The other remains in Area 7 are presented briefly first to place the house in its context and preview individually the types of rooms and the structural elements of domestic architecture at Halieis.

Rooms 7-2–7-5

The house comprising Rooms 7-2 through 7-5 lay at the southeastern corner of an insula of uncertain dimensions. (For a preliminary discussion, see Rudolph 1983, 68.) It was entered from Avenue C through a 1 m deep, recessed prothyron doorway (Room 7-4; Pl. 4) on its northeastern side. The relationship of this entryway with that of House 7 across the avenue, Room 7-6, is noteworthy. The two do not face one another but are set off-axis. This adds a degree of privacy to the domestic worlds housed behind them and seems to have been a general principle employed in insular architecture.[2] From Room 7-4 one passed into the northeastern end of the courtyard (Room 7-3, of which ca. 15 m^2 have been exposed). The base of a sunken pithos is preserved immediately inside, at the prothyron entry. A large room (7-2) lay southeast of and opened directly onto the courtyard. Although lacking the characteristic anteroom and incompletely excavated (ca. 18 m^2 of its area has been cleared), its size, off-center doorway, and location on the periphery of the rest of the house suggest that it served as an andron.[3] The courtyard widens as it continues southwest into the core of the house. The presence of a stone base for an upright support suggests that this broader portion of Room 7-3 was a roofed pastas porch or transverse hall open to the court on its southeast side (as is the case in House 7, Room 7-13, as well as in numerous other such instances of porches at the site). Finally, a smaller interior chamber, Room 7-5, completes those partially exposed within this house.

Rooms 7-20–7-27

To the northeast of House 7, and divided from it by a narrow ambitus (1.25 m at its widest

[1] Elements of the urban plan of Halieis are discussed in Boyd 1981, Boyd and Jameson 1981, and Boyd and Rudolph 1978, 338–44.

[2] Cf. Olynthos where, although not discussed, it is apparent from the plans, even for houses that have been remodeled. The one exception to this at Halieis is the prothyron of House A (Room 6-80), which faces another across Avenue B (Room 6-77). But this may be attributed to the later construction of House A (see below, 25–26). Similarly broken sight lines occur in several other features of house design as well, particularly in the layout of the andron and the principal dayroom (see below, 75).

[3] Cf. House 7, Room 7-9; House A, Room 6-82; the northernmost (unnumbered) room in House B and an isolated room north of House B in TR 145/355 (both of which were excavated in 1962); House C, Room 6-58; and the unexcavated room fronting Street 3 in House D. All of these have been identified as andrones and are discussed in more detail below.

point),[4] several rooms belonging to one or, more likely, two houses were at least partially cleared (briefly presented in Rudolph 1983, 68). The northwest–southeast oriented wall delimiting this portion of the insula is impressive. It has been cleared for 20.30 m and exhibits ashlar orthostates all along this length. Only Room 7-20 has been fully exposed. It is a long, rectangular space (ca. 8.60 x 2.30 m), the northwestern end of which contains two features: an olive press bed and a pithos-headed well (Pl. 5). Room 7-20 was excavated to an ancient floor level only in this area, and the interpretation of the stratigraphic sequence is problematic. There is some evidence to suggest that the well itself antedates the conversion of Room 7-20 to a press room and that the pithos, actually intended for the collection of pressed oil, was inserted into the out-of-use well shaft. The precise locations of doorways connecting Room 7-20 to either Rooms 7-21 or 7-22 (which lie to the northeast) are unclear. As for the suite of rooms (Rooms 7-24 through 7-27) occupying the northeasternmost portion of Area 7, and probably belonging to a separate structure, too little has been excavated to specify their relationship with Rooms 7-20 through 7-23. It should be noted that Room 7-24 has a cobbled pavement with two sunken pithoi indicative of a work area, perhaps a press room (Pl. 6).

House 7

House 7 covers an area of approximately 231 m^2, or ca. 16 x 13 m on its southwest and southeast sides.[5] It lies at the southwest corner of an insula (perhaps measuring ca. 30 x 75 m) containing as many as ten houses. It has been pointed out that the plan of House 7 corresponds remarkably well with that of the Olynthian *Typenhaus* located at the corners of insulae at that site.[6] Despite this degree of similarity with houses at Olynthos and elsewhere, the rigid guidelines for house layout posited at polis sites of more Hippodamian character were not employed at Halieis. But something akin to *Typenhäuser* can be argued for the domestic architecture at Halieis (see below, chap. 3).

House 7 (Fig. 7) was entered through Room 7-6, the prothyron, an alcove recessed ca. 1 m into the face of the courtyard wall (Fig. 9, Pl. 7). The recessed prothyron entrance was a recurrent feature of the Classical house and appears at a number of other sites in addition to Halieis.[7] Virtually all of the excavated house entryways at Halieis are variations of this. Given the width of Room 7-6 at its transition to Room 7-7,[8] it is likely that it had a set of wide double-winged doors (ca. 1.95 m wide), allowing a cart to enter the courtyard. In addition, there is room to spare for a second doorway with a single-winged or single-width double door (ca. 1.15 m wide) for use by pedestrians.[9] Two stones, which may mark the position of this narrower entry, survive on line with the inner threshold of the prothyron. They occur at the same point where the ashlars of the outer threshold, which mark the wider entry, stop. That the prothyron bore its own tiled roof is only reasonable, given the nature of its construction, but this is also confirmed by evidence from vase painting and a fall of roof tiles spread in a northwest-southeast line in front of Room 7-6 on the surface of Avenue C.[10]

The spacious courtyard, Room 7-7, which with Room 7-8 covers nearly 64 m^2, provided access to all the rooms or suites of rooms in House 7. A well, just under 1 m in diameter, is in its northern corner. Its shaft was excavated for 5.56 m, down to the point of the contemporary water table (1.60 mbsl). Its bottom was not reached.

[4] Cf. Pls. 5, 13. The ambitus, as both a longitudinal and transverse alleyway, occurs at a number of other sites: e.g., Himera, Kassope, Nea Halos, and Olynthos.

[5] For the preliminary publication, see Rudolph 1983, 66–68; and Boyd and Rudolph 1978, 351–52. For the deep sounding conducted in Avenue C, abutting Room 7-9, see Rudolph 1984, especially 135–36 ("Test E"), and 169–70, with fig. 8. A brief discussion of House 7 is also provided in Nevett 1999, 98–100.

[6] Hoepfner and Schwandner 1994, 86, n. 252, with fig. 62. This resemblance can be seen especially well in Houses A viii 1 (D. M. Robinson 1946, 6–11, pls. 1–4), A viii 2 (ibid., 12–17, pls. 5–8), and B v 1 (ibid., 130–32, pls. 46, 103).

[7] See below, 59–60, for an overview of recessed prothyra constructions.

[8] The width is ca. 3.25 m where the base for the northeast door jamb survives in situ with a squared cutting for insertion of a door pivot. The L-shaped cutting that lies in front of the door pivot probably marks the position of wooden sheathing for a mud-brick door frame (cf. the similar cuttings on the threshold stone of Room 7-10). A second jamb is restored with a width of 0.25 m.

[9] This suggestion is based on examples from Olynthos where simple entries range in width from 0.90 to 1.40 m and double-width doors from 2.00 to 2.30 m. Cf. D. M. Robinson and J. W. Graham 1938, pl. 69.1–2 (House A xi 10) with Hoepfner and Schwandner 1994, 78, fig. 57, where the same doorway is used along with street widths and hypothetical cart sizes to provide a very informative reconstruction.

[10] Cf. the roofed entry depicted on a red-figured chous in New York (Metropolitan Museum 37.11.19, dated 430–420; illustrated in Hoepfner and Schwandner 1994, 96, fig. 73; and Sparkes and Talcott 1951, fig. 60). In the vicinity of Room 7-6, 2551 roof-tile fragments were recovered above the road surface of Avenue C (cf. Table 1: Locus I).

When first exposed the wellhead was in situ, although the blocks upon which it rested had shifted along with the ashlar footings of the walls in this corner of the courtyard (possibly as a result of an earthquake or simply the collapse of the house superstructure). The wellhead was made from the local rough conglomerate and plastered over. A plastered curbed edge was attached. It had a shallow depression in its southern corner, perhaps to provide a stable recess within which to stand a jar when filling it from a bucket. This attached edge had broken off and survives in three fragments.

Midway along the northeastern side of the court, just before the doorway to Room 7-16, lies a rectangular block (ca. 0.90 x 0.60 m) with notched cuttings in its north and west corners. Its top and edges had been trimmed down to form a pad of ca. 0.68 x 0.40 m. This can only be interpreted as a base for a flight of stairs ascending toward the northwest, the cuttings in its corners serving to hold and to brace the wooden runners and frame. (For the extent of second-story chambers in House 7, see below 18–19.)

A pit lies along the southern edge of the courtyard, extending northeast from Room 7-8 (Pl. 8). Roughly trapezoidal and lined with walls of irregular dry-stone masonry, it measures approximately 1.13 x 2.60 m at its bedrock or packed stone bottom (ca. 3.01 masl), tapering in slightly from the top. From the living surface of the courtyard (for which, see below) it is approximately 1.43 m deep. Its northwestern and northeastern sides were built up, or survive, as much as 0.50 m higher than its southeastern and southwestern edges. A conduit of inverted cover tiles extends from the northeastern side. At least three of its stone cover slabs remained in situ at the time of excavation. This channel continued northeast into Room 7-17 (where it lay at ca. 4.24 masl, well below floor level) and out into Street 1 where it was directed between a series of laid stones and took an easterly bend toward the city wall. The conduit and the pit connected in the northeastern wall of the latter, where an inverted cover tile was embedded at ca. 4.21 masl. Probably the tiled drain carried runoff from the pit. The identification of this pit, and others like it at the site, as a kopron, or facility for collecting and perhaps also composting household refuse, has been discussed elsewhere and is explored further below (Ault 1999b; see below, 63–65).

The flooring of the courtyard area is partially preserved. In Rooms 7-6 and 7-7, its elevation ranges from 4.58 masl near the prothyron to 4.41 masl in the northeastern portion of the court fronting Room 7-16. Consisting of a thin, irregularly worn layer of earth with lime inclusions, when well-preserved it could be described as a whitish hardpan. Its ephemeral nature accounts for the fact that it occasionally went unrecognized and was dug through. This surfacing was generally laid over an underpinning of pebbles or small rubble. Traces of it were recovered throughout Rooms 7-6 and 7-7 except for a strip southeast of the kopron and conduit. Here, an earthen level ca. 0.30 m lower than the main courtyard floor may well have been intentional.

The lower floor level along the southeast side of the courtyard is reflected in the stepping down of the kopron walls here as well as by the lower absolute level of Room 7-8. This room, approximately square, occupied the southern corner of the courtyard adjacent to the prothyron. Excavation revealed only a small section of pavement that can be associated with the latest phase of the room. The southernmost reaches of Room 7-8 were not cleared beyond exposing the footings for the exterior walls of House 7. An extensive roof-tile fall spreads east-west across this room and out into Room 7-7, over the fill of the kopron. This supports the notion that the hard white surface (ca. 4.18 masl) laid over a packing of small stones was the Level A floor of Room 7-8. Moreover, there is a clear line of demarcation in the surfacing of Room 7-7, which terminates abruptly along the northwest side of Room 7-8.

Given this transition, one stepped down into Room 7-8 if it were entered on its northwest side. Probably the room was roofed together with the prothyron, continuously but with more extensive coverage. This is demonstrated by the aforementioned tile fall (374 roof-tile fragments were found in Locus III; cf. Fig. 8, Table 1), as well as the presence of a block for a vertical support at its northern corner. The existence of walls closing off Room 7-8 remains uncertain, for these could have been constructed entirely of perishable materials (e.g., wattle or mud brick). The excavator mentioned numerous pithos fragments and a section of "chimney" in the roof-tile fall. But these do not appear in the finds notebook for the area, so their identification may have been mistaken.

Traces of earlier walls below the Level A surfaces spanned the area between the prothyron and courtyard, where a sizable ashlar block lay perpendicular to and abutting those comprising the outer threshold of Room 7-6. Another block continued the line into Room 7-7.[11] Five meters to the northeast, and picking up the alignment of the ashlars spanning Rooms 7-6 and 7-7, a short section of another early wall, this one constructed of rubble, lay adjacent to the stair base just west of Room 7-16.[12] Both of these features probably date no earlier than the middle of the 4th century (Level A/B). South of this latter stretch of early wall was located a roughly circular pit, up to 1.5 m in diameter and with a maximum depth of ca. 0.38 m. Cut into the Level A surface of the courtyard, it was ringed with stones and filled with pottery debris. While its precise function remains unknown, it may have marked the emplacement of a pithos or basin before becoming a repository for debris at the time of and following House 7's abandonment.[13]

The most impressive rooms in House 7, an andron (Room 7-9) and its antechamber (Room 7-10), are in its northwestern quarter. The antechamber was located immediately to the left upon entering the courtyard. Both rooms were spacious (ca. 21.53 and 11.93 m^2, respectively), and both possessed well-finished plaster floors and stone thresholds.[14] While neither threshold bore traces of bolt or pivot holes for doors, L-shaped cuttings on the ends of the threshold for Room 7-10 indicate the presence of a wooden door frame. In the absence of doors, cloth hangings should probably be assumed in their place (see below, 70). The walls of both Rooms 7-9 and 7-10 were plastered, but none of the wall plaster was recorded as being in situ. Accordingly, the precise decorative scheme employed for each room is unclear. Quantities of red plaster were recovered in each room, but that in Room 7-10 may belong to the southeast collapse of the party wall shared with Room 7-9. Likewise, the existence of a white dado band ca. 0.20 m in height, and present elsewhere on the site (cf. Pl. 25), is uncertain here.

The floor of the antechamber (Room 7-10) was finished with yellowish plaster and lay between 4.71 and 4.78 masl. As recovered, it showed subsidence in its southern corner and along its northeast side. The floor of the andron proper (Room 7-9) consists of white plaster and has the recessed central panel typical for andrones (2.70 x 2.80 m, at 4.80–4.90 masl). A plaster platform runs around the full perimeter of the room and averages 1 m in width. It lies as much as 0.23 m above the central area (and ranges in elevation from 4.85 to 5.03 masl). Therefore, Room 7-9 could have accommodated klinai of approximately that width, a generous proportion, and, judging from the known lengths of various klinai, was designed to hold comfortably seven such dining couches.[15] The presence of seven klinai accounts for the off-center doorway of Room 7-9, where the odd couch would have been accommodated along the southeast wall. That this doorway was set west of the axially placed doorway to Room 7-10 also allowed a degree of added privacy for symposiasts, especially if there were no substantial door here.

Along the southeastern segment of the platform in Room 7-9, below the head of the seventh kline, a channel ran between the recessed central area of the room and a sunken circular feature (Pl. 9). Here a small plain-ware jar (0.33 m in diameter; 0.31 m deep) had been plastered into the ledge. When excavated it was found to contain a small black-glazed bowl with stamped decoration (HP 2538) and a black-glazed stemless cup (HP 2540), both datable to the 4th century. Whether this feature originally had a ritual function, as a catchbasin for poured libations, or was purely utilitarian in nature, to aid in cleaning the chamber in the aftermath of the symposium, is unknown.[16]

Room 7-9 may have evolved from earlier phases into an ever more pretentious andron. This is suggested by traces of its refurbishing over time. Excavation revealed a northeast-southwest strip (between 0.50 and 0.75 m wide) in which the plaster of the latest Level A flooring had been cut away during or after the period of abandonment (Pl. 10). When the pebble underpinning for the

[11] This area was explored in TR 000/350: u. 16–20.

[12] This section of wall appeared in TR 005/355: u. 4.

[13] This was located in TR 005/355 and excavated as u. 17 and 18. No information about the profile of this feature was provided in the trench notebook, nor does it survive on site. For purposes of analysis, the artifacts recovered from its fill are included along with those from the courtyard generally in Locus IV (for which, see below, 19–20).

[14] The size of Room 7-9 compares well with Olynthian andrones, which generally measure from 19.9 to 22.6 m^2 (Hoepfner and Schwandner 1994, 98; D. M. Robinson and J. W. Graham 1938, 173–74). Cf. Bergquist 1990, 44–45, where a number of domestic andrones are cited. These are typically square and average ca. 4.5 m per side (giving an area of 20.25 m^2).

[15] Klinai ranged anywhere from 1.80 to 2.25 m in length (cf. Hoepfner and Schwandner 1994, 98; Richter 1966, 54; D. M. Robinson and J. W. Graham 1938, 173, n. 16).

[16] The andron in the House of the Comedian at Olynthos has an identical basin set into its platform, connected to the lower portion of the floor by means of a channel (D. M. Robinson and J. W. Graham 1938, 66, pls. 17, 87). The excavators interpret it as relating to housekeeping rather than ritual behavior.

latest floor was cleared in this area, portions of two simpler plaster floors underlying the extant surfacing were visible. Unfortunately, no datable material was recovered in association with these earlier floor levels.[17]

Room 7-13 is a northeast-southwest portico 2.5 m wide by 4.2 m long. Similar in both its orientation and dimensions to the domestic porticoes at Olynthos, as well as to those at other sites, Room 7-13 may be called a "pastas," although "transverse hall" is perhaps a more appropriate designation.[18] The portico was open to the courtyard along its southeastern side where the threshold is marked by a line of substantial ashlar blocks. The northwestern side had a centrally placed doorway with a stone threshold ca. 1.25 m in length. A cutting along the southwest end of the threshold may mark the original limits of the doorway here. If so, its width would have been only 0.90 m. This doorway opened onto Room 7-12, from which access was in turn gained to Rooms 7-11 and 7-14. While the southwest end of Room 7-13 abutted the andron antechamber (Room 7-10), its northeast end opened onto Room 7-15.

Room 7-13 was probably roofed by a second-story portico (Fig. 9). Therefore, its southeastern side would have had to bear one or two supports resting upon the ashlar socle. No traces of them, however, survive. The Level A living surface of Room 7-13 is marked by a patch of plaster flooring that survived in the southwestern end of the room. At 4.44–4.46 masl, it corresponds with the Level A floor of the courtyard. Traces of plaster were present along the ashlar threshold blocks shared with the courtyard as well. It should be pointed out that the latter lay at an elevation ca. 0.20–0.30 m higher than the floors on either side. The lateral spurs at the northeast end of the room that mark the transition between Rooms 7-13 and 7-15, and that must once have footed a wooden or mud-brick door frame, lie at a lower elevation (between 4.17 and 4.36 masl) and would have been out of use or at least buried in the latest phase of the house. The structure of the transition between Rooms 7-13 and 7-15 is discussed further below.

The L-shaped Room 7-12, ca. 19.72 m², is quite spacious, although not as large as Room 7-9, the andron. On its northwest side access was gained to a small chamber, Room 7-11, while from the northeast, Room 7-14 was accessible. Traces of the Level A floor of Room 7-12 were noted in two separate areas. In the southwest corner of the room, along the wall that divided it from the andron (Room 7-9), a narrow strip of plaster survived at 4.50–4.55 masl. In the northern and eastern portions, more extensive areas of flooring were recovered, although the type of surfacing encountered here was not specified in the excavation notebooks. Also in this area are two arcs of a circle formed by white pebbles laid into the floor surface. These once formed a complete circle with a restored diameter of ca. 1.60–1.70 m. The pebbles lay at an average elevation of 4.44 masl, the latest Level A living surface of House 7. Originally, then, this pebble circle lay precisely in the center of the northwest by southeast oriented portion of Room 7-12. Since the area was disturbed by roots, it is not surprising that the circle, and the ephemeral surface into which it was laid, was partially dug through. The function of the pebble circle is enigmatic. It does not appear to be part of a mosaic. Indeed, the use of mosaic remains undocumented at Halieis. Possibly it marked a location for gaming or some other activity.[19] It might belong to post-abandonment or squatter activity, but its central position in this portion of the room suggests that it dates to the period of use.

In the south-central portion of Room 7-12, where the Level A floor surface was either not preserved or not recognized, a great deal of rubble was exposed at 0.10–0.20 m lower than floor levels documented elsewhere in the room. This probably served as underpinning or a leveling dump for laying more finished surfaces. Several earlier wall

[17] The earlier plaster floors were explored in TR 005/345: u. 5, 6, and 9. They were confined to the southwestern half of the cutaway strip and lay between 4.66 and 4.83 masl. Although they lay under the rubble underpinning of the latest andron floor, they bore no underpinning themselves. Recovered artifacts were exclusively roof-tile fragments (numbering twenty-six), and these were noted to be quite worn.

[18] Coined by J. W. Graham for the houses at Olynthos (D. M. Robinson and J. W. Graham 1938, 143–51, 161–66), and based upon an observation of Vitruvius (6.7.1), the pastas distinguishes itself as a porch running longitudinally across between two-thirds and the entire length of the house. The designation "transverse hall" is used to describe rooms at Halieis that fit loosely this definition. At Olynthos, especially, the pastas house is a clearly defined type. It is distinct from the prostas type house, which, some would say, descended from the megaron arrangement of early Greek houses and comprises a shorter anteroom / porch appended to a principle living room, as in the houses at Colophon, Peiraeus, and Priene. Cf. Hoepfner and Schwandner 1994, 322–23. For further consideration of these halls / porches, see below, 65–67.

[19] "Now if they aimed a knucklebone at a marked-off circle with the object of causing it to remain inside it when it fell, they called the game . . . 'into-the-ring' " (Pollux 9.102, trans. Edmonds 1957, 403).

alignments were also explored in this area. Among these were part of the northwest and northeast sides of a room or feature (Pl. 11). The other two sides may have lain under and been incorporated into the existing dividing walls between Rooms 7-9 and 7-12 on the southwest and Rooms 7-13 and 7-12 on the southeast. For a hint as to the nature of this feature we must turn briefly to Room 7-14, lying to the northeast. Here, below the level of a plaster floor, was preserved a length of out-of-use drain composed of cover tiles. Although its surviving course is too short to determine a direction of flow, we may suppose that it was intended to carry water away rather than bring it in. It is likely that its northeastern end originally reached the alley or ambitus, but no traces of this terminus survive (the northeastern course of the drain having been truncated by the rear wall of Room 7-14). If the alignments described above are seen as an infilled negative feature rather than a room, a second kopron (from an earlier phase of the house), this will have been the logical point of origin for the drain.

If there was once a kopron in Room 7-12, the kopron in Room 7-7 may have been its successor (if House 7 was expanded to the southeast?).[20] Or it may date from a time when the plot now occupied by House 7 was taken up by two houses. Pending detailed analysis of the finds, only rough dates may be suggested for the earlier phase of House 7 and its southeastern expansion, or for the possible unification of two separate structures into a single one. Like the earlier walls encountered below the surface of the courtyard (Room 7-7), these features probably date no earlier than the mid-4th century (Level A / B).[21]

Room 7-11 is the smallest in House 7 (approximately 6.50 m^2). Entering from the northwestern side of Room 7-12 through a 1 m wide doorway, one would have stepped up to the partially preserved plaster pavement that survives in the southwestern third of the room (at ca. 4.75 masl). Based on its small size and paving Room 7-11 may have served as a bath. There were, however, no traces of plaster on the walls. In addition, Room 7-11 is four times the size of two other probable bathrooms identified at the site (in House A, Room 6-84, and House E, Room 6-17), twice that of a third (in House B), and about 26 percent larger than another tentatively identified domestic bath (in House C, Room 6-64). Nor is it located adjacent to a probable kitchen as are three of the previous examples. If we were to accept the identification of Room 7-11 as a bath, it might be that the destruction of its pavement relates to the removal of some feature, possibly a bathtub or basin.[22] From an earlier phase (probably mid-4th century), 0.30–0.40 m below the plaster pavement to the southwest, a short section of wall extends northwest from the southeastern side of Room 7-11.[23]

Room 7-14 is the final chamber in the trio of rooms to which the pastas / transverse hall (Room 7-13) gave access. Lying in the contracted northeastern corner of House 7, it measures approximately 8.4 m^2. It was set off from Room 7-12 by a short spur wall, the footings of which lie at and below the Level A floor surface, and its doorway was ca. 1.5 m wide. Traces of a plaster floor were observed in the southern half of the room and lay at approximately the same elevation as the Level A floor of Room 7-12. Curiously, on top of this surface was built another short spur of wall parallel to, but 0.75 m northeast of the section of wall that defined the doorway (this wall does not appear on any of the plans reproduced here). It is below this level that the aforementioned (Level A / B) tile drain was located, having been set into a roughly laid fieldstone pavement. A final noteworthy feature of Room 7-14 is a channel-like cutting along the top inside edge of the ashlar foundations that form the northeast boundary of the room. Spanning three blocks and lined with plaster, its precise purpose remains unknown.

From the northeastern end of the portico (Room 7-13), one entered Room 7-15 (ca. 18.2 m^2). The room is distinguished by a short spur wall projecting southwest from the northwest-southeast rear wall of the room. There also seems to have been a modification involving the doorway (see below). Establishing the latest Level A floor was particularly difficult here as it seems to have consisted of a series of very ephemeral surfacings of hard-packed earth with lime inclusions. Two

[20] An infilled kopron is also posited in the courtyard of House C at Halieis (Room 6-53), taken out of use with the construction of a cistern, which was either built into or adjacent to it. See below, 35.

[21] The early phase of Room 7-12 was explored in TR 010 / 350: u. 6, 8, and 12. Material recovered in association with the earlier phase of Room 7-14 (from TR 010 / 355: u. 3, 6, and 7) included a silver stater of Thebes (HN 1975-124; ca. 400–390), a bronze coin of Aigina (HN 1975-113; post 404), and two bronze tokens of Halieis (HN 1975-108, HN 1975-109).

[22] No tubs or tub fragments are known from the site; for examples from Olynthos, see D. M. Robinson and J. W. Graham 1938, 200–201. For an overview of the rooms identified as baths at Halieis, see below, 68–69.

[23] This appeared in TR 010 / 350: u. 7.

or three such thin surfaces were noted in the course of excavating Room 7-15, in addition to another more substantial surface that appeared in a deep sounding in the eastern corner of the room. The latest likely floor level lies within the range of, if a bit lower than, elevations noted elsewhere for surfacings in House 7 (4.38 and 4.42 masl being the two most representative points in Room 7-15 upon which elevations were taken).

As noted above in the discussion of Room 7-13, the footings for door jambs between this portico and Room 7-15 were out of use by the latest Level A phase of House 7, having been buried by the rising floor level. In their place, at a higher elevation (4.38–4.54 masl, versus the 4.17–4.26 masl of the original jamb foundations), rests a series of three blocks set ca. 1.25 m farther northeast into Room 7-15. Spaced so as to provide an opening of 0.75 m (echoing that provided by the original jambs), these blocks could represent the position of a later doorway for Room 7-15. In addition, they could have functioned as internal supports for the posited second story of House 7. This modification would have added ca. 2 m^2 to the area of Room 7-13 and aligned the doorway of Room 7-15 in a vertical plane with that of Room 7-14, providing increased stability for the wide span that existed here. Indeed, the aforementioned spur wall along the northeast side of Room 7-14 was probably added for just such a reason.

Finally, a deep sounding in the eastern corner of Room 7-15 revealed a section of plaster floor (at 4.06 masl) and a short stretch of wall with a possible doorway associated with, if not earlier than, the flooring itself.[24] Preliminary examination of the pottery from these levels suggests a date not earlier than the mid-4th century for the features (Level A/B).

Rooms 7-16 and 7-17 have a combined area of 20.43 m^2 and are located along the eastern corner of House 7. Although in some respects quite distinct, they need to be treated as a unit since they share a feature unique among the houses thus far excavated at Halieis: a stone-built hearth. Since there are no traces of industrial activity, Rooms 7-16 and 7-17 may be identified as a kitchen. They are set off from the complex of rooms accessible from the portico (Room 7-13). Room 7-16 was provided with a doorway ca. 0.80 m wide, although the irregular survival of walls along the northeast side of the courtyard hampers precise interpretation here. Room 7-17, on the other hand, was entirely open to the courtyard along its southwest side. Portions of the L-shaped stretch of wall that divides the two rooms are of flimsy rubble construction and survive at a low elevation. This suggests that the wall may have served for partitioning rather than load bearing.

The northeast end of the partition wall between Rooms 7-16 and 7-17 terminates in the hearth, of which two upright slabs on its north and southwest sides, as well as two blocks at its eastern corner, survive in situ (Pl. 12). The rest of the hearth perimeter, which measured approximately 1 m on each side, was formed either in rubble or slabs that have since been robbed away. These dimensions are confirmed by a square, 0.25 m thick ash deposit, as well as the eastern corner blocks that were set into a partially preserved plaster pavement (Pl. 13). The elevation of the latter (at 4.40–4.48 masl) again corresponds to the range supplied by other surviving latest floor surfaces in House 7. This whitish plaster surface was laid atop a bedding of rounded water-worn cobbles and probably terminated along its northwestern edge (where it follows the line of the hearth). Originally it must have continued some distance southwest in Room 7-17 where it overlay the drain associated with the kopron in the courtyard. The floor of Room 7-16, by contrast, seems to have been partially flagged. This flagging lies in the area south of a low rubble socle that divides the room but does not abut its rear wall. It may simply have served to delimit the extent of the flagging. That the stony surface was not merely underpinning is suggested by a concentration of artifact material clustered just southwest of the hearth at ca. 4.40 masl. The northern half of Room 7-16 appears to have had an earthen floor.

The second-story rooms of House 7, reached by the stairway on the northeast side of the courtyard, probably mirrored the arrangement of those below (Fig. 9). Internal partitioning would have been placed only on top of load-bearing walls on the ground floor. This may explain the profusion of spur walls in the rooms so far discussed. Not only did these walls divide rooms internally and from one another, but they also served to support the floor above, especially over broad vacant spans below. The second story probably included chambers above Rooms 7-9 and 7-10 through Room 7-15 but did not extend further. This hypothesis is supported by the change in construction of the exterior wall foundations. This

[24] These features were investigated in TR 010/360: u. 3, 5, and 9.

occurs precisely at the transition from Room 7-15, where conglomerate ashlars were used, to Room 7-16, where there is only a meager rubble socle. In addition, in the hearth area there is no evidence for the elaborate flue arrangement employed on the second story of houses at Olynthos.[25] Probably the kitchen was a simple one-story construction with a flat or sloping roof provided with a smoke hole. Or smoke may have escaped through the open southwest side of Room 7-17.

Artifact Assemblages: Quantification and Distribution

The quantification and distribution of finds from the latest occupation levels in House 7 are presented in Tables 1–3 and Appendix II.A.[26] Some of the basic facts and figures to emerge from this material include the following. There were 6230 pottery items recovered from the latest phases of the house. By counting rims and bases (as discussed above, 8–9), one arrives at a minimum number of vessels represented of 824.[27] This MNV comprises forty-nine different shapes in the three basic fabrics: fine, plain, and coarse ware (see Table 19 for the variety of vessel forms within each house). The most numerous types are fine-ware cups associated with drink consumption (209 MNV in nine shapes) and cooking (164 MNV in four coarse-ware shapes including lids). These are followed by fine-, plain-, and coarse-ware vessels for the serving and pouring of drinks, the 148 MNV including fine-ware serving containers such as kraters. The next largest category (91 MNV) is plain and coarse wares associated with food preparation other than cooking. The open vessel forms (that is, bowls) will often have doubled as serving vessels. Following in frequency are fine-ware vessels for the serving and consumption of food (87 MNV). Storage containers in plain and coarse ware occur at the lowest frequency, 79 MNV. This small number may reflect their much greater size, durability, and longevity. They did not have to be replaced as often as finer vessels. The breakdown just discussed is summarized by the following:

6230 pottery items
- = 824 MNV (in 3 wares and 49 shapes)
- = 209 MNV (25.4%) associated with drink consumption (fine-ware cups only)
- = 164 MNV (19.9%) associated with cooking
- = 148 MNV (18.0%) associated with serving and pouring drink (including fine-ware drink-serving containers)
- = 91 MNV (11.0%) associated with food serving and preparation other than cooking
- = 87 MNV (10.6%) associated with fine-ware food serving and consumption
- = 79 MNV (9.6%) associated with storage of food and drink

In terms of distribution over the house, the largest horizontal concentration of pottery was from Rooms 7-7 and 7-8 (Loci III and IV) or the courtyard area in general. With a combined MNV of 253, virtually all types of vessels were present. The same holds true for the 230 MNV filling Locus VII, the negative feature in Room 7-7 identified as a kopron.[28] The combined 483 MNV from Loci III, IV, and VII accounts for almost 60 percent of the vessels from House 7. These numbers indicate the areas used for discard. In addition, these areas constituted the central space and primary thoroughfare of the house in which virtually all activities would have taken place at one time or another (and where all manner of vessels would, consequently, have been broken and/or disposed of). Vessel types that occur in the courtyard in particularly significant quantities are those associated with the storage of food and liquids. The 35 MNV from Locus IV for plain- and coarse-ware storage containers, primarily amphoras, indicates that a fairly large number must have been stored in the courtyard to have left so many traces.[29]

Unfortunately, artifacts from Locus III shed no light on the precise function of Room 7-8. Nor was it possible in the course of excavation to be

[25] For the somewhat controversial Olynthian flues, see J. W. Graham 1954, 328–46; Hoepfner and Schwandner 1994,100–102, with fig. 64; D. M. Robinson and J. W. Graham 1938, 189–97; and D. M. Robinson 1946, 380–83.

[26] A very brief overview of artifact distributions from House 7 has been presented in Ault and Nevett 1999, 50–51, with fig. 4.4 and table 4.3.

[27] This count excludes the nonpottery, "clay" classes of lamps, loom weights, miniature vessels, terracotta figurines, roof tiles, and the like. The overall figures are reduced slightly (i.e., to 754 MNV), if one excludes Locus I material, all of which comes from Avenue C just in front of the house.

[28] See below, 64, and Ault 1999b, especially 553–54, and 567, appendix 1 (for an inventory of its contents).

[29] Nearly half of these came from the fill of the pit feature in the north central portion of Room 7-7 (TR 005/355: u. 17, 18; and discussed above, 15). Yielding more than two hundred sherds altogether and with a MNV of 29, a MNV of 14 of these were associated with storage, including fragments of at least eleven plain-ware amphoras, one coarse-ware pithos, and two coarse-ware pithos lids.

certain that a separate room was emerging here, given the lack of walls on either the northwest or northeast sides partitioning it from the courtyard. Thus, the artifacts from Locus III include material from portions of the courtyard and probably some of the upper fill of the kopron in addition to Room 7-8. Finally, since the southernmost reaches of Room 7-8 were not taken down to the Level A floor surface, we do not have a significant sample of material from the room.

The classes of pottery from two other areas in House 7 are more informative. Rooms 7-16 and 7-17 have already been discussed as comprising the kitchen facilities for the house. This identification is born out by the 24 MNV for cooking recovered there (Loci V, VI, and XXIV–XXVIII).[30] Other vessels that would have played a role in food preparation are the 9 and 10 MNV in plain-ware shapes associated with the preparation and serving of food and the pouring and serving of drink, respectively. That a certain amount of food and drink consumption also took place in Rooms 7-16 and 7-17 is confirmed by the MNV for these fine-ware categories (7 and 20 MNV for food and drink, respectively).

Room 7-12 was the real center of food and drink consumption for the household, aside from the andron (which was probably used only for special occasions and yielded only a very small amount of material).[31] Here were recovered 22 MNV associated with fine-ware drinking shapes, plus another 5 MNV of fine-ware food serving vessels (grouped stratigraphically into Loci XVII–XIX). Although these numbers are no greater than those of similar categories in the kitchen, they are larger in comparison to those from other inner rooms of the house (that is, Rooms 7-9, 7-10, 7-14, and 7-15). This suggests that the inhabitants had a preference for this area. In addition, the position and configuration of the porch or hall (Room 7-13) supports the identification of Room 7-12 as the principal dayroom for indoor activities beyond the kitchen (see below, 67–68).

Both Rooms 7-14 and 7-15 are ideally situated for storage since they occupy the most interior locations of the house. Nevertheless, Room 7-14 (Locus XX) contained few artifacts to help clarify its function. Room 7-15 (Loci XXI–XXIII) yielded much pottery of all types, but none in a number significant enough to aid in its identification (MNV 61; cf. note 30). Since only three storage vessels were found there (based on the MNV count), it was probably not a storeroom. Perhaps Room 7-15 served as a secondary living area (a thalamos?) for the ground floor.[32]

Among other classes of artifacts there are no particular clusterings in any area. Instead, they were spread throughout the house. Three lamps each are represented by fragments from Rooms 7-8 (Locus III) and 7-13 (Loci XV–XVI). But this is not significant since most of the other rooms yielded at least one or two lamp fragments. Similarly, the only concentration of loom weights occurred within the kopron (four examples), with seven more spread evenly over most of the house. Curiously perhaps, given its identification as a principle living and working space within the house, none were found in Room 7-12.

Miniature vessels, including a lamp from the courtyard, were abundant (MNV 22). Rooms 7-11 and 7-12 yielded four examples of two types: kotyle and jug. The two terracottas from the house, the base of a seated figure (HC 856) and a mold (HC 647), came from the kitchen (Rooms 7-16 and 7-17) and dayroom (Room 7-12), respectively.

Metal objects were most numerous in the area of Rooms 7-8 and 7-16/17 with sixteen and twenty-three items recovered, respectively. One of the three bronze objects from Room 7-8 was a rooster figurine (Locus III, HM 1256) and another was a fragmentary scabbard (HM 1527; called a "sheath" in Table 1). In Room 7-16, just southwest of the hearth, lay a concentration of metal objects comprising at least ten iron nails (Locus XXV). Their grouping suggests a collapsed shelf or other small wooden structure. A small bronze "cup" was found to the north, along the back northwest-southeast wall of Room 7-16 (Locus XXVI, HM 1287).[33] Within the ashy fill of the hearth lay a

[30] The MNV for cooking shapes between Rooms 7-16/17 and Room 7-15 presented here is at odds with that I argued for elsewhere at an earlier date (Ault 1987). It invalidates the thesis there that Room 7-15 may have served as a second, possibly seasonal (i.e., winter) kitchen. The 11 MNV from Loci XXI–XXIII for pottery associated with cooking in Room 7-15 is the result of a much more thorough analysis than was previously conducted. Moreover, such an internalized, isolated location for a second food preparation area is made increasingly unlikely by evidence that suggests the courtyard or pastas porch as a more likely location (cf. the scenario presented for House A, Room 6-81c, Locus VI; and House C, Room 6-53, Locus XI).

[31] Cf. Loci IX–XIV, which correspond to Rooms 7-9 and 7-10 and which had a MNV of only 14.

[32] Cf. Plato *Protagoras* 315D (cited below, 72).

[33] Although I have not examined this piece, it is described as straight sided and undecorated with a diameter of 0.055 m. I suspect that it may have served to sheath a wooden door pivot and as such is quite out of position. For an example from Priene, now in the Berlin Antikensammlung, see Raeder 1984, 60, cat. no. 318, pl. 2b.

fragmentary iron spearhead (Locus XXVIII, HM 1285). Other iron implements recovered from House 7 include a chisel from Room 7-14 (Locus XX, HM 1508) and a sickle blade from Room 7-13 (Locus XVI, HM 1290). Just outside the doorway into Room 7-16 was recovered a bronze relief ornament with a lotus bud (Locus V, HM 1375), perhaps broken off a drop-handle or mirror. Slightly southeast, along the dividing wall between Rooms 7-7 and 7-16, a small knob-handled lead "lid" (Locus XXV, HM 1293) was found. Three bronze coins, two of Hermione (Locus XXV, HN 1975-97; and Locus XXIV, HN 1975-134; both dated 350–300) and one of Tiryns (minted at Halieis) (Locus XXIV, HN 1975-135) also came from Room 7-16.

Area 6

(Figures 2–5; Plates 1, 14–31, 44, 54, 62)

Area 6 at Halieis, also known as Field 24, comprises a continuous trench, ca. 110 m long, oriented northeast-southwest (Figs. 2–5; Pls. 21, 22). Varying from approximately 10 m wide at the south to 24 m wide at the north, it cuts across portions of three blocks of insular housing, two streets (Streets 3 and 4), and one avenue (Avenue B). Its northeastern end terminates in a small block of houses and a probable military structure, the Northeast Command Post. (See McAllister 2005, chap. 4.)

Portions of as many as fifteen houses were recovered with the excavation of Area 6, nine belonging to a trapezoidal insula (ca. 30 x 90 m) that may have contained as many as twelve houses. Approximately one-third of this insula was cleared to reveal three relatively complete house plans (Houses C, D, and E). In addition, fronting Avenue B at the northeastern end of Area 6, lies one completely recovered house (House A), while a large portion of the neighboring house to the north (House B) has also been excavated. Of these five houses, four of them (Houses A, C, D, and E) are considered in detail below. Because House B was excavated in two disparate campaigns (1962 and 1975), it lacks the continuity of record keeping, especially for the finds recovered, necessary for the detailed study applied to the other houses. In what follows, House B and the portions of nine other houses are presented briefly, although with no specific discussion of assemblages.[34]

House B (Rooms 6-89–6-93 and part of Area T [Fig. 3; Pls. 14–20]) was excavated during two field seasons, separated by thirteen years. Its northern extent was explored in 1962 while Rooms 6-89 through 6-93 were not cleared and identified until 1975.[35] It was a large house entered from Avenue B through a wide (incompletely excavated) prothyron doorway (Room 6-89) that led to a spacious courtyard extending across Rooms 6-90 and 6-91. Two rubble walls were built along the southeastern side of the court, into a corner and against the party wall shared with House A (Rooms 6-83 and 6-87). These defined an upright construction of ca. 1.25 x 2 m. It has been referred to as the only "indication of a staircase" excavated at Halieis (Boyd and Rudolph 1978, 349). This observation needs to be corrected on two counts: there are several identifiable stair bases in houses at the site and this is unlikely to be one of them. It neither resembles the known examples, nor does it make good sense in terms of its placement. Rather, given its location in the court and near the door, this feature may have served as a kopron (refuse pit) even though it is not sunken into the courtyard floor, as are all the other examples identified at Halieis.[36]

Room 6-91, inside the courtyard, has traces of a colonnade on its northwest, northeast, and southeast sides (Pl. 14). With intercolumniations between ca. 2 to 2.5 m, it may have had three columns on the northeast wing and two each on the northwest and southeast wings (counting corner columns twice). This near-peristylar arrangement is suggested by the foundations and

[34] In 1979, portions of another three houses were excavated by the Fourth Ephoreia of the Greek Archaeological Service in a plot (hereafter Ephoreia Field) lying just northwest of Area 6. Two of these lay in a previously unexplored insula north of Street 5 (cf. Fig. 2: Ephoreia Field). As yet unpublished, these excavations remain beyond the scope of this study.

[35] The 1962 excavation consisted of a few trenches in what was called "Area T" for Thomas W. Jacobsen, who was trench master. See Boyd and Rudolph 1978, 349, with fig. 3, where House B is estimated to have covered ca. 215 m^2.

[36] A similar construction lay in the southeast corner of Room c in House A iv 9 at Olynthos. Described as "an angle of light rubble and plaster" (D. M. Robinson and J. W. Graham 1938, 88, with 198, pls. 24b, 92, 93) and measuring ca. 1 x 2 m, the floor of the feature was laid with a drain. The interpretation of Room c has been contested. Graham believed that it was a second kitchen in the house, the adjacent Room b serving as a flue (ibid., 87–88). Cahill, however, has located here a light-well suite of the type he has identified elsewhere at the site (2002, 110). Similarly, interpretations as to the nature of the feature within Room c have ranged from kylikion, to stair base, to a domestic shrine, and now, a kopron. Given its flimsy construction, it may be that similar examples were overlooked in other houses excavated at the site (cf. the comments about the varying degree of care with which excavation took place in Cahill 1991, 115–30; 2002, 61–65).

a Doric capital and column fragments recovered from the area. A well was partially excavated at the northernmost corner of Room 6-91, within the colonnade. A broad doorway (ca. 3 m wide) with a stone threshold lay off this northeastern portico. It gave access to Room 6-92 (Pls. 14, 15). Room 6-92 seems to be a pastas porch or transverse hall, although its northwestern end has not been cleared. A rectangular marble basin or trough lay at its southeastern end. Also, a weight block from a press was found, probably not in situ, in the open portion of Room 6-91. (A similar weight block was found in the kitchen [visible in Pls. 17, 18 but not included in Fig. 3], but the house had no other traces of press installations.) These features suggest domestic industry in House B as well. Only a tiny portion of Room 6-93 was excavated. It is one of a probable series of rooms reached from Room 6-92.

The northwestern portion of House B was cleared in 1962 (Pls. 17, 18). Proceeding counterclockwise from Room 6-91, across the plaster pavement of its northwest portico lay a square room, averaging ca. 4.45 m on each side (Pls. 16, 17). Lacking a threshold block, it appears to have been flush with the pavement of the portico. Its dimensions, finish (i.e., its pavement), and off-center doorway suggest that this was an andron. It is almost identical in size to Room 7-9, the andron of House 7, although lacking the raised platform for klinai. But not all andrones at Halieis, or elsewhere, possessed such a platform.

Adjacent to this room lay a suite of rooms that, again because of its similarity to a known configuration at Halieis and elsewhere, is identifiable as a kitchen and bath complex (Pls. 18–20). Almost identical to Rooms 6-83 and 6-84 in House A to the south, it is larger, ca. 26 m^2, but has a similar discontinuous plaster pavement confined to the northwestern wall of the kitchen (which was also divided by a short spur), the entry to the bath, and the bathroom proper.

The final room exposed in House B, the precise configuration of which remains uncertain, lies between the kitchen / bath complex and Room 6-90. Its relationship to the other rooms is similar to that of Room 6-85 in House A. Like Room 6-85, it is small (ca. 6.25 m^2). Presumably it faced onto and was accessible from the courtyard.

Rooms 6-65–6-66 (Fig. 4; Pl. 23) and 6-72–6-79 (Fig. 3; Pls. 24, 25) belong to as many as three houses occupying the southeast corner of a largely unexplored insula lying between Avenues B and C and Streets 4 and 5.[37] Rooms 6-65 and 6-66 are surely from a separate dwelling, of which only this small area was excavated. There are two adjacent basins sunken into the plastered floor in the corner of Room 6-66 (Pl. 23). This is likely to have been a workroom, perhaps, given their prevalence elsewhere on the site, housing an oil-press.

Rooms 6-72 through 6-79 probably belong to the east corner house of the insula. Entering from Avenue B through a well-preserved prothyron (Room 6-77), one passed into the spacious, rectangular Room 6-76. Its ample dimensions (ca. 24.4 m^2) suggest that it could have been an unroofed court. Alternatively, it was roofed but did not support a second story. If so, Rooms 6-75 and 6-78 would have comprised the courtyard of the house.[38] It may even be that the entire area of Rooms 6-76, 6-75, and 6-78 was unroofed court space. The base of a large pithos was found in the eastern corner of Room 6-78. A section of a smaller pithos was located in the south corner of Room 6-76 (Pl. 24). It had been cut and fitted atop conglomerate slabs to serve as a well mouth. The shaft of this well was explored only to a depth of 0.74 m below the surrounding floor level (to 0.15 mbsl).

A suite of three interconnecting interior rooms, 6-72 through 6-74, is accessible from the southwestern side of Room 6-76. The partial excavation of the area does not provide a well-defined plan. Traces of plaster were preserved on all the extant walls of both Rooms 6-73 and 6-74 (Pl. 25). Room 6-79, too, is difficult to read, not least because it is unclear to which of the corner houses of this insula it belonged. Nevertheless, as excavated, the combination of ashlar footings and well-finished plaster pavement is similar to that associated with Rooms 6-14 and 6-15 at the southern end of Area 6 (for which, see below, 25), tentatively identified as belonging to an andron and its anteroom.

Rooms 6-67–6-71 (Figs. 3, 4) all belong to the north corner house in the insula bordered by Avenues B and C and Streets 3 and 4. As no prothyron was noted along Street 4, this house, like most corner houses, would have been entered

[37] Three rooms from the north corner house of this insula were partially revealed in the unpublished excavations by the Greek Archaeological Service (Fig. 2). A weight block from a press installation survives in the middle room.

[38] For the results of a deep sounding conducted in Room 6-78 and Avenue B, see Rudolph 1984, especially 128–30 ("Test B") and 151–55, with fig. 4 and pl. 32b.

from the avenue onto which it faced (Avenue B in this case).[39] Because excavation of these rooms was limited, there is little to add beyond noting the large size of Room 6-70 (ca. 36 m² of which has been cleared); that Room 6-71 in the north corner of the house (of which only the north and west corners have been exposed), with its northwest length of ca. 4.5 m, could have been an andron; and that Rooms 6-67, 6-68, and 6-69 at the west of the house appear to be smallish interior rooms. (It is possible that Room 6-69 was the west corner of the southeast-facing courtyard.) Although we have too little of the house to be sure of its plan, there are traces of walls visible on the surface beyond the limits of Area 6 and to the southeast of Rooms 6-67–6-71 (cf. Fig. 2). These probably do mark the southeasterly extent of this dwelling.

Rooms 6-46, 6-47, 6-49, 6-51, and 6-52 (Fig. 4; Pl. 44), lying to the southwest of and neighboring House C, present numerous difficulties in interpretation. Owing to the limits of excavation, none of the frontage (along Street 4) of the building to which they belong has been revealed. Portions of two rooms, 6-51 and 6-52, mark the northern limits of the known structure.

The largest unit in this complex, Room 6-46, lies just southeast of Rooms 6-51 and 6-52 and covers ca. 34 m². It was furnished with a well in its west corner, a built feature constructed perpendicular to its northeastern wall, and portions of two drains that were exposed on either side of this feature.[40] The northernmost of these drains was a stone-lined channel laid into the floor. It continued northeast into the porticoed portion of Room 6-53, off the courtyard in House C to the northeast (Fig. 13). This drain was out of use by the latest Level A occupation phase of both rooms. The south drain consisted of a channel cut into a series of blocks laid end to end. (Compare the similar drain associated with House E to the southwest, spanning Rooms 6-10 and 6-13; see below, 52.) Apparently originating in the east corner of Room 6-46, it sloped down toward its outlet (the well?). Perhaps it was intended to carry off water from the roofs of neighboring houses, four of which converged here (represented by Rooms 6-48, 6-50, 6-53, and the court, Room 6-46).

At the center of Room 6-46 is a low platform or trough made up of three fine-grained conglomerate slabs. It resembles the slab-built trough in House D, Room 6-26, that has been associated with an olive-press installation in the adjacent Room 6-29 (see below, 41). Perhaps the feature in Room 6-46 was used in the processing or preparation of some commodity and, as such, would indicate yet another instance of domestic industrial activity at Halieis. All these features suggest that Room 6-46 was an unroofed court (although there is no clear doorway between it and Room 6-52).

Room 6-47, a square chamber of ca. 10 m², seems to mark the southern limit of this building. It was accessible from the southwestern portion of Room 6-46. Room 6-49, of which only 2 m² have been cleared, appears to have been small and narrow. Its relationship to this complex of rooms is unclear (particularly since it is separated from Room 6-46 by a very thick rubble wall). Finally, it should be noted that a number of walls belonging to earlier (Level C?) phases were revealed in Rooms 6-46 and 6-52.

Rooms 6-40 and 6-45 (Figs. 4, 5; Pls. 26–28, 44, 54) are at the center of the insula that takes up most of Area 6. They comprise a long rectangular corridor, ca. 45 m² of which have been exposed, and are flanked by houses along the 12.5 m of their excavated length. The southern extent terminates abruptly against the northwest wall of Room 6-32 in House D. If Rooms 6-40 and 6-45 did once reach all the way north to Street 4, they would have extended to over 22 m in length. The northern limits of this space appear to continue well beyond the excavated portion of Area 6. At present, neither its full length nor the means by which it was accessed are known.

Rooms 6-40 and 6-45 are divided by two overlapping, poorly aligned stretches of rubble wall located in the northern half of the space. These, in turn, appear to overlie (and so are later than) a regularly laid foundation course of poros blocks of the sort commonly employed elsewhere at Halieis. Whether Room 6-45, and so Room 6-40 also, was in some way connected with the complex of rooms that lie to the east (Rooms 6-46, 6-47, 6-49, and 6-51 through 6-52) is unclear. On the basis of the irregular rubble walls that define its western limits, however, Room 6-45 appears to be a later insertion into Room 6-40 (late Level A or even an

[39] But cf. the south corner house of the insula exposed in the Ephoreia Field (Fig. 2), the prothyron of which faces onto Street 5.

[40] Excavation of the well in 1974 (TR 085/335) yielded a large quantity of organic remains including woodwork (e.g., planking and a notched support for stair treads) and wooden objects, notably a comb (HV 311) and mallet (HV 323), among other items, and animal bones.

abandonment phase?) when the original extent of the space once occupied solely by Room 6-40 had been compromised.

The most prominent feature of Room 6-40 is a finely cut square base of hard gray limestone, 0.5 m long on each side (Pls. 27, 28). It was situated centrally within the width of the corridor here (at 074/329). A shelly limestone pillar was originally leaded into a cutting in the base. (The cutting is 0.25 m on each side.) A fragment of the pillar survived in situ at the time of excavation. Just west of the base, a pair of stones appears to mark the foundation of some small structure. Although the associated artifacts do not help to identify the area, parallels with the hitherto unique "stele shrines" from the Potters' Quarter at Corinth suggest that Room 6-40 may have had some cult significance.[41] Spatially, however, Room 6-40 is quite similar to long, corridor-like rooms at Olynthos that have been interpreted as communal storage areas (see below, 72, with note 79). Thus the function of Room 6-40 (and 6-45) remains undecided.

Rooms 6-34 (Fig. 5; Pls. 29, 54) and 6-37–6-39 (Fig. 5; Pl. 54) occupy the southeastern reaches of one of the centrally located houses along the northwestern side of the insula between Avenues B and C and Streets 3 and 4. Although the front of this house has not been excavated, it is likely that it would have been entered from Street 4. The only internal communication between the excavated rooms is the doorway between Rooms 6-37 and 6-38. Only Room 6-38 was completely excavated. Its dimensions are ca. 8.25 m^2. Room 6-37, given its southerly location, may have been the courtyard. In the east corner of Room 6-34, which is presumed, but not certain, to have been a part of this unit, were the remains of an enormous sunken pithos (diameter 1.45 m) in situ (Pl. 29).

Rooms 6-41–6-44, 6-48, and 6-50 (Figs. 4, 5; Pls. 30, 44, 54) are probably the northernmost portions of two houses: Rooms 6-41 through 6-44 and 6-48 are from one dwelling, and Room 6-50 is from an adjacent structure. Both buildings lay within the southeastern row of houses in this insula, opposite the partially excavated structures discussed above and neighboring Houses C and D. Although none of their frontage has been exposed, they were probably entered by doors facing onto Street 3.

Only Room 6-41 was completely excavated (Pl. 30). Although rather small, at 5.8 m^2, its latest habitation level yielded many artifacts including a small Ionic capital (HS 529), a cache of more than twenty bronze fishhooks (HM 1260–1282), and seven coins (HN 1975-3, 1975-4, and HN 1975-11–1975-15) representing the mints of Troizen, Halieis, and Epidauros.[42] On its southeast side, Room 6-41 was connected to Room 6-43. This latter room may have been a pastas porch or transverse hall. Its arrangement is similar to the hall of House D to the southwest, as well as numerous other halls or pastas porches at the site. Rooms 6-42 and 6-48 would also have opened onto it. In turn, Room 6-43 should have faced south onto a courtyard, only a tiny corner of which is represented by Room 6-44. Part of a plaster platform emerging in the northeastern limits of Room 6-43 (as excavated) resembles those encountered elsewhere, especially in Room 6-29, House D, where a similar porch also served as a press room (see below, 41). Room 6-48, at the north corner of the house, appears to have been quite large (the excavated area is ca. 14.7 m^2). The foundations for some small feature were built into its west corner.

Room 6-50 is at the west corner of the neighboring house to the northeast. Because it was located near the southeastern boundary of the excavated area, only ca. 3.9 m^2 were cleared here, exposing a well shaft and its stone head.

Rooms 6-1–6-6 (Fig. 5; Pls. 31, 62) at the southern end of Area 6 are from the west corner house of an insula bordered by Avenues B and C and Streets 2 and 3. As with other corner houses, this, too, was probably entered through a doorway facing onto the fronting avenue. The overall plan of the existing rooms is fragmentary. Rooms 6-4 and 6-5 provide a good sense of their original full shape and dimensions. Rooms 6-1 and 6-2 survive as probable rectangular chambers along the northwestern portion of the house. Room 6-2 was presumably accessible from Room 6-1, although there may been passage between Room 6-2 and the longitudinal corridor Room 6-3. Room 6-1 would perhaps have functioned as a pastas porch or transverse hall facing south onto a courtyard.[43] The L-shaped corridor Room 6-3, unusual in plan, probably led to Room 6-4 at its eastern (unexcavated) portion.

[41] See C. K. Williams 1981, where these cult installations are interpreted as ancestor shrines (cf. below, 51, for the inscribed blocks from House E, Room 6-24). In this case, the foundations west of the stele in Room 6-40 could have supported a small altar.

[42] This material was recovered in TR 075/335: units 6–8. The corroded bundle of fishhooks is illustrated in Cartledge 1998, 27.

[43] A section of probable Level C wall was revealed in the northwestern area of Room 6-1.

Squarish and with an area of ca. 16.5 m^2, Room 6-4 served as a press room (Pl. 31). Its brown sandstone press bed (ca. 1.15 m in diameter) was set into the northwest corner and plastered into the pavement that surrounds it. The southern edge of the pavement itself was curbed and plaster continues up the exposed western wall of the room. The spout of the press extends over a basin (ca. 0.45 m in diameter) sunken into and made from the plaster. Presumably, given the layout of press rooms elsewhere at the site, at least one larger sunken vessel lay to the east of the press bed,[44] within the unexcavated grid square to the north (045/315, upon which an olive tree grows to this day). There were no traces of the weight block to which a press beam would have been attached. If the arrangement was similar to that of the Industrial Terrace press room, it could be located within the unexcavated northeastern portion of Room 6-4 (Ault 1999b, 562–64; Jameson 2001b).

Room 6-5 is a small square chamber, ca. 2.5 m on each side, that marks the north corner of the house. It was apparently accessible from the press room, Room 6-4, and had no other features of note. Room 6-5 lay to the northwest of Room 6-6, of which only a tiny area (ca. 1.5 m^2) was excavated.

Rooms 6-7, 6-8, 6-14, and 6-15 (Fig. 5, Pl. 62) belonged to a house neighboring that represented by Rooms 6-1 through 6-4. Room 6-7, the only one of these to have been fully cleared, is yet another fine example of a prothyron entry, recessed about a meter from the house frontage along Street 3. It may have had both a double-wide entry for vehicles (ca. 2.00 m wide?), as well as a separate doorway for pedestrians (ca. 0.75 m wide?). An anta block lay in situ on the northeast side of the prothyron, while a small block with a cutting for the door pivot mechanism survived on the southwest. Beyond Room 6-7, only a very small area of Room 6-8 was exposed.

Portions of what appears to be a two-room suite belonging to this house were also revealed northeast of Rooms 6-7 and 6-8. Of Rooms 6-14 and 6-15, a combined total of approximately 3.2 m^2 were exposed. Room 6-14 appears to have been a shallow rectangular porchlike room, perhaps only 1.5 m deep. Room 6-15 had both a plaster floor and plastered walls. This arrangement is what we would expect to encounter for an andron and its anteroom. Such a location, just within the doorway, is a logical one, typical at Halieis (for instance, House 7, Rooms 7-9 and 7-10) and elsewhere.

House A

(Figures 2, 3, 10–12; Plates 1, 32–43)

House A and the house in Area 7 provide the only fully recovered plans of dwellings at Halieis. House A is located at the northeastern end of Area 6, at the intersection of Avenue B and Street 4 (Figs. 2, 3). It is the smallest domestic structure known from the site. Measuring ca. 14.5 x 9.25 m on its southwest and southeast sides, and covering approximately 133 m^2, House A occupied an area little more than half the size of most other houses excavated at Halieis.[45] Although it has some similarities in plan, it stands as a diminutive neighbor to the comparatively sprawling House B to the north.

The location of House A may, in part, explain its small size. For rather than lying within a regular block of insular housing, it occupies a narrowing northwest-southeast oriented strip of land between the insulae of the northeast quarter and the city wall. Within this strip, to the southeast of House A, there would have been enough room for as many as three small squarish insulae (if Streets 2 and 3 indeed continued eastward into this area). In the area of House A and to the northwest, however, the contraction of the parcel may have, temporarily at least, impeded the construction of private dwellings. This is suggested by evidence from deep soundings conducted in the courtyard of House A (Room 6-81b) and Street 4. Here, the existing road metal was cut for laying in the foundation blocks of the southern corner of House A only in the second half of the 4th century.[46]

[44] E.g., Room 6-29 in House D, in the complex on the Industrial Terrace, and possibly in Room 7-20 as well. See above, 13 (Room 7-20) and below, 41 (House D, Room 6-29); and Ault 1999b, 559–64.

[45] For brief discussions of House A, see Rudolph 1983, 69; and Boyd and Rudolph 1978, 347, with fig. 3. For deep soundings conducted there in a portion of Room 6-81 and Street 4, see Rudolph 1984, especially 126–28 ("Test A"), and 147–48, with fig. 3, and pl. 32a. See also Nevett 1999, 100–101, with fig. 27 (in both text and plan, the "well" in Room 6-83 should be located in Room 6-88).

[46] Rudolph 1984, 126–28, with fig. 3. This foundation trench cut through two layers of road metaling (ibid., fig. 3, a and b), which roughly correspond to Levels A and B, and into a sterile stratum (ibid., fig. 3, d). Between b and d lay a third packing of road metal, not cut by the foundation trench of House A (ibid., fig. 3, c), which corresponds to Level C at the site (6th to mid-5th century). The relationship between the rubble alignment at the intersection of Avenue B and Street 4 (Boyd and Rudolph 1978, 344; visible here in Pl. 32) and the strata from this deep sounding has not yet been explored. This feature is the only one of possible architectural significance encountered among deep soundings in the streets at Halieis. It may reflect Level D activity (7th to the first half of the 6th century); but cf. Rudolph 1984, 139–40, where its structural significance is questioned.

The sequence of intramural growth that has been detected at Olynthos provides a parallel. There, during the Peloponnesian War, the zone between insulae and city wall, which had been laid out in 432 as free space, was built up with houses (the so-called "Row A" and "East Spur Hill" houses).[47] At Halieis, too, both the wedge of land in the northeast quarter and the more limited intramural area bordering the circuit in the northwest quarter, where underwater work combined with aerial photography have provided the basic plan, are filled with domestic structures, suggesting more agglutinative and less planned construction.[48] If, indeed, the intramural strips of the lower town that did not comprise full insulae were built up only later, this would support arguments for the alternate occupation and abandonment of the eastern and western halves of the city, with consequent influxes of population behind the walls surrounding them.[49]

Access to House A from Avenue B was gained through a well-preserved prothyron (Room 6-80; Pl. 33). The entry is recessed 0.75 m from the avenue and was, therefore, roofed over. It has a conglomerate threshold, 1.85 m in length, worn with wheel ruts (ca. 1.45–1.50 m apart) at either end. Flanking the threshold are two limestone blocks, both of which have cuttings probably for the jambs of a wide double-winged doorway. Northwest of and continuing the line of the conglomerate threshold block lies a 0.75 m stretch of rubble. This has been interpreted as a rubble wall foundation, thereby making "the outer opening . . . wider than the inner" (Boyd and Rudolph 1978, 347). Alternatively, it may mark the threshold for a second, narrower doorway. House 7, too, seems to have two different thresholds.[50] A fine-grained conglomerate slab, 2.07 m in length, lay along the southwest side of the negative feature in Room 6-81. It is identifiable as the fallen jamb from the northwest side of the doorway.[51]

From the prothyron one passed into Room 6-81 (Pls. 33, 34). As in other houses with a southern entry, the area beyond the prothyron served as a courtyard. The probable extent of the open court associated with Room 6-81 is the southern rectangular area covering approximately 15.75 m^2 (Fig. 11, Room 6-81b). This was bounded along its northwestern side by functionally distinct spaces, all apparently roofed. Due northwest lay a rectangular space (with an area of ca. 13.02 m^2), also originally designated as part of Room 6-81 (Pl. 35). But its location suggests that it is a pastas porch or transverse hall (Fig. 11, Room 6-81c). Two square bases in fine gray limestone that survive in situ on line between Rooms 6-81b and 6-81c demonstrate that the hall was roofed. Unlike House C, Room 6-53, however, there is no trace of supporting members in Room 6-81. These may well have been of wood. Different surfacings as well as elevations separate these two portions of Room 6-81. The surface of Avenue B, which continued right up to the threshold block of the prothyron, remains essentially unchanged within the courtyard.[52] Also attesting to its continuity with the street surface is the fact that the courtyard follows the sloping grade of Street 4 to the southeast, 0.10 m below that of Avenue B (to ca. 0.50 masl). North of the square bases, in the pastas portion of Room 6-81 (i.e., Room 6-81c), the floor level drops another 0.10 m to an irregular surfacing of cobbles in an earthern matrix (lying at an average of 0.40 masl).

Recessed into the interior face of the ashlar socle in both Rooms 6-81b (on the southeast side of the court) and 6-81c (on the northeast side of the pastas) are large semicircular cuttings, two in each room (Pls. 32–35). One cutting in Room 6-81c spans two blocks and shows traces of drilling, implying that the blocks were worked in situ rather than reused. Given their semicircular shape,

[47] For discussion of the growth at Olynthos between the Archaic period and 348, and a look at the Row A houses in particular, see Hoepfner and Schwandner 1994, 71, with figs. 53, 54, and 89–91, with fig. 68. Cahill is not convinced that the intramural zone was built up significantly later than the rest of the North Hill settlement (1991, 162, n. 62; 2002, 45, n. 71).

[48] A plan of the submerged remains in the northwest quarter appears in Jameson 1969, 326–27, figs. 5, 6. In 1977 "a detailed re-examination of the submerged remains in the northwestern part of the city" was made (Boyd and Rudolph 1978, 338). While this considerably clarified the orthogonal plan south of Avenue I (as reflected in Fig. 1), there has been no analysis of the numerous houses that lie here.

[49] Although based primarily on a study of the fortifications and only including material excavated through 1972, McAllister's postulated sequence provides the best diachronic overview of urban growth and decline for Halieis yet put forth (McAllister 1973, 142–52, with illustrations 15–18; cf. McAllister 2005). For the inclusion of free space within city walls, to allow for subsequent growth as well as the protection of livestock, see Hodkinson 1988, 47 (citing Martin 1973, 110). At Priene, for example, only fifteen of thirty-seven intramural hectares were built upon (Hoepfner and Schwandner 1994, 193).

[50] See above, 13, with Fig. 7 and Pl. 7.

[51] An identical jamb, also fallen, lay along the southwestern side of the prothyron in House E (see below, 48). Both the jambs from Houses A and E bear cuttings running the full length of their interior faces, probably to provide a better fit for the inward opening wooden doors.

[52] See Rudolph 1984, especially 127, fig. 3, where layers a, b, and c equate to deposits of road metaling.

the cuttings were probably made for the placement of pithoi or amphoras.[53]

Southwest of the pastas portion of Room 6-81 lay a pit (Pl. 37), similar to that already described in House 7 (Room 7-7). Presumably this was the kopron of House A. Its internal dimensions are ca. 1.5 x 1.5 m and it is lined with stone to a depth of 1.35 m (elevations taken at the bottom ranging from 1.28 to 1.38 mbsl). A substantial ashlar block built into the bottom of the pit divides it in half and could conceivably have footed a mud-brick partition. Around the top of the pit, the stone lining forms a low barrier projecting from ca. 0.20 to ca. 0.40 m above the surrounding floor level. Like another kopron from the site, that in House D, Room 6-26 (see below, 40, 46), the example in House A was virtually filled with roof tiles (Pl. 36).[54] But unlike the koprones from Houses 7 and D, which were both situated in unroofed areas of their courtyards, the example in House A seems to have lain under the putative portico of the second story. This suggestion depends in part upon the interpretation of the narrow rectangular space southwest of the kopron (Fig. 11, Room 6-81a).

In a building with such modest proportions as House A, efficient use of space would have been paramount. Such a requirement holds not only for the ground floor, but mandates the presence of a second story. (Possibly flat roofing, interspersed with the attested pitched and tiled variety, also served as an extension of living space.) The 1 x 2.25 m rectangular area bounding the western side of the kopron would have been admirably suited to the location of a staircase (cf. Fig. 10). Because of the prothyron these posited stairs could only have ascended southeast off the small southwest extension of Room 6-85. With second-story rooms covering the entire northern two-thirds of House A (Fig. 12), a northeast-southwest portico or hall (providing access to rooms further north) would have been situated directly above the kopron and pastas area of Room 6-81.

In the eastern corner of House A lay Room 6-82 (Pl. 38). Roughly square with an area of approximately 6.25 m^2, its interior walls were footed on a substantial rubble and ashlar socle that abuts the equally massive foundations of the house perimeter. Plaster pavement survives in the northern corner. Its elevation, ca. 0.58 masl, suggests that the original floor level was ca. 0.10 m above that of the courtyard. Below the plaster, a section of pebbly underpinning extends southeast, but excavation in the southwestern half of Room 6-82 revealed no further traces of flooring. (Part of a sunken vessel, identified in the trench notebooks as belonging to a pithos or storage bin, found in this area apparently comes from an earlier phase of the room.) A patch of plaster, probably over the threshold of the room, was found at the southern end of its northwest-southeast interior wall. This suggests that plaster once covered the entire floor.

It has been debated whether Room 6-82 was an enclosed room entered across a threshold on its southwestern side, as suggested by the regularity of the footings here and the plaster patch, or served instead as a raised platform within the courtyard. Given its substantial footings, I doubt the latter notion.[55] In fact, the footings are more suggestive of a pyrgos, the towered strong rooms known from houses at Colophon, the Vari Cave, and other farmstead sites (including examples in the Southern Argolid), than the foundations for a platform.[56] While I do not identify Room 6-82 as a pyrgos, the suggestion emphasizes the load-bearing capacity of its walls. What I am strongly inclined toward, however, is to recognize in Room 6-82 a three-kline andron. Its dimensions would accommodate couches along the northwest, northeast, and southeast walls, with a doorway 0.50–0.90 m wide placed along the southern half of the southwest wall. Three-kline andrones of similar dimensions are attested from Priene (Hoepfner and Schwandner 1994, 216–17, especially fig. 212). In this context, it

[53] I would like to thank Dr. L. A. Turner who brought this to my attention.

[54] Although this is explicitly stated in the trench notebook, unfortunately no finds from the fill of the kopron were recorded (they appear to have been mislabeled or misplaced between the time of excavation and processing). Accordingly, Locus IV is omitted from Tables 4–6, House A.

[55] Cf. Boyd and Rudolph 1978, 347; but see also Rudolph 1983, 69, where Room 6-82 is identified as a kitchen. The masonry style of the northwest wall of Room 6-82 is similar to the southeast wall of Room 6-88, suggesting that both were part of a similar phase of building or remodeling.

[56] For pyrgoi at Colophon, see Holland 1944, passim (e.g., House II: Room g, especially 130, where the upper chamber is interpreted as women's quarters or the gynaikonitis; House III: Room h; House IV: Room i); and at the Vari House, see J. E. Jones et al. 1973, passim (Room VII; especially 438–39). Probable towered farmsteads have been reported in the vicinity of Halieis by the Southern Argolid Survey (van Andel and Runnnels 1987, 107; and Jameson, Runnels, and van Andel 1994, passim, but see, e.g., 536 [Site A67], with 535, fig. A.42). For other Greek houses with towers, see J. E. Jones 1975, especially 117–22 (on Attica); and the general survey by Nowicka 1975.

should also be pointed out that at Colophon andrones and pyrgoi are synonymous structures, relatively detatched from the house, the former occupying the ground-floor of the latter.[57]

The rooms representing the domestic core of House A were clustered in the northwest (Pl. 42). Room 6-85, mentioned briefly above, is a square chamber except for a slight southwesterly extension that perhaps provided access to the stairwell. Its total area is 5.7 m². A 1 m wide doorway located in the east corner would force one to enter obliquely from the porch (of Room 6-81), having just navigated the edge of the kopron. There is another possible doorway along the northeastern side of the room that, judging from the masonry, may have been blocked up. In places Room 6-85 was excavated to a depth that revealed that its ashlar orthostates had been placed on the massive blocks that, elsewhere at Halieis, were generally confined to foundations for the exterior walls of houses. Because of its location at the intersection of no less than four trenches and subsequent piecemeal excavation, the floor level of Room 6-85 was not certainly established. In the west corner of the room, a whitish surfacing was reached at ca. 0.38 masl (Pl. 40), but its presence was not confirmed elsewhere. Therefore, it is not clear whether this level represents the latest Level A surface not reached or recognized in adjacent trenches, or, given the significantly higher elevation of the foundation blocks noted above (at 0.50–0.58 masl on their upper surfaces), an earlier floor.

To the northeast of Room 6-85 is Room 6-86, a hallway (1 x 2.75 m) connecting Room 6-81c with the suite of Rooms 6-83 and 6-84 (Pl. 39). Although accessible for its full width at the southeastern end, passage into Room 6-83 at the northwest was constricted to an uncomfortable 0.65 m. (An even more narrow doorway was employed in House E between Rooms 6-16 and 6-17; see below, 49.) As was the case in Room 6-85, determining the latest Level A floor of Room 6-86 proves problematic. The best candidate, an irregular plaster surface, lay in the northwestern portion (at ca. 0.11 masl). The southeastern half of the room was not excavated deeply enough to pick up the likely continuation of this floor level, or the transition that would have been necessary between the porch (Room 6-81c) and Room 6-86. Given the 0.30 m difference between the posited floor levels for the two, such a transition would most likely have taken the form of a step down. There is indeed a step at the northern end of Room 6-86, where the hall gives way to Room 6-83, but it is a step up to the higher elevation of that room (to ca. 0.30 masl at this point). The lower elevation posited for Room 6-86, compared with Rooms 6-81 to the south and 6-83 to the north, is reasonable if we consider it as a unit with Rooms 6-87 and 6-88 to the northeast, both of which lie at comparable levels.

From the hall (Room 6-86) we move into the complex of Rooms 6-83 and 6-84 (Pls. 40–42). Room 6-83 is the largest in House A (16.00 m²), while Room 6-84 is the smallest (1.5 m²). In its latest Level A arrangement, the northern half of Room 6-83 bore a plastered platform similar to that in House D, Room 6-29 (see below, 41, with Fig. 15). The surface of this feature lay at an elevation ranging from 0.39 masl along its western edge to 0.23 masl in its northeastern corner. Although not finished with the same degree of care as the example in House D, traces of a cobbled curb are apparent along its curving southern edge.

Also like House D, two vessels were sunk into the platform of Room 6-83. The first of these, in the eastern corner of the platform, was a small pithos in situ with its mouth at floor level. It was 0.43 m in diameter at its rim, 0.56 m at its greatest internal diameter, and 0.69 m deep. A circular cutting 0.90 m in diameter indicates the presence of the second vessel centrally placed at the northwestern side of the room. A section of a large pithos or storage bin, preserved in its full circumference (0.73 m in diameter and 0.34 m high), was found straddling the southeastern edge of the platform and the adjacent floor level (represented on the actual-state plan of House A, Fig. 10, as an open circle; cf. Pls. 39–41). It seems likely that this is a fragment of the vessel once housed in the empty cutting just mentioned, perhaps only partially sunken, and probably broken at the time of its attempted (abandonment/post-abandonment period?) removal.[58]

[57] Cf. note 56 above. Such an arrangement at Halieis would mandate that the House A pyrgos chamber(s) could only have been reached from the second floor gallery area. At Colophon, where the pyrgos is directly accessible from stairs adjacent to the andron, this appears to have been the only portion of the house to have risen above a single story.

[58] Although the pit that housed the pithos or bin was excavated to a depth of 0.75 m (0.48 mbsl), the excavator stated that only the first 0.42 m can have belonged to the feature proper, since at this depth a portion of a large coarse-ware vessel protruded from the side of the feature (TR 125/355: open deposit 3). I suggest that this fragment probably belonged to the bin itself. Unfortunately, no other fragments of the vessel were noted in the pit or from Room 6-83 in general. The vessel section remains in Room 6-83 as it was found and therefore has no inventory number.

Both the northeast and southwest walls of Room 6-83 flanking the platform retained traces of plaster, but none were noted on the northwest wall. In the first instance that of the floor gave way to a finer yellowish plaster on the wall, while in the second the floor plaster was finished in one with its continuation up the wall (here preserved to a maximum height of 0.40 m above the pavement). In this phase, the rest of the room bore an earthen floor (ranging from 0.35 masl in the southwest to 0.25 masl in the northeast), as was indicated by the level at which the storage bin rim lay.

For all its similarity to the platform with sunken vessels in House D, Room 6-29, there is no evidence whatsoever for a working press installation in Room 6-83. Unlike House D, there is no press bed and no impression of one (see below, 41). Nor is there a weight block. In spite of this, it may well be that the arrangement that survives in Room 6-83 represents an in-progress remodeling for a press installation, lacking only the press equipment proper.[59] Such an installation would probably have had to include provisions for a press like that observed on the Industrial Terrace, with the press bed in the north corner, between the sunken vessels, and the weight block and press beam occupying the southwestern portion of the room.[60] Otherwise, the weight block and press beam would have blocked entry to Room 6-83 altogether.

From the south corner of Room 6-83, one stepped up into the small rectangular chamber, Room 6-84 (Pl. 40). The step itself was plastered along its northwest vertical face and gave access to the fully paved room. Within Room 6-84 the floor plaster lay at an average of 0.61 masl except for a slightly raised band at the southern end (elevation ca. 0.66 masl). Traces of plaster on its walls suggest that the entire room was once so finished. It has been suggested that Room 6-84 was a bath and, in conjunction with the identification of Room 6-83 as a kitchen, strongly resembles the Olynthian kitchen-complex.[61] This point is discussed below (68).

Excavation revealed an earlier sequence of sub-floors and floors in Room 6-83. An attempt to represent each appears in Fig. 10, and they are partially visible in Pl. 32. The first of these, in descending stratigraphic order, comprises an L-shaped area of rubble underpinning in the south corner of the room (at ca. 0.30 masl). This rubble layer continues below the pavement of Room 6-84 to the south. Along its northern edge it overlies a matrix of larger rubble (at ca. 0.18 masl) that in turn extends below the paved platform of Room 6-83. No traces of plaster were found upon either, but they must represent underpinning for a floor (or floors) prior to or accompanying the latest Level A arrangement of the room. Remains of such a floor may exist along the northeast-southwest dividing wall between Rooms 6-83 and 6-85, where traces of plaster were noted at ca. 0.18 masl on its northwestern face. Along the east-central portion of Room 6-83, at ca. 0.12 masl, and extending northwest below the paved half of the room, lay an early section of plaster pavement. Both of its exposed edges are regular and aligned with the room itself suggesting that they were intentionally finished as such. In sum, the evidence from Room 6-83 indicates that it had seen considerable remodeling and must, therefore, have been a room of intensive use, if not of some importance.

A final pair of rooms occupies the north corner of House A (Pl. 42). The first of these, Room 6-88 (ca. 9.3 m^2; Pl. 43), was entered at its south corner from the pastas porch (Room 6-81c). As was suggested for the transition between Rooms 6-81 and 6-86, there seems to have been a rubble threshold with a step down at the doorway (1.25 m wide) of Room 6-88. But only a hint of it was revealed in the north-south boundary between the two five-by-five-meter trenches (120/360 and 125/360). The floor of Room 6-88 comprises an inelegant cobbled surface of rubble in a whitish earthen matrix, lying at an average of 0.15 masl. This rough surfacing may, in part, be accounted for by the presence of a well in the west corner of the room. The northwest-southeast wall appears to bend around a portion of the well's circumference. A fragmentary pithos rim and numerous body sherds were recovered from the area. Some of the sherds were embedded around the well-

[59] I have made this suggestion elsewhere (Ault 1999b, 564, n. 54). Independent of my own work, Foxhall also recognized the layout of Room 6-83 as resembling a press room (Foxhall 1993, 187).

[60] For publications discussing the press room on the Industrial Terrace, see below, 79, note 30.

[61] Boyd and Rudolph 1978, 347. Both in size and arrangement, similar pairings are to be found in Houses B and E at Halieis and perhaps also in one of the houses exposed in the "Ephoreia Field." For the kitchen complex at Olynthos, see the discussions by Mylonas (in D. M. Robinson 1946, 369–98; where it is, rather problematically, termed the "oecus-unit") and J. W. Graham (1954, 328–46; who defines the difficulty of Mylonas's terminology at the outset).

mouth, probably to reinforce the opening. While the domestic wells of Halieis were generally located around the periphery of the courtyards, at least one other example from the site seems to have been within the roofed interior of a house (in Room 6-50 to the southwest). Probably these wells were dug earlier and kept in use while houses were remodeled around them. In addition, they may reflect the exploitation of the water table, more accessible in certain places than in others.[62]

Access to the northernmost room of House A, Room 6-87 (ca. 11.70 m^2; Pl. 42), was from Room 6-88 across a rubble threshold through a 1.25 m wide doorway. This threshold retained the higher floor level of Room 6-88.The missing transitions between Rooms 6-81, 6-86, and 6-88 were probably similar to this. Entering Room 6-87, one stepped down about 0.07 m onto a plastered floor. The elevation of this pavement ranged from 0.09 masl, just inside the doorway, to 0.11 masl at its northern limits. Unfortunately, it is not preserved over the full area of the room. Confined to the northern and eastern portions of the chamber, a section of earlier plaster flooring protruded to the west, lying about 0.05 m below the later pavement. Traces of red and yellow wall plaster were recovered from the room, some of the red adhering to the northwest-southeast wall shared with Room 6-83. The finds recovered from Room 6-87 suggest that it was the principle living chamber, or "dayroom." This identification is discussed below (31).

Artifact Assemblages: Quantification and Distribution

The artifacts recovered from the latest Level A horizon in House A are presented in Tables 4–6 and Appendix II.B. From the category of pottery, 3062+ items were recorded. The MNV represented is 434, these ranging over thirty-nine different shapes (cf. Table 19).[63] The majority of vessels represented are fine-ware drinking cups (122 MNV) and coarse-ware cooking shapes (99 MNV). The cups occur in ten different shapes while cooking vessels represent only four varieties (including lids). The next most numerous category involves vessels associated with the serving and pouring of liquids (65 MNV including serving containers). These are followed by 47 MNV of fine-ware vessels for food serving and consumption, 45 MNV for food and liquid storage containers, and 24 MNV for plain- and coarse-ware vessels used in serving and/or food preparation other than cooking. The data are summarized by the following:

3062+ pottery items
- = 434 MNV (in 3 wares and 39 shapes)
- = 122 MNV (28.1%) associated with drink consumption (fine-ware cups only)
- = 99 MNV (22.8%) associated with cooking
- = 65 MNV (15.0%) associated with serving and pouring drink (including fine-ware drink-serving containers)
- = 47 MNV (10.8%) associated with fine-ware food serving and consumption
- = 45 MNV (10.4%) associated with storage of food and drink
- = 24 MNV (5.5%) associated with food serving and preparation other than cooking

Spatially, the distribution of pottery helps to confirm what discussion of the architecture of House A has already suggested. The largest concentration of MNVs occurs in Loci I (70 MNV) and II (61 MNV), which for the most part represent debris from Avenue B and Street 4. Very little of this material was actually recovered in Rooms 6-80 or 6-81. Artifacts from these loci are likely the combined result of cleaning associated with Level A occupation of House A (and adjacent areas) and abandonment activities at the site. The most significant distribution of pottery associated with the latest occupation of House A proper is found in Room 6-81c (Locus VI, with 78 MNV), Room 6-83 (Loci XI–XIV, with 56 MNV), and Room 6-87 (Locus XVIII, with 47 MNV). In these three areas activities involving intense pottery use were focused. The most notable variations that occur here are between cooking and storage vessels. As is to be expected, the 15 MNV for cooking from Loci XI–XIV support the identification of Room 6-83 as the kitchen.[64] Only 8 MNV for cooking were

[62] As stated above (note 55), the southeast wall of Room 6-88 is built in a technique like that of the northwest wall of Room 6-82. Both differ considerably from those elsewhere in the house and may be the result of alterations to a preexisting plan.

[63] If one excludes the substantial amount of material from Loci I–II, which lie primarily in Avenue B and Street 4, the MNV is reduced to 303. It should be pointed out that Loci III and X contained no finds and thus were omitted from the tables (along with Locus IV, the kopron fill that was never processed).

[64] In addition, a small open deposit of material in Room 6-83, along the southwest wall making its transition to Room 6-84, included five whole fine-ware vessels: two mugs (HP 2989 and 2990), a squat lekythos (HP 2987), a painted askos (HP 2988), and a miniature trefoil-mouthed oinochoe (HP 2986).

recovered from Locus XVIII (Room 6-87). The 19 MNV for cooking from Locus VI suggests that the pastas, Room 6-81c, may also have been utilized as an area for food preparation.[65] This situation is not surprising, since the space offered a covered but well-ventilated area (cf. Room 7-17 in House 7, the portico of Room 6-53 in House C, and Room 6-30 in House D). There are parallels in the houses of Colophon and Priene, where a hearth or oven was sometimes located in the prostas.[66]

It is also the pastas that contained the greatest MNV for storage (10, comprising mainly plain-ware amphoras), concentrated in the southeast corner along Room 6-82.[67] Along with the 8 MNV from Locus XVI (which, with a total MNV of 18, yielded relatively small amounts of anything else), forty percent of the evidence for storage vessels from House A is accounted for, and these two areas would have been logical locations for storing provisions.[68] The high figures in Locus VI for pottery of all types may testify to routine cleanup and abandonment processes in the rooms to the north. But this space stood at the principle intersection of the house. Considering the small size of House A, it probably served not simply as a thoroughfare but as a primary living space as well.

Room 6-87 yielded a substantial MNV for fine-ware shapes associated with food and drink consumption (22 from Locus XVIII), the largest MNV in House A for fine-ware pouring vessels (5), and, together with Room 6-88 (Locus XVI), produced the greatest number of red-figured fragments (7 MNV, including a skyphos and, possibly, a krater—nearly half of those from the house). A great variety of other artifact types was also recovered from Room 6-87, including eight coins, fragments of a lekanis/pyxis, a pyxis lid, a lekythos, an amphoriskos foot, and four loom weights. The whole complex of artifacts suggests the activities of women.[69] In addition, the area was enhanced with plastered floors and painted plastered walls. Room 6-87, therefore, may be identified as the primary dayroom of the house.[70]

None of the other classes of artifacts from House A reveal any particular patterns. Only two lamps are represented from rooms within House A (Rooms 6-86 and 6-88, Locus XV and XVI, respectively), while a miniature lamp came from the kitchen, Room 6-83 (Locus XI, HL 310). Room 6-83 also yielded a miniature jug (HP 2986), while Room 6-87 (Locus XVIII) contained at least three possible miniatures: two jugs (one of which was inventoried as HP 2527) and a skyphos. Seventeen bronze coins were recovered from House A. (Eight of these, as already noted, came from Room 6-87.) This is the largest number found in any house at the site. It is uncertain whether this concentration is related to the proximity of the Northeast Command Post, where coins were minted (J. A. Dengate in McAllister 2005), even though five Tirynthian coins of Halieis were found in Room 6-87, while another four were scattered over the house.[71] Other mints represented from the latest levels of House A include Aigina (six examples dated post-404), Hermione (a single coin, HN 1975-88, dated 350–300), and Troizen (one example, HN 1975-86, dated 370–300).

House C

(Figures 2, 4, 13, 14; Plates 1, 44–53)

House C lies along the northwestern range of the insula defined by the course of Avenues B and C and Streets 3 and 4. Facing onto Street 4, it is the

[65] In addition to another 3 MNV for plain- and coarse-ware vessels associated with the preparation and serving of food, and 7 MNV for fine-ware food serving vessels, MNVs associated with the serving and consumption of drink in Locus VI are quite high (36 total MNV for fine-, plain-, and coarse-ware varieties ranging from cups to jugs).

[66] For cooking hearths in the prostas porches at Colophon, see Holland 1944, 124 (House IV, Room b) and 136 (House III, Room b). For Priene, see Hoepfner and Schwandner 1994, 216; and Wiegand and Schrader 1904, 291–92.

[67] In addition, we should recall here the semicircular cuttings noted above, recessed into the foundation ashlars of the northeastern wall of Room 6-81c (as well as the southeastern wall of Room 6-81b), which may have been made for storage vessels.

[68] Perhaps because House A was relatively small, the pastas had to be used for storage. It is possible that the three coarse-ware pithos rim fragments from Locus XVI (Room 6-88) may be associated with the pithos-headed well located there.

[69] For a listing of inventoried objects from the Level A–A/B strata organized by house and locus, see Appendix II. The House A inventoried finds are compiled there as Appendix II.B.

[70] While it could, of course, be the case that objects fell from the second-story chamber, which probably existed above Room 6-87, or occurred there as the result of secondary deposition, we can not determine this securely from the available evidence.

[71] J. A. Dengate believes that there may be a connection to the city mint: "the house may have been that of a merchant or trader who availed himself of the proximity to the mint to enhance his business" (personal communication). In addition, he also notes that from the neighboring House B was recovered a bronze weight (HM 1186) inscribed "tritaion" (probably "one-third"), suggesting that it may have been the residence of an official responsible for the public weight standard. Finally, Houses A and B backed onto a small open square upon which the mint faced. This area could conceivably have been devoted to the conduct of business involving trade and coinage. This is discussed by J. A. Dengate in McAllister 2005.

only well-explored house at Halieis to have a north-oriented frontage. After Houses 7 and A, it provides the third most completely recovered house plan from the excavations.[72] Nearly square, 15 x 14.5 m along its northwest frontage and southwest sides, House C originally covered ca. 208 m^2. Approximately 80 percent of this (or ca. 169 m^2) has been cleared. Most of Room 6-55 in the west corner and portions of Rooms 6-53, 6-57, and 6-58 in the east lay outside the limits of Area 6. In addition, the presence of an olive tree on a two-by-three-meter plot above the east corner of Room 6-63 prevented excavation here. Like the other houses in Area 6, House C exhibits the terracing between allotment parcels along insulae. Neighboring houses to the northeast lay about 0.30 m lower than House C, houses to the southwest about 0.30 m higher.

House C was entered through a canonical recessed prothyron, Room 6-62, 1 m deep, with a maximum internal width of 4.5 m. The bases for one of its outer and both of its inner jambs are preserved in situ (Pl. 45). Those for the inner jambs bear small rectangular cuttings that perhaps served for the insertion of metal door pivots. One pier capital (HS 467) and a fragment from another (HS 480), which may have crowned the outer jambs, were found in the prothyron itself (Locus I). Although lacking stone thresholds with the indicative wheel ruts, and slightly more narrow than the minimum width of prothyra in Houses 7 and A (ca. 3.25 and 2.87 m, respectively), there is still enough space between the inner jambs of Room 6-62 (ca. 2.40 m) to envision a double door for admitting a cart. The presence of a second narrow doorway for pedestrians (ca. 0.62 m wide) remains a possibility.[73]

A small square chamber, Room 6-61 (ca. 6.2 m^2), lay immediately to the right upon entering House C. Tucked in so as to utilize the southwest end of the prothyron construction, its doorway (1.25 m wide) bore a rubble threshold set at floor level. The floor itself was laid with a hard whitish surfacing identical in makeup and elevation to that encountered in Room 6-63 (see below).

It should be noted at this point that the entire façade of House C along Street 4 was footed on a series of large ashlar blocks like those utilized elsewhere at the site for stretches of (generally exterior) walls. These are shown in Fig. 13 and are visible in Pl. 44. The top of this footing lay at or just below the floor level of the rooms and the surface of the street. Presumably the next course would have consisted of ashlar orthostates, for mud brick at such a low elevation would have been particularly susceptible to degradation from rain, dampness, and traffic in the streets. The absence of these orthostates all along Street 4 here is accounted for by what would have been the fairly easy task of robbing them from collapsed houses. In instances when such orthostates survive, their surface visibility is frequently clear even today where they continue to emerge through the topsoil (as is made clear in Figs. 1, 2, and Pl. 44).

Passing through Room 6-62, one entered a large squarish chamber, Room 6-63 (ca. 24.8 m^2). Because of practical considerations, courtyards were located in the southern portion of houses (see below, 60–61). Therefore, the entrance of a house occupying the northern half of an insula would not have been directly onto the courtyard, but through an intermediate chamber, which led to the rest of the house. This principle was also employed at Olynthos, although there the corresponding rooms are more like hallways. At Olynthos these rooms have been reconstructed as bearing a second story, which continued over and therefore roofed the prothyron as well.[74] Since Room 6-62 appears to have been roofed, it seems reasonable to restore second-story chambers over it and Room 6-63.[75]

[72] See Boyd and Rudolph 1978, 349–50, with fig. 3, for a brief discussion of the plan of House C; for deep soundings conducted there, see below, note 78. For another brief notice of House C, see Rudolph 1983, 70, where it is referred to as "House #2, Street #4, Insula B-C/3-4."

Cf. the discussion by Hoepfner and Schwandner (1994, 82–86) for the importance of house orientation in determining aspects of house layout. Variant types of house orientation are well represented in Areas 6 and 7, according to location within the insular blocks: the frontage of House 7, a south corner house, has a southwest orientation (House A, although not belonging to a full insula, has the same orientation); Houses D and E, lying along the southeastern range of an insula, are oriented to the southeast; and House C, situated along the northwestern side, faces northwest. Excavation did not produce a fully recovered house plan situated along the north or east corners of an insula, as for example, the houses located at the intersection of Avenue B and Street 4, and represented by Rooms 6-67 through 6-71 and Rooms 6-72 through 6-79, respectively.

[73] For a table of prothyra dimensions at Halieis, see below, 59.

[74] For examples from Olynthos, see Hoepfner and Schwandner 1994, 85, fig. 63 (Houses A v 3, A v 7, B vi 3, B vi 5, and B vi 7). For reconstructed elevations and a model of Olynthian houses employing these principles, see ibid., 86, fig. 64, and 95, fig. 70; and D. M. Robinson and J. W. Graham 1938, 99, fig. 4. Houses situated on the northwest and northeast corners of insulae naturally allowed more flexibility in the placement of their entryways.

[75] Nine hundred and seventy-one roof-tile fragments were recovered from strata associated with Level A of Room 6-63 (Locus II; see Table 7 below).

A hard whitish surfacing of earth, plaster, and pebbles covered the floor of Room 6-63 (at ca. 1.44 masl). Into this level was set a series of covering stones marking the course of two drains laid below floor level and constructed of narrow rectangular stone slabs set end to end (Pl. 46). Spaced 1.5 m apart, the drains, with excavated lengths of 3.5 and 5 m, ran roughly parallel to one another. The channels for each were traced north to a point where they emptied into a rubbly earthen matrix below the outer threshold of Room 6-62 and the road metaling of Street 4. While their point of origin is uncertain, a portion of the western drain was noted below the dividing wall between Rooms 6-60 and 6-63. Perhaps they served as outlets for the courtyard (Room 6-53), which lay at an elevation 0.30–0.40 m higher than Room 6-63. Equally obscure is their (presumably contemporaneous) date of construction and original function. Since a number of cover slabs for each drain survived in situ at floor level, they were apparently in use during the Level A occupation of the house. Whether they were intended merely to act as conduits for rain water that puddled in the house during rainstorms, or should be connected with some other domestic activity, is unknown. Similarly, their relationship with the two slab-lined channels found in the portico of Room 6-53 is unknown. (The latter are thought to have been out of use in the latest Level A phase of House C; see below.)

The balk of earth that preserves an olive tree hampers the interpretation of the eastern portion of Room 6-63. It appears, however, that a low rubble sill ran northeast from the east corner of Room 6-60, among a jumble of early walls (for these, see below) and tumbled rubble. This sill served both as a step up to and a terrace for floor levels ca. 0.20 m higher than that of Room 6-63. Its course marks the northwest side of Room 6-59, a trapezoidal corridor ca. 10 m^2, that gave access to the rest of the house.

Room 6-60 was the first room to open off this corridor. Rectangular, with an area of 7.4 m^2, it was furnished with an ample 1 m wide doorway in its southeast corner. (A 0.35 m gap in the wall adjacent to Room 6-63 does not mark a door; probably it was chinked with rubble.) Although Room 6-60 lay in the square area that had been subdivided into Rooms 6-61 through 6-63, it stood apart from these rooms because of its higher floor level. Its latest floor lay at an average of 1.64 masl, making it continuous with that of Room 6-59. Traces of whitish earthen surfacing were noted in both rooms at this elevation. During its final phase, a pithos stood in the south corner of Room 6-60 (Locus VI).[76] Also, fragments of a broken dacite hopper mill (HS 463) were set up end-to-end along the central longitudinal axis of the room. (Both the pithos and mill fragments are visible in Pl. 47.) Clearly dug into the floor, the pieces were perpendicular to an underlying Level C wall found here upon subsequent excavation. They did not fully divide the room, occupying only the central meter of the room's 3.75 m length. These fragments could have acted as a base for vertical supports to shore up a sagging second-story floor above, carried a nonbearing wall screening a portion of the room, or served as a basis for something else.[77]

Although all the rooms as described in this area of House C belong to Level A, some Level C deposits with associated architectural remains were excavated in Rooms 6-59 through 6-61 and 6-63. The walls revealed here have the same orientation as those in the 4th-century House C and seem to respect the course of Street 4 to the northwest. Because they were cleared only in small soundings, there are not enough of these Level C walls to link up into any coherent plan. Nor is it certain how many building phases they may represent.[78]

At the northeastern end of Room 6-59 about 2.5 m^2 of a small rectangular chamber, Room 6-64, were cleared. It is defined primarily by a white plaster floor that slopes down from 1.79 masl at its southeast end to 1.70 masl toward the northwest. The lower end is set off from the rest of the pavement by an edge, perhaps of a shallow trough. This pavement probably continues for only a short distance north below the standing balk left for the olive tree. What remains unclear about the perimeter of Room 6-64 is its relationship with the adjacent rooms. The party wall with

[76] This pithos, in a very fragmentary state, apparently was not inventoried. It is represented by at least two hundred sherds recorded in the finds notebooks for TR 090/345: u. 12; and TR 095/345: u. 2 and 3.

[77] A millstone was reused in the construction of a partition or nonbearing wall between the pastas and court of House A iv 9 at Olynthos; see D. M. Robinson and J. W. Graham 1938, 87, with pl. 80.8.

[78] For a full discussion of the sounding conducted in Street 4 and Room 6-61, see Rudolph 1984, 130–33 ("Test C"), especially fig. 5 (which graphically illustrates the relationship of the Level C walls of House C to its 4th-century plan), and 155–64. The Level C remains in Rooms 6-59, 6-60, and 6-63 were explored in TR 090/350, 095/345, and 095/350.

Room 6-69 in the neighboring house exists only as a low rubble socle, but traces of its mud-brick superstructure were observed by the excavator. Where the floor met this wall, there survived a line of vertically oriented plaster, suggesting that at least one wall of Room 6-64 was finished in one with its floor. The southeast end of Room 6-64 stops neatly on line with the large ashlar blocks that mark the limits of Room 6-58. If Room 6-58 was an andron (see below for this identification), a doorway between the two rooms would have been unlikely. A rubble wall defining the southwestern side of Room 6-64 survives at an elevation lower than the pavement of the room. Midway along this stretch of wall is a gap of ca. 0.50 m where the rubble lies 0.20 m below that of the wall on either side. Providing that the room was not entered at its northwest end from Room 6-63, it is logical to interpret this gap as a threshold by which one stepped up into the small chamber. The parallel between Room 6-64 and other rooms of similar dimensions and finish from the site is clear: all seem to have served as baths.[79]

From the southwestern end of Room 6-59, one passed into the courtyard of House C, Room 6-53 (Pls. 48, 49). This was nearly square except for a slight extension of its southeastern corner, which encroached upon a neighboring house (represented only by Room 6-50). The complete area of Room 6-53 was 54.21 m^2. Its most striking architectural feature was the colonnaded portico that extended along the southwest wall, and of which virtually all supporting elements have been recovered. Its central span was carried on two conglomerate columns, the rough fluting of which was finished with stucco. The columns are 2 m high and have base diameters between 0.30 and 0.40 m. When excavated, both lay oriented to the southwest where they had fallen from their foundation blocks.[80] Doric capitals that once crowned the columns were recovered as well, one from Room 6-54 (Locus IX, HS 470; visible in Pls. 50, 53) and one from the cistern fill in Room 6-53 (Locus XIV, HS 531).[81] At its north end the colonnade terminated in a rectangular sandstone pillar, the broken halves of which (HS 468, 469; Pl. 50) were found lying before the base from which it had fallen. The pillar has a restored height of 1.99 m. Its three exposed sides were finished in a coat of stucco. A pier capital also recovered from the cistern fill (Locus XIV, HS 543) may once have crowned this member. No trace of a matching pillar was found in the south, where the architrave must have been built into the party wall with Room 6-50 of the house lying due southeast. But one of two cuttings in the south wall of the courtyard aligns with the colonnade and confirms that provision was made for some vertical supporting element here. The intercolumniation for the porch would have been ca. 2.4 m. There is no indication that it rose beyond a single story in height.

The roofing of the colonnade, which sloped down to the northeast, apparently slid off into the eastern portion of Room 6-53 where more than 3261 roof-tile fragments were found spread across the surface of the courtyard (in Loci XII/XIII). (The northernmost limits of this tile fall are visible in Pl. 52.) In stark contrast, only seventy-six tile fragments were recorded from comparable strata in the area covered by the portico (Locus XI). In the clearing of the tile fall, areas of the familiar whitish pebbly flooring appeared. These ranged in elevation from 1.73 to 1.83 masl over the entire unroofed portion of the courtyard. No such surfacing was noted beneath the portico.

Only one cistern has been securely identified at Halieis. This was located roughly in the center of Room 6-53, positioned so as to take good advantage of rainwater draining from the roof of the portico, as well as to drain the surrounding courtyard floor. Its oval mouth is defined by a series of encircling blocks and measured nearly a meter at its greatest diameter. Flask-shaped in profile, the cistern had a maximum depth of 5.00

[79] For a general discussion of baths at Halieis, see below, 68–69.

[80] The southernmost column has a preserved height of 1.54 m. It was augmented by a single drum, 0.46 m high, added to its distal end. This was recovered in the cistern fill (Locus XIV). It bears a square dowel hole on its bottom surface (ca. 0.065 x 0.070 m), for which there is no corresponding cutting on the column top. The drum almost certainly was part of the column, however, because its addition would raise the column height to 2 m, matching the other column and the pillar at the north end. At the time of this writing, all these column members (except for the capitals) remain on site in Room 6-54 and have not been inventoried.

[81] In addition, a second, fragmentary Doric capital was recovered in the cistern fill (Locus XIV, HS 542), while another example came from Room 6-59 (Locus VII, HS 528). Their original location, if integral to House C, remains in question. One of the capitals for the courtyard columns, the example found in Room 6-54 (Locus IX, HS 470), may be archaic, suggesting its probable reuse (Boyd and Rudolph 1978, 350). Such recycling of architectural elements within the Halieis houses finds a possible parallel in House D, where a fragmentary painted sima tile, late 6th century, was recovered from the kopron in Room 6-26 (Locus II, HC 739; for which, see below, 46).

m.[82] Its sides were lined with plaster and the shaft proper was equipped with two pairs of footholds on the same northeast-southwest axis of the house as a whole. The cistern floor (at ca. 3.26 mbsl) was finished with an off-center depression intended to collect settled impurities.

It has been proposed, quite reasonably, that the cistern occupies the area formerly taken up by a sunken feature, identified elsewhere as the kopron, similar to those known from House 7 and Houses A and D (Rudolph 1983, 73). The western edge of this posited kopron may be preserved in the line of three ashlar blocks on top of which the colonnade was erected (perhaps the blocks forming the cistern mouth were reused from the kopron). The southeastern portion of this kopron had been infilled, although its full extent was not confirmed through excavation. The fill of the cistern (Locus XIV) was largely earth and rubble but also contained 1478 roof-tile fragments and, as noted above, architectural elements from the colonnaded portico that rose above it.[83]

In the southeastern corner of Room 6-53 was a plaster platform (ca. 2 x 2 m, at 2.00 masl) with a curbed edge (Pl. 51). In its east corner were two ashlar blocks forming a right angle and standing 0.20 m above the platform surface. These blocks were plastered on their exterior faces. At the west corner of the platform was a circular basin, also plastered, ca. 0.50 m in diameter and 0.30 m deep. The whole ensemble suggests accoutrements accompanying a well and compares favorably with the much less elaborate plaster attachments to the wellhead in House 7 and the pavement and catch-basin combinations associated with wells from portions of two houses excavated in Area 4.[84] Unfortunately, this feature could not be completely excavated because it extended beyond the limits of Area 6.

At the north corner of Room 6-53 are two features from the Level A phase of House C. Two depressions, connected to each other, are aligned with the northeastern section of the party wall between Rooms 6-53 and 6-54 (Pl. 52). Together they are 2.40 m long with a maximum depth of 0.34 m. They were lined with the same whitish lime and earth matrix as the courtyard floor around them. Although their precise function is unclear, they were perhaps associated with some sort of storage. Perpendicular to the doorway of Room 6-54 and just southwest of the paired depressions lies a block with two shallow cuttings at either end of its top surface. (This should not be confused with a weight block from an olive press, for the cuttings in it are mere depressions, not lewis holes.) The block must have served as a stair base with the cuttings marking the emplacement of parallel runners for the stairway proper. This location would have been the ideal one for a stairway ascending northeast, leading to second-story rooms over the northern range of the house (that is, above Rooms 6-54 through 6-56 and Rooms 6-60 and 6-61). I remain skeptical about the presence of a second-floor chamber over Room 6-63, which may have born no more than a high ceiling in order to continue the roof line over chambers that existed above Rooms 6-57 through 6-59 and Room 6-64 as well.[85] Still, except for Room 6-53, there is no technical reason for not continuing the second story over the entire house. The walls of House C would have provided ample support for it and the internal spans of the rooms are not too great.

In addition to, and perhaps associated with, the infilled kopron posited for Room 6-53, the line of two drains was recovered. They were constructed of stone slabs like those already noted in Room 6-63. Perhaps they represent subsequent

[82] For flask-shaped cisterns at Athens, see Camp 1977, 145–46 (140 Hellenistic examples were known from the area of the Agora at that time); at Morgantina, Tsakirgis 1984, 335 (where nearly all houses explored appear to have had at least one); and Olynthos, D. M. Robinson and J. W. Graham 1938, 307–9, with pl. 76.1 (where domestic wells were unknown, and only eight of the houses excavated though 1934 were equipped with cisterns). The average capacity of examples from Athens and Olynthos ranged from 23,000 to 26,000 liters.

[83] The presence of this cistern, inserted during the later life of House C and adjacent to the unexcavated well discussed in the next paragraph, may be evidence for a drought at Halieis. It has been argued that drought and famine afflicted Attica as well as the Argolid in the 4th century (Camp 1982). In addition, at Halieis the fresh water table, lowered during a drought, may have been contaminated by its proximity to the sea.

[84] For the well in House 7, see above, 13–14; for Area 4 (also known as Area M, for its supervisor Michael Cheilik), see Boyd and Rudolph 1978, 345, with 348, fig. 3; Jameson 1969, 328, pl. 85a; and J. H. Young 1963, 3–5 (especially 4, for the best published plan and views).

[85] In the houses at Olynthos, second-story chambers are assumed to have been present above the entryway of houses along the north side of an insula. Compare the arrangement in houses at Kassope and Ammotopos (Orraon) where stairways were located internally, in the eponymous *Herdraum* (also referred to as the oikos). While single-storied, this core room of the household rose to the height of the second story in order to accommodate the ascent of stairs to chambers there. For Kassope and Ammotopos (Orraon), see Hoepfner and Schwandner 1994, 146–52; Hoepfner et al. 1999a, 374–78; and Hoepfner et al. 1999b, 395–411.

phases of the same drain that fed into the kopron southeast of their preserved limits. The latest of the two drains was traced for a distance to the southwest where it ran under the party wall with Room 6-46 in the neighboring house. Both appear partially dismantled as found, were themselves infilled, and bore no cover slabs (unlike the drains in Room 6-63). Thus, they seem truly out of use by the latest Level A occupation phase of House C.[86]

In the southeastern quarter of Room 6-53 was, apparently, the only access to Room 6-57 and, in turn, to Room 6-58. (Room 6-57 was probably separated from Room 6-59 by a curtain wall. A scanty line of rubble between the two attests to the presence of this wall as well as its ephemeral nature.) Room 6-57, a shallow chamber, was entered through a 0.90 m wide doorway. Approximately two-thirds of its original extent has been exposed (or about 5.70 m^2 of possibly about 8.70 m^2). The Level A floor of Room 6-57 was recovered in only a small area, other passes having terminated ca. 0.10 m above its surface. This bit of plaster pavement (ca. 1.70 masl) was cleared just west of the plastered stone threshold shared with Room 6-58, along the edge of which it has subsided or been destroyed. Because so little of the floor surface was excavated, we can not reconstruct the transition from Room 6-53 to Room 6-57 (presumably it was a step down). For the same reason, we have no information about the presumed nonbearing wall between Rooms 6-57 and 6-59.[87]

Although only 5.3 m^2 of Room 6-58 have been recovered, it was clearly square in plan and would have covered at least 20 m^2. Its floor, which lay at ca. 1.75 masl, was executed in white plaster laid over a pebbly underpinning. As noted above, the threshold between Rooms 6-57 and 6-58 was also carefully finished in plaster but bore no traces of cuttings for a door emplacement.[88] Although lacking the platform for klinai with which the andrones in House 7 and Area T were finished, the dimensions of Room 6-58, its location in a corner of the house, the degree of finish, and the presence of Room 6-57 as an antechamber make its identification as an andron unambiguous.[89] The northeast-southwest wall of the room survives as a line of ashlar foundations for an orthostate course now, presumably, robbed out. (One orthostate block survives in the west corner of the room.) These foundations lie as much as 0.15 m below the floor level of all tangential rooms (compare the similar situation along the frontage of House C). In the western corner of Room 6-58 the plaster floor laps up over these footings, but elsewhere it has been cut in a strip paralleling the edge of the blocks, probably the result of robbing (there is similar trenching on the north side of the wall in Room 6-59).[90] Although no traces of wall plaster were noted in Room 6-58, this is probably because its excavation was only partial.

Across the courtyard and opening off its northwestern side lay Room 6-54 (Pls. 50, 53). A long rectangular chamber with an area of ca. 19.50 m^2, its size, shape, and location are compatible with those for a porch or hall. The passage between Rooms 6-53 and 6-54 measured 1.40 m wide and crossed a rubble threshold to a whitish surfacing of lime and earth at roughly the same elevation as the court, if slightly lower in places (ranging from 1.72 to 1.77 masl). On all the walls of Room 6-54 red and white painted plaster survived in situ. It seems likely that there may have been a white dado with red plaster continuing above (as observed elsewhere at the site). Quantities of red plaster were also observed in the mud-brick fill of the room and in the courtyard where large fragments lay face up, occasionally adhering to decayed mud brick (implying that the south walls of Room 6-54 collapsed outward into the courtyard). The line of an earlier wall was exposed just below, and perhaps protruded slightly through, the latest Level A floor of Room 6-54. Its orientation, while northwest-southeast, is slightly askew from the other early walls

[86] The drains of Room 6-53 probably carried runoff from the higher elevations of Room 6-46. See above, 23, for a discussion of Room 6-46 and its features. As noted previously, there is no evidence that physically connects the two drains in Room 6-53 with those in Room 6-63.

[87] And perhaps the finds recovered from Locus XV (Tables 7, 8), which represent the strata associated with and just above the Level A surface of Room 6-57, would have yielded more meaningful information as well.

[88] In 1992, on a visit to the site of Halieis, I noticed that the plaster threshold of Room 6-58 had weathered enough to reveal an underpinning of tile fragments that provided a leveling course for the plaster finish. One vertically laid tile under plaster was also observed adjacent to the threshold on the southwest face of the dividing wall between Rooms 6-57 and 6-58. Presumably the threshold and wall were plaster, finished in one.

[89] For the andron in "Area T," see below, 69–70. Both in its dimensions and finish and especially in the absence of a raised platform for klinai, Room 6-58 is quite similar to the andron identified in House B (see above, 22).

[90] A sandstone basin (HS 546) was exposed by the robbing along the northeast-southwest wall of Room 6-58. It was presumably deposited here as fill to level up and underpin the latest floor of the room.

revealed in House C. Also unlike these earlier remains, it was not associated with Level C artifacts. Its significance remains unknown.

The northwestern side of Room 6-54 gave way to two rooms. The first of these, Room 6-55, occupied the contracted west corner of House C. Only a small portion of the chamber was cleared. Its original area may have been ca. 6.5 m^2. Its floor level was not ascertained (the excavated surface ranged between 1.43 and 1.49 masl). The doorway, 1.15 m wide, was formed by returns from the side walls of the room. The southeastern half of the party wall shared with Room 6-56 was of flimsy construction but had a facing of red plaster, some of which adhered to mud-brick coursing that survived on a low rubble footing.

Room 6-56, ca. 9.3 m^2, was entered from Room 6-54 through a 1.25 m wide doorway. Because its floor appears to have sloped from southwest to northeast, and because the room was virtually filled with artifacts that lay on top or were embedded in the floor surface (for this, see below), determining the precise Level A extent of Room 6-56 was hampered. The makeup of this floor, which seems to have lain between 1.40 and 1.68 masl, was similar to flooring elsewhere in the house: a pebbly whitish hard-pack of lime and earth. A squarish patch midway along the eastern wall of the room, where no trace of flooring could be found, may mark the position of some no longer extant feature. In contrast to Rooms 6-54 and 6-55, there was no indication that the walls of Room 6-56 were plastered.

Artifact Assemblages: Quantification and Distribution

At first glance, the pattern that emerges from the artifacts of the Level A deposits in House C seems suggestive more of abandonment than of primary deposition. (See Fig. 14; Tables 7–9, and Appendix II.C.) But the circumstances of deposition, as discussed in the methodology section (chap.1), may admit some artifacts as indicative of activity areas. Therefore, we should expect some primary activity to be reflected among secondary depositions. The situation is also complicated by the absence of artifact data for portions of the house that either remained unexcavated (most of Room 6-55; and portions of Rooms 6-58, 6-63, and 6-64) or failed to reach Level A (a small area in the north corner of Room 6-54 and probably most of Room 6-57).[91]

Despite these lacunae, 5935 items were recorded under the category of pottery. From these can be estimated a MNV of 492 that spans forty-four different shapes from the three ware types and all functional categories (see Table 19). The majority of vessels represented are varieties of fine-ware cups for drink consumption (122 MNV) and plain- and coarse-ware storage containers (100 MNV). Coarse-ware cooking pots (79 MNV) and vessels connected with the serving, pouring, and containing of drink (74 MNV) are roughly equivalent. In addition there are fine-ware vessels associated with food consumption (47 MNV) and plain- and coarse-wares used in connection with serving food and its preparation other than cooking (32 MNV). The overall assemblage breakdown is summarized as follows:

5935 pottery items
- = 492 MNV (in 3 wares and 44 shapes)
- = 122 MNV (24.8%) associated with drink consumption (fine-ware cups only)
- = 100 MNV (20.3%) associated with storage of food and drink
- = 79 MNV (16.1%) associated with cooking
- = 74 MNV (15.0%) associated with serving and pouring drink (including fine-ware drink-serving containers)
- = 47 MNV (9.6%) associated with fine-ware food serving and consumption
- = 32 MNV (6.5%) associated with food serving and preparation other than cooking

Plain-ware storage vessels were concentrated in the courtyard (Room 6-53, as represented by Loci XI–XIII) and plain-ware food preparation and serving vessels in Room 6-63 (Locus II) and the cistern fill (Room 6-53, Locus XIV). Aside from these clusters, the greatest concentration of all MNVs by functional category was in Room 6-56 (Locus IV). This preponderance of artifacts must be described as "fill" in the true archaeological sense of the word. Since there is so much material in such a small area, it seems likely that many of the 158 MNV represented there stem from limited depositional circumstances rather than primary use activity or gradual accumulation.[92]

What remains in question is the nature of the event and origin of the contents for the dump of debris in Room 6-56. "Debris" seems to be the

[91] Room 6-64 (Locus VIII) yielded no finds from its Level A stratum and is therefore omitted from the tabulated summaries.

[92] This deposit was briefly considered in Ault and Nevett 1999, 49, with fig. 4.3.

right word, as only two whole vessels were recovered there.[93] Another ten could be reconstituted as profiles. But these represent only a dozen of the 1053 pottery items from the room (not including miniature vessels). Does the bulk of this material imply that Room 6-56 had gone out of use and served as a dump prior to abandonment, or could it indicate accumulation of House C debris contemporary with or even postdating abandonment of the dwelling? Or is it a dump used by neighboring houses? Stratigraphic evidence here is not very helpful as the top of the deposit was encountered within the first 0.30 m below the surface (that is, just below the disturbed topsoil) and ranged over a depth of ca. 0.40 m, at which point it lay on top of and was imbedded into the floor of Room 6-56. The clear robbing of the house façade for building material, which took place all along the line of Street 4, also hampers determining the relationship of strata between the street and Room 6-56. There is no strong evidence that the dumping evident in Locus IV took place at a time postdating the collapse and robbing of House C (and is therefore more likely to be of extrahousehold origin). Accordingly, it is assumed that the material in Room 6-56 was in some way integral to the household inventory but not necessarily related to the function of the particular room in which it was deposited.[94]

Although the function of Room 6-56 can not be specified, it is significant that its walls were not plastered and painted as were those of Rooms 6-54 and 6-55, with which it forms a unit. Perhaps it was, in its latest phase, no more than a storeroom. For unknown reasons seldom used and no longer considered important, it could have been seen as an ideal location for dumping.

The second highest frequency of pottery debris (106 MNV) was encountered in the courtyard proper, the eastern half of Room 6-53 (Loci XII–XIII). A similar situation occurs in House 7 (and elsewhere) and probably relates not only to a high rate of discard in the courtyard but also to its function as a thoroughfare and to the multiplicity of activities carried out there. As with House 7, we find in the courtyard area a significantly greater number of storage vessels than elsewhere. The 23 MNV present account for more than 21 percent of all the pottery from the two loci and 23 percent of all storage vessels in the house (the latter percentage reduced by the 16 MNV from the dump in Room 6-56, Locus IV). Even more significant is the material from Locus XIII alone, which consists of the two lined hollows below the putative stairwell in the northeast corner of the courtyard. Of the 35 MNV from Locus XIII, eleven plain-ware amphoras are represented. It is likely that this was a storage area, perhaps for amphoras in particular.[95]

In comparing the porticoed southwestern half of Room 6-53 (Locus XI) to its unroofed northeastern half (Loci XII and XIII) and the rest of House C (except for Room 6-56), we find another potentially significant difference in the functional distribution of pottery. Locus XI has 13 MNV for coarse-ware cooking pots. This figure stands out particularly in comparison with the low number of other pottery types recovered from Locus XI. As was the case in House A, where the pastas porch (Room 6-81c) seems to have been utilized as a cooking area, so, too, some food preparation probably took place in the portico.[96]

It is difficult to interpret the MNV of eleven cooking pots (and little else) from Locus X because this locus overlaps Rooms 6-53 and 6-54. Since there is no evidence for a well-defined kitchen area within House C, it may be that Room 6-54 served as a cooking area (although this seems at odds with its painted plaster finish). If this MNV represents an accumulation of material in the eastern half of Room 6-54, and if the area had been fully cleared to the Level A floor, such speculation could move into the realm of distinct possibility. It is hard to believe that a dwelling so large and pretentious as House C had no fixed kitchen. Indeed, it may also be that the unplastered Room 6-56 was the base of household food preparation and the other debris there simply masks primary deposition of cooking vessels, of which 32 MNV were recovered, and other associated types.

[93] The whole vessels include a black-glazed stemless cup (HP 2190) and an askos with red-figured decoration (HP 2186).

[94] The overall totals for House C and the frequency of types across various functional categories of pottery from Locus IV (e.g., 58 MNV for drink consumption, 32 MNV for cooking, 23 MNV for serving and pouring drink, etc.) are similar to those produced at other houses. This implies that there was no significant selection for or exclusion of material in the "dump." That is, it is an accurate cross section of household debris.

[95] The space below the proposed stairway in House E, Room 6-20, seems to have been similarly used; see below, 50–51.

[96] Although the 13 MNV for cooking vessels from Locus XI is not substantially greater than the 10 MNV from Loci XII and XIII, which comprise the courtyard proper, it is significant that the cooking vessels from the portico (Locus XI) account for more than 30 percent of the 43 MNV there, while the latter 10 MNV make up only a little more than 9 percent of the 106 MNV from the court (Loci XII/XIII).

From Locus IX, which does lie almost exclusively in Room 6-54, nearly 50 percent of the recovered MNVs represent plain-ware amphoras, three of which survive as profiles (HP 2343 was inventoried). It is noteworthy that the number of storage vessels in House C accounts for 20 percent of the overall MNV assemblage. This is 20–50 percent greater than that from the other houses studied (see Table 19) and suggests the prosperity of the household, a distinction already implied by the domestic architecture.

The locations and quantities of other finds in House C do not create any clear patterns. Again, it must be pointed out that the detection of more subtle spatial groupings may have been obstructed by the dump in Room 6-56 (Locus IV). A marvelous but heterogeneous variety of metal objects occurs in Locus IV, including three iron blades, two of which were perhaps pruning knives (HM 981, HM 1011, and HM 1525), two bronze drop handles (HM 982 and HM 1009), three probable furniture bosses (HM 1030, HM 1197, and HM 1206), a latchstring plate (HM 1010), and an earring (HM 1199). Among the potential complex of objects with feminine or boudoir associations, pottery figures prominently (see Table 9) and includes an amphoriskos (HP 2930), a lekanis/pyxis, a lekanis/pyxis lid with red-figured decoration (HP 2204), and a lekythos. Yet the jumble of material within which all these occur makes it impossible to discern any point but their presence.

The complex of spaces making up the northeast side of the house, that is, Rooms 6-59 through 6-64 (which correspond to Loci I, II, and V–VIII), were comparatively bare of artifacts. The 79 MNV from the area represents a mixed group of vessels and accounts for only 16 percent of the total MNV for House C. In addition, other classes of objects are singularly lacking. Storage vessels, both coarse-ware pithoi and plain-ware amphoras, are well represented with 14 MNV coming from Rooms 6-59 through 6-61. The evidence suggests that this portion of the house was less a living area and more an artery to the domestic core, with ancillary spaces set aside for work and stores.

We do not yet fully understand the abandonment and subsequent history of House C, even though there are more discernable traces here than in the other houses studied. In connection with this, it should be reiterated that numerous stone architectural elements were recovered from the cistern (Locus XIV). At least some of these, if not all, are definitely associated with House C. Similarly, joins of a fine-ware tray were made between Loci XII/XIII (HP 2253; where it has been recorded under "Fine-Ware Other") and the cistern. These instances indicate deliberate dumping (as a result of scavenging?) into the open cistern of architectural members as well as debris already deposited in the courtyard at a time when the house must have been largely in ruin.[97]

House D

(Figures 2, 5, 15–18; Plates 1, 29, 54–61)

House D and its neighbor, House E (Fig. 19, Pl. 62), are situated along the southern half of the insula containing House C. Sharing a party wall that also serves as a terrace wall, the two houses are the most fully recovered examples of contiguous domestic structures at the site. More significant is the degree to which their plans are at variance with the three houses already discussed. The differences in layout stem from the bipartite arrangement of each house. Although the remains in each case seem to reflect two separate houses, in neither is it absolutely certain that single households are represented. The plots occupied by Houses D and E, however, are roughly equivalent in size to those of Houses 7 and C. Accordingly, the notion of single houses has been retained in the following discussions and in the compilation of finds data from each area. (The significance of the two plots having been so partitioned is considered below.)

Because of the limits of Area 6, one-quarter of the estimated 204 m^2 area of House D remains unexcavated.[98] Although this includes most of its frontage along Street 3, the overall dimensions of the house can, with surety, be ascertained as ca. 16.25 x 13.5 m on the northwest and southwest sides, respectively. As recovered, the complex comprises a southwestern half, nearly all of which has been revealed (except for the southeast corner of Room 6-26), and the less completely cleared northeastern half. The foundations that divide the area of House D into two give it a terraced effect, floor levels in the west lying some 0.30 m higher than those in the east. In order to envision the complex as a unified whole, it is essential to

[97] The eighty-three Roman and Byzantine sherds from otherwise good Level A/B contexts in House C make up a far greater quantity of intrusive pottery than in the other houses studied, but they are not necessarily another manifestation of the same phenomenon.

[98] Briefly discussed in Boyd and Rudolph 1978, 350, with fig. 3.

interpret these foundations as not having supported mud-brick coursing for a standing wall over their full length. Between Rooms 6-26 and 6-31 they acted as a retaining wall and a step.

Room 6-26 is virtually certain to have served as a courtyard. It is the largest room in the southwestern half of House D and probably the complex as a whole. Nearly square and originally covering some 39 m^2, its excavated area is approximately 30 m^2. Traces of an entry were preserved in its south corner, the only part of House D that was cleared to Street 3. This doorway is located along the same aperture in the house frontage that also provided access to Room 6-22 of House E (see below, 51). It now consists of a light rubble threshold separating Street 3 from Room 6-26. Originally, the width of the doorway was perhaps as great as 1.5 m, but this is difficult to ascertain because of the limits of excavation.[99] This arrangement for access into the southwestern portion of House D seems awkward. First, there is a large negative feature just beyond the entry, and second, an ashlar block projects from the northeast-southwest scarp.

This ashlar block, oriented northwest into Room 6-26, may relate to the partitioning of the courtyard, for lying east of it is an area of plaster pavement (at 3.01–3.10 masl). Although not exposed over its full extent, the surfacing probably covered the entire southeastern corner of Room 6-26. Possibly this area was protected by a lean-to roof similar to Room 7-8 in the courtyard of House 7. The Level A floor elsewhere in Room 6-26 was hard-packed earth. It lay at an average elevation of 3.00 masl, flush with the top of the retaining wall for the negative feature.

The negative feature is similar to the two previously discussed in House 7 and House A and can be identified as a kopron (see below 63–65; see also Ault 1999b, especially 550–53). Occupying ca. 5.00 m^2 in the southwestern portion of Room 6-26, it is five-sided and somewhat irregular but aligns with the room in general (Pl. 56). It is surrounded by massive ashlar blocks one course high except for the southwestern side, which incorporated the party wall with House E (Rooms 6-21 and 6-22). Here the blocks stood three courses high. Numerous smaller stones and rubble clustered around the southeastern edge of the feature. They may represent the remains of a barrier constructed on top of the ashlar circuit (or they may be part of the collapse of a nearby rubble wall). Averaging just over 1.00 m deep, the bottom of the feature was a hard stony soil.[100] As with the koprones in Houses 7 and A, no traces of hydraulic cement were noted, nor was the bonding of the walls so tight that the feature could have held water. Also, like the other koprones, the feature was virtually packed with artifact debris, primarily roof tiles and pottery (Pl. 55; see below, 46, with Table 10: Locus II).

A well occupied the northwestern corner of Room 6-26. It was covered by two squarish blocks laid flush with the surrounding floor level and set end to end so as to form a rectangular slab of ca. 1.00 x 1.75 m. Traces of plaster covered their junction and were noted around the well mouth itself. Excavation of the well was carried out to a depth of ca. 4.30 m below the level of the wellhead (to 1.38 mbsl), at which point its bottom had not yet been reached.[101] As excavated, its fill was primarily earth (cf. Table 10, Locus III). At the southern end of the platform created by the slabs covering the well, two blocks of the kopron circuit were positioned as if steps leading down into the feature.

In the northeastern quarter of Room 6-26, along the northwest-southeast partition wall with Room 6-31, is a crudely built rubble spur. Apparently structural, it suggests the presence of a stairway ascending northeast along the dividing wall between Rooms 6-26 and 6-29. Southeast of this proposed flight of stairs is a foundation course of massive conglomerate ashlars that bisect the complex of House D. On top of the northernmost block were traces of additional courses in mud-mortared rubble that may have been part of the stairwell construction. Also, a stone that could have served as a stair base survives at what would have been the southwestern end of the flight (at 3.15 masl).

Portions of at least two fine-grained conglomerate slabs were revealed between these features. They were recessed 0.10–0.20 m into the latest Level A surface of Room 6-26 and lie flat at 2.82–2.92 masl. Since they run parallel to the

[99] At the edge of the trench is a block that marks the resumption of the frontage of House D and also the northeast side of the doorway into Room 6-26. It is visible on the present ground surface and can be seen in the scarp to continue down to the ancient level of Street 3 and the floor of Room 6-26.

[100] In the trench notebook for 060/325, this soil is said to have been identified by a geologist as forming "the natural preliminary to the bedrock."

[101] Excavation of the well was halted at this depth owing to incoming ground water and the lack of pumping equipment to enable continued work in the shaft.

dividing wall with Room 6-29, they probably were part of a feature connected with the facility in the next room, 6-29.

Room 6-29 lay to the north of Room 6-26. A rectangular chamber measuring 14.31 m^2 and set lengthwise against Room 6-26, Room 6-29 resembles a porch. It was entered through a 1.80 m wide doorway footed on a rubble threshold, from which one stepped down to a pebbly earthen floor at ca. 2.87 masl. Two additional chambers (Rooms 6-27 and 6-28) opened off its northwestern side. The northeastern portion of Room 6-29 houses the most extensively recovered and best-preserved remains of a domestic industrial installation from the lower town of Halieis (Pl. 59). On top of a plaster platform, the carefully executed curving edge of which survives intact, was situated a spouted marble press bed for extracting olive oil. The weight block, to which one end of a wooden press beam was originally attached, survives in situ 4 m away, against the doorway between Rooms 6-27 and 6-29.[102] The press bed itself, ca. 1 m in diameter and 0.30 m thick, exuded the oil through its spout into a pottery basin (0.41 m in diameter and 0.29 m deep) sunk into the plaster platform. When exposed, the press bed contained a roughly circular piece of congolomerate that was probably part of the overall pressing mechanism.[103] A rectangular depression in the rubble wall behind the press bed perhaps marks the socket for the opposite end of the press beam. (The surviving height of the rubble wall is well below the surface of the bed.) A large pithos (0.70 m in diameter and 0.78 m deep) sunk into the floor adjacent to the press bed presumably served as a settling basin for the pressed oil. On the walls around the press were traces of thick white plaster, adhering in places to mud-brick coursing. This plaster appeared to bond with that on the platform proper. In places, as many as three coats were visible, suggesting that the press complex had been in use for some time. Finally, within the curve of the platform edge, an ashy lens (ca. 0.50 m in diameter and 0.02 m deep) was explored, but nothing was found to reveal its origin or function.

The conglomerate slabs in the northern corner of Room 6-26 may have been part of this complex. I am inclined to interpret them as belonging to a crushing trough for the "milling" of olives prior to their actual pressing.[104] Although the location of a crushing trough below the stairway posited here seems awkward, given the relative infrequency of the oil production process, the inconvenience was probably slight (see below, 80–81).

Room 6-27 (9.50 m^2) lay in the northwestern corner of House D. Its doorway is defined, on the southwest, by the northeast extension of House E, Room 6-24, into Room 6-29. The northeastern side of the doorway was originally formed by a return in the dividing wall between Rooms 6-27 and 6-28. This passage may have been narrowed from a width of about 1.35 to 0.85 m by the olive-press weight block (although the block may have shifted slightly out of its original position). Unfortunately, Room 6-27 was not excavated completely to the depth of its Level A floor. Only in its western portion was a small triangle taken down to ca. 2.71 masl, at which point the soil matrix was noted to be compact and filled with large pebbles. This is probably the Level A floor surface but can not be confirmed as such without clearing the rest of the room (which lies ca. 0.30 m higher) to a comparable depth.

Room 6-28 completes the suite of rooms accessible from Room 6-26 and completes the southwestern half of House D. It is 7.6 m^2 with a packed earth floor. Although it was not set off from Room 6-29 by any sort of threshold, it must have sloped down slightly to lie at ca. 2.82 masl. In

[102] For more extended discussions on the workings of presses from the site and of the role played by olive cultivation and processing in the domestic economy of Halieis, see below, 79–81; Ault 1999b; and Jameson 2001b.

[103] Another artifact probably associated with the oil production process, and found adjacent to the press in Room 6-29, was a large marine shell, identified either as a conch, tonna, or whelk. Until recent times these were used to skim oil off the water also exuded as part of the pressing process. Although noted in the excavation notebook for TR 065/330: u. 17, it was not recorded as such in the accompanying finds notebook. An uninventoried "conch" skimmer came from the L-shaped room just south of the press room on the Industrial Terrace (Jameson 1969, 323), while another was recovered in House E, Room 6-13 (Loci III–IV, HV 307), a room with a markedly industrial character (see below, 52–53, 56).

[104] A similar feature has also been noted in Room 6-46 (southwest of House C; see above, 23), within a structure to the northeast, only partially excavated. Such troughs, presumably because they were movable and multipurpose furniture, are rarely encountered in situ. While the more specialized milling device, the trapetum, is now attested from Late Classical contexts (Foxhall 1993,190–91; 1997, 259; contra Forbes and Foxhall 1978, 41–42), it, too, is rare. An upstanding crushing trough not dissimilar to the possible examples at Halieis has been identified by Forbes and Foxhall in the Hellenistic house at Praisos, in the same room as remains of an oil press (ibid., 41, with fig. 3; cf. Bosanquet 1901–1902, 259–70). Recent excavations on Cyprus have brought to light other crushing troughs; cylindrical rollers of calcarenite have been found in association with them (Hadjisavvas 1992, 7–8, citing examples from Syria and Israel as well).

contrast with the overall utilitarian character of architectural remains in the southwestern half of House D, both the north and east walls of Room 6-28 retained traces of red painted plaster above a white dado. Such a finish indicates that, at least at some point, it was considered more than simply a room adjacent to the olive press.[105] That a room of some luxury was part of this distinctive three-room suite suggests that the main chamber (Room 6-29) was not originally intended to be a press room.[106]

Moving into the northeastern half of House D, one is confronted by the remains of a number of rooms, including 6-30 through 6-33. As exposed, these four rooms seem to have a longitudinal orientation, perpendicular to which is set a triad of rooms at the northwest: 6-35a, 6-35b, and 6-36. The width of these rooms was limited by the southerly extension of Room 6-40, the long, corridor-like construction that encroaches from the northeast. As noted above, 23–24, Room 6-40 (together with Room 6-45) surely represents an area of some importance. Indeed, it was significant enough to have precluded the presence of another sizable chamber in House D, as well as in neighboring houses on both the north and south sides of the insula.

Of the southeast chambers, Room 6-30 has been fully cleared and Room 6-32 mostly so (only its eastern corner remains concealed beyond the boundary of Area 6). Rooms 6-31 and 6-33 are incompletely cleared, because of the trench boundary, and thus are more problematic. Room 6-31 must have been a sizable chamber, continuing southeast to the frontage of House D along Street 3. About 10.00 m^2 were cleared, yielding numerous ashlar blocks, much rubble, and a significantly large quantity of roof tiles.[107] The excavators of Room 6-31 suggested that it served as a dump just before or after the final abandonment of the site. An approximate floor level can be reconstructed at between 2.57 and 2.79 masl. This surface was represented in the south of the room by a sterile whitish deposit and, in the north, by a hard grayish level. The somewhat haphazard line formed by several blocks between Rooms 6-31, 6-32, and 6-33 seems to have been employed as a threshold demarcating passage from one area to another.

Room 6-30, a small rectangular chamber (ca. 3.90 m^2), was accessible from the northwest corner of Room 6-31. Filled with debris similar in character to that recovered in Room 6-31, Room 6-30 also contained the remains of a hearth. Nestled into its western corner was a U-shaped line of fired earth measuring ca. 0.65 x 0.75 m, open on its southeast side. Around this was a perimeter constructed of mud brick or simply earth. The hearth area was packed with pottery in an ashy matrix (Table 10: Loci X/XI). When the hearth was cleared to its base, chunks of calcined stone were revealed (at ca. 2.64 masl). A floor level for Room 6-30 was reached at ca. 2.77 masl (with elevations ranging from 2.60–2.85 masl), which suggests a gentle upward slope from southeast to northwest between Rooms 6-31 and 6-30.

Among the stone architectural members recovered from Room 6-30 were three pier capitals (HS 477, HS 488, and HS 489). A fourth uninventoried example was found in Room 6-31. Fragments of at least one probable door jamb (HS 518) were found in Rooms 6-30 and 6-31.[108] The original location of the pier capitals and jamb fragments remains in question, but it is possible that at least two of the capitals as well as the door jamb belonged to a recessed prothyron entrance.[109] The prothyron entry of House D would have been located along its southeastern frontage, probably at the southern limits of Room 6-31 (where it is shown in the reconstruction of House D, Fig. 18; see below).

Very little architectural information was recovered from the small excavated portion of a

[105] An additional pass excavated within Room 6-28 itself went through the latest Level A floor and yielded many artifacts (TR 065/325: u. 21), including a Neo-Babylonian or Assyrian cylinder seal of pink quartz (HS 517, a cast of which is illustrated in Rudolph 1975, pl. 43b), a pyramidal loom weight (HC 842), an iron sickle blade (HM 1350), the shaft of a bronze nail (HM 1361), and two bronze coins of Tiryns (minted at Halieis; HN 1975-153 and HN 1975-154).

[106] Compare the in-progress conversion of the kitchen to a press room in House A (Room 6-83). See above, 29.

[107] Ca. 444 kg of roof-tile fragments were recovered from a single pass over portions of Rooms 6-30 and 6-31 (TR 065/330: u. 8; cf. Table 10: Locus IX).

[108] Only one of these, the uninventoried capital from Room 6-31, appears on Table 10, Locus IX. The other stone architectural elements were recovered in strata that could be assigned to levels lying above the Level A habitation deposits of Room 6-30.

[109] Pier capitals were found near prothyra entries in House 7, House C, and House E, and fallen stone jamb blocks have been associated with the entries to Houses A and E. Some of the fragments discussed here could also have been used to embellish the doorway between Rooms 6-32 and 6-36, which is fitted with a stone threshold and retains a fragmentary stone jamb in situ along its northeast side. Arguing against the placement of the pier capitals from Room 6-30 into a prothyron or other doorway arrangement is the fact that all three have continuous moldings on four sides. (They might have been reused in a doorway, however.)

narrow chamber designated as Room 6-33. It lies southeast of and parallel to Room 6-32 between two stretches of ashlar wall. The southwest wall of Room 6-33 bore on its southwestern terminus a small upside-down block inscribed with the letters EP (HS 516; recovered from TR 065/335: u. 4). The area could have been used as a stairwell to second-story chambers.[110] There is a second possibility, as well. Long and narrow (only 0.75 m wide), Room 6-33 has all the earmarks of a transitional space. The unexcavated area between Rooms 6-31 and 6-33, and the projected line of Street 3 and the eastern limits of House D, takes up ca. 25.00 m^2. This space is similar in size as well as in location to the andrones in House 7 and House C. Therefore, it may be that Room 6-33 served as the anteroom to an unexcavated andron. If so, it would have been entered from the side rather than on axis like the andron itself. Similarly arranged anterooms exist in most of the houses at Olynthos (but for those on the corners of insulae).[111] This scenario does not account for the southern wall spur (which bore the EP-inscribed block, and which should at some point return to the southeast if it belongs to the putative andron). But pending further excavation, or a more plausible reconstruction, the identification stands.

We may therefore offer a tentative layout for the unexcavated portions of House D as follows: Room 6-31, with a recessed prothyron entry, must have been a continuation of the courtyard from Room 6-26 to the southwest, while Room 6-33 marked the location of a stairwell or served as anteroom for an unexcavated andron that lay at the east corner of House D, along its frontage on Street 3.

With the remaining three rooms of House D, we stand on firmer ground. Room 6-32, covering ca. 12.48 m^2, compares in its orientation and dimensions to a pastas porch or transverse hall,[112] even though the light and warmth of its southern exposure would have been diminished by the posited stairwell or anteroom, Room 6-33, and the andron. It would have been entered from Room 6-31 across a roughly laid series of three "threshold" blocks. Its floor level lay at roughly the same elevation as Room 6-31 (varying from 2.54 to 2.72 masl). Like Room 6-31, this was characterized by surfaces ranging from hard-packed gray in the portion shared with Room 6-33 to a hard whitish deposit in its central area. Against the base of the northeastern wall of Room 6-32, which served as a party and terrace wall with the neighboring house,[113] were three Laconian pan tiles standing on end and slightly overlapping one another. These were probably laid in to protect the rubble and mud-brick fabric of this portion of the wall against moisture (rather like a baseboard). To the original excavator, the presence of the tiles suggested that Room 6-32 had been unroofed, but this seems unlikely considering its probable identification as a porch or hall. The placement of the three tiles suggests that some wet activity took place in this area.

Along the northwestern edge of Room 6-32 lay the entrance to Rooms 6-35 and 6-36. This was finished with a stone threshold (at 2.63 masl) that carried an upright jamb block on its northeast side. The doorway was ca. 1.40 m wide.[114] In its latest Level A phase (Fig. 16), Room 6-36 was a large rectangular chamber covering ca. 21 m^2. Its floor was of hard-packed earth and lay at elevations between 2.35 and 2.45 masl, with a gradual slope down from south to north. Located in the east corner of Room 6-36 was a shallow pit, ca. 0.50 m in diameter and 0.12 m deep. Perhaps this marked the position of a pithos. A doorway, ca. 1.40 m wide, located immediately to the left upon entering Room 6-36 (that is, in its southwestern corner) gave access to Room 6-35b. The southern jamb was demarcated by a short spur of rubble wall projecting northwest from the dividing wall between Rooms 6-35 and 6-30.

The Level A plan of Room 6-35 comprised two separate chambers (Fig. 16; Pl. 29). The northwestern half, Room 6-35a, was roughly square with an area of ca. 7.20 m^2. It was set off from the southeastern half, Room 6-35b, by an inserted rubble wall that left the latter as an L-shaped chamber of ca. 5.96 m^2. The latest floor

[110] Tsakirgis, however, has pointed out that stairwells, as opposed to stairways located within larger rooms such as courtyards, normally appear only in the context of Hellenistic housing (1984, 395, with 416–17, n. 113; citing examples at Morgantina, Delos, and Priene).

[111] Cf. the arrangement for Olynthian houses occupying the southern side of insulae, such as houses A vi 2, A vi 4, A vi 6, A vii 2, and A vii 4 (illustrated in Hoepfner and Schwandner 1994, 62, fig. 61).

[112] Examples of which have been identified in House 7, Room 7-13; House A, Room 6-81c; House C, Room 6-54; and in the southwestern half of House D, Room 6-29.

[113] As represented by Rooms 6-41 through 6-44, and Room 6-48 (see above, 24); it should be noted that the floor of Room 6-43 lay ca. 0.40 m below that of Room 6-32.

[114] As suggested above, 42 note 109, it is possible that some of the architectural members recovered from Rooms 6-30 and 6-31 were associated with this doorway.

levels lay between 2.40 and 2.50 masl in Room 6-35b and between 2.50 and 2.55 masl in Room 6-35a. Both were paved with a whitish surfacing of lime-flecked earth. A shallow pit (ca. 0.65 m in diameter and 0.09 m deep) was dug into the eastern corner of Room 6-35b, perhaps to support a vessel. In the western corner of Room 6-35b, a triangular grinding slab of white marble remains in situ at ca. 2.62 masl. Traces of mud-brick coursing were found on the inserted wall dividing the chamber in two, but no sign of a threshold for a doorway was apparent. A doorway does, however, appear to exist in the northwest-southeast wall dividing Room 6-35a from Room 6-36. Here there is a length of 1.30 m that lies ca. 0.20 m lower than the rest of the rubble wall. This threshold gap is bounded on its northwest side by a squarish upright identifiable as a jamb block.

Deep soundings carried out in the south-eastern portions of Rooms 6-35b and 6-36 revealed at least two phases of alteration in the form of the rooms prior to their final Level A arrangement (Fig. 16; Plates 29, 60). Associated with these were numerous resurfacings of both lime-tempered and lime-free earthen matrices, which accounted for a 0.20–0.40 m rise in the floor level over time. These remodelings affected the shape of Room 6-36, particularly at the southeast end. In its earliest version (Fig. 16: Level C), Room 6-36 was closed off by two returns that gave it a broad doorway, ca. 1.75–2.00 m wide. While this arrangement might have created a narrow chamber between Room 6-36 and Room 6-32 to the south (measuring ca. 0.85 x 3.50 m), it may have preceded the existing layout of Room 6-32. In a subsequent stage (Fig. 16: Level B), the northwestern two-thirds of Room 6-36 were partitioned off altogether from its southeast end (a probable doorway was noted in the northeastern portion of the dividing wall there). Preliminary analysis suggests that each of the three major architectural phases revealed within Room 6-36 should correspond to Levels C, B, and A, respectively, but this has yet to be confirmed by detailed study of the associated pottery.[115]

Remodeling in the second (Level B?) phase affected the plan of Room 6-35, which, prior to the existing Level A dividing wall, may have been a unified space. In this phase, a small southwest projecting spur constricted access into the northwestern two-thirds of the room and created a third corridor-like space fronting Rooms 6-35 and 6-36. The surviving state of Rooms 6-27 and 6-28 in the southwestern half of House D may approximate the appearance of Rooms 6-35 and 6-36 at this stage. We may see here another three-room suite of the sort already encountered at Halieis (also in House C, Rooms 6-54 through 6-56) and documented elsewhere in the Greek world.[116]

The most extensive deep sounding carried out in the lower town of Halieis was in this area. Therefore, the internal modifications revealed in Rooms 6-35 and 6-36 have been discussed in detail in order to illustrate their nature and degree, as well as to note that similar circumstances will have been operating in virtually all other houses at the site. These certainly bear on the form assumed by the houses in their latest habitation phases and may help to account for the seeming irregularities in plan that they frequently present to us.

Despite the physical and spatial separation between the two halves of House D, which is underscored by the finds data discussed below, it is probable that the complex comprises a single domestic unit or at least a single property holding. The plot size of ca. 204 m^2 is within the dimensions necessary for dividing the insula into twelve houses. Even more persuasive is the fact that no well was discovered in the northeastern half of House D. The profusion of wells at Halieis (ten were found in Areas 6 and 7 alone) indicates that they were a necessary component of each household and that each household was responsible for its own water supply. These household wells are generally situated around the edges of courtyards. Since apparently there was no well in the northeastern half of House D, it is probable that this area was connected to the southeastern half with its courtyard and well.[117]

An overview of House D is necessary to clarify the difficult points of its plan in the late 4th century. Its most prominent feature is the broad, terraced courtyard area, Rooms 6-26 and 6-31. Room 6-26, with its unpretentious entry, kopron, and well, was certainly unroofed (but for its eastern corner where a lean-to construction seems likely). Room 6-31, where an unexcavated prothyron entrance has been posited, would also have been unroofed but for the prothyron

[115] The report and plans for deep soundings carried out in Rooms 6-35b and 6-36 are in the notebook for TR 070/330: u. 24 through 54 (although as part of this deep sounding, work was conducted in TR 065/330 and TR 070/335 as well).

[116] See below, 67, for an interpretation of these suites.

[117] See below, 62–63, on household water supply.

proper.[118] Communication between the two halves of the house would have been across these two areas of courtyard. A section of the foundation that divides them probably served as a retaining wall and step rather than as a load-bearing wall.[119] It is likely that there were second-story chambers over both halves of House D. The plan of the whole complex is well suited to their presence over the suites of northwestern rooms (that is, Rooms 6-27 through 6-29, 6-32, 6-35 and 6-36, and possibly even continuing southeast over the putative andron). The best locations for stairways would have been in the northern corner of Room 6-26 (to which the rubble spur against the retaining wall between Rooms 6-26 and 6-31 may relate) or in the narrow confines of Room 6-33.

Artifact Assemblages: Quantification and Distribution

In its latest period of occupation, House D seems to have been divided into a predominantly industrial area in the southwest and a more domestic area in the northeast. (See Fig. 17, Tables 10–12, and Appendix II.D.) This is confirmed by the distribution of pottery over the Level A stratum of the house.[120]

From the more than 4536 pieces of pottery recovered, representing fifty-four different vessel types (Table 19), a MNV of 601 can be obtained. As is the case in the other houses so far considered, most of the vessels are fine-ware cups (162 MNV). Coarse-ware cooking pots (106 MNV) and plain- and coarse-ware storage containers (63 MNV and 37 MNV, respectively) are roughly equivalent. Seventy-three MNV are associated with the serving and pouring of drink, while 64 MNV are fine-ware shapes associated with the serving and consumption of food. Finally, 52 MNV comprise plain- and coarse-ware vessels associated with the serving and preparation of food other than cooking. These figures are summarized by the following:

4536+ pottery items
= 601 MNV (in 3 wares and 54 shapes)
= 162 MNV (27.0%) associated with drink consumption (fine-ware cups only)
= 106 MNV (17.6%) associated with cooking
= 100 MNV (16.6%) associated with storage of food and drink
= 73 MNV (12.1%) associated with serving and pouring drink (including fine-ware drink-serving containers)
= 64 MNV (10.6%) associated with fine-ware food serving and consumption
= 52 MNV (8.7%) associated with food serving and preparation other than cooking

Spatially, the greatest concentrations of pottery were encountered in the adjacent Rooms 6-36 (Locus XVI: 174 MNV) and 6-35b (Locus XIV: 102 MNV). In the southwestern half of House D, except for the fills of the two large negative features, the kopron (Locus II: 144 MNV) and the well (Locus III: 15 MNV), only 66 MNV were recovered.[121] The distribution of this material, based as it is on very small quantities, does not reveal any significant spatial patterning. Very few fine-ware vessels are represented from Loci I, IV–V, or VIII (15 MNV total), and most other functional classes are equally low. Plain- and coarse-ware storage vessels, with 16 MNV, are more abundant as we might expect from the businesslike nature of the area. As a whole, the pottery from the southwestern half of House D attests to a multiplicity of activities there. But either because this was not the main living area or because the accumulated debris was cleaned up and dumped into the kopron, consequently erasing traces of primary-use deposition, little can be said about the distribution of artifacts across these rooms.

[118] It seems quite probable that the full façade of House D along Street 4 would have presented a roofed edge running from the doorway in the southwest corner of Room 6-26 to the posited andron in the southeast (cf. Fig. 18).

[119] Perhaps additional steps would have been added in wood or stone. Their remains may be part of the scatter of stone building material present in Room 6-31. It is important to note that not all foundations supported bearing walls. On this point, see Aschenbrenner 1976. Discussing Karpofora, a Messenian village under ethnoarchaeological study, he noted that "at least 25% of the total linear meters of foundation is not utilized for full walls or walls associated with roofed areas" (ibid., 161).

[120] Room 6-28, with its red and white plastered walls, as already noted, must have played a more strictly domestic role at some point prior to the latest period of habitation.

[121] This MNV would surely have increased somewhat with the complete clearance of Room 6-27 to its Level A floor surface. It is worth noting that from the small area in the west corner of the room that was cleared down to the floor level, 5 MNV were recovered from Locus IV and two of these were complete: a plain-ware strainer (HP 2352) and amphora (HP 2336).

The fill of the kopron in Room 6-26 is both copious and interesting enough to merit special attention.[122] From Locus II more than 1500 pottery artifacts were recovered, in addition to more than a thousand roof-tile fragments. There were also less numerous small objects such as loom weights and miniatures. (Pls. 55 and 56 show the feature in the course of and following excavation, respectively.) The pottery from Locus II represents at least thirty-five percent of all the pottery recovered from the latest habitation levels of House D. Of the 144 MNV from the kopron, only four complete or nearly complete (but fragmentary) vessels were recovered, while another seventeen could be reconstituted as full profiles.[123]

Many of the roof tiles that filled the top of the kopron actually spilled out onto the courtyard surface and so may have been introduced into the deposit with the collapse or deliberate dismantling of nearby roofs. This was demonstrated (as part of an unpublished study) by Louis Jerkich, who examined the roof-tile debris from the upper strata of the kopron and was able to reconstruct portions of seventeen Corinthian pan and nine Corinthian cover tiles (some of which are seen in Pls. 57 and 58).[124] From the extensive fill of the kopron was a small amount of pottery from the 5th century (including a possible Laconian krater, HP 2889), probable Mycenaean sherds, and a fragmentary sima tile painted with a red and black palmette-and-lotus frieze (HC 739). Preliminary study of this piece suggests a date of ca. 520 (Jerkich 1974). Such a decorated element probably came from a pretentious, but by the late 4th century rather venerable, public building. It is not impossible that the sima had been reused in some capacity, even in a domestic context, but it does cast some doubt on the integrity of the deposit in this kopron. Other material recovered from the kopron included a lamp fragment (HL 246), three loom weights (HC 654, HC 681, and HC 898), various metal objects including one coin (HN 1974-10, a bronze issue from Troizen dated 370–300), and (unusually) only a small amount of identifiable organic material (in the form of shell and carbonized wood and seeds, but no bone).

In contrast to Rooms 6-26 through 6-29, the quantity and variety of material recovered from Level A living surfaces in the northeastern half of House D suggest residential activity at a degree of intensity comparable to that encountered elsewhere at the site. As noted above, the bulk of this material occurred in Rooms 6-35b (Locus XIV) and 6-36 (Locus XVI). These two rooms had 276 MNV, which accounts for 46 percent of the total MNV from House D (or sixty-two percent if the material filling the negative features represented by Loci II and III is excluded). The nature of such a concentration needs to be examined further.[125] The debris is certainly not the product of primary deposition alone but must in part be the result of maintenance or cleanup of floor surfaces in general. Rooms 6-32 (Locus XIII) and 6-33 (Locus XII), although just across the threshold from Rooms 6-35 and 6-36, produced only 15 MNV. This suggests that their floors were swept clear of debris. The same or similar maintenance processes may account for the concentration of artifacts within the kopron of Room 6-26 (Locus II). At which point in the history of the city this cleanup took place can not be specified, but it probably occurred just before, during, or after the abandonment of Halieis (perhaps in the context of scavenging activities or squatter occupation).

At the same time, there is no doubt that the artifact material from Loci XIV and XVI originally belonged to the primary living space of House D. Both the character of the architecture and that of the artifacts support this assertion. There are thirty-five whole vessels and two whole lamps from these loci (twenty-one of the vessels, plus the lamps, came from Room 6-35b; the other fourteen vessels came from Room 6-36). Even though numerous items from certain functional categories are lacking, these thirty-five vessels are probably a representative portion of a contemporaneous pottery collection from a typical Halieis household. In fact, the manner in which the pieces were distributed across Room 6-35b and the southeastern end of Room 6-36 suggests that they form a single deposit. The variety, and especially the small size, of the vessels indicates that there may have been a shelf collapse, perhaps originating in the southern corner of Room 6-35b (Pl. 61), with other vessels placed on the southeastern wall of

[122] This deposit is discussed briefly in Ault 1999b, 552–53, and 568, appendix 1 (an inventory of its contents).

[123] See Appendix II.D for a listing of inventoried finds from House D, Locus II, where a number of these vessels are represented.

[124] Jerkich 1974. The pan tiles were 0.56–0.64 m wide and 0.673–0.78 m long. The sides were 0.06–0.07 m high. The cover tiles were ca. 0.70 m long and 0.17–0.18 m wide. They were ca. 0.08 m high. In contrast to these tiles, other artifact debris from this kopron, as well as from that in House 7, was much more fragmentary.

[125] This assemblage was briefly treated in Ault and Nevett 1999, 48, with fig. 4.2 and table 4.2.

Room 6-36 as well.[126] The following section lists the whole vessels from Loci XIV and XVI by ware, function, and shape and includes their inventory numbers (compare Appendix II.D):

FINE WARE
Food
Serving and Consumption:
  7 bowls (HP 2500, HP 2502, HP 2552, HP 2553, HP 2555, HP 2556, HP 2557)
  4 saltcellars (HP 2496, HP 2548, HP 2551, HP 2566)
Drink
Consumption:
  3 bolsals (HP 2573, HP 2583, HP 2599)
  7 skyphoi (HP 2554, HP 2637, HP 2638, HP 2639, HP 2640, HP 2690, HP 2886)
  2 stemless cups (HP 2557, HP 2558)
Serving and Pouring:
  1 trefoil oinochoe (HP 2481)
Other
  1 askos (HP 2565)
  1 pyxis lid (HP 2576)
  1 squat lekythos (HP 2587)

PLAIN WARE
Food
Preparation and Serving:
  2 mortars (HP 2560 [or shallow bowl], HP 2561)

COARSE WARE
Food
Cooking:
  1 lid (HP 2522)
  3 lopades (HP 2591, HP 2647, HP 2650)
Food and Drink
Containing and Storage:
  1 askos (HP 2666)
  1 pithos lid (HC 827)

This list displays the interrelated functions of the whole vessels in Rooms 6-35a and 6-36 and supports their identification as a collection. But the remaining 240 MNV do not exhibit such cohesion. What is more, there are numerous other artifact types from Loci XIV and XVI: six loom weights; seven MNV for lamps (including the two whole examples noted above); eight MNV for miniatures; the base of a seated or reclining figurine; and, in addition to nine bronze coins, more than thirty metal objects including a razor, spearhead, shovel, and tongs (all in iron), two bronze strigils, three drop handles, and a possible ring foot from a bronze vessel.[127] Like the assemblage in House C, Room 6-56 (Locus IV; for which, see above 37–38), some of the material here has all the earmarks of a dump deliberately located in the two rooms. But the presence of the whole vessels and other largely intact, more valuable objects suggests that these loci combine several different depositional circumstances, ranging from primary to secondary in character. Elsewhere, I have referred to this complex assemblage as representing "a palimpsest of habitation, caching, dumping and clean-up or maintenance of debris" (Ault and Nevett 1999, 48).

In Room 6-35a, the relatively low number of 28 MNV recovered in Locus XV indicates that it was spared the degree of secondary dumping that took place in Rooms 6-35b and 6-36, although fragments of at least six plain-ware amphoras came from strata lying above the floor level deposits. The other finds from the room only suggest that in regard to its artifacts (as well as its location), Room 6-35a lies in the domestic core of the house. The bronze needle (HM 1444), earring pendant (HM 1145), and fragmentary ostrich egg (HV 312) recovered there seem to support this identification. Taken together with the cooking area attested by the hearth in Room 6-30 (Loci X–XI), which also appears to have been the focus of dumping activity attendant on or postdating abandonment, the northeastern half of House D presents a compact domestic area independent of, but still linked to, the southwestern half of the complex.[128]

House E

(Figures 2, 5, 18–20; Plates 1, 62–71)

Like its neighbor House D to the northeast (Fig. 15, Pl. 54), House E belongs to the southeastern half of an insula bounded by Avenues B and C and Streets 3 and 4. These two houses are the most completely cleared of those that lay along this side of the block. According to the interpretation offered here, House E comprises three distinct

[126] Cf. the even more likely shelf collapse in House E, Locus XVII, between Rooms 6-16 and 6-20 (see below, 55).
[127] This listing is so extensive that inventory numbers have not been included. See Appendix II.D for a complete listing of inventoried objects, by locus, from the Level A–Level A/B strata.
[128] It is worth pointing out here that the northeastern half of House D, having covered some 120 m^2, is only slightly smaller than the area of House A (at ca. 132.5 m^2).

areas: the core of the house accessed from a courtyard (Rooms 6-16 through 6-20, and Rooms 6-23 though 6-25); a two-room suite located in the east corner of the house plot (Rooms 6-21 and 6-22); and a wing to the southwest, of which all or portions of three rooms have been exposed (Rooms 6-11 through 6-13).

As excavated, nearly three-quarters of House E have been recovered.[129] Measuring ca. 15 x 13.25 m along its southeast frontage and northeast limits, respectively, the exposed area accounts for 148 of its estimated 203 m^2 original extent. The house was entered from Street 3, over a rubble threshold into the L-shaped courtyard (Rooms 6-19 and 6-20; Pl. 63). The entryway itself, in its present state, is best described as a sub-prothyron type, since the doorway shows only a slight recession into the façade of the house. Because its internal width was approximately 2 m, there would have been enough space to equip it with a single set of wide double doors. A block on the northeastern side of the doorway has a square cutting and a pivot hole. The matching block on the southwestern side of the doorway also has a square cutting, but clear traces of a pivot are not in evidence. In its original state the doorway may have more closely resembled a typical prothyron than the surviving remains attest. The southwestern doorjamb lay nearby where it had fallen on line between Rooms 6-19 and 6-20.[130] Likewise, a limestone pier capital (HS 465) was recovered just east of the jamb block inside the doorway. If restored (as has been presumed on the actual-state plan, Fig. 19), the doorjamb would stand a full meter back from the street and, in conjunction with the dividing wall between Rooms 6-20 and 6-22, surely supported the small roof typical of prothyra constructions. This arrangement confirms the presence of a recessed entryway, merely more narrow and shallow than other prothyra encountered at the site (compare the reconstruction of House E, Fig. 18).[131] In front of the doorway and running southwest along the frontage of House E was preserved the course of a drip line or shallow gutter, edged in places with field stones.[132]

Rooms 6-19 and 6-20, with a combined area of 31.98 m^2, comprised the courtyard of House E. Traces of a whitish, lime-flecked earthen surfacing, which once formed a continuous layer, appeared over most of Room 6-20, its elevation ranging from 3.21 to 3.45 masl. Room 6-19, in which are situated a well and plaster-lined conglomerate trough, appears to have had a less consistently finished floor level (Pl. 64). It may have had an earth and lime floor only around the well, while concentrations of large flattish stones found in the northern portion of the room may represent a rougher surfacing in this area. The northwest end of Room 6-19 may have been covered by a shallow lean-to roof. At the northeastern end of the party wall between Rooms 6-18 and 6-19 is a southeast projecting spur, set in just above floor level (at ca. 3.48 masl; Pl. 66). This may have provided support for extending the roof of Room 6-18 in this direction or for footing an independent construction.

The well located in Room 6-19 bore a plastered conglomerate wellhead (Pl. 65). As a finishing touch, a specially cut ceramic rim, perhaps reused from a pithos, was affixed to its mouth. During or postdating the final phase of occupation in House E, the wellhead had been covered by an improvised arrangement of pan tiles atop which was laid a flat stone. When excavated, the floor around the wellhead was found to be subsiding into the shaft itself. Removal of the wellhead fully exposed the shaft, which was, in turn, excavated to a depth of at least 3.25 m (0.50 masl being the last elevation accounted for in the excavation notebooks). Lined with hydraulic plaster, its fill was primarily earthen. Relatively little artifact material was recovered from the well (Locus VII; cf. Table 14), but because its bottom was not reached, the primary fill, if there was one, was not encountered. Just north of the well lay a large stone trough (measuring approximately 1.00 x 0.60 m, 0.60 m in height, and 0.35 m deep) lined with plaster. The remains of a pithos were recovered midway along the western wall of Room 6-19.

From an earlier phase of the courtyard, a small, rectangular, stone-lined sunken feature (ca.

[129] House E is briefly discussed in Boyd and Rudolph 1978, 350–51, with fig. 3.

[130] The jamb block is 1.38 m long, 0.36 m wide, and 0.18 m thick. It is seen in the position in which it was found in Pl. 64, but was subsequently moved several meters to the north (and broken in the process) where it appears in Pls. 63 and 67. It is similar to the example identified in House A (see above, 26), especially with regard to the longitudinal cuttings along both of its interior edges. As noted in the discussion of House A, these probably facilitated a tighter fit for wooden elements of the door and its framework.

[131] I emphasize this point because it has been stated elsewhere that House E did not have a prothyron entry (Boyd and Rudolph 1978, 350).

[132] Alternatively, this channel may mark the trenching used to remove the ashlar orthostates that have been robbed out in places along the façade of House E.

1.00 x 0.60 m) was excavated in the northwest quadrant of Room 6-20 (Pl. 67). It was located against the partition wall with Room 6-18 and capped by a rubble layer, some of which bore the same lime and earthen surfacing as the surrounding yard. The feature was emptied of its dark silty fill (Locus XI, which yielded few artifacts) to a rocky bottom at a depth of over 1 m below the floor level (at 2.06–2.14 masl). Small by the standards of domestic koprones documented elsewhere at Halieis, it may have served as a bothros, which was emptied more often than a kopron. It went out of use before the latest Level A phase of the house.[133] In addition, two closed deposits were excavated in the north corner of Room 6-20 (visible in the central foreground of Pl. 67).[134] Both of these lay below the Level A floor surface. The first, ca. 0.90 m in diameter and excavated to a depth of 0.45 m (2.69 masl), was a pit of inverted bell shape. Its fill consisted primarily of roof tiles packed in vertically on edge. Just south of this lay another pit of comparable diameter and profile. It was filled mostly with soil and was less deep than the first (its bottom lay at 2.78 masl). Its southern half was covered with a rectangular block, identified below as a stair base, set in at floor level. Both features probably served as bothroi from earlier phases of the house (Level B?).

Proceeding clockwise around House E, the first room accessible from the courtyard was Room 6-18 (Pls. 63, 66). A small, squarish chamber (ca. 3.70 m^2), it was entered through a doorway (0.65 m wide) in its eastern corner. Its threshold consisted of an irregular rubble sill over which one appears to have stepped down from Room 6-20. Room 6-18 was divided on the north from Room 6-17 by an insubstantial northeast-southwest nonbearing wall, a later addition that subdivided what may formerly have been a single chamber into Rooms 6-17 and 6-18 (for this, see below). Its southeastern wall terminates at the east in a southward spur, which not only helps to demarcate the two areas of the courtyard, Rooms 6-19 and 6-20 but, as noted above, may also have had a structural function. Room 6-18 contained a deep Level A stratum of dumped occupation debris (Locus IX, averaging 0.49 m; cf. Table 14). No definite floor level was encountered, and excavation was terminated at a level of grayish clay that covered most of the room. In its latest phase, then, the floor of Room 6-18 must have been earthen and lay at a level as much as 0.40 m below the courtyard to the east and Room 6-17 to the northwest (2.83 masl being the lowest elevation recorded in Room 6-18).

Room 6-23 was entered directly from the courtyard through a broad doorway ca. 1.40 m wide. It was a rectangular chamber oriented northwest-southeast and may have covered ca. 12.5 m^2. Its northern half lies beyond the boundary of Area 6 and remains unexcavated. The excavated portion (7.9 m^2) shows that Room 6-23 was an intermediate chamber that lay between the court and other rooms and suites of rooms to which it provided access. (In this respect it functioned like a pastas porch, or transverse hall.) Its floor consisted of a matrix of earth with pebble and small stone inclusions that sloped off ca. 0.05–0.10 m from the surface of the courtyard.

Access to Room 6-16 was probably along the northwestern side of Room 6-23, beyond the point where the two rooms were divided by a narrow orthostate (and beyond the limits of Area 6; Pl. 67). Only a small triangle comprising 2.8 m^2 of Room 6-16 was cleared. But if this room was restored as a rectangular chamber extending northwest to the probable limits of House E, its area could have covered as much as 15.8 m^2. In the southwestern portion of Room 6-16 survives an area of white plaster flooring (lying at ca. 3.42 masl). Along its finished and curving edge is visible an underpinning of large pebbles, typical for such surfaces at the site.

Whatever its original extent, Room 6-16 formed a unit with the tiny, 1.6 m^2, Room 6-17 to its south (Pls. 63, 68). The two were linked by the plaster pavement of Room 6-16, which sloped down to Room 6-17 where it was formed into a raised curb or threshold at the narrow doorway between the two. From Room 6-16, one would have stepped down to the pavement of Room 6-17, which lay at ca. 3.26 masl. The doorway had a minimum width of 0.31 m at the level of the threshold where it was constricted by a plaster ledge running along the northwestern wall of Room 6-17. It widened to a maximum preserved

[133] The feature was excavated in Tr 055/320: u. 18–20. Given the presence of large stone-lined koprones present in virtually all other houses considered here, the bothros of Room 6-20 may represent the contraction of an earlier such feature. The very stony nature of exposed but unexcavated levels along the eastern side of Room 6-18 and in the northern portion of Room 6-19 may reflect its presence (cf. House 7, Room 7-12, and House C, Room 6-53; for these, see above, 16–17, 35).

[134] These were explored in TR 060/320, as "open deposits" [sic] 2 and 3.

width of 0.62 m above the height of this ledge. In addition to their flooring, wall plaster was continuous between the two rooms, having been molded around both the west and east door jambs. In Room 6-17 the walls were finished in white plaster except for a section on the northwestern face of the nonbearing wall dividing it from 6-18. The latter two rooms once communicated with one another, if they were not, indeed, a single chamber. This is suggested by the fact that in its flimsiest southwestern extent, the nonbearing wall was clearly built on top of the pavement of Room 6-17. Moreover, plaster on the southwest wall of Room 6-17 continues beyond the point where the nonbearing wall abuts the single ashlar block of the southwestern wall shared by Rooms 6-17 and 6-18.

The northwestern wall of Room 6-17 was finished with a plaster ledge ca. 0.12 m wide running the length of the room at a height of ca. 0.14 m above floor level. Plastered into this ledge, at the corner of the wall and just above the threshold of Room 6-17, was a small black-glazed bowl. The plastered finish of the room, its floor, ledge, and the vessel set into this ledge, all become relevant when considering the feature that survived in situ in the center of the room at the time of its excavation: a cylindrical base for a ceramic louterion. Although the basin proper had been broken away and was not recovered, the pedestal, with its double-molded foot, is well preserved.[135] When lifted, its impression in the plaster floor was clearly visible, confirming that it was an integral part of the room. It seems likely, then, that Room 6-17 functioned as a bath, not with a tub but with a splash basin. The elaborate plastering would have kept the fabric of the walls—susceptible as they were to dampness—dry, and the small bowl set into the plaster ledge could have held a sponge or even oil used in bathing.[136] Baths and kitchens were frequently paired at Olynthos and have been found together at Halieis (as in Houses A and B). Therefore, it seems reasonable to suggest that Room 6-16, adjoining Room 6-17, served as the household kitchen. Additional support for this identification is provided by its associated artifact assemblage (from Loci XV, XVI, and XVII), which is presented in detail below.

Like the kitchen and bathroom, Room 6-25, at the northern corner of House E, was reached through Room 6-23. Of its probable 8.8 m^2 (the northwestern extent of the room continues beyond the limits of Area 6), ca. 5.6 m^2 were excavated. Architecturally there were no notable features about Room 6-25.[137] The southeast side of its doorway was recovered as was a thin and patchy earthen floor that lay ca. 0.20–0.30 m lower than that of Room 6-23. Two small limestone blocks finished with red plaster were found within the rather sparse debris (Locus XXI, HS 460 and HS 462), but their significance is uncertain.

Room 6-24 lay southeast of Room 6-25 and was entered from the east corner of Room 6-23 through a 1 m wide doorway. Nearly square and with an area of 9.0 m^2, it was set off from Rooms 6-20 and 6-23 by a short, freestanding, L-shaped stretch of wall. Because of its location at the intersection of four five-by-five-meter grids, Room 6-24 was excavated in piecemeal fashion. This added to the difficulty of determining an elevation for the Level A floor, which appears to have been largely earthen (although some traces of lime-flecked earth were noted, suggesting the presence of heavily worn or multiple surfacings). The latest floor seems to have lain at ca. 3.00 masl, an elevation lower than the courtyard or Room 6-23.

Between Room 6-24 and the courtyard (Room 6-20) is a small area 1m^2. Located here was a pithos, partially sunken into the floor and partially built into the dividing wall with Room 6-21.[138] In addition, large rubble further constricted passage here. It seems unlikely that this uncomfortable space was a second doorway to Room 6-24. Instead, it probably marks the location of a stairwell. Additional evidence for this is a rectangular block situated just around the corner and set in at the floor level of Room 6-20. This probably served as a stair base.[139] Thus, the area

[135] Although the louterion base seems not to have been inventoried, it is kept in the Porto Cheli Halieis storeroom. Unfortunately, the whereabouts of the black-glazed bowl from Room 6-17 is unknown.

[136] Sponges appear frequently in palaestra scenes on vases. Closer to the domestic context, a red-figured stamnos by a painter of the Polygnotan Group shows three hetairai bathing at a louterion (Munich 2411, from Vulci; ca. 440; *ARV*² 1051, no. 18). One of them holds a stick with an applicator end to her hair. This has been interpreted as the application of oil, probably perfumed, as part of the bath (*CVA* Munich 5 [Germany 20], 37–38, pl. 247 [Germany pl. 2411]; cf. Boardman 1989, 81, fig. 156).

[137] Although not noted in the excavation notebook for TR 065/320, a sizable iron fragment from an unidentifiable object is embedded in the northeast corner of the west wall of Room 6-25.

[138] Presumably the pithos postdates the out-of-use pits mentioned above, one of which is actually under the stair base. It is the pithos that is shown on Fig. 19.

[139] As already noted, this stone was placed on top of the out-of-use bothros. Although it bears no cuttings to support this identification, its size (ca. 1 x 0.5 m, dimensions comparable to other stair bases identified at the site) and position make it a likely candidate.

may be envisioned with a northwest ascending flight of stairs that made a northeasterly return to a landing associated with the upper-story rooms (as indicated on Fig. 19). Such an arrangement would have used the freestanding wall to the north as a brace for the stairway as well as a support for the second story. On the ground floor, below the stairway, the space could have been used as a small closet or cupboard (containing the pithos) that opened into Room 6-24.[140] The likely extent of second-story chambers in House E is discussed further below.

The most unusual feature of Room 6-24 is the presence of two inscribed rectangular blocks (HS 532 and HS 533; Pls. 69, 70). These were set end to end, below but with their upper surfaces essentially level with the latest Level A floor of the room, midway along the dividing wall with Room 6-25. The inscription(s) were laid out in two lines that continued around three sides of one block and from one face to the adjoining side of the second. Although difficult to read and even more so to interpret (abbreviations appear to have been used in several instances), the writing seems to include the invocation of a familial Zeus, the Dioskouroi, and an ancestral hero.[141] Preliminary analysis of the lettering, roughly cut by the same hand on both blocks, has suggested to Jameson that this was "the work of a man who had learned to write in the fifth century and was writing now in the second quarter of the fourth century" (Jameson 2001a, 198). This agrees with an earlier Level A or Level B date for the interment of the inscription. Tucked in between and behind the blocks were two miniature kotylai, while along their southwestern side was an inverted bolsal (HP 2530).[142] Although whatever construction(s) to which they once belonged had been dismantled in the latest habitation phase of House E, the blocks must have marked a site for ritual activity and are manifestations of domestic cult.

No other rooms were accessible from the courtyard of House E. But there remain two additional suites that cluster around its sides. The first of these, Rooms 6-21 and 6-22, occupied the southeastern limits of the house plot and apparently had no intercommunication with the house proper. Instead, these chambers (measuring 10.2 and 8.8 m^2, respectively) were entered directly from Street 3. Along the façade of House E, in the southeast corner of Room 6-22 and perpendicular to the party wall with House D, is an opening, ca. 1.5 m wide, bearing a rubble threshold. The two rooms themselves communicated through a doorway, 0.70 m wide, set at the northeastern end of their dividing wall.

A section of plaster pavement survives in Room 6-22. Finished with a raised threshold into Room 6-21, the pavement continues for a short distance south, where it terminates abruptly. It lies at an elevation of 3.14–3.25 masl. The party wall with House D also bore traces of plaster where it was adjacent to the pavement. At first exposure the pavement suggested to its excavators that it might have functioned as a basin that drained into the negative feature in Room 6-26 of House D (subsequently identified as a kopron), on the other side of the party wall. In fact, the surface of the pavement is not regular enough to drain in any particular direction. It shows signs of being only partially preserved along the southwestern and southeastern edges, where traces of rubble underpinning protrude from beneath. The rubble matrix exposed over the rest of the chamber marks what was originally a subfloor level below continuation of the plaster or, alternatively, represents packing below a simpler earthen surfacing.[143] Room 6-22 contained a heavy concentration of roof tiles (927 fragments were recovered from Locus XIII; cf. Table 13). In Room 6-21, the smaller number of tiles (about 300 fragments were recovered from Locus XIV) seems to have fallen on top of a sterile layer of mud-brick wall collapse (rather than directly upon the floor). The earthen floor of Room 6-21 was 3.00–3.10 masl and overlay a stony subsurface in a dark soil matrix.

The second complex of rooms associated with House E was discovered at the southwestern

[140] The similar use of such space below a flight of stairs has been documented in House I at Kassope, where a number of pithoi and amphoras were found (Hoepfner and Schwandner 1994, 148, with figs. 141, 141a). Cf. also Colophon, where the stairs of House IV: Room e, turned to create a landing with a small chamber beneath (Holland 1944, 127, with pl. XI).

[141] Information concerning the inscribed blocks was kindly supplied by M. H. Jameson. For the text, see Jameson 2001a.

[142] Although not assigned inventory numbers in the find-notebook entries for TR 060/320: u. 23, where three fragments of Corinthian miniature kotylai are listed, two miniature kotylai are specified in the trench notebook. One of these kotylai is visible in Pls. 69 and 70, where it lies atop the juncture of the two blocks. The inverted bolsal can be seen in Pl. 69. There was much additional pottery associated with this level, but it has no demonstrable relationship with the inscribed blocks.

[143] An inverted cover tile set perpendicular to the dividing wall with Room 6-21 lay on top of the stony underpinning for the floor of Room 6-22. Although continuing below the wall proper, it did not reemerge in any fashion in Room 6-21. Possibly it marks the line of a drainage channel out of use in the latest phase of the rooms.

corner of the building. Portions of two chambers (Rooms 6-11 and 6-12), all of a third (Room 6-13), and a section of a longitudinally oriented alleyway or ambitus ("Room" 6-10, of which a 5 m stretch lay within Area 6) comprise this area. Almost nothing is known about Room 6-11 because of its position along the limits of the trench. Room 6-12, an intermediate chamber between Rooms 6-11 to the northwest and 6-13 to the southeast, is the largest of the excavated rooms. Most of its area, ca. 12.00 m^2, has been exposed. It possessed one point of entry in its north corner, through a 1.0 m wide doorway shared with Room 6-11. Set off from Room 6-13 by a short dividing wall (in its original state possibly lengthened by the rubble and ashlar tumble that lay about the area), Room 6-12 also had an external doorway in its southwest corner. An ashlar and rubble wall formed the southwestern bounds of Rooms 6-12 and 6-13. One block is set ca. 0.35 m lower than the others and would have served as the threshold for a doorway about 0.80 m wide. Although no definite floor surface for Room 6-12 was ascertained, Level C deposits were reached in two of the units excavated within the room (in TR 055/315: u. 10, 12). These strata were quite stony and recall the fill or underpinning characteristic of subfloor levels encountered elsewhere. Overlying layers that would have comprised the Level A earthen floor of Room 6-12 suggest that its elevation lay between 3.60 and 3.80 masl.

Room 6-13, 8.4 m^2, lay along the course of Street 3 but seems not to have had direct access to it (Pl. 71).[144] No traces of a doorway were discerned in the low, southwest-northeast rubble foundation socle that divided it from the street and abutted the more substantial walls of House E proper to the east. Along the eastern side of Room 6-13 are remains of a plaster pavement that lay at an elevation ranging from 3.76 to 3.88 masl. Not preserved to its original dimensions, the pavement extended at least 1.0 m north into Room 6-12 where portions of its pebbly underpinning survive. Off its western edge, the original limits of which could not be determined, lay a conduit composed of ashlar blocks with a channel cut into their upper surface.[145] The remaining area of Room 6-13 was, according to the excavators, "filled with small rounded stones" (at elevations ranging from 3.72 to 3.83 masl), suggesting underpinning for continuation of the plaster or for an earthen surfacing. Since traces of flooring tangential to the conduit are not preserved, we do not know whether the drain itself lay at or below the floor level of Room 6-13 (although it presently lies at an average of 0.03 m below the elevation of the surviving pavement). The course of the conduit exited Room 6-13 in its southwestern corner, where the resulting gap in the wall foundations appears to have been bridged and leveled up with roof tiles (which survived in situ at the time of excavation). Accordingly, the drain was in use during the Level A occupation of Room 6-13. Upon entering "Room" 6-10, the channel course took a 60° bend to the northwest. At this point, excavators noted that its surface was covered with flattish stones spanning the channel itself. Intended to carry off some liquid from Room 6-13 to a point west of Room 6-10, the precise destination of the drainage remains unknown.[146] A very small part of Room 6-9 was uncovered here, west of the drain. Although almost wholly unexcavated owing to the limits of Area 6, it surely marks the eastern corner of the southwest corner house of the insula. Beyond its surviving ashlar wall could have been located another drainage feature into which the conduit emptied. Curiously, the channel cutting also extends to the southeastern terminus of the conduit's western half. This 0.30 m long section, which still lies in Room 6-13, is considerably shallower than elsewhere along the channel course. Perhaps this indicates a change of plan in the conduit design, since it does not actually lie in Street 3 where it might have channeled off rainwater that accumulated there.

"Room" 6-10, where the excavated extent of the conduit ended, is long and rectangular (4.8 m^2 have been recovered). This shape is more suggestive of an alleyway between houses, an ambitus, as that behind House 7, than it is an internal, roofed chamber. Both Room 6-10 and the alley behind House 7 are approximately 1.25 m wide. We do not have definite evidence for its opening onto Street 3 because the frontage of Room 6-13 was footed on comparatively light rubble and its continuation here is uncertain. The transverse alleys bisecting insulae at Olynthos were walled up at either end, according to the

[144] For the report on a deep sounding carried out in Room 6-13 and Street 3, see Rudolph 1984, especially 133–35 ("Test D"), and 169–70, with fig. 7, and pl. 32.c.

[145] A similarly constructed drain was found in Room 6-46, in a partially excavated building lying midway along the northwestern side of this same insula (see above, 23).

[146] Elevations within the channel itself (3.73 masl at its northeastern end, dropping to 3.66 masl where it exited Room 6-13, and 3.63 masl near its northwestern terminus) confirm the direction of flow.

excavators (D. M. Robinson and J. W. Graham 1938, 36–37). If the posited doorway in Room 6-12 were the exclusive means of entry into this portion of House E, the alley should not have been closed off at all (and it is this arrangement depicted in the reconstruction of House E, Fig. 18). Room 6-10 seems to have had a surfacing of the lime and earth admixture noted elsewhere at the site (lying at ca. 3.58 masl), as did the alley behind House 7. A sizable deposit of artifact debris lay upon this surface (Locus I; cf. Table 13). It should probably be associated with the abandonment of the area, but not necessarily with House E, and is discussed below in connection with the finds.

It is difficult to determine the role played by the southwestern suite of rooms. Room 6-11, at the northwestern end of the unit, could link the whole to House E proper. But only a tiny triangle of its area (amounting to 1.8 m^2) was exposed, and there, the floor level was not reached. Room 6-11 might have been accessible from Room 6-16, actually been part of it, or even have been accessible from a corridor along the back of the house (via Room 6-23). Unfortunately, we are unable to say for certain. Alternatively, it may be that this group of rooms did not communicate with the core of House E at all but merely shared a party wall with it. It may be that Rooms 6-11 through 6-13 stood as chambers separate from House E proper (but perhaps shared with it the same roofing system). This theory is supported by the differing floor levels within the structure. Those in the courtyard lay anywhere from 0.40 to 0.60 m lower than the pavement in Room 6-13. This same difference holds between the elevation of the plaster floors in Room 6-13 and Rooms 6-16/17. As in the several other instances already noted between and within the houses in Area 6, floor levels drop incrementally to the northeast as the site slopes down toward the ancient waterfront. Thus, the party wall between the southwestern range of rooms and the rest of House E served as a terrace wall that fully bisected the house. Such an arrangement is very similar to that in House D, except that the two halves there do communicate across the wide courtyard (Rooms 6-26 and 6-31).

The foregoing suggests that Rooms 6-11 through 6-13 stood apart from House E proper. As is more clearly the case for the southwestern half of House D (Rooms 6-26 through 6-29), this portion of the building had an industrial character. This is suggested by the plaster pavement and conduit of Room 6-13. Room 6-13 is, in turn, integrally linked to Room 6-12, especially if the latter had a doorway opening on to the alley (Room 6-10). Thus, the southwestern block may have been rental property or under the proprietorship of the owner of House E. The same holds for Rooms 6-21/22. Clearly segregated from the living space of the house, even if they are more integrated into its fabric than Rooms 6-11 through 6-13, they may have comprised some sort of shop.[147]

If the structural fabric of House E is viewed in this way, a final observation may be made regarding the extent of probable second-story rooms (compare the reconstruction, Fig. 18). These could have been confined to the core of the household, and, following the seasonal and climatic logic of Aristotle and Xenophon (see below, 60–61), they would have lain over the northern range of rooms—that is, Room 6-16, possibly Rooms 6-17 and 6-18, and Rooms 6-23 through 6-25. But in addition, the second story might have extended over Rooms 6-11 through 6-13 (providing that the effects of the terracing at ground level were compensated for in elevation). Rooms 6-21 and 6-22 could also have risen to two stories in height. The continuation of second-story chambers over the southeast rooms and southwest wing would probably have been all the more likely if the entire tract were under single ownership.[148]

Artifact Assemblages: Quantification and Distribution

In Tables 13–18, which display the quantification and distribution of artifact material from House E Level A, data on the southwest area (Rooms 6-10 through 6-12, which equate to Loci I–V and VIII) and the southeastern rooms (Rooms 6-21 and 6-22, as represented by Loci XIII/XIV) are presented separately from the central block of the house. (See

[147] It should here be pointed out that the shops and manufactories appended to houses at Olynthos, to which Rooms 6-21 and 6-22 in House E do bear a resemblance, were located along both the main avenues and the side streets (see Hoepfner and Schwandner 1994, 112, with fig. 89). Cahill has shown that such shops tend to be more frequent along the avenues and appear to increase in number closer to the putative "agora" (1991, 372–75, with fig. 72; 2002, 274–75).

[148] The second story could conceivably have wrapped around the courtyard of the entire house, including the full southwestern wing and Rooms 6-21 and 6-22, but there is no firm basis for this reconstruction. Compare the isometric restoration of an insula at Olynthos, where a variety of equally workable arrangements are shown for the extent of second-story chambers, including flat roofs used as extensions of living space (Hoepfner and Schwandner 1994, 87, fig. 64).

also Fig. 20 and Appendix II.E.) From the category of pottery, a total of 4187 items were recovered, 2886 from House E proper and 1301 from the two "wings." From these figures may be calculated a total MNV of 580, which span fifty-one different vessel types (Table 19). The central block of House E produced 374 MNV and 206 MNV were recovered from the other two areas.

Of the 374 MNV from House E proper, the majority occurred in the courtyard area: Room 6-19 (Locus VI), with 62 MNV; and Room 6-20 (Loci XIIa-c) with 90 MNV. Additional concentrations were found in Room 6-18 (Locus IX), with 73 MNV, and Room 6-24 (Locus XX), also with 73 MNV. The MNV for other rooms, although considerably less, is not insignificant. Overall, the largest class represented comprises fine-ware drinking cups (97 MNV). Coarse-ware cooking vessels (66 MNV), fine-, plain-, and coarse-ware shapes for the serving and pouring of drink (64 MNV), and plain- and coarse-ware storage containers (63) occur in nearly equal amounts. The numbers are lower for fine-ware vessels connected to the serving and consumption of food (34 MNV) and for plain and coarse wares for food serving and preparation other than cooking (23 MNV). The following figures summarize the foregoing:

House E: Core
2886 pottery items
= 374 MNV
= 97 MNV (25.9%) associated with drink consumption (fine-ware cups only)
= 66 MNV (17.6%) associated with cooking
= 64 MNV (17.1%) associated with serving and pouring drink (including fine- and plain-ware drink-serving containers)
= 63 MNV (16.8%) associated with storage of food and drink
= 34 MNV (9.1%) associated with fine-ware food serving and consumption
= 23 MNV (6.1%) associated with food serving and preparation other than cooking

Several patterns emerge from these vessel types, the clearest being those associated with storage, which cluster in the southwestern courtyard chamber, Room 6-19 (Locus VI), with a MNV of 31. This number is much greater than the other classes of vessels that occurred there: those associated with food preparation, cooking and serving, and drink consumption and serving. All these were present but in negligible frequencies. The greatest concentrations of these latter vessel types occurred across the other portion of the courtyard, Room 6-20 (Locus XII), and in Rooms 6-18 and 6-24 (Loci IX and XX, respectively).

Room 6-18 (Locus IX), with its 73 MNV including only two whole vessels, is very suggestive of a dump.[149] The depth over which the material occurred (ca. 0.50 m), as well as its concentration into such a small area, suggests that this was not a primary deposition. The character of the assemblage from Room 6-18 resembles the probable dump in Room 6-56 in House C (see above, 38). In addition, unlike the pottery from Room 6-24, which also yielded 73 MNV, the finds from Room 6-18 do not form a pattern.

Room 6-24 (Locus XX) furnished a considerable MNV for both fine and plain wares associated with the serving and consumption of drink and for food consumption and preparation (accounting for 58, of the total 73 MNV, or 78 percent). By contrast, only small frequencies were associated with cooking (2 MNV) and storage (5 MNV). Among the remaining 8 MNV, which belong to the largest number of "other" vessel categories in the house, are represented fine-ware examples of an askos-guttus (HP 2543), a skyphos-shaped pyxis (HP 2191), a lekanis/pyxis, and a lid; and in plain ware, a pyxis and two lids. The nature of this assemblage clearly suggests primary interior living space, much like others that we have been able to identify elsewhere at the site on the basis of artifact remains.[150] Any connection between the traces of domestic cult present in the room (the buried but inscribed blocks HS 532, 533) and its "dayroom" functions remains tentative.

Room 6-16 has already been discussed as the location of the kitchen for House E, primarily in light of its proximity to the bath, Room 6-17. Although only a portion of its extent was cleared, from the pottery artifacts recovered (Loci XV and XVI had 17 MNV), the most numerous class of vessels were associated with cooking (7 MNV).

[149] A bronze coin of Arcadius (HN 1975-110, minted at Herakleia in A.D. 383) was recorded among the finds recovered in Room 6-18. While this suggests a later disturbance here, only three late Roman sherds were recovered in strata assigned to Level A of House E, and none occurred in Locus IX. Thus, if there was disturbance here, it was very limited.

[150] Cf. House 7, Room 7-12 (see above, 20) and House A, Room 6-87 (see above, 31).

Among these, although not a vessel per se, was a nearly complete eschara or portable brazier (HP 2892). Although the type occurs rarely at Halieis, its presence here suggests why hearths were not always found in houses at the site.[151]

Locus XVII merits special attention because it supports the identification of Room 6-16 as a kitchen.[152] An open deposit of material located in the west corner of the courtyard, Locus XVII appears to have spread in a line southeast along the wall of Rooms 6-17 and 6-18 (Pl. 67). As isolated, it yielded 17 MNV, of which eleven were whole vessels. The following list organizes these vessels by ware, function, and shape and includes their inventory numbers (cf. Appendix II.E).

FINE WARE
Food
Serving and Consumption:
- 1 saltcellar (HP 2154)

Drink
Consumption:
- 2 bolsals (HP 2151, HP 2156)
- 1 stemless cup (HP 2164)

Serving and Pouring:
- 2 jugs (HP 2157, HP 2158)

Other
- 1 squat lekythos (HP 2153)

COARSE WARE
Food
Preparation and Serving:
- 1 bowl (HP 2170)
- 1 strainer (HP 2155)

Cooking:
- 1 griddle (HP 2159)
- 1 lopas (HP 2161)

All four coarse-ware vessels, plus a lekane (HP 2163) that survived in profile, can be associated with food preparation and cooking. Because the deposit of Locus XVII actually began on top of the wall dividing Rooms 6-16 and 6-17 from Room 6-20, it seems likely that it came from the southeast collapse of a mud-brick wall in Room 6-16 (its southeast wall near its east corner) and the attendant concentration of pottery was probably on a shelving unit on that wall.[153]

The excavation strategy employed at Halieis, based on five-by-five-meter grid squares that defined individual trenches, did not allow the full linear spread of Locus XVII to be pursued southeast where it entered a new grid square. But it seems likely that several additional whole vessels encountered in the northern portion of Room 6-20 (Loci XIIa, b) may relate to this collapse deposit as well. These include two fine-ware cups, a skyphos painted with a net pattern (HP 2189) and a cup kantharos (HP 2166), as well as a large coarse-ware lopas (HP 3006). Elsewhere in Room 6-20 the nature of debris recovered is in keeping with the degree and variety of material present in the courtyards of the other houses at Halieis already examined.

From Room 6-23 (Loci XVIII and XIX) three, nearly complete, but fragmentary, amphoras (HP 2350, HP 2351, and HP 2355) were recovered in the relatively sterile mud-brick fill above the Level A floor. The circumstances of their deposition may reflect a collapse similar to that suggested for the deposit of Locus XVII. Room 6-25 (Locus XXI), despite its size, produced the smallest amount of material from House E (yielding only 11 MNV) except for the bath, Room 6-17 (Locus X, with 1 MNV).

Other classes of artifacts from House E proper are diverse: a MNV of eleven lamps (the only whole example coming from Room 6-24, Locus XX, HL 309), ten MNV for five varieties of miniatures variously distributed about the house, a painted terracotta bird figurine (Room 6-23, Locus XVIII, HC 651), and a circular terracotta stamp with a kneeling female figure (Room 6-20, Locus XIIc, HC 815). Twenty-five loom weights were recovered, seventeen of which occurred in the courtyard Room 6-20 (between Loci XIIb, c). A single biconical loom weight from the house was stamped with an eagle and rooster (Room 6-25, Locus XXI, HC 652).

A number of stone tools were found, especially in Room 6-24 (Locus XX). The same

[151] Built hearths have been documented in three instances: in House 7, between Rooms 7-16 and 7-17 (see above, 18); in House D, Room 6-30 (see above, 42); and seemingly in the house in Area 4 adjacent to a well complex (Jameson 1969, 328; J. H. Young 1963, 4–5, with plan). A large portion of a second eschara was recovered from the dump of debris in the ambitus "Room" 6-10 (Locus I, HP 2202). See Rudolph 1984, 124, fig. 1, and Boyd and Rudolph 1978, 336, fig. 1 for site plans with area designations.

[152] See Ault and Nevett 1999, 48, with fig. 4.1, for a brief presentation and interpretation of the material from Locus XVII.

[153] Since the top of the deposit characterized as Locus XVII actually lay on the dividing wall between Rooms 6-16 and 6-17, and Room 6-20, and continued over ca. 0.55 m in depth, it seems to have fallen from a height as well as from north of where it lay. For a shelving collapse excavated in one of the Late Helladic period houses at Tsoungiza (Archaia Nemea), see Wright 1982, 387–94. For a brief discussion of shelving, along with select artistic representations, see Richter 1966, 78–79.

room also yielded numerous metal objects, including two bronze door(?) bosses (HM 1147a, b), which lay directly on top of the inscribed blocks (HS 532, 533 discussed above), a bronze drop handle (HM 1211), and fragments of a bronze grater (HM 1205). From the house as a whole, four iron cutting implements were recovered: a cleaver from Room 6-18 (Locus IX, HM 1523), a "sword" and a curved blade from the courtyard Room 6-20 (Locus XIIc, HM 1000 and HM 1531, respectively), and another generic blade form from Room 6-24 (Locus XX, HM 1532). There were also five bronze coins of the Classical period: one from Arcadia (Room 6-19, Locus VI, HN 1974-15; minted 363–280), two Halieis Tirynthian issues (Room 6-18, Locus IX, HN 1974-19; and Room 6-20, Locus XIIa, HN 1974-25), and two of the relatively rare Halieis "H" issues (Room 6-19, Locus VI, HN 1974-9; and Room 6-24, Locus XX, HN 1974-21). In addition, two bronze tokens stamped with an amphora/T were recovered from Room 6-24 (Locus XX, HM 1202, 1203).[154]

The suite of rooms occupying the eastern corner of House E, Rooms 6-21 and 6-22, yielded a MNV of 74 (Loci XIII and XIV). There is nothing from the contents of the two chambers to support their architecturally based identification as shops, as made above, nor are there any striking differences in the nature of material recovered between them. On the contrary, the vessels represented span the typical domestic assemblage, all types being present. Indeed, the three whole vessels recovered there, a Corinthian pyxis (Room 6-21, Locus XIV, HP 2471), a pyxis lid (Room 6-22, Locus XIII, HP 2428), and a plain-ware thurible (Room 6-22, Locus XIII, HP 2430), suggest that the chambers were living space.[155] The following list illustrates the functional breakdown of the assemblage:

House E: Southeast "Shops"
457 pottery items
- = 74 MNV
- = 23 MNV (31.1%) associated with drink consumption (fine-ware cups only)
- = 13 MNV (17.6%) associated with cooking
- = 12 MNV (16.2%) associated with serving and pouring drink (includes fine- and plain-ware drink-serving containers)
- = 7 MNV (9.6%) associated with fine-ware food serving and consumption
- = 6 MNV (8.2%) associated with storage of food and drink
- = 5 MNV (6.8%) associated with food serving and preparation other than cooking

From Rooms 6-12 and 6-13 were recovered 83 MNV (Loci II, V, and VIII; and Loci III and IV, respectively). By far the bulk of this material came from Room 6-12. As in Rooms 6-21 and 6-22, all classes of pottery were present, but none occurred in a density that suggested the choice of particular locations for specific activities. In the southwestern portion of the house, however, there is a significant amount of metal-bearing slag and fragments of unidentified metal (rare finds elsewhere on the site). More than sixteen pieces of slag were identified in Rooms 6-12 and 6-13. In addition, it is likely that more slag could be found among the more than twenty fragments of unidentified metal also recorded as coming from these rooms. Such a quantity could well be associated with low-level metal smithing and accords with what has already been noted about the industrial character of Room 6-12 and 6-13. Also recovered from Room 6-13 was a large marine shell, identified as a whelk (Loci III/IV, HV 307) and possibly used as a ladle. Other examples are associated with two of the oil-press installations at Halieis, where, according to ethnographic parallels, they appear to have functioned as skimmers (see above, 41, note 103).

At the same time, on the basis of the pottery recovered, both of the "wings" of House E show a strong domestic character in addition to what has already been adduced about their possible industrial and mercantile functions. Perhaps they were rental property and were used, at least in part, as dwellings. There is also the perpetually vexing question of metics' and slaves' quarters. Where did they live? How might they be identified archaeologically? It may be that Rooms 6-11 through 6-13 and Rooms 6-21 and 6-22 are examples of such areas, although the identification is still uncertain.[156]

The last deposit to be considered is Locus I, the dump of debris upon the surfacing of the alleyway "Room" 6-10. Here 49 MNV were

[154] J. A. Dengate has identified similar tokens from the lower town and acropolis; he suggests that they were issued when other coinage was in short supply to be redeemed for full value later (see Dengate in McAllister 2005).

[155] It is, of course, possible that these artifacts fell from second-story rooms above.

[156] On slaves' quarters, see Jameson 1990a, 103–4; for metics', Thür 1989. In general, see Hoepfner and Schwandner 1994, 329–30.

recovered with no whole vessels. Although these artifacts might reflect abandonment activity in Rooms 6-12 and 6-13, they could equally well have come from neighboring houses since "Room" 6-10 was probably outside. Of special note here are the 13 MNV for vessels associated with storage of food and drink (comprising 1 MNV for a plain-ware amphora, 2 MNV for plain-ware hydriai, and 10 MNV for coarse-ware pithoi).

The following figures give a breakdown by functional class for MNVs from Loci I–V and Locus VIII:

House E: Southwest Rooms
844 pottery items
= 132 MNV
= 29 MNV (22.0%) associated with serving and pouring drink (includes fine-ware drink-serving containers)
= 28 MNV (21.2%) associated with drink consumption (fine-ware cups only)
= 22 MNV (16.7%) associated with cooking
= 20 MNV (15.2%) associated with storage of food and drink
= 9 MNV (6.8%) associated with food serving and preparation other than cooking
= 8 MNV (6.1%) associated with fine-ware food serving and consumption

– CHAPTER THREE –

Synthesis of Room Types, Features, and Functions

> It is well to understand tactics too; for there is a wide difference between right and wrong disposition of the troops, just as stones, bricks, timber and tiles flung together anyhow are useless, whereas when the materials that neither rot nor decay, that is, the stones and tiles, are placed at the bottom and the top, and the bricks and timber are put together in the middle, as in building, the result is something of great value, a house, in fact.
>
> XENOPHON *Memorabilia* 3.1.7

In this chapter I offer an interpretive synopsis of the houses at Halieis.[1] In addition, I explore the ways in which the attendant artifact evidence sheds more light on the activities within each household. Also intended here is an integration of the Halieis houses into the growing corpus of domestic structures from the Classical Greek world, which provides an opportunity to make a number of observations about household organization generally. It is clear that there is no evidence for *Typenhäuser* at the site of Halieis along the lines of those postulated by Hoepfner and Schwandner for Olynthos, Peiraeus, Priene and a host of other poleis.[2] At the same time, there are a number of recurrent features in the plans of the Halieis houses that compare well with Greek houses elsewhere. These include such elements of design and layout as the positioning of certain rooms within houses, the appointment of rooms, and predictable clusterings or suites of rooms. Coupled with the distribution of artifacts, these features are all indicative of spatially differentiated activity areas within the houses and, in turn, of household organization or oikonomia given substance via architecture. In addition, when compared with similar aspects of layout, design elements, and room groupings in Classical houses at other sites, they speak for the existence of a fluid koine of domestic architecture. Although this koine was affected by local convention, environmental determinants, and physical needs, I would argue that the combination of oikonomia and isonomia is at least in part responsible for the many similarities witnessed in Classical housing.[3]

Thus, while there is a great difference between laying out city plans and determining the internal arrangement of individual houses, the organization of the household provided the fundamental design for modeling the organization of the polis. At Halieis as well as at numerous other sites it is important to note that this level of organization was achieved independently of a planner and social theoretician with the status of

[1] The translations used for the epigrams in this chapter are as follows: Xenophon, Marchant 1938; Euripides, D. M. Robinson 1946, 417, no. 68; Eupolis, D. M. Robinson 1946, 414, no. 60; Leonidas of Tarentum, D. M. Robinson 1946, 422, no. 85; Vitruvius, Rowland and Howe 1999; Crates, Sparkes and Talcott 1951, at figs. 43, 44 (text, Edmonds 1957, 158, no. 14); Aristophanes, Sparkes and Talcott 1951, at figs. 49–51 (text, Edmonds 1957, 674, no. 360); Menander, Allinson 1930; Plato, Lamb 1927; Aristotle, Rhodes 1984.

[2] Hoepfner 1986; Hoepfner 1999c, 201–440, esp. 201–6; and Hoepfner and Schwandner 1994. Cf. critiques of the existence of "type houses" in the reviews by Bommelaer (1988) and Étienne (1991, 39–43); and in Cahill (2002, 82–84).

[3] For isonomia, see above, 4, as well as the literature cited in the previous note.

Hippodamos of Miletos and is the likely result of conceptualization at a more grass-roots level.[4]

Entry: Prothyron

What are you doing by the prothyron, dear? Are you sweeping the entrances to the house or throwing water on the ground like a slave girl?

EURIPIDES frag., *POxy.* 6:35, lines 15–18

As is by now evident, the principle entryway to all the houses examined here, indeed all the houses at Halieis for which this portal has been recovered, is characterized by marked similarities. This is the roofed and recessed prothyron that has been identified with a type best paralleled at Olynthos and found at a number of other sites as well.[5] In addition to the examples from Houses 7, A, C, and E, similar arrangements are preserved in another six incompletely explored houses at Halieis.[6] Table A below gives the dimensions of the best-preserved prothyra from the site. Ranging in width from 1.8 to 3.25 m, all are wide enough to accommodate the passage of a cart into the courtyard or entry hall.[7] Accordingly, a stall or location for tethering a draft animal such as a donkey or mule may also be posited just within the doorway.[8] With a depth of 0.5–1.0 m from street to doorway, each prothyron would have provided a shallow roofed portico for those returning home or for visitors, shielding them from the elements.[9]

Just as the form of the Halieis prothyron is not in question, nor are the doors with which it

Table A. Dimensions of Halieis Prothyra by Room.

Room	Entry Width	Vehicle Entry Width	Pedestrian Entry Width	Depth
7-4	2.50	2.50	not present?	1.00
7-6 (House 7)	3.25	1.87	1.12	1.00
6-7	2.75	2.00(?)	0.75(?)	1.00
6-20 (House E)	1.85	1.85	not present	0.50
6-62 (House C)	2.40	1.50(?)	0.62(?)	1.00
6-77	2.25	2.25	not present	0.75
6-80 (House A)	2.87	1.80	0.75(?)	0.75
6-89 (House B)	3.00	3.00	present?	1.00?

The first dimension, "Entry Width," takes the point of maximum constriction and does not account for the possibility of separate pedestrian and wheeled vehicle entries. The second and third dimensions, "Vehicle Entry Width" and "Pedestrian Entry Width," give the respective widths for examples where it is likely that such entries existed. Where only one entry exists, it is listed twice in the first and second dimensions since all such examples are wide enough to accommodate wheeled traffic. Finally, for the fourth dimension, depth is measured from the edge of the street to the likely position of the door.

[4] For Hippodamos of Miletos, see especially Gehrke 1989; Hoepfner and Schwandner 1994, 301–2; and McCredie 1971. Cahill (1991, esp. 4–104; and 2002, 3–22) persuasively addresses the issues of urban planning and architectural form via the primary sources and archaeological evidence.

[5] Cf. Ault 1999a, 537–39. For prothyra at Olynthos, see Hoepfner and Schwandner 1994, 96–97; D. M. Robinson and J. W. Graham 1938, 154–56. The term "prothyron" occurs often in the primary sources, ranging from Homer (e.g., *Iliad* 24.323) to Vitruvius (6.7.5). See the examples collected in a "Reference List of Some Greek Words Concerned with the House," D. M. Robinson 1946, 468 (where the citation of an occurrence in *Iliad* 1.103, should be *Odyssey* 1.103).

Recessed prothyra entries can also be found in houses at Colophon (Holland 1944), Eretria (Ducrey, Metzger, and Reber 1993; Reber 1998), Morgantina (Tsakirgis 1984), Nea Halos (Reinders 1988), Peiraeus (Hoepfner and Schwandner 1994), Priene (Hoepfner and Schwandner 1994), and Pergamon (Pinkwart and Stammnitz 1984).

[6] From Area 7: Room 7-4; from Area 6: Rooms 6-7, 6-77, and 6-89 (House B); and from the east corner house of the insula exposed in the Ephoreia Field. An example from a now submerged house in the northwest quarter of the city, facing onto Street C, is illustrated in Boyd and Rudolph 1978, pl. 89.a.

[7] House C, since it lies on the north side of the insula, is the only excavated example from Halieis where an entry hall precedes the courtyard. Such an arrangement would probably have impeded a cart's access to the courtyard.

[8] Vitruvius (6.7.1) is perhaps vindicated on this point, but Robinson and Graham only cautiously hazard the identification of stables at Olynthos (1938, 210–11, with n. 108). Cf. Hoepfner and Schwandner (1994, 97), who are rather more sure of themselves, and Jameson's point (1990a, 111, n. 11) about the likely reality of animals being kept in the courtyard. It is also worth recalling here the mule tethered in a room off the courtyard, killed in the collapse of a late Roman house at Kourion, Cyprus, in the earthquake of A.D. 365 (Soren and James 1988, 88).

[9] Cf. the discussion of House 7, Room 7-6, above, 13, with note 10.

was fitted. The site does not provide monolithic stone thresholds with easily legible cuttings. Instead, we find individual stone elements. These would have provided less stability for the door and its framework and would have been more susceptible to post-abandonment robbing. Nevertheless, the doors must have been of the substantial double-winged variety so often depicted in vase painting. Life-sized examples of such doors survive in marble from numerous Macedonian chamber tombs (occasionally with their bronze fittings intact) and are preserved in wood from the houses at Dura-Europos.[10] The identification of double-winged doors at Halieis is based both upon the width of doorways and the presence of cuttings for pivots on which they opened and closed.[11] Although stone pivot holes are preserved in only one instance (in House E), jamb blocks in doorways elsewhere preserve similar cuttings that were designed to receive bronze fittings including pivots.[12]

The existence of two sets of double-winged doors, a wider one for wheeled traffic and a narrower door for pedestrian access, can only be hypothesized. This is, as already noted, owing to the piecemeal preservation of the stone members of the doorway. Such arrangements have been postulated, however, for Houses 7, A, and C, where the widths are great enough to have accommodated two sets of double doors.[13] Wheel ruts are actually preserved on the threshold block of House A, and perhaps also in House 7.[14] The prothyron of House E, being more narrow than the others, was probably fitted with only a single pair of wide, double-winged doors.

The Courtyard: Aule

A court facing the sun.

EUPOLIS frag. 378

The courtyard is another typical element of the Halieis houses. In fact, domestic courtyards with their shaded porches were ubiquitous throughout the Mediterranean world in antiquity, much as today they remain a part of the traditional vocabulary of the region's vernacular architecture (cf. Ault 1999a). The preference for courtyard-centered houses in the Mediterranean results not only from their suitability to the prevailing climate and to the needs of social convention, but also because of their very practical multipurpose nature. Nearly all Classical houses revolved both physically and socially around the axis of the courtyard. For example, because Greek houses had few windows, the court provided the primary source of light and air for the rooms opening off it (cf. Löhr 1990). As a consequence of this, few rooms communicated with one another since they were never more than one room away from the court.[15] This, in turn, made the court the principal artery for circulation within the house (and all the more so since stairs leading to second-story quarters were generally located here).

The importance of the courtyard is reflected by its size, which usually occupies up to twenty-five percent or more of the total house plot.[16] As shown in Table B below, at Halieis the courtyard is almost always the largest single area of the house. Following the dictum expressed by a number of authors, and thus no doubt reflecting common knowledge, the optimum placement of the court was in the southern

[10] Examples from vase painting are plentiful: e.g., Hoepfner and Schwandner 1994, 106, fig. 83; 155, fig. 147. In marble: from the Heroön at Kalydon (now in the Agrinion Museum; illustrated in Hoepfner and Schwandner 1994, 155, fig. 149) and tombs at Dion (Dion Museum), Aghia Paraskevi (Thessaloniki Museum; cf. Sismanides 1986), and Verghina (Andronikos 1984). For wooden double-winged doors from Dura Europas see Rostovtzeff et al. 1936, pl. 29. For doors in general see Ducrey, Metzger, and Reber, 1993, 63–65; Hoepfner and Schwandner 1994, 106, 155–56, 314–15; Reber 1998, 120–25; D. M. Robinson and J. W. Graham 1938, 249–63; Schwandner 1978, 109; Schwandner 1999b; and Tsakirgis 1984, 320–21.

[11] As the following passage illustrates, doors should properly have opened inwards: "Hippias, the Athenian, put up for sale the parts of the upper rooms which projected into the public streets, and the steps and fences in front of the houses, and the doors which opened outwards. The owners of the property therefore bought them, and a large sum was thus collected" ([Aristotle] *Oeconomica* 2.2.4, 1347a, trans. Barnes 1984). For similar regulation of private construction encroaching on public thoroughfares, cf. Aristotle *Athenaion Politeia* 50.2 (cited below, 73); and Heraclides Ponticus 1.10.

[12] For a bronze pivot from Priene (now in the Antikenmuseum, Berlin) see Raeder 1984, 60, no. 318, with 64, pl. 2b. See also the variety of door fittings from Olynthos, including pivots, illustrated in D. M. Robinson and J. W. Graham 1938, pls. 70–72.

[13] Similarly, two sets of double-winged doors may also have been present in the house represented by Room 6-7 (cf. Table A above).

[14] Possible wheel ruts in the coarse conglomerate blocks that make up the outer threshold of House 7, Room 7-6, do not show the same degree of definition as they do on the finer-grained threshold of House A, Room 6-81.

[15] Jameson 1990a, 100. This is an index of the house's high or relatively easy "permeability" (cf. Hillier and Hanson 1985, who relate spatial permeability cross-culturally as an index to forms of social organization).

[16] At Olynthos, courtyards range widely from less than two to thirty-six percent of the total house area (Houses A viii 6 and A v 8, respectively; Cahill 1991, 443–45, and cf. 2002, 78). The average Olynthian courtyard occupied between sixteen and thirty percent of the total house area.

portion of the house (literally, giving the house a southern "aspect"). In this way, "the sun's rays penetrate into the pastadas (porticos) in winter, but in summer the path of the sun is right over our heads and above the roof, so that there is shade" (Xenophon *Memorabilia* 3.8.9).[17]

Table B. Areas of Rooms/Features by House and Room Type.

	House 7	House A	House C	House D	House E
Room type					
Prothyron	4.04	2.25	4.73	–	0.55
Room #	7-6	6-80	6-62	–	no #
Court	54.34	15.75	54.21	59.63	31.98
Room #	7-7	6-81b	6-53[a]	6-26/6-31[b]	6-19/20
Kopron	2.94	2.25	–	5.00	–
(m^3)	(4.20)	(3.04)	–	(5.00)	–
Transverse Hall	10.35	13.02	23.15/19.88	14.31/12.48	–
Room #	7-13[c]	6-81c	6-53W/6-54	6-29/6-32	–
Kitchen	20.43	16.00	–	3.90	n.a.
Room #	7-16/17	6-83	–	6-30	6-16
Bath	6.52	1.49	4.27+	–	1.62
Room #	7-11?	6-84	6-64	–	6-17
Dayroom	19.72	11.70	cf. 6-53W/	20.99	9.00
Room #	7-12	6-87	6-54	6-36	6-24
Andron	21.53	6.25	20.64?	n.a.	–
Room #	7-9	6-82	6-58	no #	–
Anteroom	11.93	–	8.73?	n.a.	–
Room #	7-10	–	6-57	6-33?	–
Total m^2 of house	231	133	208?	204?	203?

All measurements, but "Total m^2 of house," are internal and do not include doorways. Measurements are approximate, having been made from 1:50 actual-state plans. The measurement for the prothyron is based on the maximum width and depth from street. The designation "n.a." indicates dimensions that are either not preserved or too uncertain.

[a] Room 6-53 E alone has an area of ca. 31.06 m^2.
[b] Room 6-31 has an area of ca. 20.63 m^2. Neither dimension accounts for the size of the posited recessed prothyron entry along Street 3.
[c] With a possible extension in its latest phase into Room 7-15, the area of transverse hall is ca. 13.84 m^2.

[17] Cf. Eupolis frag. 378, which opens this section; Xenophon *Oeconomicus* 9.4 ("I pointed out to her that the entire house has its façade facing south, so that it was obviously sunny in winter and shady in summer" [trans. Pomeroy 1994]); [Aristotle] *Oeconomica* 1.6.31–33, 1345A ("With a view to well-being and health, the house ought to be airy in summer and sunny in winter. This would be best secured if it faced south and is not equal in breadth to its depth" [trans. Barnes 1984, with emendations including reading κατάβορρας as "south" rather than "north"]); and Aeschylus *Prometheus Bound* 450–51 (where the hero tells of a time when "Knowledge had they neither of houses built of bricks and turned to face the sun . . . " [trans. Smyth, 1938]). Cf. the discussion in D. M. Robinson and J. W. Graham 1938, 144–46. Hoepfner and Schwandner effectively illustrate the seasonal logic of these arrangements in the context of a house at Priene (1994, 318–19, with fig. 303). Cahill also notes the likely impact of perceived health concerns on the orientation not only of houses but cities as a whole (1991, 32–33, with n. 59, where he cites, in particular, the Hippocratic corpus and similarly directed Chinese cosmology; cf. 2002, 14, with n. 50).

Because the court is frequently the first major household space entered upon leaving the street, it offers an immediate and total transition from the public sphere to the private realm and, as such, provides a maximum of privacy in urban settings characterized by crowded conditions (Rapoport 1969, 81). And while the house itself stood as a private haven from the public world, it too was marked by semipublic and private spheres, particularly when strangers (that is, all nonkin-group males) came to call. This is why the entry to the house was onto the courtyard, the most public of private-sphere spaces. Essential to the privacy it afforded, the courtyard of the Classical Greek house was surrounded by a high screen wall.[18] Since mud brick was the primary building material for the house, this wall would have been capped by terracotta tiles in order to hinder the erosion that would have been a constant threat to the entire structure.

In addition to serving as the primary source of light and air, to providing communication between rooms, and offering privacy from the outside world, the courtyard was also the principle work space for the household. It marked an area where the out-of-doors had effectively been brought within the confines of the home. Here, all manner of domestic activities from the processing and storage of crops to food preparation, cooking, eating, and craft work, including wool working and weaving, and even the washing and drying of clothes could have been carried out.[19]

The surfacings of the courtyard were appropriate, but not exclusive, to the many functions conducted there. All the courtyards at Halieis were paved with the mud and lime admixture typical of most floors at the site. The advantage of tempering flooring earth with crushed lime must relate to its added resiliency, especially where moisture was a problem. Although not generally noted in excavation reports, such a flooring composition was probably often employed at other sites as well.[20] At Olynthos, among the houses excavated through 1934, twenty-five percent of courtyards had earthen surfacings, while fifty percent were cobbled; another three examples were floored with lime plaster, and two bore mosaic pavements (D. M. Robinson and J. W. Graham 1938, 158). The courtyards of the two houses of Insula I near the Silenus Gate at Thasos had flagged surfaces, as did the Vari House.[21] What have been described as "rough stone pavements" occur in the courtyards of three Hellenistic houses at Ilion and are quite similar to two floors at Halieis that could be described as "cobbled."[22] These latter are only roughly so and occur in roofed spaces of House A: the transverse hall, Room 6-81c, and Room 6-88, which contained a well.

Courtyard Installations

Wells, Water Supply, and Drainage

Built installations appropriate for a courtyard setting generally include wells and cisterns.[23] Other than the instance noted above from House A, Room 6-88, and three other possible exceptions, seven of the eleven wells that have been located in the lower town of Halieis are in a courtyard or its periphery.[24] With plaster-lined shafts and footholds, the mouths of these wells are more or less elaborately finished, ranging from the pithos-headed well of House A to the detailed plaster-work on the well head in House 7 and on the well platform in House C. Excavated to depths of between three and five meters, none of the Halieis

[18] Cf. Solon 3.26–29, "In this way public calamity comes to each man's home, and the street-doors no longer can hold it back; over the high courtyard wall (ἕρκος) it leaps, and assuredly it finds even one who flees to the innermost corner of his bedchamber (θάλαμος)" (trans. A. M. Miller 1996, with emendations).

[19] The presence of wells and cisterns in courtyards (discussed below) suggests that this was the area for household washing. See also Crouch's comments, accompanied by a reconstruction drawing, on drying clothes in the courtyard and their potential for humidifying the house (1993, 249, with 247, fig. 17.5). Other evidence for domestic industry is examined below; see especially, 77–81.

[20] For a brief discussion of domestic flooring, see Schwandner 1999a, where lime and earthen admixtures are noted (specifically at Kassope) as well. Elsewhere, the use of these materials has been recorded in houses at Himera (Allegro et al. 1976, 590) and Ilion (Aylward 1999, 165).

[21] For Thasos, see Grandjean 1988, 110–12 (Ilot I: Hs. b); 195–96 (Ilot I: Hs. a); both were paved with slabs of gneiss and marble (ibid., pl. II). For the Vari House, see J. E. Jones et al. 1973, 359; 362, with fig. 2; 366–68 (Area VIII).

[22] At Ilion, these are the courtyards in the house in Area H2, the Gateway House, and the Quarry House (Aylward 1999, 166, 169, 172).

[23] For a preliminary report on the water resources of the Southern Argolid, see Harper 1976. An important recent contribution to the study of ancient water management is provided by Crouch 1993. For general studies of wells, cisterns, and water supply, see Camp 1977 and M. Lang 1968, as well as the brief assessment in Ault 1999a, 541.

[24] The apparent exceptions are all located in incompletely excavated houses (in Area 7: Room 7-20, where the well appears to be out of use in the latest phase of the house; in Area 6: Rooms 6-50 and 6-76), so it is impossible to state for certain the nature of the rooms in which they occur. It should be noted here that none of the structures on the Industrial Terrace appear to have contained wells, nor has a water supply been identified on the acropolis (C. Dengate et al., n.d.).

wells was cleared to its bottom. For comparison, it is worth noting that Athenian household wells of the Classical period averaged twelve meters in depth (Camp 1986, 149).

The presence of one well per household at Halieis implies that each family was responsible for its own water supply. In contrast to sites such as Olynthos and Morgantina, where fountain houses rather than domestic wells have been located, Halieis may not have had a communal water-supply system.[25] This may explain the scarcity of hydriai in the inventories of domestic pottery. Only six hydriai are accounted for from three of the five houses from which artifact assemblages have been studied and presented here (two hydriai are represented from House 7). As their name implies, these were the jars designed specifically for carrying water from the fountain house and could weigh a hefty sixty pounds when full.[26] With the presence of domestic wells, however, they were easily, and no doubt gratefully, replaced by buckets and smaller jugs. Also, in contrast to Olynthos and Morgantina, where cisterns are fairly frequent, only one cistern has been excavated at Halieis (in Room 6-53, the courtyard of House C).[27]

Apparently, although individual households at Halieis were responsible for their own water supply, neighboring structures did share drainage responsibilities. Room 6-46 provides evidence for this. Located in the building southwest of House C, at least one drainage channel continues from Room 6-46 into the courtyard of House C. There is also a separate channel, similar in construction to that of Room 6-13, between Room 6-46 and the house(s) lying to the south (represented by Rooms 6-41 through 6-44, 6-48, and 6-50). The latter conduit may represent a replacement of that between Rooms 6-46 and 6-53, which went out of use with the installation of the cistern in House C (as noted above, 36), and attests to the flexibility of drainage arrangements between neighbors.

The importance of ensuring adequate drainage in houses, where the gentle action of standing puddles or the violence of rainwater gushing from roofs could undermine walls, is suggested in the "astynomic" inscription from Pergamon.[28] Among the concerns it addresses are assessing the responsibility for damage to communal house walls (or party walls) that could occur by remodeling, unchecked water flow, or any of a number of accidents.

Koprones

> So, too, everyone will say that in agriculture there is nothing so good as manure.
>
> XENOPHON *Oeconomicus* 20.10

In addition to wells, another prominent feature found in household courtyards at Halieis is the kopron. While I have reported on the significance of koprones in detail elsewhere (Ault 1999b), some of this bears repetition here. As already noted, in a number of the houses there are stone-lined features sunken into the surface of the courtyards. Originally identified as "cellars," the three examples in Houses 7, A, and D have been fully cleared to their earthen bottoms, which lie one to nearly one and a half meters below the surrounding floor level.[29] Their sizes range from 2.25 m^2 to ca. 5.0 m^2, giving them a capacity of 3.0–5.0 m^3. Upon excavation, all three features brimmed with artifact material (see, for instance, Pl. 55).

From the example in House D, Room 6-26, more than 1500 sherds were recovered. There were, in addition, more than a thousand roof-tile fragments (see above, 46, with Pls. 55–58; Tables 10–12: Locus II; Ault 1999b, 568, appendix 1). Many of the roof tiles may actually have been introduced into the deposit from the roof collapse of House E (above

[25] For the fountain house at Olynthos and the aqueduct that fed it, see D. M. Robinson 1946, 95–114; for Morgantina, see Tsakirgis 1984, 340, with n. 187. For the Classical fountain houses of Athens, see Camp 1977, 106–42.

[26] Keuls 1985, 233. Sparkes and Talcott note that, in Athens, the shape goes out of use late in the 5th century (1970, 201).

[27] For cisterns at Olynthos, see D. M. Robinson and J. W. Graham 1938, 307–9, where, up to 1934, they were found in seven houses. For Morgantina, see Tsakirgis 1984, 334–41. The domestic water supply of Classical Athens is treated by Camp 1977, 142–59, where a proposed 4th-century lowering of the water table has been connected with its over-exploitation and possible drought on the basis of domestic cisterns replacing wells. Camp (1982) also suggests a relationship between the Athenian drought and the abandonment of Halieis.

[28] *SEG* xiii, 521; the translation and commentary I have consulted is in Klaffenbach 1953. The inscription is a 2d-century C.E. copy of an early 2d-century B.C.E. original.

[29] Boyd and Rudolph 1978, 347 (House A), 350 (House D), and 351 (House 7). In addition to these three examples, the replacement of a kopron in House C, Room 6-53, by a cistern has already been discussed (see above, 35). I would also like to identify possible koprones in House B, Room 6-90 (see above, 21), and in a poorly defined house partially excavated by the Greek Archaeological Service in 1983 northwest of Area 6 (in the Ephoreia Field). A seventh example may be posited in the square, stone-lined "well" that lay north of the hostel/hestiatorion in the submerged sanctuary of Apollo (see Jameson 1974, 115, where the feature is marked as "i" on the accompanying plan). Noted to have been filled with pottery, it is also said to have "contained a sticky grayish clay unlike the soil from the rest of the sanctuary area" (J. A. and C. Dengate, personal communication, 1992).

Rooms 6-21 and 6-22), which shared a party wall with the feature.[30] These 1500+ pottery items account for nearly thirty-five percent of the ceramic assemblage recovered from the latest habitation levels of the house. The MNV for the fill is 144.

The artifacts from a second such feature, located in House 7, Room 7-7, are comparable (see above, 19; with Pl. 8 and Tables 1–3: Locus VII; Ault 1999b, 567, appendix 1). More than nine hundred sherds and three hundred roof-tile fragments came from its fill, the former accounting for approximately fifteen percent of the excavated pottery assemblage from the latest use phase of the house. In this case, the roof-tile fragments should be integral to the deposit since they occurred in far fewer numbers than in House D, and no complete or nearly complete tiles were recovered. Nor was the location of the feature, off to the side of the courtyard in a house at the corner of an insula, as likely to become a repository for roof-collapse debris. The MNV of the pottery in the fill can be calculated at 230. No whole vessels were recovered from the deposit, although eleven fine-ware examples survived as profiles. In addition, lamp fragments, loom weights, and metal objects were present, as was a small quantity of bone. In short, the fill recovered from the two negative features in the courtyards of Houses D and 7 represents a cross section of the non-perishable household inventory.[31]

I was not satisfied with interpreting these structures as cellars for several reasons. First, there were other areas of the houses in question better suited to storage (see below, 70–72). Second, and more important, they would have been damp: the example in House 7 is clearly associated with a drainage channel connecting it to the adjacent street (Figs. 6, 7). Nor can the features have served as cisterns. Although they are stone lined in each case, there are no traces of hydraulic plaster, and, as already noted, the floors are earthen. The features did serve as "soak-aways" (Alcock, Cherry, and Davis 1994, 169), but that function is, I believe, ancillary to their main one. Finally, the debris that comprises so much of the fill of these features has all the earmarks of deliberate discard. That is, it is a concentration of unusable material.

In considering the function served by these constructions, a study by E. J. Owens on the organization of urban refuse disposal in Classical Athens is pertinent (Owens 1983; cf. Vatin 1976). Owens points out that although the collection of garbage was supervised by the state (in Athens, at least, by the astynomoi or epistatai kopronon), a large part of the operation may have been in the hands of private entrepreneurs (the koprologoi) who were able to turn a profit first by collecting waste material and then by recycling and reselling it as fertilizer.

Owens notes that the collection facility was called a "kopron" and cites several examples from Attic mortgage horoi.[32] He also identifies archaeological examples from published accounts of three houses at the north foot of the Areopagus in Athens and at the 5th-century "palace" at Larissa-on-the-Hermos.[33] Among the posited Athenian koprones, which tend to be located in the courtyard or in the street just in front of the doorway, a number are stone lined.[34] Hoepfner and Schwandner have also suggested that there were koprones in the houses at Olynthos. Although not defined as negative features, the structures are located below the roofed portion of the courtyards adjacent to prothyra entries.[35]

Elsewhere, on Thasos, a stone-lined construction 1.70 x 1.25 x 0.75 m deep was discovered in one of the houses just within the Silenus Gate, in a courtyard adjacent to the doorway to the street.[36] While its function was not discussed by the excavators, I am inclined to see the sunken features at both Thasos and Halieis as koprones.

[30] This tile fall, which could also be interpreted as a series of deliberate postcollapse dumpings, is discussed in Jerkich 1974.

[31] Unfortunately the artifacts from the third such feature excavated at the site, in House A, Room 6-81, were lost before being processed.

[32] Owens 1983, 48, with notes 42 and 44. These include *IG* II[2] 2496 (in Peiraeus), *IG* II[2] 2742 (Finley 1952, 142, no. 86); and Fine 1951, 8, no. 16.

[33] Owens 1983, 47, with notes 31 and 36. For the Areopagus houses, see note 34 below. For Larissa-on-the-Hermos, see Boehlau and Schefold 1940, 88, fig. 5.

[34] H. A. Thompson 1959, 101–2 (where the features are referred to as "cesspools"), with pls. 17 and 21:a–b. Thompson also points out two similar constructions in houses in the "Industrial District" west of the Areopagus (1959, 102, n. 26; citing R. S. Young 1951, 194–95, with fig. 7, and pl. 66d [House A], and 201 [House B]).

[35] Hoepfner and Schwandner 1994, 97, with fig. 74; see also Carroll-Spillecke 1989, 44. This arrangement is much like the one that existed between Rooms 7-6 and 7-8 of House 7 at Halieis. Olynthian koprones, if they did share the same floor level as the courtyard, must have had provisions for drainage onto the street. A possible alternate form for koprones at Olynthos, with a parallel in House B, Room 6-90, at Halieis, is discussed above (21, note 36).

[36] In Insula II, House a, period 3 (dated mid-4th century; Grandjean 1988, 223, 230, with pls. 74:5 and 77 [phase 4.1]). Apparently, one could have stepped down into the feature from two treads located along its western side. This arrangement compares well with what may be steps in the west corner of the sunken feature in House D at Halieis.

After the initial identification of koprones at Halieis, examples have also been tentatively recognized at Stymphalos and Gravina di Puglia.[37]

The kopron should be viewed not as a lowly cess- or garbage pit. Instead, it contributed to the domestic economy by providing a receptacle for the collection of household refuse, which was subsequently composted for use as fertilizer. Indeed, these installations ultimately served to enhance agricultural productivity in the chora of Halieis. Kopros, then, like "manure," "fumier," and "κοπρία" did not refer strictly to animal or human waste as it has generally been defined.[38] Particularly in the context of the kopron, kopros should include all debris deposited into it: animal and vegetal matter such as kitchen refuse and table scraps, and waste materials from domestic industrial activity, as well as human and animal excrement. It is also likely that other items to be discarded—broken pots, for example—went into the kopron.[39] When domestic kopros was added to naturally accumulating debris in gardens and fields—fallow crops (also known as "green manure"), brush, weeds, prunings, and the dung of grazing animals—a plentiful and powerful source of fertilizer was made available.[40]

In an agriculturally based polis such as Halieis, one of hundreds occupying the landscapes of the Greek world, the incentive to maintain a facility for collecting household waste is as obvious as are the advantages of kopros, especially considering the limited area of arable land available to the Haliots (see below, 80). In the vocabulary of the methodologies and interpretations current in landscape archaeology, the concentrations of artifact material recovered from the Halieis koprones provide an urban correlate to and generating mechanism for the off-site pottery scatters documented by numerous regional survey projects in the Mediterranean that are interpreted as the result, at least in part, of manuring practices.[41]

It is through the courtyard that the Greek house and its occupants most directly interacted with the external physical environment. Internally, while courtyard houses may compartmentalize domains hierarchically to some degree, they also exhibit the segmentation of space in an egalitarian fashion. In what follows we continue to see that the artifact evidence from Halieis works in tandem with the architectural to clarify the function of various parts of the house.

Portico: Transverse Hall

> With such as these one should deck a pastas, an andron, a court, or a bridal chamber. But let the bloody spoils of horse-pursuing Ares adorn his temple.
>
> LEONIDAS OF TARENTUM (*Anthologia Graeca* 9.322.7–10)

The eminent scholar of Greek domestic architecture, J. W. Graham, once wrote, "The court is

[37] The possible kopron at Stymphalos, which remains unexcavated owing to the high water table at the site, is briefly discussed in H. Williams 1996, 95–96, and illustrated in plan in H. Williams et al. 1997, 25, fig. 1. For the sterculinum at Gravina di Puglia, see Small et al. 1994.

[38] Cf. the fragment of Eubulus *Cercopes:* "Next I went to Thebes, where they dine the whole night through, and all the day, and where every man has a kopron right at the door; for a full mortal there is no comfort greater than that; when a man has to go a long way to relieve himself, gasping loudly and biting his lips, he makes a spectacle altogether ludicrous" (Athenaeus 10.417, trans. Gulick 1930). This passage appears to have influenced the view espoused by Robinson, who, while defining "kopron" as "a place for dung," seems to prefer "privy," or "latrine" in the domestic context (D. M. Robinson 1946, 462). It seems to me that the comic effect intended by Eubulus has not been fully understood here. Others, especially Amouretti (1986, 62) and Hodkinson (1988, 49), realize that defining kopros as merely human or animal waste is too narrow. And while Alcock, Cherry, and Davis acknowledge that kopros "had a wide semantic field" (1994, 147), they continue to emphasize its fecal component above all others. Although this is accurate for the farm where animals were kept and manure collected, kopros generated by urban households would have had differing constituent elements.

[39] Cf. Epictetus 2.4.4: "What confidence am I to place in you? If you were a vessel so cracked that it was impossible to use you for anything, you would be cast forth upon the kopros heap (κοπρίας) and even from there no one would pick you up; but if, although a man, you cannot fill a man's place, what are we going to do with you?" (trans. Oldfather 1926). This passage is cited in Alcock, Cherry, and Davis 1994, 150. Their extensive consideration of the literary, ethnographic, and archaeological evidence for manuring practices provides a welcome wealth of data with which to pursue the topic further.

[40] White gives the best overview of the ancient sources on manuring supplemented by modern agronomic commentary (1970, 125–45). Although the earliest surviving agricultural treatises from the classical world are Hellenistic and Roman in date, they probably reflect a continuity of knowledge as well as practices from earlier times. Especially useful in this regard are discussions by Cato (*de Agri Cultura* 5.8; 29.1; 36.1; 37.2; 50.1), Columella (2.14–15), Theophrastus (*de Causis Plantarum* 3.9 and *Historia Plantarum* 8.6.3), and Varro (*Res Rusticae* 1.38). Columella (1.6.21; 2.14.6–8) and Varro (*Res Rusticae* 1.13.4) also give advice on the construction and maintenance of the sterculinum. See also Alcock, Cherry, and Davis 1994; Amouretti 1986, 62–63; Burford 1993, esp. 106, 122–24; and Hodkinson 1988, 49–50.

[41] This proposition has proved somewhat controversial because of the current debate about the meaning of off-site sherd scatters, also referred to as "halos." See Wilkinson 1982 and Bintliff and Snodgrass 1988 for the initial discussions; see especially Alcock, Cherry, and Davis 1994 for a critique of the "manuring hypothesis." The perimeters of the problem are surveyed in Ault 1999b, esp. 558–59.

such a ubiquitous feature of the Mediterranean house that it can not profitably be used as a criterion of distinction in discussing house types."[42] What can offer this criterion, Graham and others have argued, by virtue of its distinctness, is the type of exedral space that opens off the courtyard and provides a transitional element to one or more principle living rooms in the house. Termed the "prostas" or the "pastas," depending on its dimensions and the arrangement of rooms to which it gives access, the name of this feature is ultimately indebted to a Vitruvian assertion in the course of his comments about Greek houses.[43] As Barbara Tsakirgis has pointed out, however, this is merely an observation made by Vitruvius; he does not distinguish between the two.[44] Yet the terms have gained currency and assumed their respective places in various evolutionary trajectories and typological schemata for Greek houses.[45]

Some would place the prostas in a lineage with the Homeric tradition and the Bronze Age megaron (e.g., Drerup 1967; Hoepfner and Schwandner 1994, 323; Hoepfner 1999d, 138). Hoepfner and Schwandner (1994, 323) go on to connect prostas houses with their hypothesis of cities planned according to Hippodamian-Pythagorean tenets. In this scheme, such houses are well suited to the characteristic compact insula divided into six or more rectangular houses (cf. Peiraeus and Priene). Pastas-style houses have typically been associated with sites on the Greek mainland, their presence at Olynthos marking the initial identification of the type (see note 45). As regards typology, however, Tsakirgis (1989) has rejected the prostas as being distinct from the pastas and in so doing rejects the prostas as a particularly Ionian type. She opts instead for the "universality" of three-room suites that she terms the "prostas with dependent oikoi."[46] The pastas, meanwhile, has been seen as a formative element for the development of Hellenistic peristyle houses.[47] Graham himself (1966) took up and rejected the notion that peristyles appended to Roman houses (as at Pompeii) led to the transformation and demise of the Etruscan and Republican atrium house.

Although I do not advocate doing away with established terminology, looking at the houses of Halieis, we can see that the designation of prostas or pastas is not so easily applied. Since there are clearly elements similar to both the prostas and pastas present, however, I use the mediating term "transverse hall" to describe the room located on the north side of the courtyard that fronts a suite of two or more rooms.[48] The Halieis room closest to a true pastas is located in House A, Room 6-81c, and there the house is atypical, being more like the Row A houses at Olynthos.[49] Since these latter examples grew up along the western edge of the North Hill, they provide, as already noted, an interesting analog for the situation at Halieis where this intramural zone, too, may initially have been unencumbered by domestic structures. Room 7-13 in House 7 could also be described as pastaslike, but its length

[42] J. W. Graham 1966, 4. Cf. Nevett 1999, 21–26, with figs. 1–4, for the "normative" model of Greek house typology.

[43] "This peristyle has porticoes on three sides; on the side facing south it has two piers standing a considerable distance apart, across which beams are carried. Whatever the distance between these piers, that expanse minus one-third goes to the depth of the portico. This place is named 'prostas' by some, and 'pastas' by others" (Vitruvius 6.7.1, trans. Rowland and Howe 1999).

[44] Tsakirgis 1989. Much the same point is made by F. Lang, who provides a good overall discussion, especially regarding evolutionary typology and early examples (1996, 98–101).

[45] As defined by Graham (D. M. Robinson and J. W. Graham 1938, 143–51), the canonical pastas is a porch running longitudinally across between two-thirds and the entire length of the house. The prostas is a shorter, but frequently deeper, anteroom or porch appended to the principle living room of the house.

In a recent survey of the Hellenistic and Roman domestic architecture of Pergamon, Wulf-Rheidt (1998, esp. 158–60) strives to apply the terminology of prostas and pastas to the porches she identifies there. Especially noteworthy in light of the evidence from Halieis is the co-occurrence of both prostas and pastas porches at Pergamon alongside and in addition to peristyle courtyards. It is also significant that these porticoes continue as part of the vocabulary of domestic architecture well into the Roman period.

[46] But in her doctoral dissertation on the houses of Morgantina, she argues in favor of the influence of the pastas house on domestic architecture at that site (Tsakirgis 1984, esp. 460–65). In her most recent contribution to the problem, Tsakirgis retreats to this original position, identifying pastas houses in Sicily and stating that "The prostas with its exedral porch and inner main room does not exist in Sicily, but the three-room suite is its equivalent" (Tsakirgis 1994). Cordsen (1995) has probably influenced this change in stance.

[47] Krause 1977. In Houses B (Room 6-91) and C (Room 6-53) at Halieis colonnaded porches are present, which may represent steps in the direction of peristylar courtyards. Cf. the "pastas - peristyle" houses identified at Olynthos (D. M. Robinson and J. W. Graham 1938, 143–44), where full peristyles were realized in seven cases (Cahill 1991, 208, with n. 18).

[48] For a listing of transverse halls by house, along with their relevant dimensions, see Table B above.

[49] The Row A houses at Olynthos occupy plots on average ca. 350 m^2, compared to the 294 m^2 house plots of the North Hill insulae. House A at Halieis is only 133 m^2, 70 to 98 m^2 less than the other four most completely recovered houses treated in this study.

is abbreviated.[50] Elsewhere, in Houses C and D, Rooms 6-54 and 6-29 take the positions of prostas-type porches but are largely walled up where they would otherwise be open to the court. In addition, Room 6-54 was given a decorative treatment of red and white painted plaster and Room 6-29 was converted to a press room. Presumably, extensive remodeling in House E has left only vestiges of a transverse hall in Room 6-23 (if one ever existed here in the first place), while a similar hall, more engulfed than altered, survives as Room 6-32 in the northeastern half of House D.

In this extended discussion of the transverse hall and the admixture of pastas / prostas elements at the site I do not mean to suggest that the differing forms of the halls imply different populations at Halieis. (Newcomers might use the architectural vocabulary of their original homes, a time-honored theory that ultimately lies behind the pastas / prostas dichotomy.) Instead I want to highlight the blurred boundaries of typology. What provides, in fact, the unifying element of the transverse hall at Halieis and other sites, where pastas or prostas porches have been identified, is their function. If the prothyron giving way onto the courtyard marks the threshold between the public world and the private, the transverse hall marks an equally important transition. In this case, it mediates between the semipublic space of the courtyard and the fully private inner sanctum (which I term the "dayroom"; see below). It stands in relation to the rooms that lie beyond it as the anteroom does to the andron, only more so, in that it is perhaps the most versatile space in the house. Sheltered but open owing to its proximity to the court, it provided the best lit and ventilated workplace in the house next to the courtyard itself. That a multiplicity of activities took place in the transverse hall is apparent from evidence at Colophon and Priene, where hearths were typically located in the prostas, and at Olynthos and Halieis, where diverse and numerous artifact assemblages were often recovered.[51]

Dayroom and Adjacent Chambers Reached from the Transverse Hall

> Inside these places [the "prostas" or "pastas"] large oeci are put up, in which the lady of the house sits with her woolworkers. To the right and left of the prostas cubicula are located, of which one is called the thalamos and the other the amphithalamos.
>
> VITRUVIUS *De architectura* 6.7.2

Typically, from the north side and the ends of the transverse hall there opens a room or series of rooms among which can be identified some of the principle living chambers in the house, for example, Room 7-12 in House 7.[52] Cahill refers to this area in the Olynthos houses as comprising the "North" and "Pastas Rooms" and notes that the kitchen or andron may be located here (Cahill 1991, 206–7; and 2002, 79). At Colophon, Olynthos, Priene, and other sites, the dominant room of this group has been referred to as the "oecus" or "oikos."[53] While acknowledging the primacy of these designations, in order to employ more neutral language (as with my usage of "transverse hall"), I have chosen to refer to the main room here as the "dayroom." In any case, along with the other room types discussed, we are able to see a recurring spatial pattern (supported by artifact distributions as well as in plan) around which the house was being conceptually and physically organized.[54]

As noted above, in attempting to articulate a dynamic relationship for the syntax of domestic

[50] It has already been noted that there is some evidence for extending the length of Room 7-13 1.5 m to the northeast in its latest use phases (see above, 18). Olynthian pastades typically have their full possible lengths truncated by the addition of rooms at one or both ends.

[51] For Priene and Colophon, see above, 31, note 66. For Olynthos, see Cahill's study of the domestic assemblages (1991, 268–322; 2002, 74–147). There most of the pastades showed a marked concentration of activities ranging from cult practice to food preparation, weaving, washing, and storage.

[52] Elsewhere at Halieis this position is occupied by Room 6-87 in House A; the largely unexcavated rooms northeast of Room 6-91 in House B; Rooms 6-55 and 6-56 in House C; and Rooms 6-27 and 6-28, and 6-35 and 6-36 in House D. See Table B above for areal dimensions. While a corresponding suite is not obvious from the plan of House E, judging from its artifacts, Room 6-24 appears to have served the essential function.

[53] Jameson asserts that, "there is no clear ancient support for the use of the word" (1990a, 98, n. 5). A selection of citations from the primary sources in Greek (D. M. Robinson 1946, 465, sv οἶκος) and Vitruvius's employment of the term (6.7.2) suggest otherwise. While D. M. Robinson and J. W. Graham use the term only once, seeking to qualify its distinction from the andron, to which it had been applied by excavators at Delos (D. M. Robinson and J. W. Graham 1938, 172–73), and support its pedigree, Mylonas applies the designation "oecus unit" (D. M. Robinson 1946, 369–97) to what Graham had referred to as the kitchen complex (D. M. Robinson and J. W. Graham 1938, 185–204; J. W. Graham 1954).

[54] Tsakirgis (1989) takes Vitruvius at his word here and makes much of the "oeci magni" lying beyond the portico. In so doing she follows Krause (1977) who sees here an elemental core of, ideally, three rooms. A similar scheme has been identified at Eretria (e.g., Reber 1998, 196–97) and Pergamon (e.g., Wulf-Rheidt 1998) and is recognizable elsewhere.

architecture, we might say that the transverse hall is to the rooms that lie beyond it what the anteroom is to the andron. The dayroom, then, is equivalent to the andron on this level. It can be distinguished on relative terms within a given house by its placement, its size, and its appointments. Artifact assemblages recovered from these rooms at Halieis also help to confirm their identification. They are typically characterized by high concentrations of debris associated with the consumption of food and drink, in comparison to a lower MNV for types connected with food preparation and storage. The finds also show diversity in other classes of pottery as well as metal artifacts.

Kitchen and Bath: Ipnos and Balaneion

"The kitchen ware
Will come when bidden. Table stand by
me.
Casserole, make ready. Flour-bag, knead
the bread.
Pour, ladle. Where's the cup? Come clean.
Rise, barley cake. Now, cooking pot,
disgorge the beet.
Here, fish." "But my other side's not
cooked."
"Well, over you go, and salt and oil
yourself."

CRATES *Wild Animals*

"But a moment ago I left her
Soaping herself in the bath."

ARISTOPHANES *Lemnian Women*

Brian Sparkes once stated that "the search for the presence of [ancient Greek] kitchens from architectural features is unlikely to prove very fruitful"[55]—this, in spite of the fact that excavations at Olynthos had already documented a tripartite kitchen-complex comprising a main room, which occasionally bore traces of a central hearth, a so-called "flue," and a bathroom.[56] One of the most striking illustrations of the communality of elements of layout and design, or the koine, that I recognize for Classical domestic architecture appears in the recurrence or translation of kitchen complexes similar to those at Olynthos at Halieis. Lacking the distinctive Olynthian flue and the rarely occurring Olynthian hearth, couplings of kitchen and bath occur in three of the houses excavated at Halieis (Houses A, B, and E). Since built hearths at Halieis are as rare as they are at Olynthos (found only in Houses 7 and D), portable charcoal and brush-fueled braziers probably sufficed for most cooking. The general absence of hearths at Halieis is discussed in the context of domestic cult practice (below, 76).

And although no examples of bathtubs are attested at Halieis, the louterion base preserved in the bath of House E (Room 6-17; see above, 50, with Pl. 68) is evidence for how cleansing was accomplished. At Eretria, kitchen-bath complexes similar to those at Halieis and Olynthos have been excavated and are now published.[57] Further afield, but with marked similarities to domestic architecture at Eretria, some of the houses of Morgantina also employ this logical pairing of rooms.[58]

While there is no communication between the two, and thus their proximity to one another may be merely fortuitous, two examples of variant pairings at Halieis group together the bathroom

[55] Sparkes 1962, 132, is still the fundamental discussion of the Greek kitchen. Cf. also Sparkes 1965 and 1981. These presentations do, admittedly, illustrate the essentially movable nature of the various tasks of food preparation and cooking, something I do not intend to deny. For kitchens and cooking at Olynthos, as well as a good overview of the subject generally, see Cahill 1991, 323–36, and 2002, 80–81, 153–69.

[56] In his study of the Olynthian kitchen, it is these three spaces that Mylonas lumped together as part of the "oecus unit" (see note 53 above). Of the thirty kitchens identified at Olynthos through the excavations of 1934, seven had hearths (D. M. Robinson and J. W. Graham 1938, foldout table between 198 and 199). Hoepfner and Schwandner count only six hearths among twenty-nine "unequivocal" kitchens (1994, 100). See, however, Cahill's count of forty excavated flues (1991, 323; cf. 2002, 154), which should reflect the total number of kitchens identified at the site, that is, including those excavated in the final field season of 1938. Up through the excavations of 1934, Robinson and Graham list twenty-three bathrooms, noting that one-third of the houses at Olynthos possessed them (1938, 199, 204 [table]). Among these, twelve formed part of a kitchen complex, twelve contained traces of bathtubs in situ, while five showed gaps in their plaster pavement, indicating the likely removal of a tub (D. M. Robinson and J. W. Graham 1938, 204).

[57] House IA, Phase 3: Rooms l and m (Reber 1998, 47–48) preserved traces of a bathtub as well a specially constructed channel for heating the tub. House IB, Phase 3: Rooms u, A–C (Reber 1998, 55–57) have a hearth, bathtub, and latrine. House II, Phases 1 and 2: Rooms a and a1 (Reber 1998: 100–102) include a hearth, traces of a bathtub, and a latrine. House IV, Phase 2: Rooms 5, 5a, and b (Reber 1998, 74–76) include a hearth and traces of a bathtub. The House with the Mosaics: Rooms 14 and 16 (Ducrey, Metzger, and Reber 1993, 48) similarly show a pairing of bath and kitchen. For the kitchen complexes of Eretria generally, see Reber 1998, 137–39.

[58] Tsakirgis 1984, 383–86 (in the House of the Doric Capital, Room 12; and the House of the Arched Cistern, Room 3).

and andron.[59] Other probable baths at Halieis include an example in a house along Street 5 (in the Ephoreia Field) and a room from the house in the northwest quarter of the city (along Street d in Area 4).[60]

Just as one's ablutions would have been tended to modestly, probably with water held in basins, pots, or buckets, so too urination and defecation probably employed an ad hoc arrangement of receptacles (which, if not utilizing the household kopron directly, would have been regularly emptied into it).[61] There is no evidence for either built latrines or specialized pottery accoutrements from Halieis.[62]

Andron and Anteroom

> In contrast to the general notion that the Greek house emphasizes the private realm over and above the political or public one, the polis itself is manifest in the domestic andron.
>
> FELIX PREISSHOFEN

The institution of the symposium as both a religious and social phenomenon has a long history.[63] Archaic precedents for domestic andrones are found in ritual dining halls at a number of sites.[64] Already in the 7th century we can, with varying degrees of confidence, begin identifying them in aristocratic private houses.[65] It is only in the 5th century, however, that the andron becomes widespread, as distinctive forms of Classical houses become increasingly regularized throughout the Greek world.[66]

The andron has, in fact, been explicitly connected with the democratic institutions that underpinned the Classical city. As an essential part of the citizen household, it served to extend the political sphere into the domestic realm by providing a congenial setting for small groups of citizen males to gather in discussion of matters of state and business outside the public assembly, law court, or agora (Jameson 1990b, 190–91). That Hoepfner and Schwandner have detected in the andrones of Olynthos a structural module or building block for laying out the house as a whole is a vivid illustration of its importance.[67] For our purposes it is significant to stress the omnipresence of the andron, for while it may vary in size and appointments, it is a recurrent feature that can be identified in as many as eleven of the houses explored at Halieis.[68]

[59] House 7: Rooms 7-9, 7-10, and 7-11; House C: Rooms 6-57, 6-58, and 6-64. A similar arrangement may also be detected in House D, where Room 6-33 can be identified as a possible anteroom to an unexcavated andron in the east corner of the house, and the northeast wall of Room 6-32 (the transverse hall north of Room 6-33) shows elements of deliberate waterproofing. It should be noted that there are several examples of Olynthian pastades containing a louterion for washing (Cahill 1991: 268–322; 2002, 74–147).

[60] Owing to the incomplete excavation of both of these houses, it is not possible to specify whether or not they were conceived as part of a unit with adjacent rooms. For the architecture in Area 4 (also known as Area M), see Jameson 1969, 328, with pl. 85a; and J. H. Young 1963, 3–5 (including a plan of the area showing the probable bath).

[61] For use of the kopron as a latrine, see the passage from Eubulus *Cercopes*, cited above in note 38.

[62] Outside of the possible examples from Olynthos, mentioned below, built toilets first appear in the classical Mediterranean in Hellenistic houses at Delos, Eretria, Morgantina, and Priene. For discussions, see especially Neudecker 1994, 14–16; Reber 1998, 139–40; and Vatin 1976 (who denies their existence in the Classical period altogether). Cf. the oft-cited ceramic "toilet seat" from Olynthos (D. M. Robinson and J. W. Graham 1938, 205, pl. 55.1–1a), which provides, to my knowledge, the only example of its type. Crouch includes it in an improbable reconstruction of an "integrated" domestic bath at Olynthos (1993, 300, fig. 20.11A). There are also three spouted vessels from the site, identified as urinals because one survived in situ in House A vii 9, piercing the wall of room c to drain into the street (D. M. Robinson and J. W. Graham 1938, 205–6, pls. 54.1, 55.2–2a). Children used "potty / highchairs," which are depicted both in painted pottery (Klein 1932, frontispiece, A [in Brussels]; D. B. Thompson 1971, 22, fig. 39 [in the British Museum]) and attested from archaeological examples (D. B. Thompson 1971, 22, fig. 40 [from the Athenian Agora]). For men, specialized jugs for urination are mentioned in literature (the amis; e.g., Aristophanes *Wasps* 935, and *Thesmophoriazusae* 633) and have also been recognized in the pottery repertoire (Sparkes and Talcott 1970, 231, pl. 96, nos. 2014–15). Women (hetairai) urinating in basins are known from vase painting, e.g., on the tondo of a kylix in Berlin (Inv. 3757; *CVA* Berlin 2 [Germany 21], pl. 74.2 [Germany pl. 3757]). The basin, following Aristophanes *Thesmophoriazusae* 633, could be referred to as a "skaphion."

[63] There is much recent literature on the subject. See especially Murray 1990 and Slater 1991 for a wide range of essays on matters pertaining to symposia; and Schmitt-Pantel 1990, 1992 for institutionalized and ritual public dining as a democratic modification of aristocratic precursors.

[64] See Bergquist 1990 for a brief history of "sympotic space."

[65] See Hoepfner 1999d on the emergence of "andron culture"; Kraus 1977, 165–69, for a listing of possible early andrones; and F. Lang 1996, 116–17, on benched rooms in Archaic houses. It should be kept in mind that sympotic space need not have been architecturally fixed.

[66] On andrones in general, see Hoepfner and Schwandner 1994, 327–28; and D. M. Robinson and J. W. Graham 1938, 171–85.

[67] Hoepfner and Schwandner 1994, 86–88, figs. 65, 66. This is an example of the controversial interpretations offered by Hoepfner and Schwandner, to which many take exception (see above 3–4, note 20, and 58, note 3).

[68] The following comprises a north to south listing of all the possible Halieis andrones (house and room numbers are provided where they have been assigned): Area 5 (see note 69 below); Area T (see above, 21, note 35, and below, note 69); House B; House A: Room 6-82(?); Room 6-79(?); Room 6-71(?); House C: Room 6-58; House D: Room 6-15; House 7: Room 7-9; and Room 7-2(?).

The most elaborate andrones at Halieis are in House 7 and in partially explored structures in Areas T and 5.[69] Of the andrones identified at the site, only these three possessed the characteristic low plaster platform that ran around the perimeter of the room and upon which were placed banqueting couches ("klinai"). As previously noted, the Area T andron is also the largest example from Halieis, measuring 6.8 m across by 5.3 m deep (Pl. 72). Its platform, unlike the continuous course of that in House 7, shows a deliberate interruption at the doorway. The sunken receptacle in Room 7-9 may have served some ritual function or it may have been used for cleaning. An even more pragmatic provision for cleaning the andron was made in the Area T example. Here, a drainage channel, laid into the northwest angle of the platform, found its outlet in the corner of the room. As in House 7, the walls of this andron were painted red above a white dado course.[70] With the possible exception of the example in House A (Room 6-82, which could have accommodated only three couches), all the andrones at Halieis had seven klinai. Despite its generous size, the Area T andron, too, would have held only seven klinai. This was because a built construction took up a position on the rear (southeast) wall of the room, located between two couches. Initially proposed as the remains of an altar, Jameson later offered the identification of a kylikeion or sideboard.[71] Traces of projections in the form of animal feet flanked the semicircular base of the feature, which, on the basis of fragments recovered from the area, may have been stuccoed yellow (Pl. 73).

At least two more seven-kline andrones have been partially excavated at the site, in Houses B and C (Room 6-58). In both cases they were entered through antechambers and their floors were simply paved. I have also posited that a seven-kline andron occupied the unexcavated east corner of House D. There are four other possible examples in Rooms 6-79, 6-71, 6-15, and 7-2. Equally tenuous, perhaps, is my identification of a three-kline andron in the eastern corner of House A (Room 6-82).

Although much has been made of the exclusivity of the andron, none of the Halieis examples preserve any evidence of having been shut off by doors. That is, there are no traces of bolt or pivot holes in the surviving, and in some instances, carefully finished thresholds. Nor, seemingly, are internal doors present elsewhere in the houses. Hoepfner and Schwandner note that among Olynthian andrones only the anteroom tends to show traces of a door, while the entrance to the andron itself was probably screened only by a curtain (Hoepfner and Schwandner 1994, 98; cf. D. M. Robinson and J. W. Graham 1938, 251). Accordingly, curtain rings may well be represented among the many generic iron and bronze rings recovered from both sites (Richter 1966, 119).

Storage: Tamieion/Pitheon

And I myself, too, helping, giving this and
  that,
Into the store-room, as it chanced, had
  gone, from whence
I did not come directly, busy laying out
More food than common and inspecting
  many things
Within. Just then while I was there, a
  woman came,
Descending from an upper story, from
  above,
Into the store-room's antechamber.

MENANDER *Samia* 228–34 (13–19)

The terms "tamieion" and "pitheon" occur in the primary sources with reference to household storage areas (D. M. Robinson 1946, 470 [ταμεῖον] and 468 [πιθεών or πιθών]). But because of the frequent incongruity between the written and archaeological record, such facilities are notoriously difficult to identify. To be sure, we will continue to lack material evidence for the quantities of clothing, bedding, and many other perishable items that would have been stored in the household.[72] Food stuffs and agricultural

[69] In House 7, Rooms 7-9 and 7-10 comprise the andron and its anteroom, respectively; see above, 15. The andron in Area T was excavated in 1962 off the northwestern side of what became Area 6 in the 1970s campaigns (Figs. 2, 3). See Jameson 1969, 329, pl. 85b, and J. H. Young 1963, 5–6, with illustration. Lacking any definite continuation of the structure to which it belongs, the identification of this latter example as a domestic andron is not absolutely certain. Test excavations in 1972 explored the third such platformed andron in Area 5, along the shore to the west of Area 6 (Boyd and Rudolph 1978, 345).

[70] Note the erratum, "The walls were plastered, and painted white over a red dado" (J. H. Young 1963, 5).

[71] J. H. Young 1963, 5; cf. Jameson 1969, 329. Archaeological parallels from other andrones are unknown. For kylikeia, see Richter 1966, 81–84.

[72] Although admittedly representing aristocratic householdings, cf. the range of material assembled from domestic inventories offered for sale in the Attic Stelai (Pritchett 1953, 1956; Amyx 1958) and Ischomachus's discussion of storage in his oikos (Xenophon *Oeconomicus*, esp. 8.18–9.10). I suspect that second-story rooms were ideal for many of these sorts of items.

produce should be another matter, however, since ceramic containers can indicate where at least some of the household stores were located.

This is true to a certain extent at Halieis, where MNV counts for storage vessels reveal definite patterns. But to calculate from this evidence overall storage capacities of houses and then to discern subsistence or larger economic strategies pursued by households on the basis of potential food reserves is difficult. From the comparative gross MNV counts by vessel shape per house (Table 19), it is clear that certain storage vessels are well represented. They range from the sixteen amphoras from the latest floor levels of House A to sixty-five in House C. Pithoi, too, make a showing, but in fewer numbers. This is to be expected given their generally larger size and greater longevity than amphoras (owing to the fact that they tended to be more stationary and less portable since they were typically, at least in part, sunk into the surrounding floor). They number from only two in House 7 to fourteen in House E. It should also be kept in mind that the high cost of pithoi, if not making their acquisition prohibitive, encouraged their repair rather than replacement. In addition, if sea transport were an option, as would have been likely for departing Haliots, these expensive vessels would not have been left behind.[73] Pithos lids (up to thirteen in House D) and storage bins (five apiece from Houses 7 and D) also suggest how great a concern storage was for the household. As noted above (63), the low numbers of hydriai represented probably relate to the presence of wells in each house.

The spatial distribution of storage vessels within individual houses shows the sort of variability we should probably expect. In House 7 (not including the fill of negative features), 76 percent of all storage vessels, or 37 MNV, were recovered in the courtyard (Table 2: Loci III–IV [= Rooms 7-7/8]). In House A, as already noted, a significant concentration of the MNV for storage, represented primarily by amphoras, was recovered between Rooms 6-81c and 6-88 (Table 5: Loci VI and XVI).[74] House C appears to have had its storage facilities spread over several areas (Table 8). Along with a small number of amphoras, seven of the 12 MNV for pithoi came from Rooms 6-59 (Locus VII, 2 MNV), 6-60 (Locus VI, 2 MNV), and 6-61 (Locus V, 3 MNV).[75] Plain-ware storage containers, primarily amphoras, clustered in the eastern half of Room 6-53 (Loci XII and XIII, 21 MNV) and in Room 6-54 (Locus IX, 10 MNV).[76] Some patterning also emerges that locates a storage area of House D in Rooms 6-28/29 (Table 11). The MNV of 11 amphoras recovered here (Loci V–VII and VIII) could well relate to containing oil from the press installation in Room 6-29. This substantial number is rivaled only by another 10 MNV for cooking vessels. Finally, from the core of House E, the courtyard Room 6-19 yielded a MNV of 31 for storage containers (Table 16: Locus VI). This accounts for nearly 50 percent of the storage vessels recovered from the house, excepting the independent units represented by the east shops and west rooms.

For an interesting comparison, we can turn to the houses at Olynthos. Here, Cahill notes that there is relatively little evidence for large-scale domestic storage on the North Hill, particularly in contrast to the situation on the plain to the east below, in the so-called "Villa District," where storage facilities were clearly a greater concern to householders (Cahill 1991, 336–41, 376–77; and 2002, 233–35, 281–88). Cahill observes that traces of non-agriculturally oriented domestic industry (ranging from weaving to coroplasty) are prom-

[73] Five irreparably shattered pithoi from room j in the Villa of Good Fortune at Olynthos had prices inscribed on their rims, which give a total cost of between 210 and 215 drachmas (D. M. Robinson and J. W. Graham 1938, 214–16), and even cracked pithoi were sold according to the Attic Stelai (Amyx 1958, 168). What are probably small pithos pits are attested at Halieis, where only a few examples of the vessels not associated with press installations survived in situ (e.g., in House E, under the stairway in Room 6-20; and in Rooms 6-34 and 6-78), most notably in House D, Rooms 6-35a and 6-36. That they are not recorded from Olynthos probably relates to the limited control over stratigraphic excavation at the site. At more recent, and careful, excavations, especially those at prehistoric and early Iron Age sites, they are a regular feature (e.g., at Assiros: G. Jones et al., 1986; and the Heroön at Lefkandi: Popham, Calligas, and Sackett 1993, esp. 25–26). Similar pits have also been identified in the Hellenistic houses at Ilion (e.g., Aylward 1999, 165–66).

[74] There is a chance that the pithos counts from House A are overrepresented. From a total of fourteen MNV, seven were recovered from Rooms 6-86 (Locus XV) and 6-88 (Locus XVI). Since pithos sherds reinforced the well opening in Room 6-88 (they were found to be badly damaged at the time of excavation), and considering the flimsiness of the wall that separated Locus XV from XVI at this point, I would treat the MNV with caution.

[75] Three of the remaining five MNV for pithoi come from the cistern fill (Locus XIV).

[76] The dump of debris filling Room 6-56 (Locus IV) obviates its inclusion here. Likewise, material from the western half of Room 6-53 (Locus XI, 7 MNV), while certainly representative of some storage, is negligible by comparison.

inent on the North Hill and noticeably absent in the Villa District. He proposes that the inhabitants of the North Hill followed an attested economic strategy whereby a household would sell all of its annual produce in one transaction or series of transactions and then rely on the market to supply the household.[77]

Gallant, on the other hand, finds no lack of agricultural storage space on the North Hill. He finds evidence to suggest that producing households tried to store a ten- to sixteen-month supply of foodstuffs and calculates that the four sunken pithoi found in House A xi 10 could have contained an eleven- to thirteen-month supply of grain.[78] Unfortunately, his use of the evidence from Olynthos is rather cavalier. He reidentifies the Olynthian bath in the kitchen complex as a storeroom and claims that a number of other quite nondescript rooms served for grain storage, goes on to apply dry measures to liquid-containing vessels (i.e., the aforementioned pithoi), and extrapolates back to "compensate" and "provide a fairly accurate guide" (Gallant 1991, 96).

At the same time, there are half a dozen quite sizable rooms on the North Hill that were identified by Robinson and Graham as "unroofed pens for animals, or . . . possibly . . . for storage" (D. M. Robinson and J. W. Graham 1938, 111). That these rooms were ideally suited to serving the storage needs of not one but several families seems the most plausible interpretation.[79] Such a scenario also fits well with Cahill's notion of kin-based "neighborhoods" at Olynthos and other sites. The identification of communal storage depots in these rooms at Olynthos is perhaps paralleled at Halieis by Room 6-40, the lengthy corridor-like space located in the dead center of the one insula that has received the most extensive exposure (see above, 23–24). While the fragmentary stele and associated foundation recovered might be related to a cult installation (whether ancestral or a protective deity of the stores like Zeus Ktesios, for whom, see below, 76–77), it might also have displayed ownership or regulations pertaining to the use of the facility.

Finally, we should not neglect the likelihood that woven bags and baskets also served for dry storage and could have had a second-story location, up from the damp and further away from pests. Produce could have been stockpiled in the chora as well.[80] Given the multitude of strategies for storage and subsistence available to householders, it is not surprising that we lack clear and consistent evidence for the location of the tamieion.

Thalamoi

> . . . for you know Prodicus of Ceos is in Athens too: he was in a certain chamber formerly used by Hipponicus as a store room (tamieio), but now cleared out by Callias to make more space for his numerous visitors, and turned into a guest-room. Well, Prodicus was still in bed, wrapped up in sundry fleeces and rugs, and plenty of them too, it seemed. . . .
>
> Plato *Protagoras* 315D

The rooms for which we have the least archaeological evidence are thalamoi, or bedrooms. Most concur that sleeping quarters were often located in rooms on the second story.[81] At Halieis, lacking stratigraphic or artifact evidence to the contrary, it has not been possible to identify second-story collapse debris atop ground-floor deposits.[82] Thus, it is presumed negligible, and accordingly, the function of second-story rooms must have been primarily for sleeping, and for light and seasonal storage. At the same time, as the passage from Plato's *Protagoras* cited above also suggests, the location of sleeping chambers could be as variable as those used for storage. The andron, for example, contained dining couches that for all practical purposes were identical to beds used for sleeping.

[77] The practice is described in Plutarch *Pericles* 16 and also discussed in [Aristotle] *Oeconomica* 1344b.

[78] Gallant 1991, 96–97. Cahill observes that these pithoi most likely contained oil instead (1991, 336–37; 338, where "A ix 10" should be read as "A xi 10"; cf. 2002, 239–41).

[79] Cahill 2002, 247–48: in houses A 4, room b; A vi 8, a; A vii 3, d; A vii 8, h; A vii 9, a; and A viii 6, d. While few artifacts were recorded from these rooms, which were four to five meters wide and frequently as deep as the houses themselves, room b, in house A 4, yielded fifteen slate and terracotta pithos lids. Gallant finds the evidence for communal storage facilities in general, especially granaries, untenable (1991, 179–81). But cf. Aristophanes *Ecclesiazusae* 14–15, "When we stealthily open the stoas full of grain and flowing wine, you stand beside us" (trans. D. M. Robinson 1946, 403, no. 17).

[80] See Jameson's observations on the residence of the agricultural labor force, both slave and free (1977/78, 1992), as well as Osborne (1985), for epigraphically attested instances of buildings in the countryside dedicated to storage.

[81] Cf. the oft-cited literary testimonia of Aristophanes *Thesmophoriazusae* 478–89; and Lysias 1, *On the Murder of Eratosthenes* 9–13.

[82] The stratigraphy in room 5 of the House of the Doric Capital at Morgantina is cited by Tsakirgis as an example exhibiting second-story collapse debris (1984, 394, with n. 109).

John Boardman has gone so far as to state that, "In the simpler Greek houses, that is the majority, . . . the sleeping-room was the eating-room, the living-room, and the dying-room" (Boardman 1990, 127).

Elevation: Windows, Stairs, Second Story, and Roofing

> They prevent buildings which encroach on the streets, balconies which extend over the streets, overhead drainpipes which discharge into the street, and window-shutters which open into the street.
>
> ARISTOTLE *Athenaion Politeia* 50.2

The passage from Aristotle's *Athenian Constitution* cited above has been interpreted by Keuls as meaning that it was "specifically forbidden to have windows looking out onto the street."[83] Her reading plays into her reconstruction of women's domestic space as verging on a penal environment (see below). But taken in its proper context, that is, of constructions encroaching upon public thoroughfares, Aristotle must refer to shutters opening onto the street that could obstruct commercial and pedestrian traffic. While it is true that we have little evidence for windows in Greek houses, examples are preserved in the stone built house walls of Ammotopos and are depicted in vase painting.[84] In both the preserved and painted examples windows tend to be quite small, placed high in the walls, and taper from wider interior dimensions to narrower exterior ones. These features reflect concerns with privacy and security over and above climate control and the illumination of interior spaces (cf. Löhr 1990).

We have already seen that the houses of Halieis supply good evidence for having been provided with second stories. Stair bases can be securely identified in three of the five houses considered here (Houses 7, C, and E), and stairs can be tentatively located in Houses A and D.[85] The dimensions calculated for a flight of stairs at Olynthos, with a breadth of 0.80–1.10 m, a length of 2.50–3.50 m, and sloping at the rather steep minimum grade of 45°, accord with the evidence for stairways at Halieis (Hoepfner and Schwandner 1994, 107. Cf. D. M. Robinson and J. W. Graham 1938, 267–80). As at Olynthos, stairways in the Halieis houses tended to be located on the north side of the court (Houses 7, C, D, and E) or in the pastas / transverse hall (House A).

And while roof tiles are among the most numerous finds from the Halieis excavations, and so indicate the existence of pitched and trussed roofs, there may have been areas of thatched or flat roofing interspersed with tiled ones.[86] These would have been especially practical as measures of economy since roof tiles were expensive and, like doors and woodwork, were described as nonremovable in leases of rental properties.[87] Moreover, areas of flat roofing could add to the amount of outdoor working space available to the household, an extension of the courtyard, as it were.[88]

[83] Keuls 1985, 97. Cf. A. J. Graham (1998) who believes that a prohibition on women looking out of house windows on the "stele from the harbor" of Thasos was related to prostitutes soliciting clients.

[84] In general, see Schwandner 1999c. For Ammotopos, see Dakaris 1986 and Hoepfner et al. 1999b. Windows figure prominently as a decorative adjunct in South Italian vase painting and signify indoor settings (for a selection of examples, see Schauenburg 1972).

[85] See also above, 23, note 40. Of course, lacking built staircases, ladders would have served the same purpose. The ladder as an artistic motif occasionally appears in vase painting (e.g., Trendall 1989, pl. 364) and stands as an iconographic reference to the upstairs location of the thalamos (but not the gynaikon specifically; see below). For instances where a more symbolic reading is applied to the ladder motif, see Edwards 1984.

[86] For thatched roofs, see the presumably domestic building depicted on the interior of a cup attributed to the Brygos Painter in Milan (Mus. Arch. 266; *ARV*² 379.145; illustrated in Bérard et al. 1989, 35, fig. 41; Hoepfner and Schwandner 1994, 222, fig. 215; and Keuls 1983, 212, fig. 14.6). Hoepfner and Schwandner's reconstructed isometric elevations of insular housing effectively convey the impression of how areas of flat roofs would have appeared and been used (1994, e.g., 86, fig. 64, for Olynthos).

[87] For prices of roof tiles, see Pritchett 1956, 282–83. For examples of their perceived value as well as their integral status with regard to leased property, see Osborne 1985, 122–23 (with references).

[88] For a comparable scenario among Native Americans, see Dohm 1996. J. A. Dengate informs me that "the flat roofs of modern Turkish villages provide a relatively comfortable place for sleeping on hot nights and catch even the slightest breeze" (personal communication, 2000).

– CHAPTER FOUR –

Oikos and Oikonomia

In this final chapter I examine specific aspects of household organization—namely, the nature of male and female space and the domestic economy. While there is evidence from Halieis that can be invoked on behalf of both these subjects, a related area for which we lack archaeological correlates is that of chattel slavery. Such "invisibility" is characteristic, but we can be fairly certain that, as in other Greek poleis, both household and agricultural slaves were present at Halieis (although probably not in great numbers per household).[1] They have simply gone undetected in the material record. Perhaps we should find in the enormous pottery inventories represented from the houses (numbering into the thousands of vessels, judging from the fragments) an indication of a greater number of individuals, using and breaking pots, than merely the shifting makeup of nuclear to extended family units. Spatially there are many peripheral areas in houses where slaves could have lodged. The two small suites associated with House E (Rooms 6-21 and 6-22; and 6-11 through 6-13; for which, see above, 51–53, 56–57) provide particularly good examples where compact workshop-like spaces appear to be combined with living debris. Those slaves whose role it was primarily to tend crops could have resided in the chora as well.

Male and Female Space: Andronitis and Gynaikonitis

There has been much recent discussion aimed at elucidating aspects of gender in the Classical household.[2] Prior to this, the prevailing opinion followed those primary sources that compared distinct male and female roles in society to the sharp division between male and female space in the household. Male to female roles and spaces were seen as corresponding generally to public versus private spheres of activity. The words of Vitruvius (6.7.2; 6.7.5) and Xenophon (*Oeconomicus* 8–10) have been reiterated as though the former had first-hand acquaintance with the house type he purports to describe and the latter was not imbedding a discussion of his aristocratic estate in an essentially moralizing argument of Socrates.[3] Indeed, gender distinctions employed by classical authors nearly always tend toward their use "as similes where two contrasting opposites are being described" (Nevett 1994, 99). Even Morgan's use of Lysias 1 (*On the Murder of Eratosthenes*) to shed light on the apportionment of domestic space is of limited value since the house, located in the unplanned sprawl of urban Athens, is small and irregular (Morgan 1982).

Unquestioning adherence to the literary sources was first criticized by Jameson, then by Nevett, and subsequently by others (see above, note 2). Jameson believes that despite "the powerful social and symbolic distinctions between the two genders," they are not reflected in the layout of houses (Jameson 1990a, 104). Nevett, in her more extended treatments, draws on the apt analogy of Islamic household organization to demonstrate a subtler system of gendered space (Nevett 1994; 1999, esp. 30–31). From this, it is clear

[1] Cf. Burford 1993, 208–22; Cahill 2002, chap. 6; Cox 1998, 190–94; Jameson 1977/78; Jameson 1990a, 103–4; Jameson 1990b, 191; Jameson 1992; Morris 1998b.

[2] Cahill 2002, chap. 4; Goldberg 1999; Jameson 1990a, esp. 104; Jameson 1990b, esp. 186–92; Morris 1998b; Nevett 1994; Nevett 1995a; and Nevett 1999, esp. 14–20, 30–31, 154–55, 163–64. Lissarrague (1998) provides an iconographically based examination of the gynaikonitis.

[3] Cf. Keuls 1985, esp. 210–12; and Walker 1983. Both Tsakirgis (1989) and Reber (1988) seek to vindicate Vitruvius's discussion of the Greek house as reflecting late Classical and Hellenistic types, particularly those of southern Italy and Sicily.

that the scheduling of female activities throughout the house was flexible enough for women to avoid contact with nonkin-group males who came to call at home. She makes the point that while the andron is the room specifically set aside for use by males, the rest of the house is essentially the gynaikonitis in that "in these other areas the women of the house are present, although they are in no sense specifically dedicated to female use."[4] Ultimately we are left with the conclusion that, despite the emphasis that the primary sources put upon rigorously segregated women's quarters, this was simply not the case in reality. This supposed segregation was, in fact, a trope of Athenian aristocratic male speech and thought, used to describe an "ideal" domestic setting that no doubt few could actually attain.[5]

The evidence from Halieis supports this developing picture only in that there is little evidence for strictly enforced separation of the sexes on either architectural or artifactual grounds. While the andron tends to stand apart from the core of the house, its status as a distinct suite mandates that it do so. It is surely intentional that sight-lines into (and out of) the andron are limited by its off-center doorway. The dayroom, too, is typically removed from the courtyard by one intervening room (often a transverse hall), as well as set perpendicular to the house entry, and so invisible from it (as it is from the andron as well). But these are built-in devices that act as screens and deterrents in subtle ways. In terms of residues of material culture, while it may be possible to identify a "complex of female associated artifacts"[6] in House A, Room 6-87 (see above, 31), the distribution of finds correlates better with activity areas than it does with gender specific ones. Even associations between gender and activities implied by artifact types are not explicit, and I believe they suggest communality rather than specificity of space.[7]

Domestic Cult

> [T]he whole house was in effect the sacred precinct and the fire, in whatever form, the altar.
>
> M. H. Jameson

While there are traces of domestic cult practice at Halieis, they are not prominent in the archaeological record of the houses. Unlike Olynthos and other sites, no discernable evidence for household altars, either full size or the miniaturized arulae, was recovered in the course of excavation.[8] Terracotta figurines, which may have served religious functions, were not so numerous in the Halieis houses as at Olynthos, Priene, and elsewhere.[9] Moreover, all were so fragmentary that precise identification of their subject matter is still uncertain.[10] Miniature vessels, however, were a ubiquitous find in the houses. Their shapes range from bowls and skyphoi, to jugs, lekythoi, and lamps. A total of twenty-three miniatures were

[4] Nevett 1994, 108. Cf. Morris 1998b, 217: "Space was not rigidly divided into male and female, but into male and non-male; and space was conceived as having varying degrees of maleness, lying along a gender spectrum rather than falling into one of two distinct categories."

[5] Cf. the recent work by Scheidel (1995, 1996). Using ancillary and comparative evidence, he argues that women in classical antiquity actively contributed to the agricultural labor force, as was, and still is, the norm in peasant societies. He also seeks to demolish the idealized view of women's roles generally. The extremes of female seclusion and segregation across Islamic society are relevant here, in that they vary from being not enforced at all in secular states to brutal compulsion in more militant, fundamentalist settings. But even in the latter instances, enforcement can vary drastically according to location and social differentiation of women. In the end, the ultimate motivation behind such restrictions is similar: to protect women's honor, to restrain men from temptation, and to ensure the legitimate paternity of offspring.

[6] I borrow this phrase from L. C. Nevett (personal communication, 1992).

[7] Jameson states, "Attempts to divide space along these lines are arbitrary and obscure the flexibility of use and a broader unity" (1990a, 104).

[8] For Olynthos, see D. M. Robinson and J. W. Graham 1938, 321–25; for Priene, Hoepfner and Schwandner 1994, 219. A terracotta mold (HC 247; 0.25 x 0.21 m), depicting what may be a mythological rape scene, was found in the northwest quarter of the lower town. It has been suggested that it could have served for making relief decoration in stucco for a small chest or altar (Jameson 1969, 330, pl. 82). For house altars in general, see Jameson 1990a, 104–5; Nilsson 1960a; Yavis 1949, 175–76.

[9] The best discussion of the functions of terracotta figurines is Ammerman 1990. Cf. also Harward 1982, and Raeder 1983, 22–25.

[10] The following is a brief description of the five terracotta figurines and one mold recovered from Level A strata in the five houses treated in this study. At other sites, terracotta molds have been found in houses, such as at Olynthos (Cahill 1991, 359–60; 2002, 253–55) and Nea Halos (Reinders 1988, 117–34), and help to identify coroplasts' residences.

House 7. HC 856 (Rm. 7-17): Base and body fragment of cloaked female(?) figure seated(?) on a square base. Traces of red and white paint present. HC 647 (Rm. 7-11/12): Circular mold, egg-shaped with vegetal motif of four palmettes linked to cruciform vine pattern. Pierced on one end?

House D. HC 646 (Rm. 6-26): Fragmentary circular plaque with hand-modeled(?) relief face. Akroterion? HC 844 (Rm. 6-35 SE): Base and body fragments of a seated or reclining figure. Traces of red and yellow paint.

House E. HC 815 (Rm. 6-20): Circular stamp with impression of kneeling female figure, holds flower(?) in left hand. HC 651 (Rm. 6-23): Bird figurine (dove?), handmade(?). White slip with traces of blue and red paint.

recovered from the Level A contexts associated with House 7, twelve from House A, twelve from House C, fifteen from House D, and twenty-three from House E. While a votive function cannot be proven for all of them, nor are their findspots informative, some will surely have served the simpler ritual needs of household cult.[11]

For the preeminent household deities, several good discussions already exist.[12] Particularly useful among them is Jameson's effort to dispel the myth of the household hearth, and the round hearth in particular, while leaving intact the venerability of Hestia.[13] We have already seen that only two of the dwellings excavated at Halieis have fixed hearths, Houses 7 and D, and that the latter is of rather makeshift construction. While both were probably used for cooking, portable braziers appear to have been favored by other householders. Hearths at Olynthos are similarly rare, and even when they are present, actual cooking seems to have taken place in the flue.[14] Yet the association of Hestia with the household hearth persists. Hoepfner and Schwandner have suggested that once a city had erected its prytaneion (the council house), the actual function of the household hearth as a seat for Hestia became subsumed in the communal hearth of the prytaneion, which, like the function of the building itself, stood for all citizen families.[15] Thus, Hestia remained an integral part of domestic cult but was capable of being venerated even without the physical manifestation of her hearth.

Two aspects of Zeus as a guardian of the household also merit brief consideration here. Zeus Herkeios, of the herkos, or enclosure of the house, has been seen to preside from the area of the court.[16] Because of the mention of his altar in the court of Odysseus's house (*Odyssey* 22.334–35), courtyard altars at Olynthos, Eretria, and the similarly placed hearth-altars at Colophon and Athens have been interpreted as specific to his domain.[17] Although Jameson has expressed doubts about the ubiquity of Zeus Herkeios in domestic cult, I would point out an interesting fragment from Aristophanes' lost comedy, *Danaides*.[18] Quoted in a scholium to *Peace* 923, it states, "My witness be the Pots of Household Zeus / 'Fore which this shrine was sanctified for use" (Edmonds 1957, 643, no. 245). And although not an altar per se, a built construction of cooking pots, mortared together with earth and sherds, was recovered as a votive deposit in 6th-century levels of the Thesmophorion at Bitalemi near Gela in Sicily (Orlandini 1966, 22, pl. 14; cf. also Kron 1992, 643–48, with pl. 14). Although this pertains more to the relationship between Demeter and the household (for which, see below) and does not necessarily aid us in "placing" Zeus Herkeios, it does say something about the ad hoc nature of cult furniture and helps to pardon even the diligent archaeologist's inability to recover all but the most marked traces of domestic cult.

In a second guise, Zeus takes the epithet "Ktesios" where he is concerned with the family stores of possessions and produce (ktemata). As such, we should expect to find his veneration focused upon the tamieion or pitheon, but we have already noted the difficulty of locating an area set aside specifically for household storage. In his examination of the evidence for a cult of Zeus Ktesios, Nilsson has identified both the Dioskouroi and household snakes as epiphanies of his guardian aspect (Nilsson 1960b; 1961, 67–69. Cf. also Cook 1965, 1054–68). We may connect this

[11] See the discussion of miniature vessels, particularly in their aspect as votive dedications, in Dunbabin and Blakeway 1960, 290–91. Among the numerous sanctuary contexts in the Southern Argolid where votive miniatures have been recovered, the remains of more than 5000 miniature kotylai from the back room of the submerged temple of Apollo at Halieis are worthy of special mention (Jameson 1974, 117).

[12] E.g., Jameson 1990a, 104–6; Jameson 1990b, 192–94; Nilsson 1960b; Nilsson 1961, 65–83; and Sjövall 1931. Unfortunately, Wiencke 1947, a Ph.D. thesis on the subject, is not generally available.

[13] As cited in note 12. Tsakirgis has also been pursuing a similar theme (Tsakirgis, forthcoming, b).

[14] See above, 68, notes 55 and 56. Of the forty flues identified by Cahill at Olynthos, sixteen were recorded as containing traces of ash or burning on their floors (Cahill 1991, 323; 2002, 155).

[15] Hoepfner and Schwandner 1994, 100; cf. Jameson 1990a, 106. For a discussion of the form and function of prytaneia, see S. G. Miller 1978, esp. 4–37.

[16] Cf. Solon 3.26–29, cited above, 62, note 18.

[17] See D. M. Robinson and J. W. Graham 1938, 159, 321, and D. M. Robinson 1946, 388, for attribution to Zeus Herkeios of the courtyard altars at Olynthos (and concurrence on the identification of the hearth-altars at Colophon). For the altar from the court of the House with the Mosaics at Eretria, see Ducrey, Metzger, and Reber 1993, 65–66. For the hearth-altars from Colophon, see Holland 1944, 124, with n. 25 (House IVe); 135 (House IIIf); and 146 (House IIe). Another example from Athens has been identified in House D along the Street of the Marble Workers in the Areopagus district (R. S. Young 1951, 222). The blurred distinction between hearths and altars extends to their terminology ("eschara" can refer to either a hearth or an altar) and is especially relevant in light of Jameson's observations on the symbolism versus the reality of the household hearth among the Greeks (see above, note 12).

[18] For his reservations, see Jameson 1990a, 105, with n. 19. Nor does the evidence presented by Cook suggest domestic associations for Zeus Herkeios (1964, 39, n. 6; 1965, 72, n. 5; 727, n. 3; 807, n. 3; 892, n. 5; 1066).

with the inscribed blocks recovered in House E, Room 6-24 (HS 532 and HS 533; Pls. 69, 70), that may invoke Zeus and the Dioskouroi (see above, 51 and Jameson 2001a). Also relevant here is a recent find from the Dutch excavations of the Hellenistic city of Nea Halos in Boeotia (for preliminary reports, see Haagsma 1990, 1991; and Reinders 1988). In the summer of 1993, while exploring a house containing the first domestic hearth discovered at the site (out of seven at least partially excavated houses), a stone vessel was found sunken beneath the floor next to the hearth itself. When emptied of its earthen fill, it was found to contain two snake figurines, one of silver and the other of bronze.[19] Although the precise significance of this discovery has not yet been fully assessed, it doubtless relates to domestic cult, perhaps to Zeus Ktesios and the Dioskouroi in particular.[20]

These brief observations on aspects of domestic cult at Halieis and in general conclude by way of returning to Demeter. Evidence for aspects of her cult provides a transition to a consideration of the domestic economy and also leads toward my concluding observations below. Jameson has proposed the identification of an extramural sanctuary dedicated to Demeter on a north-facing terrace of the next hill east of the acropolis (1969, 340–41). For our purposes, however, we need rather to consider a unique group of dining structures not from Halieis but from the Sanctuary of Demeter and Kore at Corinth. Spanning the late 6th to 2d centuries, these buildings frequently comprise regularized groupings of dining hall, kitchen, and bath. On the basis of the evidence at hand, these now appear to derive from a fairly common architectural vocabulary, that of the household.[21] The kitchen/bath complex is particularly reminiscent of those identified at Halieis, as well as elsewhere. The structures at Corinth are, in essence, abbreviated houses, reduced to the most essential elements of architectural and functional syntax. In this light, it is especially interesting and significant to note that, following the 5th-century C.E. lexicographer, Hesychius of Alexandria, it may have been Demeter Epoikidia ("of the little household") who was celebrated here (Bookidis 1990, 87 [citing Latte 1966, 180, no. 5473]; 1993, 45; and Bookidis and Stroud 1997, 2, 72, 411). In addition to the domestic character of the architectural remains, if Demeter Epoikidia was venerated here, votives recovered from the site suggest that among her special aspects were those connected with agriculture, food preparation, and textile production.[22] Ultimately, it is the two activities of producing food and textiles that underpin and account for the domestic economy and that are joined together by the bond of marriage. I would even argue that they stand for isonomia at the grassroots level as a measure of equality between male and female.[23]

Domestic Economy

All subsistence activities engaged in by the ancient household ultimately qualify as contributing to domestic management, the literal definition of "economy." And while the degree to which such endeavors actually approached our contemporary understanding of "economic" has been questioned (most notably by M. I. Finley), I would assert that it is the natural tendency of households to produce beyond the level of mere subsistence.[24] This stands

[19] This find was presented in a paper read by M. Haagsma at the 95th Annual Meeting of the Archaeological Institute of America, Dec. 27–30, 1993, in Washington D.C. (Haagsma 1994).

[20] Nilsson notes that in Sparta there is evidence for the household Dioskouroi appearing as snakes and illustrates a relief from the museum of Sparta that can be interpreted as such (Nilsson 1961, 69, with 154, fig. 31). Another example is illustrated by Cook (1965, 1062, fig. 915).

[21] See Bookidis 1990, 1993 for summary discussions of the site and its attendant problems; and Bookidis and Stroud 1997 for the final report on the architecture.

[22] Nancy Bookidis has informed me that the votive material includes miniature agricultural tools as well as weaving implements (personal communication, 1993). Miniature ceramic kalathoi, in real life baskets that held the wool used in weaving, are mentioned as the most popular votive objects at the sanctuary in the early 3d century (Bookidis and Stroud 1997, 433). But aside from the miniature vessels, which were recovered by the thousands (Pemberton 1989, 64–66, 168–77), and miniature terracotta likna, representing winnowing fans used as offering trays (Brumfield 1997), the votives have not been published in detail. At the same time, it should be noted that these classes of votive material are not all that unusual. Actual agricultural implements, for example, have been recovered from the Thesmophorion at Bitalemi (Kron 1992, 636–40) as well as from the temple of Apollo at Halieis (M. H. Jameson, personal communication, 1999).

[23] The recent translation of and commentary upon Xenophon *Oeconomicus* by Pomeroy (1994; cf. Pomeroy 1995) reaches much the same conclusions, albeit phrasing them in a different manner.

[24] See, especially, Finley 1973, but also Austin and Vidal-Naquet 1977, Cartledge 1983, and Gallant 1991. The overview of the ancient economy by Morris (1994b) is also quite useful, as are Cahill's comments (2002, 223–88). As for production beyond susbsistence, the risk-management or buffering strategies advocated by many as having been pursued by households in order to avoid periodic production shortfalls (e.g., Gallant 1991; Garnsey 1988; and Halstead and O'Shea 1989) suggest that one would strive to have surpluses available, even when they were not needed for consumption by the immediate family or its socially bound constituents.

in distinction to commonly stated precepts advocating domestic self-sufficiency and an avoidance of nonagrarian mercantile or so-called "banausic" pursuits (e.g., Xenophon *Oeconomicus* 4.2–3. Cf. the discussion of the passage by Pomeroy 1994, 235–37). Like the strict division of domestic space into male and female, such notions do not reflect reality. Instead, they are moralizing proscriptions issued by politicians and philosophers to make points above and beyond mere subsistence strategies. Ultimately, then, our notion of domestic self-sufficiency is in need of revision, if not recognized as a myth and discarded altogether. In the revised interpretation, the orientation of the household would tend, in both the extremes of stressed and favorable circumstances, toward market exchange and hence, local and regional involvement. Just as the Greek household was a microcosm of the wider social and political world, so, too, the domestic economy should be considered to mirror the macroeconomy.

Among the range of pursuits engaged in by households, from textile and other craftwork, to agricultural production and processing, those that had potential for going beyond mere self-sufficiency were weaving and olive-oil production. Both these activities have left traces in the houses of Halieis and are briefly discussed below.

Home Textile Production

The histeon, or "loom room," like those given over to cooking or storage, is yet another indicator of the domestic economy.[25] Stressing the importance of textile production is fundamental to completing the picture of oikonomia. The motif of weaving recurs throughout literature and art as an indicator par excellence of the good wife and stood as one of her primary contributions to successful household management. These same associations are true not only for ancient Greece but for most of history prior to the Industrial Revolution. The archaeology of weaving in antiquity has lately begun to receive the attention it deserves. Recent scholarship not only confirms its significance but augments our appreciation of textiles in terms of the amount of work involved in their creation, value, and overall place in the world view of traditional cultures.[26]

Any actual designation of the household histeon was probably quite flexibly applied by the Greeks. The upright warp-weighted looms used in antiquity were dismantled and stored when not in use and could be fairly easily moved about even when they were in service.[27] Thus, the histeon was variably placed and referred, no doubt, to wherever the loom was at a given time.[28] In good weather, weaving could be done in or just off the courtyard. At other times, interior rooms would have been favored. Yet for the whole range of activities and products accompanying cloth making there is, in practice, but a single class of archaeological correlates: terracotta spindle whorls and loom weights.

Each of the five houses from Halieis for which the artifact assemblages have been studied in detail yielded between eight and twenty-five loom weights. Although none were encountered in clusters numerically significant enough to indicate the position of a loom (as is the case for examples from other sites cited below), they certainly attest to the presence of domestic weaving. Presumably the departing inhabitants of the city managed to take their looms along with them in their flight, an indication of the craft's valued status. The absence of spindle whorls from the assemblages altogether implies either that organic substitutes were in use or that the raw wool had already been spun into thread elsewhere.

From House A, two loom weights were found in the transverse hall (Room 6-81c), and four came from the "dayroom" (Room 6-87). Three loom weights came from the andron anteroom (Room 6-57) in House C. It should be recalled that the probable Level A floor surface was exposed in but a small area here, so only a sample of the artifact assemblage from the room was actually recovered. In House D, five loom weights came from the enormous dump in Room 6-35b. In House E, seventeen were recovered from the courtyard (Room 6-20), while three and two loom weights came from Rooms 6-24 and 6-25, respectively. Although the numbers are small, I believe that they tell us about likely work areas. The transverse hall, courtyard, dayroom, and andron anteroom would all have made ideal locations for weaving.

[25] Although the designation "histeon" is attested only in Menander *Samia* 234 (19).

[26] Barber 1991 has become a fundamental source. Cf. Barber 1992 for a synoptic version, and Barber 1994 for a more popular treatment. An earlier effort based on ethnographic work in the southern Argolid is provided by Koster 1976. Useful, but with greater emphasis on symbolic readings of textiles and their manufacture, are Jenkins 1985, Keuls 1983, and Vickers 1999.

[27] Cahill states that a loom upon which a textile was being woven could not have been moved (2002, 170), but my own discussions with weavers suggest otherwise.

[28] E.g., there is also a bed in the histeon mentioned by Menander *Samia* 225 (10). Cf. Jameson 1990a, 102–3; and 1990b, 186, with n. 18.

Olynthos provides far richer evidence for household weaving than that preserved at Halieis. Cahill's study of the remains suggests that as many as forty-three rooms in thirty-five houses showed evidence for weaving (Cahill 1991, 341–46, 356–57; and 2002, 169–79, 250–52). Of these, twenty-five rooms yielded between ten and twenty-five loom weights, while between twenty-five and forty-three were found in another seven rooms. In only one instance, the Villa CC, did the excavators recognize and record hard evidence for a possible loom in situ. Here, forty-three loom weights were found extending along a 1.1 m line. Eighty-three loom weights were recovered from four rooms situated around the courtyard of House A v 9 and indicate that as many as four looms were set up between those chambers. Also, the common pastas porch of Houses A viii 7 and A viii 9 yielded 247 loom weights, which could equip from four to a dozen looms depending on the size of the jobs underway. Cahill interprets the evidence from these latter examples as implying weaving on more than just a domestic scale.

Good evidence for household textile production also exists at Ammotopos (Orraon) (see Hoepfner et al. 1999b, esp. 408; Hoepfner and Schwandner 1994, 323, with figs. 139, 308). Both in the southeast corner of the "hearthroom" (or "oikos," room d) of House 1 and in a small chamber opening off it (room c) were found paired blocks believed to mark the position of looms. Supporting this interpretation, numerous loom weights were found in association with both features. Accordingly, the latter room has been identified as a specialized "webkammer" or histeon.[29]

Olive-Oil Extraction

At least five, and as many as eleven, olive-oil press installations can be recognized in the houses at Halieis.[30] Up to twenty more examples of press furniture have been noted on Classical to Hellenistic-period sites identified by the Southern Argolid Exploration Project within the territory of Halieis and its neighbors.[31] Recently, Foxhall has called into question the function of the Halieis presses, and the identification of urban presses in general, as having been used for oil extraction (Foxhall 1993, esp. 184–87). She attempts to resuscitate an early misidentification of the Halieis presses as belonging to a local industry producing purple dye from murex shells. This hypothesis was first published by Young with regard to the remains on the so-called Industrial Terrace.[32] Jameson began to doubt this interpretation early on and has since gone to some lengths to refute it (Jameson 1969, 324; 2001b, esp. 254, n. 5; and Jameson, Runnels, and van Andel 1994, 316–19, esp. 317, n. 21). Reese, while also acknowledging the well-attested prominence of nearby Hermioni in the murex-dye industry, does not find the evidence from Halieis compelling enough to support the hypothesis (Reese 1989, and personal communication 1991). The quantity of shells required for extracting the pigment known as "Tyrian purple" (12,000 *Murex brandaris* were needed to produce enough dye to trim a single garment [Reese 1987, 204]) is nowhere in evidence. Elsewhere, Anderson-Stojanović has shown that two other so-called dye-works, those from Isthmia and Hellenistic Mycenae, were almost certainly oil-press installations.[33]

[29] The evidence from Ammotopos has been used to posit similar arrangements for weaving in the houses at Kassope (Hoepfner and Schwandner 1994, 148; Hoepfner et al. 1999a, 376).

[30] The discussion that follows is based largely upon that of Ault 1999b, esp. 559–60, and 564–66. Those presses that can be identified as definitely surviving in situ include the following: Area 4, house (press bed; Jameson 1969, 328; J. H. Young 1963, 3–4); Area 6, Room 6-4 (press bed) and House D, Room 6-29 (entire press room cleared; it is discussed in detail above, 41; Ault 1999b, 560–62); Area 7, Room 7-20 (press bed); Industrial Terrace (entire press room cleared; Ault 1999b, 562–64; Jameson 2001b, 281–87, and 1969, 323–24; J. H. Young 1963, 6–7). Others that are less certain include: Area 6, House A, Room 6-83 (perhaps in the process of conversion to a press room, as noted above, 29); Area 6, House B, Room 6-91 (weight block); Area 6, Room 6-66 (a pair of vessels sunken into a plaster pavement); Area 6, Room 6-43 (exposed corner of unexcavated plaster pavement); Greek Archaeological Service excavations, Ephoreia Field (northwest of Area 6; weight block); Area 7, Room 7-24 (section of cobbled pavement with two sunken vessels).

[31] Jameson, Runnels, and van Andel 1994, 384–85, with table 6.6, where it is noted that press installations occur at "a ratio of one out of six [i.e., houses and sites] in both town and country" during the late Classical and early Hellenistic periods. For a historical overview of olive cultivation in the southern Argolid, see Jameson, Runnels, and van Andel 1994, 268–76. Press furniture from the Southern Argolid Survey (comprising press beds, weight blocks, and trapeta) is treated in Runnels, Pullen, and Langdon 1995, 128–33.

The most important studies of olive culture in classical antiquity generally include Amouretti 1986; Amouretti and Brun 1993; Forbes and Foxhall 1978; Foxhall (in press); and Mattingly 1996.

[32] J. H. Young 1963, 6, with 7, for a plan and photograph identifying the press remains as a "dye-works."

[33] Anderson-Stojanović 1996, esp. 91–93; 1997; and 1998. Foxhall (personal communication 1997) has stressed the multiple functions presses might have served, over and above having been designated for any single purpose (cf. Foxhall 1997, 258–59). I find such a position more accommodating but will continue to refer to the Halieis installations as oil presses.

Oil presses complemented the domestic koprones, those recurrent features in the houses at Halieis that were part of conscious efforts at increasing agricultural productivity through providing components for fertilizer (see above, 63–65). These presses, too, served as a means for processing the yield of the land. As has already been noted, however, the houses in question were clearly not laid out with press installations in mind. These are later features added in the 4th century when the processing amply attested in the contemporary chora was deemed insufficient or when any existing (and archaeologically undocumented) communal press facilities were overworked as a result of the intensification of olive cultivation and oil production.[34]

As to the forces motivating a concerted effort toward olive production and oil processing, van Andel, Jameson, and Runnels have pointed out that areas with the highest-quality cultivable soils in the territory of Halieis were fairly limited and lay about two kilometers away from the city.[35] Closer, however, were alluvial soils on hillsides and valley bottoms, which, they observe, while less well suited to grain cultivation, were ideal for olives.[36] They have further suggested that the degree of prosperity attained by Halieis in its final, 4th-century phase may have been linked to its supplying olive oil to external markets. Potential customers could have been found in Attica and its commercial dependents, which first were deprived of oil as a result of the annual ravaging of crops during the Peloponnesian War.[37] Also, the territories of Thebes and Megalopolis underwent rapid growth in the 4th century and were located in regions poorly suited to olive cultivation (van Andel and Runnels 1987, 107–9; Runnels and van Andel 1987). Finally, in the wake of Alexander the Great's conquests, vast, far-flung, and newly Hellenized areas were opened up as potential markets and sources of exchange.[38]

Much of the potential economic viability of oleiculture posited for Classical Greece hinges not only on the reconstruction of evidence for large-scale agribusiness attested in the Roman world but from more contemporary production figures.[39] Still, from 4th-century Attica comes the calculation based on [Demosthenes] 42 (*Against Phainippos*) that land planted with olive trees was worth three times the equivalent area sown with wheat (Pritchett 1956, 183–84, citing Jardé 1925, 187). From that same century have been documented widely fluctuating prices of oil, where a metretes (39.4 liters) ranged from 12 drachmas at Athens to 36 drachmas at Lampsakos to 55 drachmas at Delos (Pritchett 1956, 184). We can combine these prices with what is offered as a "highly speculative" but "conservative" estimate that in the every-other-year cycle of olive fruiting, a family might average 250–300 liters of oil from its trees.[40] Then the potential value of a household's olive harvest could itself fluctuate between 76.14 and

[34] Acheson's observation that the intramural presses at Halieis may have been used to deal with "bumper" harvests (1997, 181), which with traditional methods of cultivation come only once every few years, leads one to wonder why extra presses would not simply have been installed in the chora. Her point does emphasize, however, the brief annual period during which such installations would have been in use. Consequently, the constituent elements, except for press beds and weight blocks, are likely to have been dismantled and stored, or put to other purposes, when not being used for pressing. Elsewhere, Foxhall (1993, 194–99; 1997, 261) has attempted to identify a variety of ancillary pieces of equipment that could have been associated with pressing listed for sale in the Attic Stelai. Forbes and Foxhall (1978, 46) have also suggested that in antiquity, as is the case today, as many as ten families might have shared a press, given the expense incurred with its acquisition.

[35] See van Andel and Runnels 1987, 105–9, maps 20, 21 (also reproduced in Ault 1999b, 550, fig. 1; the best agricultural lands being associated with the areas of "deep soils"); and Jameson, Runnels, and van Andel 1994, 383–94, figs. 6.17, 6.18, back-pocket map 8.

[36] Recently, Acheson has reevaluated the agricultural potential of the soils, especially the so-called Loutro alluvium, in the vicinity of Halieis, and suggests that they were capable of sustaining greater agricultural productivity than was posited by the Southern Argolid Exploration Project (1997). Also, as is still the case in many areas today, grains or legumes were intercropped among the olive trees (Jameson, Runnels, and van Andel 1994, 385).

[37] Arguing against the notion of a generation-long gap in the ability of Attica to regain its potential for oil production, Hanson (1998, esp. 55–68, and 157–61) notes the hardiness of olive trees, the difficulty in utterly destroying them, and their properties of rapid regeneration. In spite of their long-term resilience, olive trees are notoriously sensitive, and annual disruptions coupled with their normally fluctuating productivity could have seriously curtailed their yield over the short term, even if the trees themselves remained alive. It is also worth noting here that on two occasions, in 430 and again in 425, the chora of Halieis was itself subject to ravaging at the hands of the Athenians (Diodorus Siculus 12.43.1; Thucydides 2.56.5).

[38] Numerous other areas in addition to the southern Argolid participated in the settlement boom and dispersal that characterized the century between ca. 350 and 250 (Jameson, Runnels, and van Andel 1994, 392). It is no coincidence that these are virtually all regions that have been carefully studied by archaeological surface surveys.

[39] See, for example, Mattingly (1996) for the Roman world and Forbes (1992; 1993) for cautionary observations about the role of the olive in the southern Argolid itself.

[40] Forbes and Foxhall 1978, 46–47; and this is not counting the periodic "bumper crop" years, when yields could be four or five times as great as normal (cf. Forbes 1992).

418.55 drachmas. But did the domestic (micro) economies of the citizens of Halieis, let alone the polis economy, turn on such transactions?

There is evidence that olive cultivation and oil production were ubiquitous in regions that supported the practice but neither very profitable nor dependable as a source of income (e.g., Finley 1973, 133; Foxhall 1997, esp. 261–62; and Sallares 1991, 304–9). Thus, it has been argued that the apparent Late Classical and Hellenistic boom in olive cultivation in the chora of Halieis was primarily of local significance. That is, it was meant to supply the burgeoning population of the Halias peninsula.[41] But surely Halieis benefited from its position at the mouth of the Argolic Gulf. Possessing a fine naturally sheltered bay and harbor, the position of the polis must have lent itself to more than serving as a pawn in the military aspirations of others.[42] The enormous quantities of Attic, Corinthian, Argive, and other fine-ware pottery present in the houses and all across the site indicate the ongoing commercial activity with the wider Greek world. In addition to these imported fabrics, much, if not most, of the plain- and coarse-ware pottery from Halieis would also have been acquired via market exchange. There is ultimately no reason why local surplus production of olive oil or any other commodity (such as salt, to take a toponymically appropriate example) would not have found its way onto trading vessels passing through, or even sent out by, Halieis. And while we should not overemphasize the role of the olive in linking the local economy to wider networks, everything about the domestic architecture and other evidence that we can muster to reconstruct household organization at Halieis attests to full integration within the koine of Hellenic culture.

I close with a brief recapitulation of three of the most salient features to be teased out of the archaeology of the Halieis houses. These are points that have also been suggested and supported by the work of others elsewhere, whose efforts I have tried to acknowledge throughout my own studies. In many ways, these observations may hold true not only for Halieis but for many other poleis as well. They may be especially significant in providing a non-Athenocentric example and, as such, one that is arguably more representative of the Greek social and political collective. First, the relationship between male and female in the household, rather than being one divided in opposition along spatial lines, is both a social and economic partnership. It forms the integral domestic unit upon which the polis was founded and depends. Second, it suggests a measure of equality at the domestic level that is reflected in many aspects of urban topography, from the plans of houses to the layout of cities, but also in the arena of political isonomia for which the Greeks are justly famed. Finally, it is the domestic microeconomies, oikonomia writ small, that ultimately laid the foundations for and fueled regional political macroeconomies. There can be no more fitting closure at this point than to cite the words of Jameson once again: "On a small scale, the private house shows the democratization of aristocratic values, which was in so many ways characteristic of the city-state" (1990b, 195).

[41] Acheson has formulated the most explicit version of this argument (1997). She has also emphasized the small-scale nature of the numerous agricultural establishments located by the Southern Argolid Exploration Project in the chora of Halieis (especially in comparison with what are clearly more extensive ones) and noted that they would have had the same subsistence-driven orientation as their urban agriculturally oriented counterparts.

[42] Nevertheless, it is the strategic importance attached to the location of Halieis that is behind almost all the limited references to the city in the primary sources. For the most comprehensive historical overview of the southern Argolid generally, see Jameson, Runnels, and van Andel 1994, 57–148.

– APPENDIX I –

Concordance by House of Loci, Rooms, Trenches, and Units Forming Level A–Level A/B Strata

In Appendix I, the first heading is the house, followed by Roman numerals indicating the loci belonging to each house and the rooms or areas associated with each locus. Trenches, identified by the last three digits of the north and east coordinates, and the units excavated in each trench are listed under their respective loci. All measurements are in meters. The following abbreviations are used: u. = unit/units, d. = depth, n.a. = not available (information not in trench notebooks).

A. House 7

I. Avenue C
000/345
u. 2 (0.49 d.), Level A
000/350
u. 11 (0.06 d.), Level A
u. 12 (0.01 d.), Level A
u. 3, 5, 8, and 9 also contain tile fall that forms approximate stratum with 000/345: u. 2
005/340
u. 2 (0.25 d.?), Level A
May also extend into portion of 000/340 lying in Avenue C
005/345
u. 7 (0.10 d.), Level A
u. 10 (0.08 d.), Level A
Average d. Locus I = 0.25

II. Rooms 7-6 and 7-7
000/350
u. 10 (0.09 d.), Level A
u. 10 and 14 appear on archival phase plan, but only u. 10 is Level A
Average d. Locus II = 0.09

III. Rooms 7-7 and 7-8
000/350
East Balk u. 26 (0.20 d.), Level A in Room 7-7 only (still above Level A in Room 7-8)
East Balk u. 27 (0.28 d.), Level A/B in Room 7-8
000/355
u. 4 (0.12 d.), Level A in Room 7-7 only (still above Level A in Room 7-8)
u. 5 (0.17 d.), Level A/B (Level A in Room 7-8, Level B in Room 7-7)
u. 8 (n.a.), Level A
u. 9 (0.11 d.), Level A
u. 4, 5, 8, and 9 all contain traces of kopron fill
Average d. Locus III = 0.44+

IV. Room 7-7
000/350
North Balk u. 24 (0.11 d.), Level A
u. 24 (Locus IV) underlies u. 23 (Locus X), which is Level A in Room 7-10 only
000/355
North Balk u. 11 (0.19 d.), Level A
North Balk u. 12 (0.01–0.41 d.), Level A or A/B

For computing average d. of locus, 0.20 m used for u. 12
East Balk u. 13 (0.22 d.), Level A
East Balk u. 14 (0.38 d.), Level A
u. 13 and 14 contain kopron debris; south end of u. 13 in Street 1, excavated to road metal
000/360
u. 3 (0.20 d.), Level A
u. 4 (0.14 d.), Level A
005/350
u. 5 (0.10 d.), Level A
u. 5 (Locus IV) underlies u. 2 (Locus XI), which is Level A in Rooms 7-10 and 7-9 only
East Balk u. 9 (0.16 d.), Level A
005/355
u. 3 (0.10 d.), Level A
u. 16 (0.08 d.), Level A
u. 17 (n.a., cf. u. 18), Level A
u. 18 (0.38 d. in center), Level A
Because they constitute excavation of a pit feature, u. 17 and 18 are not considered in computing average d. of locus
Average d. Locus IV = 0.27

V. Rooms 7-7, 7-15, and 7-16
005/355
East Balk u. 19 (0.10 d.), Level A (in Room 7-7 only; still above Level A in Rooms 7-15 and 7-16)
u. 19 (Locus V) overlies u. 20 (Locus XXIV) in Room 7-16 and u. 21 (Locus XXII) in Room 7-15; most debris from u. 19 probably from Room 7-7
Average d. Locus V = 0.10

VI. Rooms 7-7 and 7-17
000/360
North Balk u. 5 (0.21 d.)
Average d. Locus VI = 0.21

VII. Room 7-7 kopron
000/355
u. 15–18 (1.07 d.), Level A
Average d. Locus VII = 1.07

VIII. Room 7-7 well
005/355
u. 6–11 (5.56 d.), Level A
Average d. Locus VIII = 5.56

IX. Room 7-10
000/345
u. 3 (0.41 d.), Level A
Southeast corner of u. 3 extends into 000/350
005/345
u. 8 (0.12 d.); although included on archival phase plan, Level A was not actually reached (cf. 000/345 u. 3 and East Balk u. 13 [Locus XII], Rooms 7-9 and 7-10, where Level A was reached in Room 7-10)
Average d. Locus IX = 0.41

X. Rooms 7-7 and 7-10
000/350
North Balk u. 23 (0.24 d.), Level A in Room 7-10 only (still above Level A in Room 7-7)
u. 23 (Locus X) overlies u. 24 (Locus IV) in Room 7-7
Average d. Locus X = 0.24

XI. Rooms 7-7, 7-9, 7-10, and 7-13
005/350
u. 2 (0.13 d.), Level A in Rooms 7-10 and 7-9 only (still above Level A in Rooms 7-13 and 7-7)
u. 2 (Locus XI) overlies u. 5 (Locus IV) in Room 7-7 and u. 10 (Locus XV) in Rooms 7-13 and 7-12
u. 4 (0.08 d.), Level A (lies solely in Room 7-10 but contained few finds)
Average d. Locus XI = 0.21

XII. Rooms 7-9 and 7-10
005/345
u. 2 (0.11 d.), Level A in Room 7-9 only (still above Level A in Room 7-10, cf. comments on 005/345, Locus IX)
East Balk u. 13 (0.32 d.), Level A
Average d. Locus XII = 0.22

XIII. Room 7-9
005/340
u. 3 (0.27 d.?), Level A
005/345
North Balk u. 12 (0.14 d.), Level A
Average d. Locus XIII = 0.21

XIV. Rooms 7-9 and 7-11
010/345
u. 2 (0.10 d.), Level A
Average d. Locus XIV = 0.10

XV. Rooms 7-12 and 7-13
005/350
u. 10 (0.16 d.), Level A
u. 10 (Locus XV) underlies u. 2 (Locus XI), which is Level A in Rooms 7-9 and 7-10 only
Average d. Locus XV = 0.16

XVI. Room 7-13
005/355
North Balk u. 14 (0.27 d.), Level A/B
Average d. Locus XVI = 0.27

XVII. Room 7-11
010/345
East Balk u. 3 (0.12 d.), Level A
Average d. Locus XVII = 0.12

XVIII. Rooms 7-11 and 7-12
010/350
u. 5 (0.14 d.), Level A/B
Average d. Locus XVIII = 0.14

XIX. Room 7-12
010/350
North Balk u. 10 (0.19 d.), Level A/B
Level A in Room 7-12 (or A/B?) and Level A/B in small portion of Room 7-11
East Balk u. 11 (0.18 d.), Level A
015/350
u. 4 (0.26 d.), Level A/B
Average d. Locus XIX = 0.21

XX. Room 7-14
010/355
North Balk u. 5 (0.13 d.), Level A
015/355
u. 13 (0.13 d.), Level A
Average d. Locus XX = 0.13

XXI. Rooms 7-12, 7-13, 7-14, and 7-15
010/355
u. 2 (0.14 d.), Level A
Average d. Locus XXI = 0.14

XXII. Room 7-15
005/355
North Balk u. 15 (0.20 d.), Level A/B
East Balk u. 21 (0.25 d.), Level A/B
u. 21 (Locus XXII) underlies u. 19 (Locus V), which is Level A (probably) in Room 7-7 only
010/355
East Balk u. 8 (0.18 d.), Level A/B
Average d. Locus XXII = 0.21

XXIII. Room 7-15, alley/ambitus, and Room 7-20
010/360
u. 1 (0.20 d.), Level A in Room 7-15 only (most pottery noted from Room 7-15; tile concentrated in alley but still above Level A here and in Room 7-20)
Average d. Locus XXIII = 0.20

XXIV. Room 7-16
005/355
East Balk u. 20 (0.27 d.), Level A/B
u. 20 (Locus XXIV) underlies u. 19 (Locus V), which is Level A (probably) in Room 7-7 only
Average d. Locus XIV = 0.27

XXV. Rooms 7-7, 7-16, and 7-17
005/360
u. 2 (0.13 d.), Level A (in Rooms 7-7 and 7-17 only; above Level A in Room 7-16?)
u. 3. (0.13 d.), Level A/B (Level A in Room 7-16; Level B in Rooms 7-7 and 7-17?)
Average d. Locus XXV = 0.26

XXVI. Room 7-16 and alley/ambitus
005/360
North Balk u. 7 (0.26 d.), Level A/B
Average d. Locus XXVI = 0.26

XXVII. Room 7-17 and alley/ambitus
005/360
East Balk u. 11 (0.21 d.), Level A
Average d. Locus XXVII = 0.21

XXVIII. Room 7-17 hearth
005/360
u. 8 (0.25 d.), Level A
Average d. Locus XXVIII = 0.25

Total number of stratigraphic units in Level A–Level A/B strata of House 7 formed by Loci I–XXVIII = 67
Average depth of Level A–Level A/B strata = 0.21[1]

[1] Excludes Loci VII (Room 7-7 kopron), VIII (Room 7-7 well), and XXVIII (Room 7-17 hearth).

B. House A

I. Rooms 6-80 and 6-81, Avenue B, and small area of Street 4
115/360
u. 3 (0.14 d.), Level A stratum at end; lies in Rooms 6-80 and 6-81, Avenue B, and small area of Street 4
u. 3 (Locus I) overlies u. 4 (Locus II) in Street 4
u. 5 (0.09 d.), Level A (reaches Avenue B road metal); lies in Avenue B and Room 6-80
u. 6 (0.06 d.), Level A(?); lies in Room 6-81
u. 9 (0.09 d.), Level A (reaches Avenue B road metal); lies in Avenue B and Room 6-80
Average d. Locus I = 0.13

II. Street 4, Room 6-81, and small area of Avenue B
115/360
u. 4 (0.22 maximum d.), Level A (reaches Street 4 and Avenue B road metal); lies in Street 4 and small area of Avenue B
u. 4 (Locus II) underlies u. 3 (Locus I) in Room 6-81, Avenue B, and small portion of Street 4
u. 10 (0.64 d.), Level A in Street 4 (road metal) and Room 6-81(?); lies in Street 4 and Room 6-81
115/365
u. 3 (0.32 d.), Level A in Street 4 (road metal), still above Level A in Room 6-81(?); lies in Street 4 (open deposit 1) and small portion of Room 6-81
u. 4 (0.13 d.), Level A in Room 6-81(?); lies entirely in Room 6-81
u. 5 (0.62 d.), Level A in Street 4 (road metal) and Room 6-81(?); lies in Street 4 and Room 6-81

120/365
u. 8 (0.23 d.), Level A in Street 4 (road metal); lies entirely in Street 4
Average d. Locus II = 0.43

III. Room 6-81a
120/360
u. 7 (0.10 d.), Level A(?)
Average d. Locus III = 0.10

IV. Room 6-81 kopron
120/360
u. 8, 10, and 11, Level A debris fill feature
Very few finds recorded for u. 8, none recorded for u. 10 and 11 (omitted from finds summary)
Maximum d. Locus IV = 1.35

V. Room 6-81b courtyard
120/360
u. 12 (0.16 d.), spans Level A/B
No finds recorded
u. 16 (0.23 d.), Level A
120/365
u. 7 (0.07 d.), Level A
u. 7 (Locus V) underlies u. 3 (Locus VI) in Room 6-81 and u. 4 (Locus VII) in Rooms 6-81 and 6-82
Average d. Locus V = 0.15

VI. Room 6-81c pastas, Room 6-86, and small areas of Rooms 6-81b, 6-85, and 6-88
120/360
u. 9 (0.17 d.), Level A in Room 6-81c (possible irregular surfacing of cobbles and plaster); lies in 6-81c
u. 17 (0.51 d.), spans topsoil to Level A in Rooms 6-81c and 6-85(?), still above Level A in Room 6-86 (where it may overlie threshold/step down from Room 6-81c); lies in Rooms 6-81c, 6-85, and 6-86
120/365
u. 3 (0.19 d.), Level A in Room 6-81c; lies in 6-81
Overlies u. 7 (Locus V) in Room 6-81b
u. 6 (0.12 d.), spans Level A/B(?) in Room 6-81c; lies in Room 6-81c
125/365
u. 4 (0.31 d.), spans Level A/B in Room 6-81c, Level A in Room 6-88; lies in Room 6-81 and small portion of Room 6-88
Average d. Locus VI = 0.33

VII. Rooms 6-81b and 6-82
120/365
u. 4 (0.11 d.), Level A plaster floor in portion of Room 6-82 but may pass into Level B where floor destroyed, still above Level A in Room 6-81b
Overlies u. 7 (Locus V) in Room 6-81b
Average d. Locus VII = 0.11

VIII. Rooms 6-81a, 6-85, and small area of Avenue B
120/355
u. 13 (0.57 d.), may reach Level A in Room 6-85 (still above or well below?), mixed Level A/B in 6-81a(?) with possible robbing disturbance along house frontage in Avenue B (but cf. problems indicated by balloon photo and possible Level A plaster floor in Room 6-85 [Locus XI, 120/355, u.12])
Average d. Locus VII = 0.57

IX. Room 6-85
120/360
u. 6 (0.12 d.), possible Level A (or still above? cf. possible Level A plaster floor in Room 6-85 [Locus XI, 120/355, u.12])
Average d. Locus IX = 0.12

X. Room 6-84 and small area of Room 6-85
120/355
u. 6 (0.05 d.), Level A in Room 6-84 (plaster floor) but still above in Room 6-85(?); lies in Rooms 6-84 and small area of 6-85
Only 1 sherd (Roman) and 6 tile fragments (omitted from finds summary)
Average d. Locus X = 0.05

XI. Room 6-83, Avenue B, and small areas of Rooms 6-84 and 6-85
120/355
u. 12 (0.57 d.), Level A in Rooms 6-83 (open deposit 1), 6-84 (plaster floor), and Avenue B, possible Level A (or A/B) in Room 6-85 (plaster floor); lies in Room 6-83, Avenue B, and small portions of Rooms 6-84 and 6-85
125/355
u. 6 (0.12 d.), Level A in Room 6-83 (plaster floor); lies in Room 6-85
Average d. Locus XI = 0.35

XII. Room 6-83 open deposit 1
125/355
u. 6 - open deposit 1 (n.a.), storage bin rim resting on Level A surface of Room 6-83
Maximum d. Locus XII n.a.

XIII. Room 6-83 open deposit 2
125/355
u. 6 - open deposit 2 (0.69 d.), pithos sunk into Level A surface of Room 6-83
Maximum d. Locus XIII = 0.69

XIV. Room 6-83 open deposit 3
125/355
u. 6 - open deposit 3 (0.75 d.), circular pit cut into Level A surface of Room 6-83 (overdug, mixed Level A/B fill)
Maximum d. Locus XIV = 0.75

XV. Room 6-86
125/360
u. 3 (0.58 d.), mixed Level A/B (reaches Level B at SE end where more deeply excavated, trench notebook observes that one to two floor levels apparently dug through)
u. 8 (n.a.), Level A floor reached (irregular chalky surface)
Maximum d. Locus XV = 0.58

XVI. Room 6-88
125/360
u. 6 (0.17 d.), Level A, ends just above floor u. 10 (0.08 d.), Level A floor cleared (worn plaster over rubble underpinning, latter = Level B?)
Average d. Locus XVI = 0.25

XVII. Room 6-88 well
125/360
u. 10 and open deposits 1–3 (1.41 d.)
u. 12–15 (1.70 d.)
Maximum d. Locus XVII = 3.11

XVIII. Room 6-87
125/355
u. 4 (0.59 d.), spans Level A/B (no trace of floor)
125/360
u. 5 (0.17 d.), Level A (just above plaster floor)
u. 7 (0.09 d.), spans Level A/B (plaster floor in eastern portion)
u. 11 (n.a.), Level A floor
130/360
u. 5 (0.26 d.), Level A plaster floor, possible Level B reached where floor level not preserved
Average d. Locus XVIII = 0.37

Total number of stratigraphic units in Level A–Level A/B strata in House A formed by Loci I–XVIII = 49
Average depth of Level A–Level A/B strata = 0.27 m [2]

[2] Excludes Loci IV (Room 6-81 kopron), XII–XIV (Room 6-83 open deposit and negative features), and XVII (Room 6-88 well).

C. House C

I. Room 6-62 and Street 4
100/345
u. 4 (0.21 d.), Level A; lies in Room 6-62 and Street 4 where road metal reached and drain cover slab exposed in Room 6-62 (presence of Roman pottery indicating some contamination)
u. 5 (0.07 d.), probably still in Level A; lies in Room 6-62; bit of floor plaster along east scarp overlain by road metal and drain cover slab
Average d. Locus I = 0.28

II. Room 6-63 and small areas of Rooms 6-59, 6-62, 6-67, and Street 4
100/345
u. 6 (0.12 d.), Level A ("plaster" floor); lies in Room 6-63
u. 9 (0.10 d.), Level A in Room 6-63, but no mention of surfacing here, in Rooms 6-62, 6-67, or Street 4; lies in Room 6-63 and small areas of Rooms 6-62, 6-67, and Street 4
u. 10 (0.18 d.), Level A in Room 6-63 where cover slab for drain exposed; lies in Room 6-63 and small areas of Rooms 6-62, 6-67, and Street 4
100/350
Although u. 2 and 5 noted on archival phase plan, u. 2 lies primarily in Room 6-67, while u. 5 is tiny and yielded almost no finds (both omitted from finds summary)
095/345
u. 4 (0.29 d.), Level A ("plaster" floor); lies in Room 6-63
u. 6 (0.46 d.), Level A ("plaster" floor); lies in Room 6-63
Presence of Roman pottery (small quantity) suggests some contamination
u. 8 (0.16 d.), Level A in Room 6-63, Level B(?) in Room 6-59; lies in Room 6-63, and small portion of Room 6-59
"Threshold" between Rooms 6-59 and 6-63 appears, no mention of floor in Room 6-63
Average d. Locus II = 0.23

III. Room 6-55
095/340
u. 8 (0.35 d.), Level A(?); lies in small portion of Room 6-55 (and cuts across return wall for doorway of Room 6-56)
Only u. to reach Level A surface in 6-55 (hard packed with pebbles); possibly A/B?
Average d. Locus III = 0.35

IV. Room 6-56 and small areas of Room 6-61 and Street 4
095/340
u. 2 (0.16 d.), Level A in Room 6-56, where hard packed white layer in western half equated with floor; still above Level A in Room 6-61 and Street 4
Roman pottery and worn plain-ware fragments suggest some mixing with topsoil and intrusions from robbing that removed ashlar orthostates of wall along Street 4; u. 2 (Locus IV) overlies u. 6 (Locus V) in Room 6-61
u. 3 (0.10 d.), Level A in Room 6-56, where floor of u. 2 exposed in eastern half, still above Level A in Street 4; lies in 6-56 and small portion

Street 4
u. 9 (0.16 d.), Level A (or A/B?) in Room 6-56
Some artifacts atop, some embedded into and below floor noted in u. 2 and 3
Average d. Locus IV = 0.42

V. Room 6-61
095/340
u. 6 (0.24 d.), Level A ("plaster" floor)
Underlies u. 2 (Locus IV), which is Level A in Room 6-56 only
u. 15 (0.31 d.), Level A ("plaster" floor)
095/345
u. 5 (0.39 d.), Level A ("plaster" floor = "hard white packed surface"?)
u. 10 (0.21 d.), Level A ("plaster" floor)
Average d. Locus V = 0.29

VI. Room 6-60
095/340
u. 12 (0.49 d.), Level A/B in small area in northwest corner of room
095/345
u. 2 (0.24 d.), Level A floor? (cf. underlying u. 3 where whitish "calcrete pan" noted in south portion of room)
090/345
u. 12 (0.37 d.), Level A floor (white "plaster", possibly only south portion of room paved)
Average d. = 0.37 (without 095/340 u. 12 = 0.31)

VII. Room 6-59 and small areas of Rooms 6-58, 6-63, and 6-64
095/350
u. 8 (0.11 d.), Level A likely; area small and heavily disturbed by roots, jumbled building material; lies in Room 6-59, small area of Room 6-64, and along ashlar footings of Room 6-58 (see below, 090/350 u. 5)
090/345
u. 5 (ca. 0.25 d.), Level A floor as in Room 6-53: "hard packed plaster w/small pebbles"; lies in Room 6-59
u. 11 (0.30 d.), Level A floor, as u. 5; lies in Room 6-59
u. 14 (0.21 d.), Level A; lies in Room 6-59
090/350
u. 5 (0.27 d.), Level A in Room 6-59(?); very confused, no certain floor level, also explores ashlar footings of Room 6-58
If ashlar orthostates of Room 6-58 robbed here, disturbance likely; very few finds
Average d. Locus VII = 0.23

VIII. Rooms 6-64 and 6-69, small areas of Room 6-68, and along footings of Room 6-58
095/350
u. 2 (0.08 d.), Level A in Room 6-64 (plaster floor), above Level A in Rooms 6-68 and 6-69
Omitted from finds summary since most of u. 2 lay beyond House C
u. 11 (0.27 d.), Level A/B(?); lies in Rooms 6-59 and 6-64
Omitted from finds summary since most of u. 11 lay beyond House C
Average d. Locus VIII = 0.18

IX. Room 6-54 and small areas of Rooms 6-52 and 6-55
095/340
u. 4 (0.15 d.), Level A ("plaster" floor); lies in Room 6-55
u. 11 (0.24 d.), fails to reach Level A floor but within Level A stratum; lies in Room 6-55
090/335
u. 5 (0.32 d.), Level A in Room 6-54 (or just above? "plaster" floor not noted but only 0.03 to 0.04 above it elsewhere), still above Level A in Room 6-55; lies in Room 6-54 and small area of Room 6-55
u. 6 (0.38 d.), Level A in Room 6-54 (or as u. 5, just above it?), still above Level A in Room 6-52; lies in Room 6-54 and small area of Room 6-52
090/340
u. 6 (0.16 d.), Level A ("hard white surface"); lies in Room 6-54
North Balk u. 2 (n.a.), Level A in Room 6-54 (presumably), no information available for stratigraphic position in Room 6-55; lies in Room 6-54 and small area of Room 6-55
Average d. Locus IX = 0.26

X. Rooms 6-53 and 6-54
090/345
u. 13 (0.42 d.), Level A reached on both sides of wall in Rooms 6-53 and 6-54
Finds split between Rooms 6-53 and 6-54 (loom weight and metal objects from Room 6-54?)
Average d. Locus X = 0.41

XI. Room 6-53 southwest portico
090/340
u. 5 (0.17 d.), Level A ("plaster" floor below roof-tile fall, no tile count available)
085/340
u. 6 (0.11 d.), Level A
u. 8 (0.07 d.), Level A, no surface recognized beyond earthen one
North Balk u. 3 (0.68 d.), Level A
All North Balk finds mixed together in finds notebook; all North Balk finds included in finds summary
East Balk u. 5 (0.14 d.), Level A
080/340
u. 10 (0.48 d.), Level A (tiny unit)
Average d. Locus XI = 0.29 (TR 080/340: u. 10, excluded from average d. estimate owing to its small size)

XII. Room 6-53 courtyard, and small areas of Rooms 6-50 and 6-54
- 090/340
  - u. 8 (0.56 d.), spans topsoil to Level A; lies in Room 6-53 and small portion of Room 6-54
  - u. 8 (Locus XII) overlies u. 6 (090/345, Locus XIII: double pit feature in northern corner of Room 6-53)
- 090/345
  - u. 3 (0.46 d.), Level A ("uneven floor of hard packed plaster and small pebbles")
  - u. 3 (Locus XII) overlies u. 6 (090/345, Locus XIII: double pit feature in northern corner of Room 6-53)
- 085/345
  - u. 4 (0.09 d.), Level A (where plaster well platform exposed) and Level A in Room 6-53; lies in Room 6-53 and small area of Room 6-50
  - open deposit 2 (0.31 d.), Level A ("catch basin" in well platform)
  - u. 5 (0.11 d.), Level A (floor not yet exposed); lies in Room 6-53
  - u. 6 (0.09 d.), Level A ("plaster" floor, "white and pebbly"); lies in Room 6-53
  - u. 7 (0.31 d.), Level A; lies in Room 6-53
  - u. 12 (0.44 d.), spans topsoil to Level A (plaster floor noted)

Average d. Locus XII = 0.41 (085/345 open deposit 2 is negative feature, so excluded from average d.)

XIII. Room 6-53 double pit
- 090/345
  - u. 6 (ca. 0.28 maximum d.), Level A ("plaster" lined hollows)
  - As excavated, u. 6 extends into 090/340, underlies u. 8 (Locus XII, 090/340) and u. 3 (Locus XIII, 090/345), which are Level A in 6-53 courtyard

Maximum d. Locus XIII = 0.28

XIV. Room 6-53 cistern
- 085/345
  - u. 16–17, and cistern u. 1–12, Level A

Maximum d. Locus XIV = 5.00

XV. Room 6-57 and small area of Room 6-59
- 090/345
  - u. 4 (n.a.), Level A? (floor noted to be same composition and at same elevation as in Room 6-53); lies in Room 6-57
  - u. 8 (0.33 d.), Level A? (end elevation may be just above actual floor); lies in Room 6-57 and small area of Room 6-39
- 090/350
  - u. 4 (0.04 d.), Level A? (but cf. u. 8 where definite "plaster" surface reached); lies in Room 6-57
  - All but inventoried finds lost?
  - u. 8 (0.17 d.), Level A? ("plaster" surface at ca. 1.70 masl, ca. 0.10 m below other units here); lies in Room 6-57
- 085/345
  - u. 14 (0.11 d.), Level A? lies in Room 6-57 at same elevation as other units (except 090/350 u. 8)

Average d. Locus XV = 0.22 (excluding 090/350 u. 8 = 0.16)

XVI. Room 6-58
- 090/350
  - u. 3 (0.18 d.), Level A ("smooth layer of pebbles covered with plaster")

Average d. Locus XVI = 0.18

Total number of stratigraphic units in Level A–Level A/B strata of House C formed by Loci I–XVI = 67

Average depth of Level A–Level A/B strata = 0.29 m

D. House D

I. Room 6-26
- 055/330
  - u. 3 (0.44 d.), spans collapse debris to Level A (surface of rubble and earth)
- 060/325
  - u. 11 (0.12 d.), Level A, contaminated (see below, u. 24)
  - u. 24 (0.30 d.), Level A, contaminated
  - Both u. 11 and 24 reach Level A earthen floor that underlay roof-tile collapse but show contamination by Roman pottery; trench notebook suggests pit visible in scarp; other than roof-tile count, finds largely insignificant; both u. 11 and 24 overlie Locus II (Room 6-26 kopron)
  - u. 38 (0.21 d.), Level A
  - u. 43 (ca. 0.11 d.), Level A
- 060/330
  - u. 5 (0.11 d.), Level A (plaster surface in eastern portion)
  - Overlies Locus II (Room 6-26 kopron)
  - u. 13 (0.30 d.), Level A
  - Full find count lacking? (e.g., no tile)
- 065/325
  - u. 10 (0.40 d.), Level A
- 065/330
  - u. 6 (0.20 d.), Level A at end?
  - Pottery joins with and between u. 3, 9, and 12 noted in trench notebook but not clear from finds notebook; cf. troughlike feature exposed in u. 9 and 12 (Level A/B?); most pottery in Locus I comes from this unit

Average d. Locus I = 0.28 (if 065/330 u. 9 included = 0.29)

II. Room 6-26 kopron
060/325
u. 19, 25–34, Level A
060/330
u. 6–10, Level A
Locus II overlain by u. 11 and 24 (Locus I, 060/325) and u. 5 (Locus I, 060/330)
Average d. Locus II = 1.06

III. Room 6-26 well
060/325
u. 21, reaches Level A but contaminated by Roman pottery; cf. u. 11 and 24 (Locus I, 060/325)
u. 48–51, Level A
u. 45–47 explore below wellhead proper
Maximum d. Locus III = 4.36

IV. Room 6-27
065/320
u. 6 (0.36 d.), Level A
065/320 u. 6 the only one excavated in Room 6-27 to reach possible Level A floor
Average d. Locus IV = 0.36

V. Room 6-29
060/325
u. 39 (0.29 d.), Level A? (end elevation just above floor level of Room 6-29 elsewhere)
065/325
u. 17 (0.08 d.), Level A
u. 18 (0.10 d.), Level A
u. 19 (0.02 d.), Level A abandonment? (comprises small circle of ash, no finds)
Tile fall of u. 3 that overlay u. 17 and 18
065/330
u. 7 (0.31 d.), Level A? (or just above at end?)
u. 39 (0.09 d.), Level A
Average d. Locus V = 0.22 (excludes 065/325 u. 19)

VI. Room 6-29 basin below spout of press
065/325
open deposit 1 (0.29 d.), Level A abandonment? (few finds)
Average d. Locus VI = 0.29

VII. Room 6-29 pithos adjacent press
065/330
open deposit 1 (0.78 d.), Level A abandonment?
Average d. Locus VII = 0.78

VIII. Room 6-28
065/325
u. 20 (0.13 d.), Level A
u. 20 extends into 070/325; cf. u. 21 (0.10 d.), early Level A/Level B(?)
Average d. Locus VIII = 0.13 (with u. 21 = 0.12)

IX. Rooms 6-30 and 6-31
065/330
u. 8 (0.28 d.), Level A in Room 6-31 (still above Level A in Room 6-30?); lies in Rooms 6-30 and 6-31
u. 8 overlies open deposit 2 (Locus X hearth) in Room 6-30 and u. 37 (Locus XI) in Room 6-30
u. 25 (0.18 d.), Level A; lies in Room 6-30
065/335
u. 5 (0.10–0.18 d.), Level A; lies in Room 6-30
u. 6 (0.07 d.), Level A; lies in Room 6-30
065/335 u. 7 included on archival strata plan but probably = Level B
Average d. Locus IX = 0.17

X. Room 6-30 hearth
065/330
open deposit 2 (ca. 0.09 d.), Level A abandonment(?)
Open deposit 2 underlies u. 8 (Locus IX) in Room 6-30
Average d. Locus X = 0.09

XI. Room 6-30
065/330
u. 37 (0.13 d.), Level A
u. 37 underlies u. 8 (Locus IX), which reached Level A floor in Room 6-31 only
Average d. Locus XI = 0.13

XII. Rooms 6-32 and 6-33
065/335
u. 4 (0.13 d.), Level A
065/330 u. 20 included on archival strata plan but fails to reach Level A
Average d. Locus XII = 0.13

XIII. Room 6-32
070/335
u. 5 (0.11 d.), Level A
Average d. Locus XIII = 0.11

XIV. Room 6-35b
065/325
u. 15 (0.25 d.), Level A
065/330
u. 28 (0.06 d.), Level A
u. 29 (0.15 d.), Level A (hard white floor noted)
u. 30 (0.09 d.), Level A (excavation of "pit")
u. 36 (0.09 d.), Level A
070/325
u. 17 (ca. 0.10 d.), Level A
u. 17 underlies u. 11 (Locus XV), which is Level A in Room 6-35a only
070/330
u. 5 (0.10 d.), Level A abandonment(?). Underlies u. 4 (Locus XVI), which is Level A in Room 6-36 only; pottery deposit equates with that of u. 9 (Locus XVI) in Rooms 6-35b and 6-36
u. 6 (0.07 d.), Level A (white [plaster?] floor present)

u. 17 (0.10 d.), Level A

Average d. Locus XIV = 0.13 (065/330 u. 30 is negative feature, so excluded from average d.)

XV. Room 6-35a and small area of Room 6-35b

070/325

u. 4 (ca. 0.43 d.), Level A; lies in Room 6-35a

u. 11 (0.21 d.), Level A in Room 6-35a only, still above Level A in Room 6-35b; lies in Room 6-35a and small area of Room 6-35b, where it overlies u. 17 (Locus XIV)

u. 12 (0.03 d.), Level A; lies in Room 6-35a

Hard white floor exposed in u. 11 and 12, fragments of several joining amphoras from u. 8, 9, and 10 (over u. 11), counted as Level A in finds summary (fallen from above?)

070/330

u. 7 (0.37 d.), Level A; lies in Room 6-35a

Average d. Locus XV = 0.37

XVI. Room 6-36 and small areas of Rooms 6-32 and 6-35b

070/330

u. 4 (0.30 d.), Level A in Room 6-36 (still above Level A in Room 6-35b, where it overlies u. 5 [Locus XIV])

u. 8 (0.34 d.), Level A abandonment? lies in Room 6-36

u. 9 (0.33 d.), Level A abandonment? lies in Room 6-36 and small portion of Room 6-35b

Pottery deposit equates with that of u. 5 (Locus XIV) in Room 6-35b

u. 10 (0.20 d.), Level A ("hard packed floor"); lies in Room 6-36 and small area of Room 6-35b

u. 11 (0.54 d.), Level A ("hard packed floor"); lies in Room 6-36

All but inventoried and kept pieces lost from finds notebook?

u. 12b (0.29 d.), Level A (combination of finds from "Roman hearth" excavated in u. 12a biases material from u. 12b); lies in Room 6-36

u. 20 (0.12 d.), Level A; lies in Room 6-36

u. 23 (0.20 d.), Level A at end; lies in Room 6-36 and small area of Room 6-32

u. 26 (0.14 d.), Level A; lies in Room 6-36 and small area of Room 6-32

u. 28 (0.06 d.), Level A; lies in Room 6-36 and small area of Room 6-32

u. 30 (0.12 d.), Level A; lies in Room 6-36, entirely in 070/335 but excavated as part of 070/330

u. 33 (0.13 d.), Level A (pit/depression feature); lies in Room 6-36 and, like u. 30, is entirely in 070/335 but excavated as part of 070/330

075/330

u. 7 (0.61 maximum d.), spans Level A/B; lies in Room 6-36 (excavation of "pit" feature = Level B?)

Average d. Locus XVI = 0.41 (070/330 u. 33 and 075/330 u. 7 are negative features, so excluded from average d.)

Total number of stratigraphic units in Level A–Level A/B strata of House D formed by Loci I–XVI = 74

Average depth of Level A–Level A/B strata (excluding negative features) = 0.22

E. House E

I. Rooms 6-9, 6-10 ambitus, 6-12, and Street 3

050/315

u. 5 (0.06 d.), spans collapse debris to Level A abandonment; lies in Rooms 6-9, 6-10, 6-12, and Street 3 but primarily in Room 6-10 ambitus where it seems to recover Level A abandonment debris (u. 5 still above Level A elsewhere)

u. 5 (Locus I) overlies u. 9 (Locus II) in Room 6-12

u. 8 (0.17 d.), Level A abandonment; lies in Rooms 6-9, 6-10, and Street 3

u. 10 (0.18 d.), Level A; lies in Room 6-10

Average d. Locus I = 0.41

II. Room 6-12

050/315

u. 9 (0.21), Level A (and Level B?)

u. 9 (Locus II) underlies u. 5 (Locus I) in Room 6-12

Average d. Locus II = 0.21

III. Room 6-13 and small area of Room 6-12

050/315

u. 6 (0.04 d.), Level A (and Level B?)

u. 7 (0.08 d.), Level A (and Level B?)

Average d. Locus III = 0.12

IV. Room 6-13 and Street 3

050/315

East Balk u. 4 (n.a.), Level A

Average d. Locus IV = n.a.

V. Room 6-12 and small area of Room 6-13

050/315

u. 13 (0.35 d.), spans collapse debris to Level A

u. 14 (0.20 d.), spans collapse debris to Level A

u. 15 (0.12 d.), Level A (and Level B?)

u. 16 (0.17 d.), Level A

u. 17 (0.14 d.), Level A (and Level B?)

Average d. Locus V = 0.49

VI. Room 6-19
050/320
u. 10 (n.a.), Level A
North Balk u. 2 (0.20 maximum d.?), spans collapse debris to Level A
055/315
u. 13 (0.60 d.), spans collapse debris to Level A
055/320
u. 7 (0.10 maximum d.?), Level A
u. 11 (0.10 maximum d.?), Level A
u. 12 (0.16 d.), Level A
Average d. Locus VI = 0.34 (055/315 u. 13 is very small but makes average d. of Locus VI considerably greater; without u. 13, average d. = 0.19)

VII. Room 6-19 well
050/320
u. 12–15 (problem with elevations; 1.04–2.75 maximum d.), Level A
Maximum d. Locus VII = 1.04–2.75

VIII. Rooms 6-12 and 6-18
055/315
u. 4 (0.11 d.), Level A
u. 6 (0.12 d.), Level A (and Level B in Room 6-12? still above Level A in Room 6-18)
u. 4 and 6 (Locus VIII) overlie u. 11, 15, and 16 (Locus IX) in Room 6-18
Average d. Locus VIII = 0.23

IX. Room 6-18
055/315
u. 11 (0.20–0.36 d.), spans collapse debris to Level A
u. 15 (0.13–0.15 d.), Level A
u. 16 (0.18 d.), Level A
u. 11, 15, and 16 (Locus IX) underlie u. 4 and 6 (Locus VIII) in Room 6-18
055/320
u. 10 (0.11 d.), Level A
u. 13 (0.12 d.), Level A
u. 14 (0.08 d.), Level A
u. 17 (0.66 d.), spans collapse debris to Level A
Average d. Locus IX = 0.49 (minimum to maximum average d. without u. 17 = 0.41–0.50, minimum to maximum average d. with u. 17 = 0.49–0.55)

X. Room 6-17
055/315
u. 14 (0.16 d.), Level A
u. 17 (0.35 d.), spans collapse debris to Level A
Average d. Locus X = 0.26

XI. Room 6-20 bothros
055/320
u. 18–20 (1.13 maximum d.), Level A (or Level B?)
Average d. Locus XI = 1.13

XII. Room 6-20
055/320
u. 8 (0.10 d.), Level A
u. 16 (0.40 d.), spans collapse debris to Level A
u. 22 (0.40 d.), spans collapse debris to Level A
u. 23 (0.05 d.), Level A
055/325
u. 11 (0.17 d.), Level A
u. 15 (0.08 d.), Level A
060/320
u. 7 (0.10 d.), Level A
u. 8 (0.10 d.), Level A
Locus XII has been subdivided into XIIa–c in order to study spread of finds across courtyard
XIIa = 060/320 u. 7, 8
XIIb = 055/320 u. 8
055/320 u. 16
XIIc = 055/320 u. 22, 23
055/325 u. 11, 15
Average d. Locus XII = 0.28

XIII. Room 6-22
055/325
u. 16 (0.13 d.), Level A
u. 18 (0.10 d.), Level A (or A/B?)
u. 25 (0.15 d.), Level A
u. 29 (0.42 d.), Level A
Average d. Locus XIII = 0.27

XIV. Room 6-21 and small area of Room 6-22
055/325
u. 27 (0.40 d.), Level A/B; lies in Room 6-21
060/320
u. 22 (0.71 d.), Level A/B; lies in Room 6-21
060/325
u. 15 (0.17 d.), Level A; lies in Room 6-21 and small area of Room 6-22
u. 17 (0.12 d.), Level B; lies in Room 6-21
Although artifacts from u. 17 are exclusively Level B, it is included in finds summary since other units in Room 6-21 = Level A/B and entire chamber cleared to same depth
u. 44 (0.54 d.), Level A/B; lies in Room 6-21
Average d. Locus XIV = 0.49

XV. Room 6-16 and small area of Room 6-17
060/315
u. 4 (0.11 d.), Level A; lies in Room 6-16 and small area of Room 6-17
u. 5 (0.04 d.), Level A/B; lies in Room 6-16
Average d. Locus XV = 0.15

XVI. Room 6-16 and small area of Room 6-20
060/320
u. 5 (0.22 d.), Level A/B in Room 6-16 (still above in Room 6-20)
Underlies Locus XVII (Room 6-20 open deposit) but overlies Locus XIIa (Room 6-20) in southwest corner of 060/320
Average d. Locus XVI = 0.22

XVII. Room 6-20 open deposit
060/320
open deposit 1 (0.55 maximum d.), Level A
Overlies Locus XVI (Room 6-20)
Maximum d. Locus XVII = 0.55

XVIII. Room 6-23 and small area of Room 6-24
060/320
u. 9 (0.18 d.), Level A
Amphora joins with u. 6, and u. 7 and 8?
Average d. Locus XVIII = 0.18

XIX. Room 6-23
060/320
u. 18 (0.58 d.), spans collapse debris to Level A
Average d. Locus XIX = 0.58

XX. Room 6-24
060/320
u. 17 (0.29 d.), Level A
u. 19 (0.26 d.), Level A
u. 21 (0.88 d.), Level A/B
060/325
u. 16 (0.12 d.), Level A
u. 40 (0.34 d.), Level A
065/320
u. 9 (0.26 d.), Level A
065/325
u. 5 (0.06 d.), Level A
Average d. Locus XX = 0.37

XXI. Room 6-25 and small area of Room 6-23
060/320
u. 16 (0.14 d.), Level A, lies in Room 6-25
065/320
u. 5 (0.23 d.), Level A, lies in Room 6-25 and small area of Room 6-23
u. 10 (0.37 d.), spans collapse debris to Level A, lies in Room 6-25
Average d. Locus XXI = 0.25

Total number of stratigraphic units in Level A–Level A/B strata of House E formed by Loci I–XXI = 68
Average depth of Level A–Level A/B strata (excluding negative features) = 0.31 [3]

[3] Excludes Loci VII (Room 6-20 well), XI (Room 6-20 bothros), XVII (Room 6-20 open deposit), and Locus IV (Room 6-20 and Street 3, for which no depth available).

– APPENDIX II –

Inventoried Finds from Level A–Level A/B Strata by House and Locus Houses 7, A, C, D, and E

Inventoried finds are grouped by the loci associated with each house. Each find belongs to a unit (u.) within a trench (identified by the last three digits of the north and east coordinates). Halieis inventory numbers are preceded by letters indicating the category of object (HC = Halieis clay, HL = lamp, HM = metal, HN = numismata [coins], HP = pottery, HS = stone, HV = various).

The following abbreviations are used in Appendix II: AE = bronze, BF = black figure, BG = black gloss ("glaze"), CW = coarse ware, FE = iron, FW = fine ware, PB = lead, PW = plain ware, RF = red figure.

Dates are given in parentheses if there are close, dated parallels (primarily Attic). Where possible, pottery fabric is identified (Attic, Corinthian, and so forth). "Eastern Peloponnesian" refers to a fabric that may be local but has not yet been distinguished from Laconian or Argive (Rudolph 1974, 127). "Profile" means that the vessel is not whole but its profile is preserved. The descriptions are taken from the initial inventory and do not represent final publication.

A. House 7 (cf. Appendix I.A and Fig. 8)

Locus I

HP 2197 (000/350 u. 11)
CW chytra, nearly whole

HP 2373 (005/345 u. 10)
FW BG kantharos handle

HP 2614 (005/340 u. 2)
FW BG oinochoe handle with graffito

HP 2615 (005/340 u. 2)
FW BG shallow askos foot/body/shoulder (400–350)

HP 2625 (000/345 u. 2)
PW handle, impressed pattern (Prehistoric?)

HP 2651 (000/345 u. 2)
FW rim (open vessel), banding (Geometric?)

HP 2918 (000/345 u. 2)
FW RF bell-krater: rim with laurel leaf pattern

HP 2919 (000/345 u. 2)
FW RF closed vessel neck, laurel leaf pattern

HP 2922 (000/345 u. 2)
FW BG small bowl with incurving rim profile, Attic

HL 267 (000/350 u. 12)
BG lamp body fragment

HL 380 (000/345 u. 2)
BG lamp rim fragment

HS 519 (000/345 u. 2)
limestone architectural fragment

HS 539 (000/345 u. 2)
limestone pier capital

HM 1358 (005/340 u. 2)
AE sheet with FE nail

HM 1383 (000/345 u. 2)
PB strip

HN 1974-13 (000/350 u. 12)
AE Tiryns (4th)

HN 1975-127 (000/345 u. 2)
AE Hermione (350–300)

Locus II
HS 632 (000/350 u. 10)
u. 29 (0.42 d.), Level A
obsidian bladelet fragment

Locus III
HP 2563 (000/355 u. 9)
CW lekanis(?) lid, traces of painted bands
HP 2643 (000/355 u. 5)
FW open vessel body fragment, painted (Geometric?)
HP 2655 (000/355 u. 5)
FW BG trefoil oinochoe/chous fragments (350–325)
HP 2656 (000/355 u. 5)
PW spouted lekane rim, body, handle (burned)
HP 2662 (000/355 u. 5)
CW basin profile
HP 2846 (000/355 u. 9)
FW RF closed vessel body fragments, tongue pattern, drapery
HP 2881 (000/355 u. 9)
FW BG saltcellar profile (350–325)
HP 2897 (000/355 u. 9)
FW one-handled cup profile, Corinthian
HP 2899 (000/355 u. 9)
PW amphora foot, very worn
HC 884 (000/350 u. 26)
conical loom weight
HL 341 (000/355 u. 9)
BG lamp rim/nozzle
HM 1256 (000/355 u. 5)
AE rooster figurine
HM 1259 (000/355 u. 5)
FE two-headed nail/clamp
HM 1367 (000/350 u. 27)
FE nail
HM 1368 (000/350 u. 27)
FE nail
HM 1369 (000/350 u. 27)
2 FE nails
HM 1370 (000/350 u. 27)
AE nail
HM 1372 (000/350 u. 27)
FE scoop fragment
HM 1384 (000/350 u. 27)
FE rod
HM 1393 (000/350 u. 27)
FE strip
HM 1394 (000/350 u. 27)
FE spike
HM 1527 (000/355 u. 4)
AE "sheath" fragment (for curving FE blade?)
HN 1975-106 (000/355 u. 5)
AE Hermione (350–300)

Locus IV
HP 2216 (005/355 u. 3)
FW RF krater body fragments with cross-plate meander
HP 2364 (005/355 u. 3)
FW RF krater body fragments with laurel leaf pattern near rim, cross-plate meander on body, female(?) figure advancing to right and figure with spotted leggings; joins with HP 2613?
HP 2545 (000/360 u. 3)
miniature trefoil oinochoe, Corinthian
HP 2593 (000/355 u. 14)
PW amphora rim, neck, handles
HP 2594 (000/355 u. 14)
CW lekane/tub profile
HP 2613 (005/355 u. 17 open deposit)
FW RF krater fragment with cross-plate meander, palmette scroll in handle zone, leg of draped female(?) figure advancing to right; joins with HP 2364?
HP 2621 (005/355 u. 17 open deposit)
FW RF hydria/pelike(?) rim fragment with tongue pattern, Attic (5th ?)
HP 2662 (000/355 u. 5)
CW basin/tub profile
HP 2672 (005/355 u. 18 open deposit)
FW BG shallow askos (400–350)
HP 2900 (005/355 u. 18 open deposit)
PW amphora rim, neck, handles, body fragments
HP 2903 (000/355 u. 14)
FW BG stemless cup profile, Argive
HP 2907 (005/355 u. 18 open deposit)
CW lopas profile
HP 2908 (005/355 u. 18 open deposit)
CW jug base, body fragments
HC 833 (000/350 u. 24)
pyramidal loom weight
HL 289 (005/355 u. 3)
BG miniature lamp
HL 336 (000/350 u. 24)
BG lamp profile
HL 338 (005/355 u. 17 open deposit)
BG lamp, nearly whole
HM 1038 (005/355 u. 3)
FE rod/spit handle
HM 1293 (000/355 u. 12)
FE nail
HM 1299 (000/355 u. 12)
FE nail fragments
HM 1310 (000/350 u. 24)
FE nail
HM 1313 (000/350 u. 24)
AE disk edge fragment with PB plated box motif(?) (est. diam. 0.08 m)
HN 1975-157 (005/355 u. 16)
AE Tiryns (4th)

Loci V, VI, XXIV, XXV, XXVI, XXVII, XXVIII
HP 2572 (005/360 u. 11)
FW BG mug profile, Laconian
HC 786 (005/360 u. 3)
conical loom weight with graffito

HC 856 (005/360 u. 11)
base/body fragment of female(?) figure, seated(?) on square base, cloaked, white and red paint (450–425)
HL 332 (005/360 u. 7)
BG lamp nozzle
HL 337 (005/360 u. 2)
semiglazed lamp body fragment
HS 515 (005/360 u. 8 hearth)
shelly limestone fragment (from hearth circuit?)
HM 1224 (005/360 u. 3)
FE nail
HM 1225 (005/360 u. 3)
FE nail
HM 1226 (005/360 u. 3)
FE nail head
HM 1229 (005/360 u. 3)
FE nail
HM 1231 (005/360 u. 3)
FE nail head
HM 1236 (005/360 u. 3)
FE nail head
HM 1239 (005/360 u. 2)
PB "lid" with knob (for pyxis?)
HM 1285 (005/360 u. 8 hearth)
FE spearhead fragment
HM 1287 (005/360 u. 7)
AE "cup," straight sided (max. diam. 0.055)
HM 1324 (000/360 u. 5)
AE coiled wire
HM 1375 (005/355 u. 19)
AE relief ornament with lotus bud; from vessel (handle attachment) or mirror handle?
HN 1975-97 (005/360 u. 3)
AE Hermione (350–300)
HN 1975-134 (005/355 u. 20)
AE Hermione (350–300)
HN 1975-135 (005/355 u. 20)
AE Tiryns (4th)

Locus VII
HP 2682 (000/355 u. 15)
FW BG Attic-type skyphos base/body (375–350)
HP 2683 (000/355 u. 15)
FW RF bell krater rim and body fragments with laurel leaf and tongue patterns, unidentified scene (includes drapery?)
HP 2684 (000/355 u. 15)
FW BG bowl body fragment with stamped palmette circle
HP 2687 (000/355 u. 16)
FW BG body fragment (from lid or askos top?); ribbed, stamped with ovules and palmette
HP 2688 (000/355 u. 16)
FW RF krater(?) body fragment with foot of draped figure, horse's legs and tail in added white, cross-plate meander
HP 2894 (000/355 u. 16)
FW RF body fragment (open vessel), palmette
HP 2895 (000/355 u. 17)
Blister ware squat lekythos rim, neck, shoulder, handle
HP 3036 (000/355 u. 17)
FW RF open vessel body fragment, two lines at right angle
HC 867 (000/355 u. 15)
conical loom weight
HC 869 (000/355 u. 15)
conical loom weight
HC 870 (000/355 u. 15)
pyramidal loom weight
HC 871 (000/355 u. 15)
pyramidal loom weight
HL 347 (000/355 u. 16)
BG lamp
HL 355 (000/355 u. 17)
BG lamp rim/body
HL 356 (000/355 u. 15)
BG lamp rim/body
HL 357 (000/355 u. 15)
BG lamp rim/body
HL 358 (000/355 u. 15)
BG lamp rim/body
HL 360 (000/355 u. 16)
BG lamp base/body
HM 1389 (000/355 u. 17)
AE cylindrical handle?
HM 1397 (000/355 u. 16)
FE socket
HM 1404 (000/355 u. 18)
AE rivet/nail
HM 1416 (000/355 u. 17)
FE nail/tack

Locus VIII
HP 2633 (005/355 u. 6)
FW krater rim fragment, Corinthian/Argive? (Late Geometric I)
HP 2920 (005/355 u. 6)
FW RF bell krater rim fragment, laurel leaf pattern?
HC 751 (005/355 u. 9)
drain pipe(?) fragment
HC 840 (005/355 u. 6)
conical loom weight
HL 383 (005/355 u. 6)
BG lamp rim/body
HS 608 (005/355 u. 6)
obsidian blade segment
HM 1067 (005/355 u. 9)
AE sheet fragments

Loci IX, X, XI, XII, XIII, XIV
HP 2538 (005/345 u. 13)
FW BG small bowl with stamped palmette cross (4th)
HP 2540 (005/345 u. 13)
FW BG stemless cup, Argive

HC 813 (005/350 u. 2)
pyramidal loom weight
HS 521 (000/350 u. 23)
limestone pier capital
HS 574 (005/345 u. 12)
grinding slab, rectangular fragment
HM 997 (005/345 u. 2)
FE spike
HM 1227 (005/350 u. 2)
AE nail
HM 1254 (005/350 u. 2)
AE drop-handle(?) fragment with lotus bud terminal
HM 1298 (000/350 u. 23)
FE spike
HM 1512 (005/350 u. 2)
FE handle(?) fragment

Loci XV, XVI
HP 2568 (005/355 u. 14)
PW body fragment, red fabric, impressed linear motif
HP 2577 (005/355 u. 14)
FW kotyle body fragment with ray pattern (Middle Corinthian?)
HP 2686 (005/350 u. 10)
FW miniature lekythos with net pattern (375–350)
HP 3033 (005/350 u. 10)
FW RF open vessel body fragment, drapery?
HC 877 (005/350 u. 10)
pyramidal loom weight
HL 351(= HL 375) (005/350 u. 10)
BG lamp rim/body
HL 354 (005/350 u. 10)
BG lamp rim/body
HL 374 (005/350 u. 10)
BG lamp rim/body/handle
HS 581 (005/350 u. 10)
obsidian bladelet segment

HM 1290 (005/355 u. 14)
FE sickle blade fragments

Loci XVII, XVIII, XIX
HC 647 (010/350 u. 5)
mold, rectangular to egg shaped with four palmettes linked to cruciform vine pattern; saw-toothed edge to mold motif proper; pierced on one end?
HC 892 (010/350 u. 5)
CW pithos lid fragment
HS 493 (010/350 u. 5)
stone button
HS 551 (010/350 u. 10)
stone rubber/polisher
HM 1330 (010/350 u. 10)
FE socketed tip (staff end?)
HM 1362 (010/350 u. 10)
AE sheet with embossed palmette-floral design
HM 1379 (010/350 u. 10)
FE nail

Locus XX
HM 1508 (010/355 u. 5)
FE chisel

Loci XXI, XXII, XXIII
HP 2582 (010/355 u. 2)
FW RF bell(?) krater rim, laurel leaf pattern
HP 2627 (010/355 u. 2)
FW BG pelike foot
HP 2673 (005/355 u. 21)
FW RF skyphos rim/body fragments, female head facing right
HL 352 (010/355 u. 8)
BG lamp rim/body
HM 1008 (010/360 u. 1)
AE jug neck (Roman?)

B. House A (cf. Appendix I.B and Fig. 11)

Locus I
HP 2371 (115/360 u. 6)
FW BG saltcellar profile, Attic (350–325)
HN 1974-3 (115/360 u. 6)
AE Tiryns (4th)

Locus II
HP 2435 (115/365 u. 5)
FW BG squat jug
HP 2483 (155/365 u. 3 open deposit 1)
FW BG bowl body fragment with graffito
HP 2485 (115/365 u. 3 open deposit 1)
CW strainer rim
HP 2531 (115/365 u. 3)
CW storage bin fragments
HP 2532 (115/365 u. 3 open deposit 1)
CW column krater fragments
HP 2533 (115/365 u. 3 open deposit 1)
PW amphora neck/shoulder
HP 2534 (115/365 u. 3 open deposit 1)
PW small mortar
HP 2804 (115/360 u. 10)
PW amphora rim, shoulder, handle
HP 2933 (115/360 u. 10)
FW RF krater(?) body fragments, sphinx body in added white, meander, drapery
HP 2946 (155/365 u. 3)
FW RF oinochoe(?) body fragment, female head facing right
HC 824 (120/365 u. 8)

pyramidal loom weight
HL 405 (115/365 u. 3 open deposit 1)
lamp base
HS 580 (115/365 u. 3)
obsidian blade fragment
HS 592 (115/365 u. 3)
flint flake
HM 1139 (115/365 u. 3)
FE nail head
HM 1140 (115/360 u. 3)
FE shaft
HM 1150 (115/365 u. 3)
FE nail
HM 1300 (115/365 u. 5)
FE nail or handle fragment?
HM 1355 (115/360 u. 10)
FE nail
HM 1360 (115/360 u. 10)
AE finger ring, engraved bezel
HM 1380 (115/360 u. 10)
FE spike

Loci III, IV
no inventoried finds

Locus V
HV 313 (120/365 u. 7)
glass vessel fragments (intrusive?)

Locus VI
HP 2935 (120/360 u. 17)
FW BG lekanis pyxis fragments (Eastern Peloponnesian?)
HP 3009 (125/365 u. 4)
FW RF closed vessel body fragment, palmette?
HP 3010 (125/365 u. 4)
FW RF bowl/skyphos(?) body fragment, curved lines above parallel bands
HP 3018 (120/360 u. 17)
FW RF krater(?) body fragment, meander
HC 875 (120/360 u. 9)
conical loom weight
HC 933 (125/365 u. 4)
conical loom weight
HM 1218 (120/365 u. 6)
FE nail
HM 1409 (120/360 u. 17)
AE sheet, embossed dots
HM 1429 (120/360 u. 17)
PB bar
HN 1975-86 (120/365 u. 3)
AE Troizen (370–300)
HN 1975-91 (120/365 u. 3)
AE Tiryns (4th)
HN 1975-94 (120/365 u. 6)
AE Aegina (after 404)
HN 1975-99 (120/365 u. 6)
AE Aegina (after 404)

Locus VII
HM 1220 (120/365 u. 4)
FE nail

Loci VIII, IX, X
no inventoried finds

Locus XI
HP 2893 (125/355 u. 6)
PW amphora rim, shoulder, handles
HP 2986 (120/355 u. 12 open deposit 1)
miniature trefoil oinochoe, Corinthian (late 4th)
HP 2987 (120/355 u. 12 open deposit 1)
FW BG squat lekythos (jug type), incised X and zigzag below handle (mid-4th)
HP 2988 (120/355 u. 12 open deposit 1)
FW BG guttus-type askos, vertical lines and rays on shoulder (400–350)
HP 2989 (120/355 u. 12 open deposit 1)
FW BG Pheidias-shape mug, ribbed (450–425)
HP 2990 (120/355 u. 12 open deposit 1)
FW BG Laconian mug (late 5th–early 4th)
HP 3155 (125/355 u. 6)
FW BG ribbed oinochoe profile
HL 310 (125/355 u. 6)
BG miniature lamp body fragment, Corinthian
HM 1163 (125/355 u. 6)
AE distaff(?) tip
HM 1200 (125/355 u. 6)
AE disk fragments (mirror?), incision
HM 1511 (125/355 u. 6)
FE clamp, fitting, or reinforcement

Locus XII
no inventoried finds

Locus XIII
HN 1975-37 (125/355 u. 6 open deposit 2)
AE Aegina (after 404)

Locus XIV
no inventoried finds

Locus XV
HP 2473 (125/360 u. 3)
CW louterion rim
HP 2506 (125/360 u. 3)
miniature dish
HP 2513 (125/360 u. 8)
FW RF shallow askos body, crouching dog opposing cat on both sides (or cat vs. cat?) with graffito (late 5th?)
HL 314 (125/360 u. 3)
BG lamp rim/nozzle
HS 526 (125/360 u. 3)
limestone fragment
HS 572 (125/360 u. 8)
volcanic grinding slab fragment

HN 1975-72 (125/360 u. 3)
AE Tiryns (4th)
HN 1975-88 (125/360 u. 8)
AE Hermione (350–300)

Locus XVI
HP 2529 (125/360 u. 6)
FW pyxis lid profile, Corinthian
HP 2602 (125/360 u. 6)
FW RF krater(?) body fragments showing furniture leg? drapery lines?
HP 2617 (125/360 u. 6)
miniature kotyle
HP 2992 (125/360 u. 10)
FW RF open vessel body fragments, drapery in added white with yellow lines, oval object decorated with bands, zigzags, and rows of dots (decorated vessel or omphalos?)
HP 2993 (125/360 u. 10)
FW BG ribbed mug body fragment
HL 324 (125/360 u. 6)
BG lamp nozzle/handle
HM 1347 (125/360 u. 10)
AE sheet fragments with nail holes
HN 1975-77 (125/360 u. 6)
AE Tiryns (4th)

Locus XVII
HP 3011 (125/360 u. 10 open deposit 2)
FW BG ribbed mug foot/body (460–420)
HC 934 (125/360 u. 10 open deposit 2)
pyramidal loom weight
HL 406 (125/360 u. 10 open deposit 1)
BG lamp rim, Corinthian
HL 407 (125/360 u. 10 open deposit 2)
BG lamp rim, nozzle, body
HV 328 (125/360 u. 14)
bone die

Locus XVIII
HP 2494 (125/355 u. 4 and 125/360 u. 5)
FW BG bowl profile, rouletting, Attic? (350–325)
HP 2516 (125/360 u. 5)
FW BG stemless cup profile
HP 2517 (125/360 u. 5)
FW BG squat olpe foot/body
HP 2518 (125/360 u. 5)
FW BG small bowl with incurving rim profile, stamped palmette cross, graffito
HP 2519 (125/360 u. 5)
FW BG bowl, one-handler, Eastern Peloponnesian
HP 2527 (125/360 u. 7)
BG miniature trefoil oinochoe, Corinthian?
HP 2649 (125/360 u. 5)
FW RF skyphos rim, palmette?
HP 2954 (125/355 u. 4)
FW amphoriskos foot, Corinthian
HC 773 (125/360 u. 5)
pyramidal loom weight
HC 774 (125/355 u. 4)
pyramidal loom weight
HC 821 (130/360 u. 5)
pyramidal loom weight
HC 825 (130/360 u. 5)
pyramidal loom weight
HM 1154 (125/355 u. 4)
FE nail shaft
HM 1183 (125/355 u. 4)
AE sheet fragments (from vessel?)
HM 1184 (125/355 u. 4)
FE sheet/band fragments
HM 1186 (125/360 u. 7)
AE weight
HM 1187 (125/360 u. 5)
AE nail
HM 1315 (130/360 u. 5)
AE reinforcement ring with four prongs
HM 1321 (130/360 u. 5)
FE spike
HN 1975-73 (125/360 u. 5)
AE Aegina (after 404)
HN 1975-75 (125/360 u. 7)
AE Tiryns (4th)
HN 1975-76 (125/360 u. 5)
AE Tiryns (4th)
HN 1975-79 (125/360 u. 7)
AE Tiryns (late 5th–early 4th)
HN 1975-82 (125/360 u. 5)
AE Tiryns (4th)
HN 1975-149 (125/360 u. 11)
AE Aegina (after 404)
HN 1975-151 (125/360 u. 11)
AE Aegina (after 404)
HN 1975-152 (125/360 u. 11)
AE Tiryns (4th)

C. House C (cf. Appendix I.C and Fig. 14)

Locus I
HL 256 (100/345 u. 4)
BG lamp foot
HS 480 (100/345 u. 4)
limestone pier capital fragment
HS 492 (100/345 u. 5)
limestone grindstone fragment
HM 1028 (100/345 u. 4)
AE sheathing fragment, repoussé rosette

Locus II
HP 2465 (100/345 u. 10)
FW RF open vessel fragment, spotted animal (panther?)

HM 1238 (100/345 u. 10 [from Room 6-67, not House C])
AE reinforcement ring with four prongs
HM 1240 (100/345 u. 10 [from Room 6-67, not House C])
AE disk with two holes; scale pan?

Locus III
HM 1048 (095/340 u. 8)
PB fragments (11 unidentified)
HM 1052 (095/340 u. 8)
PB scrap fragment

Locus IV
HP 2186 (095/340 u. 2)
FW RF shallow askos, ovules and tongue pattern
HP 2190 (095/340 u. 2)
FW BG stemless cup
HP 2196 (095/340 u. 3)
CW louterion rim fragment (built into wall of Room 6-56)
HP 2204 (095/340 u. 3)
FW RF lekanis or pyxis lid, ovules and tongue pattern
HP 2207 (095/340 u. 3)
FW BG saltcellar profile (350–325)
HP 2340 (095/340 u. 3)
FW amphoriskos fragments, traces of glaze, Corinthian
HP 2341 (095/340 u. 3)
FW BG fish plate rim fragment, Attic (early 4th)
HP 2342 (095/340 u. 3)
FW BG bowl or plate foot fragment, Eastern Peloponnesian?
HP 2413 (095/340 u. 2)
FW BG plate foot/body fragment, rouletting
HP 2414 (095/340 u. 2)
FW RF shallow askos fragments, ovules and laurel leaf pattern, Attic
HP 2415 (095/340 u. 2)
FW BG cup-kantharos(?) foot/body fragment, routletting, Attic
HP 2509 (095/340 u. 9)
FW BG bolsal foot fragment, stamped palmette cross
HP 2544 (095/340 u. 9)
FW BG mug profile, Laconian
HP 2680 (095/340 u. 3)
PW storage bin fragments
HP 2944 (095/340 u. 3)
CW lid profile
HC 920 (095/340 u. 2)
pyramidal loom weight
HL 261 (095/340 u. 2)
BG lamp fragments
HL 321 (095/340 u. 9)
BG lamp rim/body fragment
HM 980 (095/340 u. 2)
PB band, scrap?
HM 981 (095/340 u. 2)
FE sickle blade
HM 982 (095/340 u. 2)
AE drop handle
HM 983 (095/340 u. 2)
PB fragment
HM 984 (095/340 u. 2)
FE rim fragments; cauldron, pipe?
HM 1007 (095/340 u. 3)
AE ring, chain or earring?
HM 1009 (095/340 u. 3)
AE drop handle
HM 1010 (095/340 u. 3)
AE latchstring plate
HM 1011 (095/340 u. 3)
FE small pruning knife, sickle shaped
HM 1012 (095/340 u. 2)
FE spike
HM 1030 (095/340 u. 2)
AE boss
HM 1034 (095/340 u. 2)
PB lump
HM 1036 (095/340 u. 3)
FE nail
HM 1190 (095/340 u. 9)
FE bent rod; spit handle?
HM 1197 (095/340 u. 9)
AE boss with FE shaft
HM 1198 (095/340 u. 9)
FE chain links
HM 1199 (095/340 u. 9)
AE earring
HM 1206 (095/340 u. 9)
AE boss with FE shaft
HM 1209 (095/340 u. 9)
AE flat ring, washer?
HM 1213 (095/340 u. 9)
PB trapezoidal piece, weight?
HM 1449 (095/340 u. 3)
FE coil
HM 1525 (095/340 u. 2, 3)
FE blade

Locus V
no inventoried finds

Locus VI
HP 2254 (095/345 u. 2)
FW BG krater neck/body, Laconian?
HP 2542 (090/345 u. 12)
PW amphora handle, stamped
HP 2581 (090/345 u. 12)
FW BG saltcellar profile (375–325)
HP 2801 (095/345 u. 2, 3)
FW BG bell krater fragments, Laconian (4th)
HP 3161 (095/345 u. 2)
PW amphora neck fragments with stamp, Corinthian
HP 3162 (095/345 u. 2)
PW amphora neck/shoulder fragment
HS 463 (095/345 u. 3)
dacite hopper-mill

Locus VII
HC 960 (095/350 u. 8)
 CW pithos foot fragment
HS 524 (090/345 u. 11)
 limestone fragment
HS 528 (090/345 u. 11)
 limestone Doric capital
HM 1311 (090/345 u. 14)
 FE nail
HM 1494 (095/350 u. 7)
 FE blade

Locus IX
HP 2343 (095/340 u. 4)
 PW amphora fragments
HP 2800 (090/340 North Balk u. 2)
 FW BG skyphos profile, Attic (ca. 330)
HM 1453 (090/340 North Balk u. 2)
 FE sheet fragment
HM 1492 (090/335 u. 6)
 FE nail
HN 1974-6 (090/340 u. 6)
 AE Tiryns

Locus X
HP 2802 (090/345 u. 13)
 PW amphora rim/neck/handle
HC 849 (090/345 u. 13)
 pyramidal loom weight
HN 1975-119 (090/345 u. 13)
 AE Tiryns (4th)

Locus XI
HP 2176 (085/340 u. 8)
 FW RF bell krater body fragments, drapery
HP 2183 (095/340 u. 6)
 CW lid
HP 2281 (090/340 u. 5)
 PW amphora fragments with graffito
HP 2361 (090/340 u. 5)
 FW BG stemless cup rim/body/handle, Argive
HP 2362 (090/340 u. 5)
 FW BG bowl foot fragments, stamped palmette
HP 2366 (085/340 North Balk u.3)
 FW BG bolsal profile, rouletting and stamped palmette cross (380–350)
HP 2923 (085/340 u. 6)
 FW RF open vessel body fragment, drapery
HP 2928 (085/340 u. 6)
 PW amphora neck/shoulder/handle root
HL 251 (085/340 North Balk u. 3)
 BG lamp with graffito
HS 468, 469 (090/340 u. 5)
 sandstone pilaster fragments with plaster
HS 613 (085/340 u. 6)
 flint flake
HM 1044 (085/340 East Balk u. 5)
 FE bell-shaped object; bell, cover, crucible?

Locus XII
HP 2253 (090/345 u. 3)
 FW circular tray, white slipped with impressed leaf pattern and two PB clamps (joins with 090/345 u. 6 and 085/345 u. 12)
HP 2345 (090/340 u. 8)
 CW lopas (joins with 090/345 u. 6)
HP 2359 (090/345 u. 3)
 PW amphora fragments
HP 2360 (090/345 u. 3)
 PW amphora fragments
HP 2367 (090/340 u. 8)
 PW lid profile
HL 255 (085/345 u. 7)
 BG lamp nozzle
HC 876 (085/345 u. 12)
 conical loom weight
HC 893 (085/345 u. 6)
 pyramidal loom weight
HC 737 (085/345 u. 4)
 Laconian cover tile

Locus XIII
no inventoried finds

Locus XIV
HP 3163 (085/345 u. 11?)
 PW amphora rim/neck/shoulder, handles?
HP 3164 (085/345 u. 11?)
 PW trefoil jug with high handle
HS 541 (085/345 u. 7)
 limestone Doric capital
HS 542 (085/345 u. 10)
 limestone Doric capital fragment
HS 543 (085/345 u. 11)
 limestone pier capital
HS 544 (085/345 u. 12)
 limestone rectangular block fragments

Locus XV
HP 2967 (090/350 u. 4)
 CW lopas profile (400–350)
HP 2984 (090/350 u. 4)
 FW BG fish plate profile (ca. 325)
HC 649 (090/345 u. 4)
 conical loom weight
HC 891 (085/345 u. 14)
 conical loom weight fragment
HC 915 (090/350 u. 4)
 pyramidal loom weight fragment
HL 250 (090/345 u. 4)
 BG lamp body fragment

Locus XVI
no inventoried finds

D. House D (cf. Appendix I.D and Fig. 17)

Locus I
HP 2178 (065/330 u. 6)
FW BG cup-kantharos with rouletting and stamped palmette circle (375–350)
HP 2475 (065/325 u. 10)
PW storage bin fragments
HP 2479 (060/330 u. 13)
PW amphora rim/neck/shoulder/handle
HC 646 (065/330 u.6)
circular plaque fragments, frontal face hand-modeled in relief (lid or akroterion?)
HC 862 (060/330 u. 13)
drainage pipe? fragments
HS 597 (060/330 u. 13)
obsidian core flake (rejuvenated)
HM 1005 (065/330 u. 6)
AE ring
HM 1141 (060/330 u. 13)
FE nail fragment
HM 1439 (060/330 u. 13)
AE fish hook fragment
HM 1445 (060/330 u. 130)
FE boss

Locus II
HP 2213 (060/325 u. 31)
CW strainer fragments
HP 2809 (060/325 u. 27)
FW BG saltcellar with graffito (425–350)
HP 2821 (060/325 u. 29)
PW amphora body fragment with graffito
HP 2888 (060/325 u. 34)
FW BG lekanis pyxis profile
HP 2889 (060/325 u. 27, 28, 30, 34, 35)
FW BG krater fragments
HP 2891 (060/325 u. 29, 30)
CW griddle
HP 2896 (060/325 u. 30, 34, 35)
PW jug
HP 2912 (060/325 u. 30)
PW one-handled bowl
HP 2924 (065/325 u. 34)
CW lid profile
HP 2927 (060/325 u. 28)
PW amphora fragments
HP 2937 (060/325 u. 30)
FW feeder, black and red bands, Corinthian
HP 2941 (060/325 u. 30)
CW strainer fragments
HP 2955 (060/325 u. 34)
PW body fragment, incised circle
HP 2957 (060/325 u. 30)
FW RF skyphos rim fragment, palmette
HP 3159 (060/325 u. 29)
PW amphora neck/handles
HL 246 (060/325 u. 19)
BG lamp base
HC 654 (060/325 u. 29)
pyramidal loom weight with BG
HC 681 (060/325 u. 29)
pyramidal loom weight
HC 898 (060/325 u. 31)
conical loom weight
HC 739 (060/325 u. 28)
sima tile fragments, painted palmette and lotus frieze, Corinthian (ca. 520)
HM 1002 (060/325 u. 29)
AE ring
HM 1025 (060/325 u. 30)
AE handle
HM 1027 (060/325 u. 29)
AE fish hook fragment
HM 1029 (060/325 u. 29)
AE earring
HM 1033 (065/325 u. 29)
FE nail
HM 1035 (065/325 u. 29)
FE handle
HM 1056 (060/325 u. 31)
AE grater fragments
HN 1974-10 (060/325 u. 29)
AE Troizen (370–300)

Locus III
HC 900 (060/325 u. 49)
spool
HC 902 (060/325 u. 49)
pyramidal loom weight

Locus IV
HP 2336 (065/320 u. 6)
PW amphora
HP 2352 (065/320 u. 6)
PW strainer fragments

Locus V
HP 2348? (065/330 u. 7)
CW pithos lid rim or opaion tile fragments (joins with Locus VI?)
HP 2604 (065/325 u. 18)
FW kotyle profile, traces of BG(?), Corinthian
HP 2618 (065/325 u. 18)
CW griddle base/body fragments
HP 2624 (065/325 u. 18)
FW BG small bowl with incurving rim profile, graffito (425–400)
HC 743 (065/330 u. 7)
opaion tile or pithos lid
HC 744 (065/330 u. 7)
opaion tile or pithos lid
HM 1294 (065/325 u. 18)
FE nail
HM 1296 (065/325 u. 18)
AE nail

HM 1301 (065/325 u. 18)
FE blade or bar

Loci VI–VII
no inventoried finds

Locus VIII
(*inventoried finds from below latest floor surface, Level A/B or B?)
HC 842* (065/325 u. 21)
pyramidal loom weight
HS 517* (065/325 u. 21)
pink quartz "neo-Assyrian" cylinder seal
HM 1335 (065/325 u. 20)
AE ring
HM 1350* (065/325 u. 21)
FE sickle blade
HM 1361* (065/325 u. 21)
AE nail shaft
HM 1363 (065/325 u. 20)
AE ring
HN 1975-121 (065/325 u. 20)
AE Tiryns (4th)
HN 1975-153* (065/325 u. 21)
AE Tiryns (4th)
HN 1975-154* (065/325 u. 21)
AE Tiryns (4th)

Locus IX
HP 2607 (065/335 u. 5)
FW BG bolsal with stamped palmette cross (420–400)
HP 2619 (065/335 u. 5)
FW RF body fragment
HC 784 (065/335 u. 5)
conical loom weight
HS 488 (065/330 u. 8)
shelly limestone pier capital

Locus X
HP 2203 (065/330 u. 8 open deposit 2)
Blister ware oinochoe profile
HP 2260 (065/330 u. 8 open deposit 2)
FW biconical pyxis profile, Corinthian
HP 2278 (065/330 u. 8 open deposit 2)
FW RF pelike fragments including neck/shoulder; side A, myth/battle scene; side B, facing figures

Locus XI
HP 2824 (065/330 u. 37)
FW RF open vessel? body fragments, seated male? facing standing/dancing female?
HP 3038 (065/330 u. 37)
FW RF open vessel? body fragments, unidentified detail lines

Locus XII
HP 2503 (065/335 u. 4)
FW BG cup-kantharos, rouletting and stamped palmette cross (350–325)
HS 516 (065/335 u. 4)
shelly limestone block with inscribed letters

Locus XIII
HP 2469 (070/335 u. 5)
PW amphora rim/neck/shoulder/handle
HP 2663 (070/335 u. 5)
PW small amphora rim/neck/shoulder/handle/body

Locus XIV
HP 2474 (070/330 u. 5)
FW RF open vessel body fragments, palmette
HP 2481 (070/330 u. 5)
FW BG trefoil oinochoe, ribbed (325–310)
HP 2490 (070/330 u. 5)
FW BG shallow askos fragments, tongue pattern (400–375)
HP 2498 (070/330 u. 5)
FW RF open vessel body fragment, draped figure
HP 2546 (065/330 u. 29)
miniature kotyle
HP 2547 (065/330 u. 29)
miniature kotyle
HP 2548 (065/330 u. 29)
FW BG saltcellar profile (425–400)
HP 2549 (065/330 u. 29)
FW BG footless bowl or kyathos cup profile, Eastern Peloponnesian
HP 2550 (065/330 u. 29)
FW RF open vessel body fragment, palmette?
HP 2551 (065/330 u. 29)
FW BG saltcellar, graffito
HP 2552 (065/330 u. 29)
FW BG small bowl with incurving rim, stamped palmette cross (375–350)
HP 2553 (065/330 u. 29)
FW BG small broad-based bowl profile, stamped palmette cross (350–325)
HP 2554 (065/330 u. 29)
FW BG large late Attic-type skyphos, Eastern Peloponnesian (ca. 330)
HP 2555 (065/330 u. 29)
FW BG small broad-based bowl, stamped palmette cross, Eastern Peloponnesian (ca. 380)
HP 2556 (065/330 u. 29)
FW BG small bowl with incurving rim, graffito
HP 2557 (065/330 u. 29)
FW BG stemless cup, Eastern Peloponnesian
HP 2558 (065/330 u. 29)
FW BG stemless cup, Eastern Peloponnesian
HP 2559 (065/330 u. 29)
FW BG askos foot fragment
HP 2560 (065/330 u. 29)
PW mortar/shallow bowl
HP 2561 (065/330 u. 29)
PW mortar

HP 2565 (070/330 u. 17)
FW BG guttus-type askos body, Attic? (375–350)
HP 2566 (070/330 u. 17)
FW BG footed saltcellar, graffito, Attic (375–350)
HP 2569 (070/330 u. 5)
FW RF skyphos(?) body fragments, palmette
HP 2573 (070/330 u. 17)
FW BG bolsal, rouletting and stamped palmette cross (380–350)
HP 2576 (070/325 u. 17)
FW BG pyxis lid
HP 2585 (065/330 u. 29)
FW BG krater rim
HP 2586 (065/330 u. 29)
FW BG cup-skyphos fragments
HP 2589 (070/330 u. 17)
miniature kotyle
HP 2590 (070/330 u. 17)
FW BG shallow askos fragments (400–375)
HP 2591 (065/330 u. 29)
CW lopas
HP 2597 (070/330 u. 17)
FW BG small bowl with incurving rim, graffito, Eastern Peloponnesian (375–350)
HP 2598 (070/330 u. 5)
FW BG bowl fragments, graffito, Eastern Peloponnesian
HP 2599 (070/330 u. 5)
FW BG bolsal, stamped palmette cross, graffito, Attic (380–350)
HP 2605 (070/330 u. 17)
FW BG bolsal fragments, stamped palmette cross, Attic? (early 4th)
HP 2612 (065/325 u. 15)
PW amphora rim/neck/shoulder/handles
HP 2635 (070/330 u. 5)
CW lopas profile
HP 2646 (065/330 u. 29)
miniature bowl
HP 2647 (065/330 u. 29)
CW lopas
HP 2650 (065/330 u. 29)
CW lopas
HP 2653 (065/330 u. 29)
FW RF bell krater rim
HP 2660 (070/330 u. 5)
BG column krater rim/handle/body fragments
HP 2678 (070/330 u. 17)
PW amphora neck/shoulder/handle
HP 2930 (070/330 u. 5)
FW BG fish plate profile, Attic? (375–350)
HP 3019 (070/330 u. 17)
FW BG plate rim fragments
HC 788 (065/330 u. 28)
conical loom weight
HC 811 (070/330 u. 17)
conical loom weight
HC 812 (065/330 u. 29)
conical loom weight
HC 820 (070/325 u. 17)
conical loom weight
HC 844 (070/325 u. 17)
base/body fragments of seated or reclining figure with red and yellow slip
HL 315 (065/330 u. U29)
miniature lamp
HL 323 (070/330 u. 17)
PW lamp without handle
HL 345 (065/330 u. 29)
BG lamp
HS 573 (070/325 u. 17)
sandstone grinding slab fragment
HM 1189 (070/330 u. 5)
AE strigil fragment
HM 1232 (065/330 u. 29)
AE boss
HM 1233 (065/330 u. 29)
PB pot clamp
HM 1245 (065/330 u. 29)
FE spearhead
HM 1248 (070/330 u. 17)
FE shovel
HM 1249 (070/330 u. 17)
FE rod and miscellaneous FE fragments
HM 1251 (070/330 u. 17)
AE drop handle
HM 1327 (070/325 u. 17)
AE drop handle
HN 1975-95 (065/330 u. 29)
AE Tiryns (4th)
HN 1975-101 (065/330 u. 29)
AE Tiryns (4th)
HN 1975-102 (065/330 u. 29)
AE Epidauros (323–240)
HN 1975-104 (070/330 u. 17)
AE Tiryns (4th)
HN 1975-105 (065/330 u. 29)
AE Troizen (370–300)

Locus XV
HP 2195 (070/325 u. 4)
miniature jug
HP 2421 (070/325 u. 11)
FW BG Attic-type skyphos profile (375–350)
HP 2468 (070/325 u. 9, lies above Level A)
PW amphora rim/neck/handles
HP 2478 (070/325 u. 10, lies above Level A)
PW amphora rim/neck/handle
HC 776 (070/325 u. 11)
conical loom weight
HS 530 (070/325 u. 11)
stone vessel rim fragment
HM 1031 (070/325 u. 4)
AE ring
HM 1133 (070/325 u. 11)
AE disk
HM 1134 (070/325 u. 11)
AE nail

HM 1145 (070/325 u. 12)
AE earring pendant
HM 1144 (070/325 u. 12)
FE ring
HM 1146 (070/325 u. 12)
PB fragment
HM 1444 (070/325 u. 11)
AE needle
HN 1974-7 (070/325 u. 4)
AE Aegina (after 404)
HN 1975-2 (070/325 u. 12)
AE Tiryns (4th)
HV 312 (070/325 u. 4)
ostrich egg fragments

Locus XVI
HP 2496 (070/330 u. 9)
FW BG saltcellar, footed (375–350)
HP 2500 (070/330 u. 10a)
FW BG small bowl with incurving rim profile, stamped palmette cross, graffito, Eastern Peloponnesian (350–325)
HP 2502 (070/330 u. 10a)
FW BG small bowl with incurving rim, Eastern Peloponnesian
HP 2522 (070/330 u. 10a)
CW lid
HP 2564 (070/330 u. 9, 11)
CW lid profile (350–325)
HP 2583 (070/330 u. 10a)
FW BG bolsal, stamped palmette cross, Attic (ca. 400?)
HP 2587 (070/330 u. 11)
FW BG squat lekythos
HP 2588 (070/330 u. 11)
CW lid profile
HP 2592 (070/330 u. 11)
FW RF krater body fragments; palmettes in handle zone, tongue pattern frames bottom of scene with female figure stooping/seated on left, faced by male legs (running?), horse's hind legs, and seated female(?) to right
HP 2609 (070/330 u. 21)
FW RF bell krater rim with laurel leaf pattern and two female figures facing right, separated by cross motif
HP 2631 (070/330 u. 9)
FW BG stemless cup profile, Eastern Peloponnesian
HP 2637 (070/330 u. 23)
FW BG Attic-type skyphos, Attic? (400–375)
HP 2638 (070/330 u. 23)
FW semi-glazed kotyle, Corinthian (350–325)
HP 2639 (070/330 u. 26)
FW semi-glazed kotyle, Corinthian
HP 2640 (070/330 u. 26)
FW semi-glazed kotyle, Corinthian (4th)
HP 2666 (070/330 u. 33)
CW askos (320–275)
HP 2670 (070/330 u. 33)
FW RF open vessel body fragment with PB clamp, tongue pattern bordering unidentified scene
HP 2674 (070/330 u. 28)
FW RF closed vessel body fragments, drapery details
HP 2676 (070/330 u. 10a)
CW griddle profile (490–450)
HP 2690 (070/330 u. 26)
FW kotyle, Corinthian
HP 2694 (070/330 u. 9)
PW amphora rim/neck
HP 2807 (070/330 u. 30)
PW amphora foot fragment
HP 2808 (070/330 u. 30)
PW amphora foot fragment
HP 2815 (070/330 u. 30)
FW bowl rim, traces of red bands
HP 2818 (070/330 u. 9)
miniature kotyle
HP 2886 (070/330 u. 23)
FW BG Attic-type skyphos (ca. 320)
HP 2915 (070/330 u. 33)
FW lid, traces of red and brown bands, Corinthian
HP 2916 (070/330 u. 10a)
FW BG small bowl with broad base profile
HP 2971 (070/330 u. 26)
FW RF body fragments of large, thin-walled, closed vessel; tongue pattern, nude female figure, drapery and unidentified scene
HP 2973 (070/330 u. 28)
FW ray-based kotyle body fragment, Corinthian
HP 2980 (070/330 u. 30)
FW RF closed vessel body fragments, unidentified scene
HC 789 (070/320 u. 10a)
pyramidal loom weight
HC 827 (070/330 u. 9)
CW pithos lid
HC 853 (070/330 u. 28)
spool
HL 326 (070/320 u. 10a)
BG lamp rim/filling hole
HS 523 (070/330 u. 9)
limestone architectural fragment
HS 560 (070/330 u. 11)
limestone handstone, plano-convex
HS 565 (070/330 u. 28)
volcanic handstone fragment, elliptical
HS 585 (070/330 u. 11)
obsidian bladelet segment
HM 1188 (070/330 u. 8)
AE nail or tack
HM 1201 (070/330 u. 9)
AE nail or attachment
HM 1214 (070/330 u. 9)
FE nail
HM 1223 (070/330 u. 9)
FE nail

HM 1230 (070/330 u. 10b)
AE boss with FE shaft
HM 1242 (070/330 u. 10a)
AE reinforcement ring fragment with prongs
HM 1247 (070/330 u. 9)
FE nail
HM 1326 (070/330 u. 20)
AE drop handle
HM 1364 (070/330 u. 30)
AE strigil
HM 1365 (070/330 u. 28)
AE nail
HM 1366 (070/330 u. 28)
AE nail
HM 1373 (070/330 u. 28)
FE nail or clamp
HM 1374 (070/330 u. 26)
AE vessel ring foot (cf. HM 1399)
HM 1376 (070/330 u. 23)
AE strip with FE rivet
HM 1377 (070/330 u. 30)
FE razor
HM 1513 (070/330 u. 30)
FE hook
HM 1514 (070/330 u. 10a)
FE tongs
HM 1515 (070/330 u. 10a)
FE spit or handle
HN 1975-85 (070/330 u. 9)
AE Tiryns (4th)
HN 1975-92 (070/330 u. 10a)
AE Tiryns (4th)
HN 1975-100 (070/330 u. 10b)
AE Epidauros (323–240)
HN 1975-116 (070/330 u. 20)
AE Tiryns (4th)

E. House E (cf. Appendix I.E and Fig. 20)

Locus I
HP 2202 (050/315 u. 5)
CW eschara profile
HC 888 (050/315 u. 8)
pyramidal loom weight
HL 284 (050/315 u. 8)
BG lamp base/body fragment
HM 1516 (050/315 u. 5)
AE tack

Loci II/V/VIII
HP 2595 (055/315 u. 6)
FW RF closed vessel body fragment, palmette
HS 505 (050/315 u. 9)
marble fragment with nail
HM 1250 (050/315 u. 13)
FE nail head
HM 1284 (055/315 u. 6)
FE nail fragments
HM 1522 (050/315 u. 9)
AE nail

Loci III/IV
HP 2188 (050/315 u. 7)
miniature trefoil oinochoe, Corinthian
HL 278 (050/315 u. 6)
BG lamp rim fragment
HL 280 (050/315 u. 6)
BG lamp nozzle fragment
HV 307 (050/315 u. 6)
large whelk shell, scoop?

Locus VI
HC 656 (055/320 u. 11)
conical loom weight
HL 247 (055/320 u. 11)
BG lamp rim
HS 443 (055/320 u. 11)
marble perirrhanterion rim fragment
HM 989 (050/320 North Balk u. 2)
PB sheet with AE nails
HM 990 (055/320 u. 11)
PB sheet with AE nails
HM 1001 (055/320 u. 11)
AE tack
HM 1451 (055/320 u. 12)
FE handle
HM 1520 (055/320 u. 11)
AE tack
HM 1537 (055/320 u. 12)
AE shaft fragment
HN 1974-9 (055/320 u. 11)
AE Tiryns (4th)
HN 1974-15 (055/320 u. 11)
AE Arcadia (363–280)

Locus VII
no inventoried finds

Locus IX
HP 2611 (055/315 u. 15)
FW RF body fragment
HP 2693 (055/315 u. 15)
CW chytra fragments
HP 2795 (055/315 u. 11)
FW semi-glazed bowl (Hellenistic)
HP 2936 (055/315 u. 11)
CW lopas profile
HP 3021 (055/315 u. 16)
FW BG mug lower body, Laconian (ca. 480)
HM 1333 (055/315 u. 15)
AE strip
HM 1351 (055/315 u. 16)
AE ring and sheet fragment

HM 1523 (055/320 u. 13)
FE cleaver
HN 1974-19 (055/320 u. 14)
AE Tiryns (4th)
HN 1975-110 (055/315 u. 11)
AE Arcadius, Heraclea mint (A.D. 383)

Locus X
no inventoried finds

Locus XI
no inventoried finds

Locus XIIa
HP 2189 (060/320 u. 8)
FW BG Corinthian-type skyphos with cross-hatching
HP 2884 (060/320 u. 8)
FW RF bell krater(?) body fragment, meander
HC 749 (060/320 u. 8)
Laconian cover tile fragments with BG
HN 1974-25 (060/320 u. 8)
AE Tiryns (4th)

Locus XIIb
HP 2165 (055/320 u. 8)
FW BG bolsal profile with graffito, Attic (early 4 th?)
HP 2166 (055/320 u. 8)
FW BG kantharos with rouletting (350–325)
HP 2167 (055/320 u. 8)
FW BG plate body fragment with graffito
HP 2172 (055/320 u. 8)
FW BG kantharos foot, stamped palmette cross and rouletting
HP 2491 (055/320 u. 16)
CW squat jug, round mouth
HP 2520 (055/320 u. 16)
FW BG globular lekythos neck/shoulder/body fragment (375–350)
HP 2677 (055/320 u. 16)
PW lekane profile
HP 3006 (055/320 u. 8)
CW large lopas
HP 3045 (055/320 u. 8)
FW RF bell krater rim fragment, laurel leaf pattern
HC 768 (055/320 u. 16)
pyramidal loom weight fragments
HC 769 (055/320 u. 16)
pyramidal loom weight
HC 793 (055/320 u. 16)
amphora stand? eschara?
HC 936 (055/320 u. 8)
pyramidal loom weight
HC 937 (055/320 u. 8)
pyramidal loom weight
HC 938 (055/320 u. 8)
pyramidal loom weight
HC 939 (055/320 u. 8)
pyramidal loom weight
HC 940 (055/320 u. 8)
pyramidal loom weight
HC 941 (055/320 u. 8)
pyramidal loom weight
HC 942 (055/320 u. 8)
pyramidal loom weight

Locus XIIc
HP 2632 (055/320 u. 22)
FW BG stemless cup foot
HP 3158 (055/320 u. 23
PW stamped amphora handle, Corinthian
HP 3047 (055/320 u. 23)
PW amphora rim/shoulder
HC 815 (055/320 u. 23)
circular stamp with kneeling female figure, flower in left hand?
HC 831 (055/320 u. 23)
pyramidal loom weight
HC 832 (055/320 u. 23)
conical loom weight
HC 836 (055/320 u. 23)
pyramidal loom weight
HC 837 (055/320 u. 23)
pyramidal loom weight
HC 838 (055/320 u. 23)
pyramidal loom weight
HC 839 (055/320 u. 23)
pyramidal loom weight
HS 461 (055/325 u. 15)
dacite grindstone fragments
HS 465 (055/325 u. 11)
limestone pier capital
HS 579 (055/320 u. 23)
sandstone fragment, pierced
HM 1000 (055/325 u. 15)
FE "sword"
HM 1252 (055/320 u. 22)
FE nail fragment
HM 1289 (055/320 u. 22)
FE nail
HM 1531 (055/325 u. 15)
FE blade, curving

Locus XIII
HP 2179 (055/325 u. 16)
FW BG bowl with incurving rim, rouletting and stamped palmette circle (350–325)
HP 2255 (055/325 u. 16)
FW BF cup-skyphos body fragment
HP 2273 (055/325 u. 16)
FW BG stemless cup profile, Argive?
HP 2428 (055/325 u. 29)
FW pyxis lid with red and black bands, Corinthian
HP 2430 (055/325 u. 25)
PW thurible (425–400)

HP 2580 (055/325 u. 29)
FW BG bolsal foot fragment, stamped palmette cross, graffito
HP 2883 (055/325 u. 16)
FW BG saltcellar profile (350–325)
HL 301 (055/325 u. 29)
BG lamp nozzle
HM 1135 (055/325 u. 25)
FE clamp/nail

Locus XIV
HP 2422 (055/325 u. 27)
PW louterion rim fragment with moldings
HP 2471 (060/325 u. 44)
FW patterned pyxis, Corinthian (mid-5th?)
HM 1142 (055/325 u. 27)
FE knife blade

Loci XV/XVI
HP 2892 (060/315 u. 4)
CW stand
HC 729 (060/320 u. 5)
conical loom weight
HS 561 (060/315 u. 4)
schist disk
HM 993 (060/320 u. 5)
FE strip fragments

Locus XVII
HP 2151 (060/320: open deposit 1)
FW BG bolsal, stamped palmettes and rouletting, Attic (380–350)
HP 2152 (060/320: open deposit 1)
FW BG bolsal profile, stamped palmette cross and rouletting, Attic (400–350)
HP 2153 (060/320: open deposit 1)
FW BG trefoil oinochoe, Argive?
HP 2154 (060/320: open deposit 1)
FW BG saltcellar with graffito (350–325)
HP 2155 (060/320 open deposit 1)
CW strainer
HP 2156 (060/320 open deposit 1)
FW BG bolsal with stamped palmette cross (380–350)
HP 2157 (060/320: open deposit 1)
FW globular jug profile, trace of red band, Corinthian?
HP 2158 (060/320 open deposit 1)
FW BG trefoil oinochoe body, Corinthian
HP 2159 (060/320 open deposit 1)
CW double-rimmed griddle fragments
HP 2161 (060/320: open deposit 1)
CW lopas
HP 2163 (060/320 open deposit 1)
PW lekane fragments
HP 2164 (060/320 open deposit 1)
FW BG stemless cup, Eastern Peloponnesian
HP 2170 (060/320 open deposit 1)
CW large bowl, two holes pierce rim
HP 2192 (060/320 open deposit 1)
FW BG askos spout with graffito
HC 640 (060/320 open deposit 1)
pyramidal loom weight
HL 242 (060/320 open deposit 1)
BG lamp handle

Loci XVIII/XIX
HP 2171 (060/320 u. 9)
FW BG olpe base/body
HP 2180 (060/320 u. 9)
FW BG lekanis lid, Eastern Peloponnesian (ca. 400)
HP 2184 (060/320 u. 9)
FW BG ribbed trefoil oinochoe profile (late 4 th?)
HP 2194 (060/320 u. 9)
PW lekane
HP 2280 (060/320 u. 9)
CW large chytra
HP 2350 (060/320 u. 6 [above, but associated with Level A])
PW amphora fragments
HP 2351 (060/320 u. 6 [above, but associated with Level A])
PW amphora fragments
HP 2355 (060/320 u. 6 [above, but associated with Level A])
PW amphora fragments
HP 2368 (060/320 u. 9)
FW BG bosal profile
HC 651 (060/320 u. 9)
handmade(?) dove(?) figurine, white slip, traces of blue and red paint
HS 547 (060/320 u. 9)
grinding slab
HS 637 (060/320 u. 9)
obsidian blade segment
HM 994 (060/320 u. 9)
AE boss

Locus XX
HP 2191 (065/325 u. 5)
FW BG skyphos-shaped pyxis profile, Eastern Peloponnesian
HP 2419 (060/320 u. 17)
PW body fragment with PB clamp
HP 2420 (060/320 u. 17)
PW body fragment with PB clamp
HP 2477 (060/325 u. 40)
PW amphora rim/neck/shoulder/handle fragment
HP 2482 (060/325 u. 40)
FW BG small bowl with incurving rim (350–310)
HP 2524 (060/320 u. 21)
FW BG miniature bowl
HP 2543 (060/320 u. 21)
FW BG guttus-type askos with graffito (ca. 350)
HP 2890 (060/320 u. 21)
PW amphora rim/neck/shoulder/handle fragments

HP 2926 (060/320 u. 21)
PW amphora rim/neck/shoulder/handle fragment
HP 2978 (060/320 u. 21)
FW miniature lid, traces of red
HP 3153 (060/320 u. 21)
PW krater foot/body fragment
HC 641 (060/325 u. 16)
pyramidal loom weight with BG
HC 808 (060/320 u. 21)
pyramidal loom weight
HC 810 (060/320 u. 21)
pyramidal loom weight with stamp
HL 245 (060/325 u. 16)
BG lamp base fragment
HL 299 (060/320 u. 17)
BG lamp nozzle
HL 309 (060/320 u. 21)
BG lamp
HL 327 (060/320 u. 21)
BG lamp rim fragment
HS 446 (060/325 u. 16)
slate disk (lid? cover?)
HS 555 (060/320 u. 21)
limestone spheroid (grindstone/hammer)
HS 558 (060/320 u. 21)
volcanic conical tool
HS 588a (060/320 u. 21)
obsidian bladelet segment
HS 588b (060/320 u. 21)
obsidian flake
HM 1138 (060/320 u. 17)
FE lump
HM 1147a (060/320 u. 17)
AE boss
HM 1147b (060/320 u. 19)
AE door boss
HM 1155 (060/325 u. 40)
AE tack head
HM 1202 (060/320 u. 21)
AE token with designs
HM 1203 (060/320 u. 21)
AE token with designs
HM 1205 (060/320 u. 21)
AE grater fragments
HM 1211 (060/320 u. 21)
AE drop handle
HM 1216 (060/320 u. 21)
FE nail
HM 1221 (060/320 u. 21)
FE ring fragments
HM 1222 (060/320 u. 21)
FE nail
HM 1532 (060/320 u. 21)
FE blade fragment

Locus XXI
HP 2265 (065/320 u. 5)
FW RF skyphos fragment, profile female head (late Attic type)
HP 2331 (065/320 u. 5)
PW amphora rim/neck/shoulder/handle fragment
HP 2332 (065/320 u. 5)
PW amphora rim/neck/shoulder fragment
HP 2476 (060/320 u. 16)
PW amphora rim/neck/handle fragment
HC 652 (065/320 u. 5)
biconical loom weight, stamped with eagle and rooster
HC 687 (065/320 u. 5)
pyramidal loom weight
HL 249 (065/320 u. 5)
BG lamp nozzle fragments
HL 291 (065/320 u. 5)
BG lamp rim fragment
HS 445 (065/320 u. 5)
slate pendant, weight or sinker
HS 460 (065/320 u. 5)
limestone block plastered red
HS 462 (065/320 u. 5)
limestone block plastered red
HS 498 (065/320 u. 5)
whetstone
HM1 003 (065/320 u. 5)
FE square (washer)
HM 1004 (065/320 u. 5)
AE needle
HM 1006 (065/320 u. 5)
AE scale plate
HM 1447 (065/320 u. 5)
FE triangle
HM 1483 (065/320 u. 5)
FE shaft fragment
HN 1974-21 (065/320 u. 5)
AE Tiryns (late 5th –early 4th)

Tables

Locus	I	II	III	IV	V–VI/ XXIV– XXVIII	VII	VIII	IX– XIV	XV– XVI	XVII– XIX	XX	XXI– XXIII
Fine ware												
Food: serve/consume												
whole	-	-	-	-	-	-	-	1	-	-	-	-
profile	1	-	1	-	-	4	-	-	-	1	-	2
rim	5	1	5	9	4	15	4	-	4	4	-	4
foot	6	-	1	6	3	4	1	-	-	-	-	1
other	-	-	-	1	-	4	-	1	1	-	-	-
Drink: consume												
whole	-	-	1?	-	-	-	-	1	-	-	-	-
profile	-	-	3	1	2	3	-	-	-	-	-	-
rim	16	1	17	9	14	31	6	1	13	17	3	14
foot	2	-	9	10	4	15	5	2	2	5	-	2
other	11	1	17	17	11	22	7	3	4	23	3	2
Drink: serve/pour												
whole	-	-	1	-	-	-	-	-	-	-	-	-
profile	-	-	-	-	-	-	-	-	-	-	-	-
rim	1	-	-	3	1	2	1	1	-	1	-	-
foot	3	-	2	8	3	4	-	-	1	1	-	7
other	7	-	4	24	3	12	-	1	5	-	-	14
Drink: serve/contain												
rim	6	-	2	4	1	3	2	-	-	1	-	1
foot	1	-	2	3	1	1	1	-	-	1	-	3
other	2	1	2	6	-	3	10	-	-	1	-	-
Other												
whole	-	-	-	1	-	-	-	-	-	-	-	-
profile	-	-	-	-	1	1	-	-	-	-	-	-
rim	1	-	-	2	-	3	2	-	1	1	-	1
foot	1	1	3	4	-	2	-	-	-	2	-	4
other	150	15	77	132	82	171	37	19	56	65	20	72
Plain ware												
Food: prepare/serve												
profile	-	-	-	1	-	-	-	-	-	-	-	-
rim	3	-	8	11	6	24	-	2	-	3	-	4
foot	-	-	2	2	3	8	-	-	-	1	-	-
other	1	-	8	-	1	1	-	-	-	2	-	-
Drink: serve/pour												
rim	3	-	6	5	8	6	2	1	-	-	1	1
foot	2	1	-	4	2	19	1	2	-	-	-	3
other	-	-	1	5	1	14	6	-	-	1	1	-
Food/Drink: store/contain												
profile	-	-	-	1	-	-	-	-	-	-	-	-
rim	8	-	1	28	-	14	1	3	1	1	-	1
foot	1	-	1	3	1	3	-	-	-	2	-	1
other	29	1	68	187	3	74	-	-	1	2	-	11
Other												
rim	-	-	2	4	-	-	1	-	-	-	-	-
foot	-	-	-	4	-	-	-	-	-	-	-	-
other	542	57	189	461	272	224	55	142	63	334	40	288

Table 1. House 7: Distribution of Finds by Loci, Pottery by Ware, Function, and Anatomical Variable

Locus	I	II	III	IV	V–VI/ XXIV– XXVIII	VII	VIII	IX– XIV	XV– XVI	XVII– XIX	XX	XXI– XXIII
Coarse ware												
Food: prepare/serve												
whole	-	-	2	-	-	-	-	-	-	-	-	-
profile	-	-	1	2	-	-	-	-	-	-	-	-
rim	-	-	-	2	-	3	-	-	1	-	1	-
other	-	-	7	-	1	1	-	-	-	-	-	-
Food: cook												
whole	1	-	-	-	-	-	-	-	-	-	1	-
profile	-	-	-	1	-	-	-	-	-	-	-	-
rim	4	-	15	33	24	59	-	-	4	7	1	11
foot?	3	-	-	-	-	-	-	-	-	-	-	-
other	2	-	5	14	28	13	1	1	2	1	1	11
Drink: serve/pour												
rim	-	-	1	1	-	3	-	-	-	-	-	-
foot	-	-	1	1	-	-	-	1	-	1	1	-
other	-	-	-	1	-	2	-	-	-	-	-	1
Food/Drink: store/contain												
profile	-	-	-	2	-	-	-	-	-	-	-	-
rim	2	-	-	1	-	1	-	-	-	1	-	1
other	1	-	2	-	-	-	-	-	-	-	-	-
Other												
rim	-	1	-	-	-	1	-	-	-	-	-	-
other	60	31	123	166	176	166	88	42	59	70	4	100
Roman												
rim	-	-	-	-	1	-	-	-	-	-	-	-
other	-	-	-	-	5	-	-	4	-	3	-	5
Byzantine												
other	-	-	-	-	-	2	-	-	-	-	-	-
Modern												
rim	-	-	-	-	-	-	-	1	-	-	-	-
other	-	-	-	-	-	-	-	-	-	-	-	3
total pottery items = 6230												
Clay												
Lamp												
whole	-	-	-	1	-	1	-	-	-	-	-	-
profile	-	-	-	1	-	-	-	-	-	-	-	-
rim	1	-	3	-	1	4	1	-	3	-	-	1
foot	-	-	-	-	-	1	-	-	-	-	-	-
other	1	-	-	-	1	-	-	2	-	-	-	-
Loom weight	-	-	1	1	1	4	1	1	1	-	-	1
Miniatures												
bowl												
profile	-	-	-	1	-	-	-	-	-	-	-	-
foot	-	-	-	-	-	1	-	-	-	-	-	-

Table 1 (continued). House 7: Distribution of Finds by Loci, Pottery by Ware, Function, and Anatomical Variable

Locus	I	II	III	IV	V–VI/ XXIV– XXVIII	VII	VIII	IX– XIV	XV– XVI	XVII– XIX	XX	XXI– XXIII
Kotyle												
whole	1	-	-	1	-	-	-	-	-	-	-	-
rim	-	-	-	2	1	-	-	-	-	1	-	-
foot	-	-	1	4	-	-	-	-	-	2	-	-
Jug												
whole	-	-	-	1	-	-	-	-	-	1	-	-
rim	-	-	-	-	-	1	-	-	-	-	-	-
foot	-	-	-	-	1	-	-	-	-	-	-	-
other	-	-	-	-	1	-	-	-	-	-	-	-
Lamp	-	-	-	1	-	-	-	-	-	-	-	-
Lekythos												
whole	-	-	-	-	-	-	-	-	1	-	-	-
											(MNV = 22)	
Tile												
body	1060	23	225	241	265	163	118	200	25	189	21	48
edge	850	1	145	119	124	139	5	67	8	9	1	19
cover	640	-	9	14	17	7	1	44	-	1	1	1
complete cover	1	-	1	-	-	-	-	-	-	-	-	-
Other												
figurine base	-	-	-	-	1	-	-	-	-	-	-	-
mold	-	-	-	-	-	-	-	-	-	1	-	-
"chimney" tile	-	-	1	-	-	-	-	-	-	-	-	-
drain segment	-	-	-	-	-	-	1	-	-	-	-	-
Stone												
pier capital	1	-	-	-	-	-	-	1	-	-	-	-
architectural fragment	1	-	-	-	-	-	-	1	-	-	-	-
marble fragment	-	-	-	-	-	-	-	-	-	-	1	-
worked block	-	-	-	2	3	-	2	-	-	-	-	-
incised stone	-	-	-	-	-	-	-	-	-	1	-	-
obsidian blade	-	1	-	-	-	-	1	-	1	-	-	-
grinding slab	-	-	-	-	-	-	-	1	-	-	-	-
rubber	-	-	-	-	-	-	-	-	-	1	-	-
button	-	-	-	-	-	-	-	-	-	1	-	-
Metal												
Iron												
nail	-	3	5	3	13	1	-	1	-	2	-	2
spike	-	-	1	1	-	-	-	2	-	-	-	-
clamp	-	-	1	-	1	-	-	-	-	-	-	-
strip	-	-	1	-	-	-	-	-	-	-	-	-
ring	-	-	-	-	1	-	-	-	-	-	-	-
chisel	-	-	-	-	-	-	-	-	-	-	1	-
sickle	-	-	-	-	-	-	-	-	1	-	-	-
spearhead	-	-	-	-	1	-	-	-	-	-	-	-
socket	-	-	-	-	-	1	-	-	-	1	-	-
rod	-	-	1	-	-	-	-	-	-	-	-	-
rod/spit?	-	-	1	-	-	-	-	-	-	-	-	-
handle?	-	-	-	-	-	-	-	-	-	-	-	-
scoop fragment	-	1	-	-	-	-	-	-	-	-	-	-

Table 1 (continued). House 7: Distribution of Finds by Loci, Pottery by Ware, Function, and Anatomical Variable

Locus	I	II	III	IV	V–VI/ XXIV– XXVIII	VII	VIII	IX– XIV	XV– XVI	XVII– XIX	XX	XXI– XXIII
Bronze												
ornament	-	-	-	-	1	-	-	-	-	-	-	-
cock figurine	-	-	1	-	-	-	-	-	-	-	-	-
"cup"	-	-	-	-	1	-	-	-	-	-	-	-
jug	-	-	-	-	-	-	-	-	-	-	-	1
sheath	-	-	1	-	-	-	-	-	-	-	-	-
fishhook	-	-	-	-	1	-	-	-	-	-	-	-
coil	-	-	-	-	1	-	-	-	-	-	-	-
disk	-	-	-	1	-	-	-	-	-	-	-	-
handle	-	-	-	-	-	1	-	1	-	-	-	-
nail	-	-	1	-	-	-	-	1	-	-	-	-
sheet	-	-	-	-	-	-	1	-	-	-	-	-
embossed sheet	-	-	-	-	-	-	-	-	-	1	-	-
sheet with FE nail	1	-	-	-	-	-	-	-	-	-	-	-
rivet	-	-	-	-	-	1	-	-	-	-	-	-
Lead												
clamp	-	1	2	-	-	-	-	-	-	-	-	-
point?	-	-	-	-	-	-	-	1	-	-	-	-
"lid"	-	-	-	-	1	-	-	-	-	-	-	-
strip	1	-	-	-	-	-	-	-	-	-	-	-
Unidentified metal	2	-	1	x	2	12	-	8	-	9	-	-
Coin												
AE Hermione	1	-	1	-	2	-	-	-	-	-	-	-
AE Tiryns	1	-	-	1	1	-	-	-	-	-	-	-
Varia												
Bone												
fragments	-	-	-	-	x	-	x	1	-	-	-	-
small bag	-	-	-	-	-	1.5	-	-	-	-	-	-
medium bag	-	-	-	-	-	0.5	-	-	-	-	-	-
Shell												
Cerastoderma	-	-	1	-	-	-	-	-	-	-	-	-
Cerithium	-	-	2	-	1	1	1	5	2	2	1	2
Cockle	-	-	-	-	-	-	3	-	-	-	-	-
Conus mediterraneus	-	-	-	-	-	-	-	-	-	1	-	-
Estrea	-	-	1	-	-	-	-	-	-	-	-	-
Glycimeris	-	-	-	-	-	1	-	-	-	-	-	1
Helix	-	-	-	-	-	-	88	-	-	-	-	-
Monodonta turbinata	-	-	-	-	2	-	-	-	-	-	-	-
Mother of pearl	-	-	-	-	-	-	-	-	-	5	-	-
Murex	2	-	1	-	2	-	-	-	-	-	1	-
Patella	-	-	-	-	-	-	-	-	2	-	-	1
Pinna	-	-	2	1	1	x	-	1	1	-	-	-
Spondylus	-	-	-	1	-	-	-	-	-	-	-	-
Tonna	-	-	3	-	2	-	-	-	-	-	1	-
Venus aurea	-	-	5	-	-	-	-	-	-	-	-	-
Vertigo	-	-	-	-	-	-	42	-	-	-	-	-
unidentified	-	-	-	2	-	-	-	-	-	-	-	-
Other												
carbonized wood	-	-	-	-	-	-	x	-	-	-	-	-

Table 1 (continued). House 7: Distribution of Finds by Loci, Pottery by Ware, Function, and Anatomical Variable

Locus	I	II	III	IV	V–VI/ XXIV– XXVIII	VII	VIII	IX– XIV	XV– XVI	XVII– XIX	XX	XXI– XXIII	Total
Fine ware													
Food: serve/consume	12	1	7	15	7	23	5	1	4	5	-	7	87
Drink: consume	18	1	30	20	20	49	11	4	15	22	3	16	209
Drink: serve/pour	4	-	3	11	4	6	1	1	1	2	-	7	40
Drink: serve/contain	7	-	4	7	2	4	3	-	-	2	-	4	33
Other	2	1	3	7	1	6	2	-	1	3	-	5	31
Plain ware													
Food: prepare/serve	3	-	10	14	9	33	-	2	-	4	-	4	79
Drink: serve/pour	5	1	6	9	10	25	3	1	-	-	1	4	65
Food/drink: store/contain	9	-	2	32	1	17	1	3	1	3	-	2	71
Other	-	-	2	8	-	-	1	-	-	-	-	-	11
Coarse ware													
Food: prepare/serve	-	-	3	4	-	3	-	-	1	-	1	-	12
Food: cook	8?	-	15	34	24	59	-	-	4	7	2	11	164?
Drink: serve/pour	-	-	2	2	-	3	-	1	-	1	1	-	10
Food/drink: contain/store	2	-	-	3	-	1	-	-	-	1	-	1	8
Other	-	1	-	-	-	1	-	-	-	-	-	-	2
Roman	-	-	-	-	1	-	-	-	-	-	-	-	1
Modern	-	-	-	-	-	-	-	1	-	-	-	-	1
MNV per locus	70	5	87	166	79	230	27	14	27	50	8	61	824 (House 7 MNV)

Table 2. House 7: Minimum Numbers of Vessels Represented

Locus	I	II	III	IV	V–VI / XXIV– XXVIII	VII	VIII	IX– XIV	XV– XVI	XVII– XIX	XX	XXI– XXIII
Fine ware												
Red Figure												
hydria rim	-	-	-	1?	-	-	-	-	-	-	-	-
krater rim	1	-	-	2	-	1	1	-	-	-	-	1
krater body	-	-	-	3	-	1	-	-	-	-	-	-
skyphos rim	-	-	-	-	-	-	-	-	-	-	-	1
unidentified	4	1	2	-	1	4	-	-	-	1	1	2
											MNV = 28	
Other												
aryballos	-	-	-	-	1	-	-	-	-	-	-	-
askos whole	-	-	-	1	-	-	-	-	-	-	-	-
rim	-	-	-	1	-	1	-	-	-	-	-	-
foot	1	-	-	-	-	-	-	-	-	-	-	-
other	-	-	-	-	-	1	-	1	-	-	-	-
jar foot	-	-	-	1	-	-	-	-	-	-	-	-
ladle	-	-	1	-	-	-	-	-	-	-	-	-
lekanis / pyxis												
profile	-	-	-	-	1?	-	-	-	-	-	-	-
rim	-	-	-	1	-	1	-	-	-	-	-	1
foot	-	-	-	-	-	1?	-	-	-	-	-	-
other	-	-	-	-	-	-	-	-	1	-	-	-
lekythos												
profile	-	-	-	-	-	1	-	-	-	-	-	-
rim	-	-	-	-	-	1?	-	-	-	-	-	-
foot	-	-	1	-	-	-	-	-	-	-	-	-
other	1	-	-	2	-	-	-	-	-	-	-	1
lid												
rim	-	-	-	-	-	-	1	-	-	-	-	-
other	-	-	-	-	-	1?	-	-	-	1	-	-
storage bin												
rim	-	-	-	-	-	-	-	-	1	-	-	-
Plain ware												
askos rim	-	-	-	1?	-	-	-	-	-	-	-	-
lid												
rim	-	-	2	2	-	-	1	-	-	-	-	-
other	1	-	-	-	-	4	1	-	-	-	-	-
tray	-	-	-	-	-	1?	-	-	-	-	-	-
Coarse ware												
lid	-	-	-	-	1	-	-	-	-	-	-	-

Table 3. House 7: Other Pottery Variables

Locus	I	II	V	VI	VII	VIII–IX	XI–XIV	XV	XVI	XVII	XVIII
Fine ware											
Food: serve/consume											
whole	-	-	-	-	-	-	-	-	-	-	1
profile	2	-	-	-	-	-	-	-	-	-	2
rim	5	4	3	2	1	2	2	1	-	2	4
foot/base	2	4	1	5	-	1	-	-	-	2	1
other	1	2	-	1	-	-	1	-	-	4	2
Drink: consume											
whole	-	-	-	-	-	-	2	-	-	-	-
profile	-	1	-	1	-	-	1	-	-	2	1
rim	12	4	3	14	1	2	16	3	2	16	11
foot/base	6	2	-	5	-	2	4	2	-	7	2
other	4	10	2	10	-	2	2	3	4	4	2
Drink: serve/pour											
whole	-	1	-	-	-	-	-	-	-	-	-
profile	-	-	-	-	-	-	1	-	-	-	-
rim	1	-	-	-	-	-	-	1	-	1	3
foot/base	-	1	-	-	-	-	1	-	-	-	2
other	3	9	-	1	2	-	-	-	7	1	-
Drink: serve/contain											
rim	2	2	-	-	-	-	-	-	-	-	-
foot	-	-	-	-	-	-	-	-	-	1	-
other	-	1	-	1	-	-	-	-	2	2	1
Other											
whole	-	-	-	1	-	-	2	1	-	-	-
profile	-	-	-	1	-	-	-	-	1	-	-
rim	1	-	-	-	-	-	-	1	-	1	2
foot	3	-	-	1	1	-	-	-	-	-	1
other	91	59	8	30	1	16	38	11	13	61	65
Plain ware											
Food: prepare/serve											
whole	-	1	-	-	-	-	-	-	-	-	-
rim	4	5	1	2	1	-	-	2	2	1	1
foot	-	1	-	-	-	-	-	-	-	-	-
other	-	-	-	-	-	-	-	-	-	2	-
Drink: serve/pour											
whole	-	-	-	-	-	-	-	-	-	1	-
rim	6	2	-	11	-	-	5	-	-	-	1
foot/base	1	6	1	4	-	2	2	1	-	-	1
other	1	4	1	3	-	-	-	-	-	-	-
Food/Drink: store/contain											
rim	4	5	1	9	-	1	2	-	5	-	-
foot	-	2	1	1	-	-	-	-	-	-	-
other	7	9	-	12	-	1	2	2	-	1	1
Other											
rim	-	2	1	-	-	-	-	-	-	1	1
foot	-	-	1	-	-	-	-	-	1	-	2
other	306	172	99	191	13	-	97	51	43	86	175

Table 4. House A: Distribution of Finds by Loci, Pottery by Ware, Function, and Anatomical Variable

Locus	I	II	V	VI	VII	VIII–IX	XI–XIV	XV	XVI	XVII	XVIII
Coarse ware											
Food: prepare/serve											
rim	-	2	-	1	-	-	-	-	-	-	-
Food: cook											
rim	19	9	5	19	1	5	15	3	4	11	8
other	3	5	1	4	-	-	23	2	5	2	13
Drink: serve/pour											
foot	-	2	-	1	-	-	-	-	-	-	1
Food/Drink: store/contain											
whole	-	1	-	-	-	-	-	4	-	-	-
rim	-	2	-	-	-	-	3	-	3	-	1
other	-	-	-	1	1	-	-	50	-	100+	1
Other											
whole	-	1	-	-	-	-	-	-	-	-	-
rim	-	-	-	-	-	-	-	1	-	-	1
foot	2	1	-	-	-	-	-	-	-	-	-
other	180	31	16	100	18	15	42	36	21	84	102
Roman											
Other	-	12	-	1	-	3	-	-	-	-	-
								total pottery items = 3062+			
Clay											
Lamp											
rim	1	-	-	-	-	-	-	1	1	3	-
foot	-	1	-	-	-	-	-	-	-	-	-
Loom weight	-	1	-	2	-	-	-	-	-	1	4
Miniatures											
jug											
whole	-	-	-	-	-	-	1	-	-	-	1
foot	1	3	-	-	-	-	-	-	-	-	-
other	-	-	-	-	-	-	-	-	-	-	1?
lamp	-	-	-	-	-	-	1	-	-	-	-
kotyle											
whole	-	-	-	-	-	-	-	-	1	-	1
other	-	-	-	-	-	-	-	-	-	2	-
										(MNV = 12)	
Tile											
body	97	180	33*	95*	34	8	81	27	59	4*	65
edge	71	28	5*	2*	-	4	(+	4	1	-	2
cover	8	5	-	-	-	(+30	250	-	4	-	-
whole	4	-	-	-	-	kg)	kg)	-	-	1	1?
									(*full count lacking)		

Table 4 (continued). House A: Distribution of Finds by Loci, Pottery by Ware, Function, and Anatomical Variable

Locus	I	II	V	VI	VII	VIII–IX	XI–XIV	XV	XVI	XVII	XVIII
Stone											
altar? fragment	-	-	-	1	-	-	-	-	-	-	-
obsidian blade	-	1	-	-	-	-	-	-	-	-	-
flint flake	-	1	-	-	-	-	-	-	-	-	-
worked chips	-	-	-	-	-	-	-	-	-	2	-
worked block	-	2	-	-	-	-	-	1	-	-	-
worked stone	-	-	-	-	-	-	-	-	-	-	1
grindstone	-	-	-	-	-	-	-	1	-	-	-
rock crystal	-	-	-	-	-	-	-	-	-	1	-
Metal											
Iron											
nail	-	4	-	2	1	-	-	-	-	-	1
spike	-	1	-	-	-	-	-	-	-	-	1
clamp	-	-	-	-	-	-	1	-	-	-	-
sheet	-	-	-	-	-	-	-	-	-	-	1
Bronze											
nail	-	-	-	-	-	-	-	-	-	-	1
finger ring	-	1	-	-	-	-	-	-	-	-	-
embossed fragment	-	-	-	1	-	-	-	-	-	-	-
disk fragment	-	-	-	-	-	-	1	-	-	-	-
distaff tip	-	-	-	-	-	-	1	-	-	-	-
sheathing	-	-	-	-	-	-	-	-	2+	-	1
weight	-	-	-	-	-	-	-	-	-	-	1
reinforcement	-	-	-	-	-	-	-	-	-	-	1
Lead bar	-	-	-	1	-	-	-	-	-	-	-
Unidentified metal	-	4+	-	4+	-	-	4+	-	1	12	-
Coin											
AE Aegina	-	-	-	2	-	-	1	-	-	-	3
AE Hermione	-	-	-	-	-	-	-	1	-	-	-
AE Tiryns	1	-	-	1	-	-	-	1	1	-	5
AE Troizen	-	-	-	1	-	-	-	-	-	-	-
Varia											
bone	-	-	-	-	-	-	-	-	-	x	-
bone die	-	-	-	-	-	-	-	-	-	1	-
Shell											
Cerithium	1	1	-	4	-	-	-	-	-	-	5
Cerastoderma	-	1	-	2	-	-	-	-	-	-	-
Helix	3	-	-	-	-	-	-	-	-	-	-
Monodonta	-	-	-	-	-	-	-	-	-	1	-
Murex	-	-	-	1	1	-	1	-	-	-	-
Patella	-	-	-	-	-	-	-	-	-	2	-
Pinna	-	-	-	4	-	-	-	3	-	-	4
Spondylus	-	-	-	-	-	-	-	-	-	-	1
Vertigo	1	-	-	-	-	-	-	-	-	-	-
unidentified	-	-	-	-	-	-	1	-	-	x	-
Glass	-	-	3	2	-	-	-	-	-	-	-

Table 4 (continued). House A: Distribution of Finds by Loci, Pottery by Ware, Function, and Anatomical Variable

Locus	I	II	V	VI	VII	VIII–IX	XI–XIV	XV	XVI	XVII	XVIII	Total
Fine ware												
Food: serve/consume	9	8	4	7	1	3	2	1	-	4	8	47
Drink: consume	18	7	3	20	1	4	23	5	2	25	14	122
Drink: serve/pour	1	2	-	-	-	-	2	1	-	1	5	12
Drink: serve/contain	2	2	-	-	-	-	-	-	-	1	-	5
Other	4	-	-	3	1	-	2	2	1	1	3	17
Plain ware												
Food: prepare/serve	4	7	1	2	1	-	-	2	2	1	1	21
Drink: serve/pour	7	8	1	15	-	2	7	1	-	1	2	44
Food/drink: store/contain	4	7	2	10	-	1	2	-	5	-	-	31
Other	-	2	2	-	-	-	-	-	1	1	3	9
Coarse ware												
Food: prepare/serve	-	2	-	1	-	-	-	-	-	-	-	3
Food: cook	19	9	5	19	1	5	15	3	4	11	8	99
Drink: serve/pour	-	2	-	1	-	-	-	-	-	-	1	4
Food/drink: store/contain	-	3	-	-	-	-	3	4	3	-	1	14
Other	2	2	-	-	-	-	-	1	-	-	1	6
MNV per locus	70	61	18	78	5	15	56	20	18	46	47	434 (House A MNV)

Table 5. House A: Minimum Numbers of Vessels Represented

Locus	I	II	V	VI	VII	VIII–IX	XI–XIV	XV	XVI	XVII	XVIII
Fine ware											
Red Figure											
askos	-	-	-	-	-	-	-	1	-	-	-
krater body	-	1?	-	1?	-	-	-	-	1?	-	-
oinochoe body	-	1?	-	-	-	-	-	-	-	-	-
skyphos rim	-	-	-	-	-	-	-	-	-	-	1
skyphos body	2	-	-	-	-	-	-	-	-	-	-
unidentified	-	-	-	2	-	-	-	-	5	-	-
											MNV = 15?
Other											
amphoriskos											
foot	-	-	-	-	-	-	-	-	-	-	1
askos	-	-	-	-	-	-	1	1	-	-	-
lekanis/pyxis											
whole	-	-	-	1	-	-	-	-	-	-	-
profile	-	-	-	1	-	-	-	-	-	-	-
rim	-	-	-	-	-	-	-	-	-	-	1
lekythos											
whole	-	-	-	-	-	-	1	-	-	-	-
rim	1	-	-	-	-	-	-	1?	-	1	1
pyxis											
foot	3	-	-	-	-	-	-	-	-	-	-
lid											
profile	-	-	-	-	-	-	-	-	1	-	-
other	-	-	-	-	-	-	-	-	-	-	1
Plain ware											
lid rim/knob	-	-	1	1	-	-	-	-	-	-	1
tripod foot	-	-	-	-	-	-	-	-	1?	-	-
Coarse ware											
krater	-	1	-	-	-	-	-	-	-	-	-
krater fragment	1	-	-	-	-	-	-	-	-	-	-
louterion rim	-	-	-	-	-	-	-	1	-	-	-

Table 6. House A: Other Pottery Variables

Locus	I	II	III	IV	V	VI	VII	IX	X	XI	XII/ XIII	XIV	XV	XVI
Fine ware														
Food: serve/consume														
whole	-	-	-	-	-	-	-	-	-	-	1	1	-	-
profile	-	-	-	2	-	1	-	-	-	-	-	-	1	-
rim	-	3	-	11	1	-	-	-	-	-	4	2	1	-
foot	-	1	-	4	-	3	-	-	-	4	7	-	-	-
other	-	-	-	2	-	-	-	-	-	-	1	-	-	-
Drink: consume														
whole	-	-	-	1	-	-	-	1	-	-	-	-	-	-
profile	-	-	-	2	-	-	-	1	-	1	-	-	-	-
rim	-	4	-	48	1	1	1	3	-	4	26	3	4	-
foot	-	2	-	7	-	1	1	1	-	1	6	-	2	-
other	1	-	-	12	1	-	1	3	2	5	8	-	4	1
Drink: serve/pour														
profile	-	-	-	-	-	-	-	-	-	-	-	-	-	-
rim	-	2	-	5	-	-	-	-	-	1	1	2	-	-
foot	-	2	-	5	-	-	-	-	-	-	5	1	-	-
other	1	3	-	-	-	-	-	1	-	1	-	-	-	-
Drink: serve/contain														
profile	-	-	-	-	-	2	-	-	-	-	-	-	-	-
rim	-	1	-	2	-	-	-	-	1	1	-	-	1	-
foot	-	1	-	1	-	-	-	-	-	1	-	-	-	-
other	-	1	-	-	-	-	-	-	1	1	1	1	-	-
Other														
whole	-	-	-	1	-	-	-	-	-	-	1	-	-	-
profile	-	-	-	4	-	-	-	-	-	-	-	-	-	-
rim	-	1	-	2	-	-	-	1	-	1	-	-	-	-
foot	3	1	-	-	-	-	-	-	-	3	1	2	-	-
other	10	38	7	303	11	-	5	18	4	42	114	37	29	12
Plain ware														
Food: prepare/serve														
rim	1	5	-	2	-	1	-	1	-	-	1	12	-	-
foot	-	-	-	1	1	-	-	-	-	-	3	-	-	-
Drink: serve/pour														
whole	-	-	-	-	-	-	-	-	-	-	-	1	-	-
profile	-	-	-	-	-	1	-	-	-	-	2	-	-	-
rim	-	-	-	2	-	1	2	1	1	1	5	4	-	-
foot	-	-	-	8	2	4	-	1	-	-	2	-	-	-
other	-	1	-	3	-	1	-	2	4	6	6	-	-	-
Food/Drink: store/contain														
whole	-	-	-	-	-	-	-	-	-	1	-	-	-	-
profile	-	-	-	1	-	-	-	3	-	-	2	1?	-	-
rim	1	1	-	15	-	3	3	6	1	6	12	18	2	-
foot	-	-	-	-	-	2	-	1	1	-	7	1	1	-
other	1	-	-	94	1	2	6	12	3	15	19	124	6	25
Other														
profile	-	-	-	-	-	-	-	-	-	-	1	-	-	-
rim	-	-	-	-	-	-	-	-	-	-	-	-	1	-
foot	-	-	-	1	-	-	-	-	-	2	2	-	-	-
other	23	92	-	759	56	155	130	343	86	595	593	55	92	15

Table 7. House C: Distribution of Finds by Loci, Pottery by Ware, Function, and Anatomical Variable

Locus	I	II	III	IV	V	VI	VII	IX	X	XI	XII/ XIII	XIV	XV	XVI
Coarse ware														
Food: prepare/serve														
rim	-	1	-	-	-	-	1	-	-	1	1	-	-	-
Food: cook														
whole	-	-	-	-	-	-	-	-	-	1	1	-	-	-
profile	-	-	-	1	1	-	-	-	-	-	5	-	2	-
rim	2	1	-	31	1	2	-	1	11	12	4	2	1	-
other	112	7	-	7	-	-	4	1	7	22	11	-	-	1
Drink: serve/pour														
foot	-	-	-	-	-	-	-	-	-	-	1	-	-	-
other	-	-	-	-	-	-	-	-	-	1	-	1	-	-
Food/Drink: store/contain														
profile	-	-	-	-	-	-	-	-	-	-	-	-	-	-
rim	-	-	-	-	2	1	1	-	-	-	2	1	-	-
foot	-	-	-	-	1	1	1	-	-	-	-	2	-	-
other	-	-	-	-	-	53	-	-	-	16	-	528	-	-
Other														
rim	2	-	-	1	-	-	-	-	-	-	2	-	-	-
other	-	11	-	135	15	13	22	47	30	67	182	20	15	30
Roman														
rim	-	-	-	-	-	-	-	-	1	2	1	-	-	-
foot	-	1	-	-	-	-	-	-	-	-	-	-	-	-
other	1	14	-	8	-	4	-	10	9	15	16	-	-	-
Byzantine														
other	-	-	-	-	-	-	-	1	-	-	-	-	-	-
										total pottery items = 5935				
Clay														
Lamp														
whole	-	-	-	1	-	-	-	-	-	1	-	1	-	-
profile	-	-	-	-	-	-	-	-	-	-	-	-	1	-
rim	-	-	-	1	-	-	-	-	-	-	1	-	-	-
foot	1	-	-	-	-	-	-	-	-	-	-	-	-	-
Loom weight	-	-	-	1	-	-	-	1	1 (6-54)	-	3	-	3	-
Miniatures														
kotyle														
whole	-	-	-	1	-	-	-	-	-	1	-	-	-	-
profile	-	-	-	3	-	-	-	-	-	-	-	-	-	-
rim	-	1	-	4	-	-	-	-	-	-	-	-	-	-
foot	-	-	-	1	-	1	-	-	-	-	-	-	-	-
													MNV = 12	
Tile											*	*		*
body	208	653	-	98	123+	804	373	92	58	59	2123	1012	205	250?
weight: body (kg)	-	-	-	-	-	104	-	-	-	-	-	-	-	-
edge	15	256	-	5	50+	800	117	28	8	16	726	444	29	150?
weight: edge (kg)	-	-	-	-	-	52	-	-	-	-	-	-	-	-
cover	9	62	-	3	29	20	11	2	-	-	87	22	-	2
complete cover	-	-	-	-	-	-	-	-	-	-	1	-	-	-
other	-	-	-	-	-	-	-	-	-	1	325+	-	-	-

(*counts missing)

Table 7 (continued). House C: Distribution of Finds by Loci, Pottery by Ware, Function, and Anatomical Variable

Locus	I	II	III	IV	V	VI	VII	IX	X	XI	XII/ XIII	XIV	XV	XVI
Stone														
pier capital	1	-	-	-	-	-	-	-	-	-	-	1	-	-
Doric capital	-	-	-	-	-	-	1	-	-	-	-	2	-	-
jamb	-	-	-	-	-	-	-	-	-	1	-	-	-	-
column drum	-	-	-	-	-	-	-	-	-	-	-	1	-	-
worked block	-	-	-	-	-	-	-	-	-	-	-	1	-	-
mill	-	-	-	-	-	1	-	-	-	-	-	-	-	-
grindstone fragment	1	-	-	-	-	-	-	-	-	-	-	-	-	-
limestone fragment	-	-	-	-	-	-	1	-	-	-	-	-	-	-
obsidian blade	-	-	-	-	-	-	-	-	-	1	1	-	-	-
flint	-	-	-	-	-	-	-	-	-	1	-	-	1	-
rock crystal	-	-	-	-	-	-	-	-	-	-	-	-	1	-
other	-	-	-	-	-	-	-	-	-	-	-	x	-	-
Metal														
Iron														
nail	-	-	-	1	-	-	1	1	6 (6-54)	-	2	-	-	-
spike	-	-	-	1	-	-	-	-	-	-	-	-	-	-
chain link	-	-	-	x	-	-	-	-	-	-	-	-	-	-
cutting implement	-	-	-	3	-	-	1	1?	-	-	-	-	-	-
rim	-	-	-	1	-	-	-	-	-	-	-	-	-	-
coil	-	-	-	1	-	-	-	-	-	-	-	-	-	-
bell-shaped object	-	-	-	-	-	-	-	-	-	1	-	-	-	-
sheet	-	-	-	-	-	-	-	1	-	-	-	-	-	-
Bronze														
handle	-	-	-	2	-	-	-	-	-	-	-	-	-	-
boss	-	-	-	3	-	-	-	-	-	-	-	-	-	-
earring	-	-	-	1	-	-	-	-	-	-	-	-	-	-
washer	-	-	-	1	-	-	-	-	-	-	-	-	-	-
ring (chain?)	-	-	-	1	-	-	-	-	-	-	-	-	-	-
latchstring plate	-	-	-	1	-	-	-	-	-	-	-	-	-	-
sheathing	1	-	-	-	-	-	-	-	-	-	-	-	-	1
Lead														
weight	-	-	-	1	-	-	-	-	-	-	-	-	-	-
strip	-	-	-	1	-	-	-	-	-	-	-	-	-	-
reinforcement	-	-	-	-	-	-	-	-	-	-	-	1	-	-
unidentified	-	-	12	9+	-	-	-	4	-	5	-	3	-	-
Coin														
AE Tiryns	-	-	-	-	-	-	-	1	1	-	-	-	-	-
Varia														
bone	-	-	-	2	-	1	-	-	2	-	-	1	-	-
Shell														
Callista	-	-	-	3	-	-	-	-	-	-	-	-	-	-
Cerastoderma	-	-	-	4	-	-	-	-	-	-	-	1	-	-
Cerithium	-	-	-	3	-	-	-	1	-	-	3	1	-	-
Helix	-	-	-	-	-	-	-	-	-	1	-	-	-	-
Limpet	-	-	-	-	-	-	-	1	-	-	-	-	-	-
Monodonta	-	-	-	-	-	-	-	-	-	-	-	1	-	-

Table 7 (continued). House C: Distribution of Finds by Loci, Pottery by Ware, Function, and Anatomical Variable

Locus	I	II	III	IV	V	VI	VII	IX	X	XI	XII/ XIII	XIV	XV	XVI
Mother of pearl	-	-	-	-	-	-	-	-	-	-	1	-	-	-
Murex	-	-	-	10	-	-	-	2	-	-	-	-	-	-
Patella	-	1	-	9	-	-	-	-	-	-	-	1	-	-
Pinna	-	-	-	6	-	-	-	-	-	1	-	-	-	-
Spondylus	-	1	-	-	-	-	-	-	-	1?	-	-	-	-
Tonna	-	-	-	13	-	-	-	-	-	-	-	-	-	-
Venus verucosa	-	-	-	-	-	-	-	-	-	-	-	-	1	-
Vertigo	-	-	-	-	-	-	-	1	-	1	-	-	1	-
unidentified	21	-	2	10	-	-	1	-	-	5	4	x	1	-
Other														
plastic comb	-	-	-	-	-	-	-	-	-	-	1	-	-	-

Table 7 (continued). House C: Distribution of Finds by Loci, Pottery by Ware, Function, and Anatomical Variable

Locus	I	II	III	IV	V	VI	VII	IX	X	XI	XII/ XIII	XIV	XV	XVI	Total
Fine ware															
Food: serve/consume	-	4	-	17	1	4	-	-	-	4	12	3	2	-	47
Drink: consume	-	6	-	58	1	2	2	6	-	6	32	3	6	-	122
Drink: serve/pour	-	4	-	10	-	-	-	-	-	1	6	3	-	-	24
Drink: serve/contain	-	2	-	3	-	2	-	-	1	2	-	-	1	-	11
Other	3	2	-	7	-	-	-	1	-	4	2	2	-	-	21
Plain ware															
Food: prepare/serve	1	5	-	3	1	1	-	1	-	-	4	12	-	-	28
Drink: serve/pour	-	-	-	10	2	6	2	2	1	1	9	5	-	-	38
Food/drink: store/contain	1	1	-	16	-	4	3	10	2	7	21	20	3	-	88
Other	-	-	-	1	-	-	-	-	-	2	3	-	1	-	7
Coarse ware															
Food: prepare/serve	-	1	-	-	-	-	1	-	-	1	1	-	-	-	4
Food: cook	2	1	-	32	2	2	-	1	11	13	10	2	3	-	79
Drink: serve/pour	-	-	-	-	-	-	-	-	-	-	1	-	-	-	1
Food/drink: store/contain	-	-	-	-	3	2	2	-	-	-	2	3	-	-	12
Other	2	-	-	1	-	-	-	-	-	-	2	-	-	-	5
Roman	-	1	-	-	-	-	-	-	1	2	1	-	-	-	5
MNV per locus	9	27	-	158	10	23	10	21	16	43	106	53	16	-	492 (House C MNV)

Table 8. House C: Minimum Number of Vessels Represented

Locus	I	II	III	IV	V	VI	VII	IX	X	XI	XII/ XIII	XIV	XV	XVI
Fine ware														
Red Figure														
askos														
whole	-	-	-	1	-	-	-	-	-	-	-	-	-	-
profile	-	-	-	1	-	-	-	-	-	-	-	-	-	-
lekanis/pyxis														
lid profile	-	-	-	1	-	-	-	-	-	-	-	-	-	-
krater body	-	-	-	-	-	-	-	-	-	1	-	-	-	-
pelike rim	-	1	-	-	-	-	-	-	-	-	-	-	-	-
unidentified	-	2	-	-	-	-	-	-	-	1	-	-	-	-
Other														
amphoriskos														
profile	-	-	-	1	-	-	-	-	-	-	-	-	-	-
aryballos														
body	-	-	-	1	-	-	-	-	-	-	-	-	-	-
askos														
whole	-	-	-	1	-	-	-	-	-	-	-	-	-	-
profile	-	-	-	1	-	-	-	-	-	-	-	-	-	-
rim	-	-	-	-	-	-	-	1	-	-	-	-	-	-
other	-	-	-	2	-	-	-	-	-	-	-	-	-	-
lekanis/pyxis														
profile	-	-	-	1	-	-	-	-	-	-	-	-	-	-
other	-	-	-	1	-	-	-	-	-	-	-	-	-	-
lekanis/pyxis lid														
profile	-	-	-	1	-	-	-	-	-	-	-	-	-	-
lid														
rim	-	1?	-	-	-	-	-	-	-	1	-	-	-	-
other	-	1	-	1	-	-	-	-	-	-	-	-	-	-
lekythos														
profile	-	-	-	1	-	-	-	-	-	-	-	-	-	-
pyxis														
other	-	-	-	-	-	-	-	-	-	-	-	1	-	-
pyxis lid														
rim	-	-	-	1	-	-	-	-	-	-	-	-	-	-
tray	-	-	-	-	-	-	-	-	-	-	1	-	-	-
Plain ware														
aryballos foot	-	-	-	-	-	-	-	-	-	-	1	-	-	-
lid profile	-	-	-	-	-	-	-	-	-	-	1	-	-	-
Coarse ware														
louterion rim	-	-	-	1	-	-	-	-	-	-	-	-	-	-

Table 9. House C: Other Pottery Variables

Locus	I	II	III	IV	V–VII	VIII	IX	X/XI	XII	XIII	XIV	XV	XVI
Fine ware													
Food: serve/consume													
whole	-	1	-	-	1	-	-	-	-	-	7	-	3
profile	-	3	-	-	-	-	-	-	-	-	3	-	2
rim	3	15	-	-	-	-	1	-	-	-	7	1	6
foot	1	4	-	-	1	-	-	2	-	-	1	-	2
Drink: consume													
whole	1	-	-	-	-	-	1	-	1	-	6	-	7
profile	-	2	-	-	1	-	-	-	-	-	1	2	2
rim	-	21	2	1	2	-	4	1	-	-	20	7	40
foot	-	15	1	-	-	-	2	-	-	-	6	4	12
other	3	31	2	-	1	2	1	-	-	-	6	13	48
Drink: serve/pour													
whole	-	-	-	-	-	-	-	-	-	-	1	-	-
profile	-	-	-	-	-	-	-	1	-	-	1	-	-
rim	-	-	-	-	-	-	-	2	-	-	-	-	9
foot	-	1	4	-	-	-	-	-	-	-	2	-	-
other	-	17	-	-	-	-	-	-	-	1	5	-	6
Drink: serve/contain													
profile	-	1	-	-	-	-	-	1	-	-	-	-	-
rim	-	1	1	-	-	-	-	-	-	-	4	1	4
other	-	-	-	-	-	-	1	-	-	-	3	-	-
Other													
whole	-	1	-	-	-	-	-	-	-	-	1	-	1
profile	-	1	-	-	-	-	-	-	-	-	2	-	1?
rim	1	1	-	-	-	-	-	-	-	-	3	-	5
foot	3	1	-	-	-	-	-	-	-	-	2	-	4
other	24	89	18	5	-	6	17	21	8	4	68	12	225
Plain ware													
Food: prepare/serve													
whole	-	1	-	1	-	-	-	-	-	-	2*	-	-
profile	-	2	-	-	-	1	-	-	-	-	-	-	-
rim	-	14	-	-	-	-	4	1	1	-	1	1	11
foot	-	-	-	-	-	-	-	-	-	-	-	-	1
other	12	11+	-	-	-	-	-	-	-	-	-	-	11
Drink: serve/pour													
whole	-	1	-	-	-	-	-	-	-	-	-	-	-
profile	-	1	-	-	-	-	-	-	-	-	-	-	-
rim	4	1	-	-	-	-	-	2	-	-	4	-	5
foot	2	4	-	-	-	1	5	-	-	-	3	-	5
other	-	-	-	-	-	-	1	9	1	-	-	-	9
Food/Drink: store/contain													
whole	-	-	-	1	-	-	-	-	-	-	-	-	-
profile	-	1?	-	-	-	-	-	-	2	-	-	-	-
rim	3	5	-	-	5	4	4	1	-	2	3	-	12
foot	-	1	1	-	-	1	-	4	-	1	-	-	5
other	2	324	1	-	13	-	7	2	-	20	1	1	20

*from fill of RM 6-35 above Level A floor: 5 rim, 1 foot, 30 other

Table 10. House D: Distribution of Finds by Loci, Pottery by Ware, Function, and Anatomical Variable

Locus	I	II	III	IV	V–VII	VIII	IX	X/XI	XII	XIII	XIV	XV	XVI
Other													
whole	-	-	-	-	-	-	-	-	-	-	1	-	-
profile	-	-	-	-	-	-	-	1	1	-	-	-	1
rim	1	-	-	-	-	-	-	-	1	-	-	-	-
foot	-	1	2	-	-	-	-	1	-	-	-	-	-
other	307	533	37	21	87	28	170	21	13	-	122	22	584
Coarse ware													
Food: prepare/serve													
profile	-	3	-	-	-	-	-	-	-	-	-	-	-
rim	1	-	-	1	1	1	2	1	-	-	-	-	1
Food: cook													
whole	-	-	-	-	-	-	-	-	-	-	3	-	1
profile	-	3	-	-	1	-	-	-	-	-	1	-	3
rim	5	24	-	1	1	8	12	2	1	1	14	5	20
other	6	2	-	-	2	-	3	-	-	-	12	-	6
Drink: serve/pour													
rim	-	1	-	-	-	-	-	-	-	-	-	-	-
Food/Drink: store/contain													
whole	-	-	-	-	-	-	-	-	-	-	1	-	1
profile	-	-	-	-	-	-	-	-	-	-	1	-	-
rim	1	11	4	-	1?	-	2	-	4	-	1	-	8
foot	-	1	-	-	-	-	-	-	-	-	-	-	1
other	62	7+	-	-	4	-	20	-	3	-	-	10	20
Other													
whole	-	-	-	-	-	-	-	-	-	-	-	-	1
rim	4	1	-	-	-	-	-	-	-	-	-	-	-
other	77	139	15	7	91	25	18	2	25	6	89	73	181
Roman													
foot	1	-	-	-	-	-	-	-	-	-	-	-	-
other	11	-	2	-	-	-	-	-	-	-	-	-	-

total pottery items = 4536+

Locus	I	II	III	IV	V–VII	VIII	IX	X/XI	XII	XIII	XIV	XV	XVI
Clay													
Loom weight	-	3	1	-	-	-	1	-	-	-	5	1	1
Lamp													
whole	-	-	-	-	-	-	-	-	-	-	2	-	-
rim	-	-	-	-	-	-	1	-	-	-	1	-	2
foot	-	1	-	-	-	-	-	-	-	-	-	-	2
body	-	-	-	-	-	-	2	-	-	-	-	-	2
Miniatures													
bowl													
whole	-	-	-	-	-	-	-	-	-	-	1	-	-
rim	-	1?	-	-	-	-	-	-	-	-	-	-	-
jug													
whole	-	-	-	-	-	-	-	-	-	-	-	1	-
rim	-	1	-	-	-	-	-	-	-	-	-	-	1

Table 10 (continued). House D: Distribution of Finds by Loci, Pottery by Ware, Function, and Anatomical Variable

Locus	I	II	III	IV	V–VII	VIII	IX	X/XI	XII	XIII	XIV	XV	XVI
kotyle													
whole	-	-	-	-	-	-	-	-	-	-	3	-	-
rim	-	-	-	-	-	-	-	-	-	-	1	-	-
foot	-	1	-	-	-	-	-	-	-	-	1	1	-
other	-	2	-	-	-	-	-	-	-	-	-	-	-
lamp	-	-	-	-	-	-	-	-	-	-	1	-	-
												MNV = 15	
Tile													
body fragments	698	498	191	32	315	30	1002	32	9	45	48	202	188
stack	-	3	-	-	-	-	-	-	-	-	-	-	-
zembili	-	-	-	-	-	-	9.5	-	-	-	-	-	-
edge fragments	304	350	39	8	169	16	800	9	2	7	24	55	44
stack	-	2	-	-	-	-	-	-	-	-	-	-	-
zembili	-	-	-	-	-	-	7	-	-	-	-	-	-
cover	13	54	3	4	1	-	32	1	-	8	1	4	10
opaion?	1	-	-	-	2	-	-	-	-	-	-	-	-
painted sima	-	1	-	-	-	-	-	-	-	-	-	-	-
semi-circle?	-	-	-	-	-	-	-	-	-	-	-	1	-
Other													
drain tile	1	-	1	-	-	-	-	-	-	-	-	-	-
relief plaque	1	-	-	-	-	-	-	-	-	-	-	-	-
spool	-	-	1	-	-	-	-	-	-	-	-	-	1
figurine	-	-	-	-	-	-	-	-	-	-	1	-	-
Stone													
architectural fragment	-	-	-	-	-	-	-	-	-	-	-	-	1
pier capital	-	-	-	-	-	-	1	-	-	-	-	-	-
inscribed block	-	-	-	-	-	-	-	-	1	-	-	-	-
flint	-	-	-	-	-	-	1	-	-	-	-	-	-
obsidian blade	-	-	-	-	-	-	-	-	-	-	-	-	1
obsidian flake	1	-	-	-	-	-	-	-	-	-	-	-	-
celt	-	1?	-	-	-	-	-	-	-	-	-	-	-
vessel rim	-	1?	-	-	-	-	-	-	-	-	-	1	-
hollow block	-	-	-	-	1	-	-	-	-	-	-	-	-
grinding slab	-	-	-	-	-	-	-	-	-	-	1	-	-
"handstone"	-	-	-	-	-	-	-	-	-	-	-	-	2
quartz	-	-	-	-	-	-	-	-	-	-	-	-	1
Metal													
Iron													
nail	1	1	-	-	1	-	-	-	-	-	-	-	4
boss	1	-	-	-	-	-	-	-	-	-	-	-	-
ring	-	-	-	-	-	-	-	-	-	-	-	1	-
blade	-	-	-	-	1?	-	-	-	-	-	-	-	-
razor	-	-	-	-	-	-	-	-	-	-	-	-	1
spearhead	-	-	-	-	-	-	-	-	-	-	1	-	-
hook	-	-	-	-	-	-	-	-	-	-	-	-	1
shovel	-	-	-	-	-	-	-	-	-	-	1	-	-
tongs	-	-	-	-	-	-	-	-	-	-	-	-	1
rod	-	-	-	-	-	-	-	-	-	-	1	-	-
handle	-	1	-	-	-	-	-	-	-	-	-	-	-
spit?	-	-	-	-	-	-	-	-	-	-	-	-	1

Table 10 (continued). House D: Distribution of Finds by Loci, Pottery by Ware, Function, and Anatomical Variable

Locus	I	II	III	IV	V–VII	VIII	IX	X/XI	XII	XIII	XIV	XV	XVI
Bronze													
boss	-	-	-	-	-	-	-	-	-	-	1	-	1
nail	-	-	-	-	1	-	-	-	-	-	-	1	4
needle	-	-	-	-	-	-	-	-	-	-	-	1	-
fishhook	1	1	-	-	-	-	-	-	-	-	-	-	-
ring	1	1	-	-	-	2	-	-	-	-	-	1	-
ring reinforcement	-	-	-	-	-	-	-	-	-	-	-	-	1
strip	-	-	-	-	-	-	-	-	-	-	-	-	1
disk	-	-	-	-	-	-	-	-	-	-	-	1	-
earring	-	1	-	-	-	-	-	-	-	-	-	-	-
earring pendant	-	-	-	-	-	-	-	-	-	-	-	1	-
handle	-	1	-	-	-	-	-	-	-	-	-	-	-
drop handle	-	-	-	-	-	-	-	-	-	-	2	-	1
grater	-	1	-	-	-	-	-	-	-	-	-	-	-
strigil	-	-	-	-	-	-	-	-	-	-	1	-	1
ring foot?	-	-	-	-	-	-	-	-	-	-	-	-	1
wire	-	-	-	-	-	-	-	-	-	-	-	-	1
sheet	-	-	-	-	-	-	-	-	-	-	-	-	1
Lead													
clamp	-	1	-	-	-	-	-	-	-	-	1	-	-
slag	-	3	-	-	-	-	-	-	-	-	-	-	-
unidentified	-	-	-	-	2	-	x	-	-	-	2+	1	x
Coin													
AE Aegina	-	-	-	-	-	-	-	-	-	-	-	1	-
AE Epidauros	-	-	-	-	-	-	-	-	-	-	1	-	1
AE Halieis	-	-	-	-	-	-	-	-	-	-	-	-	1
AE Tiryns	-	-	-	-	-	1	-	-	-	-	3	1	2
AE Troizen	-	1	-	-	-	1	-	-	-	-	1	-	-
Varia													
bone	2	-	x	-	-	-	-	-	-	-	-	1	-
Shell:													
Cerastoderma	-	-	-	-	-	-	-	-	-	-	-	1	-
Cerastoderma with red pigment	-	-	-	-	1	-	-	-	-	-	-	-	-
Cerithium	-	1	-	-	-	-	1	-	-	-	-	-	2
Chlamys	-	-	-	-	-	-	-	-	-	-	1	-	-
Glycimeris	-	-	-	-	-	-	-	-	-	-	1	-	-
Mactra	-	2	-	-	-	-	-	-	-	-	-	-	-
Murex	-	-	-	-	-	-	-	-	-	-	-	1	-
Pinna	-	-	-	-	-	-	1	-	-	-	-	-	-
larval	1?	-	-	-	-	-	-	-	-	-	-	-	-
bags	-	-	3	-	-	-	-	-	-	-	-	-	1
unidentified	3	1	-	2	2	1	2	1	-	-	-	-	-
ostrich egg	-	-	-	-	-	-	-	-	-	-	-	1	-
carbonized seed	-	x	-	-	-	-	-	-	-	-	x	-	-
carbonized olive	-	-	-	-	-	-	-	-	-	-	-	-	33
carbonized wood	-	x	-	-	-	-	-	-	-	-	-	-	-

Table 10 (continued). House D: Distribution of Finds by Loci, Pottery by Ware, Function, and Anatomical Variable

Locus	I	II	III	IV	V–VII	VIII	IX	X/XI	XII	XIII	XIV	XV	XVI	Total
Fine ware														
Food: serve/consume	4	23	-	-	2	-	1	2	-	-	18	1	1	64
Drink: consume	1	38	3	1	3	-	7	1	1	-	33	13	61	162
Drink: serve/pour	-	1	4	-	-	-	-	3	-	-	4	-	9	21
Drink: serve/contain	-	2	1	-	-	-	-	1	-	-	4	1	4	13
Other	4	4	-	-	-	-	-	-	-	-	8	-	11	27
Plain ware														
Food: prepare/serve	-	17	-	1	-	1	4	1	1	-	3	1	12	41
Drink: serve/pour	6	7	-	-	-	1	5	2	-	-	7	-	10	38
Food/drink: store/contain	3	7	1	1	5	5	4	5	2	3	3	7	17	63
Other	1	1	2	-	-	-	-	2	2	-	1	-	1	10
Coarse ware														
Food: prepare/serve	1	3	-	1	1	1	2	1	-	-	-	-	1	11
Food: cook	5	27	-	1	2	8	12	2	1	1	18	5	24	106
Drink: serve/pour	-	1	-	-	-	-	-	-	-	-	-	-	-	1
Food/drink: store/contain	1	12	4	-	1	-	2	-	4	-	3	-	10	37
Other	4	1	-	-	-	-	-	-	-	-	-	-	1	6
Roman	1	-	-	-	-	-	-	-	-	-	-	-	-	1
MNV per locus:	31	144	15	5	14	16	37	20	11	4	102	28	174	601 (House D MNV)

Table 11. House D: Minimum Number of Vessels Represented

Locus	I	II	III	IV	V–VII	VIII	IX	X/XI	XII	XIII	XIV	XV	XVI
Fine ware													
Red Figure													
krater													
rim	-	-	-	-	-	-	-	-	-	-	-	-	1
body	-	-	-	-	-	-	-	-	-	-	-	-	-
kylix													
rim	-	1	-	-	-	-	-	-	-	-	-	-	-
pelike													
profile	-	-	-	-	-	-	-	1	-	-	-	-	-
skyphos													
rim	-	1	-	-	-	-	-	-	-	-	-	-	-
other	-	-	-	-	-	-	-	-	-	-	1?	-	-
unidentified	-	-	-	-	-	-	1	18	-	-	10	-	17
												MNV = 51	
Other													
askos													
profile	-	-	-	-	-	-	-	-	-	-	2	-	1
rim	-	-	-	-	-	-	-	-	-	-	1	-	-
foot	-	-	-	-	-	-	-	-	-	-	1	-	-
feeder													
whole	-	1	-	-	-	-	-	-	-	-	-	-	-
lekanis/pyxis													
profile	-	1	-	-	-	-	-	-	-	-	-	-	-
rim	1	1	-	-	-	-	-	-	-	-	-	-	-
other	-	1	-	-	-	-	-	-	-	-	-	-	-
lekythos													
whole	-	-	-	-	-	-	-	-	-	-	-	-	1
rim	-	-	-	-	-	-	-	-	-	-	-	-	1
foot	-	-	-	-	-	-	-	-	-	-	1	-	-
other	-	-	-	-	-	-	-	-	-	-	1	-	-
lid													
rim	-	-	-	-	-	-	-	-	-	-	1	-	4
other	-	1	-	-	-	-	-	-	-	-	-	-	2
pyxis lid	-	-	-	-	-	-	-	-	-	-	1	-	-
Plain ware													
krater													
rim	1	-	-	-	-	-	-	-	-	-	-	-	-
other	-	-	1	-	-	-	-	-	-	-	-	-	-
lid													
whole	-	-	-	-	-	-	-	-	-	-	1	-	-
profile	-	-	-	-	-	-	-	-	1	-	-	-	1
other	-	1	-	-	-	-	-	-	-	-	-	-	-
pyxis													
profile	-	-	-	-	-	-	-	1	-	-	-	-	-
rim	-	-	-	-	-	-	-	-	1	-	-	-	-
Coarse ware													
askos	-	-	-	-	-	-	-	-	-	-	-	-	1

Table 12. House D: Other Pottery Variables

Locus	I	II/V VIII	III IV	XIII	XIV
Fine ware					
Food: serve/consume					
profile	-	-	-	2	-
rim	1	6	-	3	1
foot	1	-	-	1	-
Drink: consume					
profile	-	1	-	2	-
rim	3	11	3	7	9
foot	2	7	1	2	3
other	5	12	2	2	17
Drink: serve/pour					
rim	-	1	-	2	-
foot	1	1	-	-	2
other	1	2	-	-	9
Drink: serve/contain					
rim	-	1	-	-	-
foot	-	-	-	2	-
other	-	1	-	-	-
Other:					
whole	-	-	-	1	1
rim	-	1	-	-	-
foot	-	-	-	1	1
other	48	35	11	22	33
Plain ware					
Food: prepare/serve					
profile	-	1	-	-	-
rim	-	3	-	-	3
foot	-	1	-	1	-
Drink: consume					
foot	1	-	-	-	-
Drink: serve/pour					
profile	1	-	-	-	-
rim	3	3	-	-	3
foot	9	5	2	-	-
other	-	3	-	-	-
Drink: serve/contain					
rim	-	-	-	-	1
Food/Drink: store/contain					
rim	3	3	1	-	2
foot	-	2	-	-	4
other	1	4	13	-	10
Other					
whole	-	-	-	1	-
rim	-	5	-	-	1
foot	6	-	-	-	-
other	236	151	24	15	197

Locus	I	II/V VIII	III IV	XIII	XIV
Coarse ware					
Food: prepare/serve					
rim	-	1	2	1	1
foot	1	-	-	-	-
other	-	-	-	1	1
Food: cook					
profile	1	-	-	-	-
rim	1	20	-	9	4
other	-	71	-	2	-
Drink: serve/pour					
rim	-	-	-	-	1
foot	1	-	-	-	1
Food/Drink: store/contain					
rim	9	1	-	-	1
foot	1	-	-	-	-
other	41	-	-	-	-
Other					
rim	2	-	-	-	-
foot	1	-	-	-	-
other	34	9	7	16	58
Roman	-	1	-	-	-

Total pottery items = 1301

Locus	I	II/V VIII	III IV	XIII	XIV
Clay					
lamp					
rim	-	-	2	1	-
foot	1	-	-	-	-
Loom weight	1	-	-	-	-
Miniatures					
aryballos					
foot?	-	-	1	-	-
jug					
whole	-	-	1	-	-
kotyle					
whole?	-	-	-	-	1
foot	-	-	1	-	-
Tile					
body	284	159	85	549	136
body (zembili load)	-	-	-	-	0.75
edge	173	82	29	374	75
cover	17	8	3	2	3
complete pan	-	-	-	1	-
complete cover	-	2	-	1	-

Table 13. House E: Southwest Rooms and Southeast Shops, Distribution of Finds by Loci. Pottery by Ware, Function, and Anatomical Variable

Locus	I	II/V VIII	III IV	XIII	XIV
Stone					
marble fragment	1	1	-	-	-
obsidian blade	1	-	-	-	-
obsidian flake	-	-	-	1	-
serpentine	1	-	-	-	-
Metal					
Iron					
nail	-	4	-	1	-
blade	-	-	-	-	1
Bronze					
nail	-	1	-	-	-
tack	1	-	-	-	-
wire (pin?)	-	-	-	1	-
Lead?					
nail	-	1	-	-	-
slag	4+	3	9+	1?	-
unidentified	2+	9+	10+	-	-
Varia					
bone	8	1	-	-	-
Shell					
Cerithium	1	2	-	-	1
Cockle	1	-	-	-	-
Cowrie	-	-	-	-	1
Helix	1	-	-	-	-
Murex	1	-	-	-	-
Spondylus	-	2	-	-	-
Vertigo	2	-	-	-	-
Whelk (large)	-	-	1	-	-
unidentified	-	1	2	1	-
carbonized seed	x	-	-	-	-

Table 13 (continued). House E: Southwest Rooms and Southeast Shops, Distribution of Finds by Loci. Pottery by Ware, Function, and Anatomical Variable

Locus	VI	VII	IX	X	XI	XII a	XII b	XII c	XV/ XVI	XVII	XVIII/ XIX	XX	XXI
Fine ware													
Food: serve/consume													
whole	-	-	1	-	-	-	-	-	-	1	-	2	-
profile	-	-	-	-	-	-	-	1	-	-	1	-	-
rim	1	-	9	1	-	-	1	1	-	-	1	4	1
foot	2	1	2	-	-	-	-	1	3	-	-	-	-
other	1	-	-	-	-	-	1	1	-	-	-	1	-
Drink: consume													
whole	-	-	-	-	-	1	1	1	-	3	-	1	-
profile	1	-	-	-	-	-	-	-	-	1	-	-	-
rim	1	1	18	-	2	5	7	3	-	-	1	21	2
foot	1	2	7	-	1	1	7	2	1	1	1	3	-
other	4	-	13	-	-	-	3	2	2	-	2	12	4
Drink: serve/pour													
whole	-	-	-	-	-	-	-	-	-	2	1	-	-
rim	1	-	2	-	-	1	-	-	-	-	-	1	-
foot	1	-	5	-	-	-	-	-	-	-	1	3	-
other	4	1	6	-	3	5	-	-	-	-	3	5	-
Drink: serve/contain													
rim	-	1	-	-	-	-	1	-	-	-	-	-	1
foot	-	-	-	-	-	-	-	1	-	-	-	-	-
other	-	-	2	-	-	1	-	-	-	-	-	2	-
Other													
whole	-	-	-	-	-	-	-	-	-	1	1	1	-
profile	2?	-	-	-	-	-	-	-	-	-	-	1	-
rim	-	-	-	-	-	-	-	-	1	-	-	2	-
foot	2	-	1	-	-	-	2	1	-	-	1	2	-
other	49	5	55	-	4	-	70	43	12	1	9	221	13
Plain ware													
Food: prepare/serve													
whole	-	-	-	-	-	-	-	-	-	-	1	-	-
profile	-	-	-	-	-	-	1	-	-	-	-	1	-
rim	3	-	1	-	-	-	-	1	-	-	1	3	-
foot	-	-	1	-	-	-	-	1	-	-	-	-	-
Drink: serve/pour													
profile	-	-	-	-	-	-	-	-	-	-	1?	-	-
rim	2	1	3	-	-	-	2	1	1	-	-	11	-
foot	-	-	5	-	-	-	1	2	2	-	-	7	-
other	2	1	2	-	1	1	-	1	-	-	-	2	-
Drink: serve/contain													
foot	-	-	-	-	-	-	-	-	-	-	-	1	-
Food/Drink: store/contain													
whole	-	-	-	-	-	-	-	-	-	-	3*	-	-
profile	1?	-	-	-	-	-	-	-	-	1?	-	-	-
rim	3	-	3	-	-	3	2	1	-	-	1	4	3
foot	19	1	3	-	-	-	2	2	-	-	-	1	-
other	1	12	5	1	-	1	-	4	-	-	2	58	1

*from fill of Room 6-23 just above Level A floor

Table 14. House E Northeast: Distribution of Finds by Loci, Pottery by Ware, Function, and Anatomical Variable

Locus	VI	VII	IX	X	XI	XII a	XII b	XII c	XV/ XVI	XVII	XVIII/ XIX	XX	XXI
Other													
rim	-	-	-	-	-	-	-	-	-	-	-	2	-
foot	1	-	-	-	-	1	1	-	-	-	-	-	1
other	210	5	262	39	7	127	180?	5	31	-	181	173	44
Coarse ware													
Food: prepare/serve													
whole	-	-	-	-	-	-	-	-	-	2	-	-	-
profile	-	-	-	-	-	-	-	-	-	1	-	-	-
rim	-	-	1	-	-	-	4	-	-	-	-	-	-
foot	-	-	-	-	-	-	1	-	-	-	-	-	-
Food: cook													
whole	-	-	1?	-	-	-	1	-	1	2	1	-	-
profile	1	-	2	-	-	-	-	-	1	-	-	1	-
rim	12	2	7	-	1	5	18	-	4	1	-	1	3
foot	-	-	-	-	-	-	-	-	1	-	-	-	-
other	3	2	16	4	2	-	46	2	-	1	-	9	1
Drink: serve/pour													
whole	-	-	-	-	-	-	1	-	-	-	-	-	-
rim	-	1	-	-	-	-	-	-	-	-	-	-	-
other	-	1	-	-	-	-	-	-	-	-	-	-	-
Food/Drink: store/contain													
rim	8	-	-	-	-	-	1	-	1	-	-	-	-
other	2	-	-	-	-	-	3	2	-	-	-	-	1
Other													
rim	-	-	1	-	-	-	-	-	1	1	-	-	-
other	183	28	43	1	2	16	3	1	63	6	21	113	17
Roman	1	-	-	-	-	-	-	-	-	-	1	-	-

total pottery items House E Northeast = 2886
total pottery items House E = 4187

Locus	VI	VII	IX	X	XI	XII a	XII b	XII c	XV/ XVI	XVII	XVIII/ XIX	XX	XXI
Clay													
Lamp													
whole	-	-	-	-	-	-	-	-	-	-	-	1	-
profile	-	-	-	-	-	-	-	-	-	1	-	-	-
rim	2	-	-	-	-	-	-	1	-	1	-	2	2
foot	-	-	-	-	-	-	-	-	-	-	-	1	-
Loom weight	1	-	-	-	-	-	9	8	1	1	-	3	2
Miniatures													
bowl	-	-	-	-	-	-	-	-	-	-	-	1	-
jug													
foot	-	-	1	-	-	-	-	-	-	-	-	-	-
other	-	-	-	-	-	-	-	1	-	-	-	-	-
krater													
rim	-	-	1	-	-	-	-	-	-	-	-	-	-
foot?	-	-	1	-	-	-	-	-	-	-	-	-	-
lid	-	-	-	-	-	-	-	-	-	-	-	1	-

Table 14 (continued). House E Northeast: Distribution of Finds by Loci, Pottery by Ware, Function, and Anatomical Variable

Locus	VI	VII	IX	X	XI	XII a	XII b	XII c	XV/ XVI	XVII	XVIII/ XIX	XX	XXI
kotyle													
whole	-	-	-	1	-	-	-	-	-	-	-	-	-
profile	-	-	-	-	-	-	-	-	-	-	-	-	1
rim	-	-	-	-	-	-	1	-	-	-	-	-	-
foot	-	-	-	-	-	-	1	-	-	-	-	-	-
other	-	-	-	-	-	-	5	-	-	-	-	4	-
Tile													
body	278	27	158	-	1	-	129	158+	6*	-	5	176	13
edge	148	6	28	-	-	-	82	21	57*	13	-	25	-
cover	1	5	-	-	-	2	22	5	8*	1	-	3	-
whole cover	-	-	-	-	-	-	-	-	-	1	-	-	-
(collected in zembili)	-	-	-	1.5	-	-	-	-	-	-	-	-	-
											*full count lacking		
Other													
figured stamp	-	-	-	-	-	-	-	1	-	-	-	-	-
bird figurine	-	-	-	-	-	-	-	-	-	-	1	-	-
amphora stand?	-	-	-	-	-	-	1	-	-	-	-	-	-
wellhead fragments	14	-	-	-	-	-	-	-	-	-	-	-	-
Stone													
pier capital	-	-	-	-	-	-	-	1	-	-	-	-	-
plastered block	-	-	-	-	-	-	-	-	-	-	-	-	2
perirrhanterion rim	1	-	-	-	-	-	-	-	-	-	-	-	-
obsidian blade	-	-	-	-	-	-	-	-	-	-	1	1	-
obsidian flake	-	-	-	-	-	-	-	-	-	-	-	1	-
volcanic tool	-	-	-	-	-	-	-	-	-	-	-	1	-
grinding stone	-	-	-	-	-	-	-	1	-	1	-	1?	-
grinding slab	-	-	-	-	-	-	-	-	-	-	1	-	-
whetstone	-	-	-	-	-	-	-	-	-	-	-	-	1
weight	-	-	-	-	-	-	-	-	-	-	-	1	1?
pierced stone	-	-	-	-	-	-	-	1	-	-	-	-	-
large stone, pierced	-	-	-	-	-	-	-	1	-	-	-	-	-
stone disk	-	-	-	-	-	-	-	-	1	-	-	1	-
Metal													
Iron:													
nail	3	-	1	-	-	-	1	4	-	-	-	2	-
handle	1	-	-	-	-	-	-	-	-	-	-	-	-
washer	-	-	-	-	-	-	-	-	-	-	-	-	1
blade	-	-	-	-	-	-	-	1	-	-	-	1	-
cleaver	-	-	1	-	-	-	-	-	-	-	-	-	-
sword	-	-	-	-	-	-	-	1	-	-	-	-	-
ring	-	-	-	-	-	-	-	-	-	-	-	1	-
slab	-	-	-	-	-	-	2	-	-	-	-	-	-
triangle	-	-	-	-	-	-	-	-	-	-	-	-	1
shaft	-	-	-	-	-	-	-	-	-	-	-	-	1
strip	-	-	-	-	-	-	-	-	1	-	-	-	-
Bronze:													
nail	-	-	-	-	-	-	-	1?	-	-	-	-	-
nail in PB	2	-	-	-	-	-	-	-	-	-	-	-	-
tack	2	-	-	-	-	-	-	-	-	-	-	1	-

Table 14 (continued). House E Northeast: Distribution of Finds by Loci, Pottery by Ware, Function, and Anatomical Variable

Locus	VI	VII	IX	X	XI	XII a	XII b	XII c	XV/ XVI	XVII	XVIII/ XIX	XX	XXI
needle	-	-	-	-	-	-	-	-	-	-	-	-	1
boss	-	-	-	-	-	-	-	-	-	-	1	2	-
handle	-	-	-	-	-	-	-	-	-	-	-	1	-
grater	-	-	-	-	-	-	-	-	-	-	-	1	-
shaft	1	-	-	-	-	-	-	-	-	-	-	-	-
sheet	-	-	1	-	-	-	-	-	-	-	-	-	-
armor (scale) plate	-	-	-	-	-	-	-	-	-	-	-	-	1
strip	-	-	1	-	-	-	-	-	-	-	-	-	-
wire	1	-	-	-	-	-	-	-	-	-	-	-	-
Lead:													
clamp	-	-	-	-	-	-	-	1	-	-	-	-	-
Slag	3	-	-	-	-	1	-	-	-	-	1	-	-
unidentified	-	18	x	-	-	x	x	-	x	-	1	4	-
Coin													
AE Arcadia	1	-	-	-	-	-	-	-	-	-	-	-	-
AE Arcadius	-	-	1	-	-	-	-	-	-	-	-	-	-
AE Halieis	1	-	-	-	-	-	-	-	-	-	-	-	1
AE Tiryns	-	-	1	-	-	1	-	-	-	-	-	-	-
AE token	-	-	-	-	-	-	-	-	-	-	-	2	-
Bone													
fragments	-	-	-	-	3	-	-	-	-	-	-	1	-
small bag	-	-	1	-	-	-	-	-	-	-	-	-	-
Varia													
Shell													
Cerastoderma	-	-	-	-	-	-	-	-	-	-	-	1	-
Cerithium	-	-	1	1	-	-	-	1	1	-	1	1	-
Clam	-	-	-	-	-	-	-	-	-	-	-	-	1
Glycimeris	-	-	-	-	-	-	-	2	-	-	-	-	-
Helmet	-	-	-	-	-	-	-	-	-	1	1	-	-
Murex	-	-	1	-	-	-	-	-	-	-	-	-	-
Ostra edulis	-	-	-	-	-	-	-	-	-	-	-	1	-
Patella	-	-	1	-	-	-	-	-	-	-	-	-	-
Pinna	-	5	-	-	-	-	-	-	-	-	1	3	-
Spondylus	-	-	-	-	-	-	-	-	-	-	1	1	1
Tonna	-	-	-	-	-	-	1	-	-	-	-	2	-
unidentified	9	-	10	-	-	-	12	3	2	5	-	-	-

Table 14 (continued). House E Northeast: Distribution of Finds by Loci, Pottery by Ware, Function, and Anatomical Variable

Locus	I	II/V/ VIII	III/ IV	XIII	XIV	Total
Fine ware						
Food: serve/consume	2	6	-	6	1	15
Drink: consume	5	19	4	11	12	51
Drink: serve/pour	1	2	-	2	2	7
Drink: serve/contain	-	1	-	2	-	3
Other	-	1	-	2	2	5
Plain ware						
Food: prepare/serve	-	5	-	1	3	9
Drink: consume	1	-	-	-	-	1
Drink: serve/pour	14	8	2	-	3	27
Drink: serve/contain	-	-	-	-	1	1
Food and drink: store/contain	3	5	1	-	6	15
Other	6	5	-	1	1	13
Coarse ware						
Food: prepare/serve	1	1	2	1	1	6
Food: cook	2	20	-	9	4	35
Drink: serve/pour	1	-	-	-	2	3
Food and drink: store/contain	10	1	-	-	1	12
Other	3	-	-	-	-	3
MNV per locus	49	74	9	35	39	206

Table 15. House E Southwest Rooms and Southeast Shops: Minimum Number of Vessels Represented

Locus	VI	VII	IX	X	XI	XII a	XII b	XII c	XV/ XVI	XVII	XVIII/ XIX	XX	XXI	Total
Fine ware														
Food: serve/consume	3	1	12	1	-	-	1	3	3	1	2	6	1	34
Drink: consume	3	3	25	-	3	7	15	6	1	5	2	25	2	97
Drink: serve/pour	2	-	7	-	-	1	-	-	-	2	2	4	-	18
Drink: serve/contain	-	1	-	-	-	-	1	1	-	-	-	-	1	4
Other	4?	-	1	-	-	-	2	1	1	1	2	6	-	18
Plain ware														
Food: prepare/serve	3	-	2	-	-	-	1	2	-	-	2	4	-	14
Drink: serve/pour	2	1	8	-	-	-	3	3	3	-	1?	18	-	39
Drink: serve/contain	-	-	-	-	-	-	-	-	-	-	-	1	-	1
Food and drink: store/contain	2	3	16	-	-	3	4	3	-	1	4	5	3	53
Other	1	-	-	-	-	1	1	-	-	-	-	2	1	6
Coarse ware														
Food: prepare/serve	-	-	1	-	-	-	5	-	-	3	-	-	-	9
Food: cook	13	2	10	-	1	5	19	-	7	3	1	2	3	66
Drink: serve/pour	-	1	-	-	-	-	1	-	-	-	-	-	-	2
Food and drink: store/contain	8	-	-	-	-	-	1	-	1	-	-	-	-	10
Other	-	-	1	-	-	-	-	-	1	1	-	-	-	3
MNV per Locus	62	10	73	1	4	17	54	19	17	17	16	73	11	374
														MNV House E = 580

Table 16. House E Northeast: Minimum Number of Vessels Represented

Locus	I	II/V VIII	III IV	XIII	XIV
Fine ware					
Red Figure					
unidentified body	-	1	-	-	-
				MNV = 1	
Other					
pyxis	-	-	-	-	1
pyxis lid	-	-	-	1	-
pyxis lid rim	-	1	-	-	-
Plain ware					
Other					
lid rim	-	1	-	-	-
louterion rim	-	4	-	-	1
thurible	-	-	-	1	-

Table 17. House E, Southwest Rooms and Southeast Shops: Other Pottery Variables

Locus	VI	VII	IX	X	XI	XII a	XII b	XII c	XV/ XVI	XVII	XVIII/ XIX	XX	XXI
Fine ware													
Red Figure													
krater													
rim	-	-	-	-	-	-	1	-	-	-	-	-	-
other	-	-	2	-	-	1	-	-	-	-	-	-	-
oinochoe	-	1	-	-	-	-	-	-	-	-	-	-	-
skyphos rim	-	-	-	-	-	-	-	-	-	-	-	-	1
unidentified	-	-	4	-	-	-	-	-	-	-	-	-	-
												MNV = 10	
Other													
aryballos	-	-	-	-	-	-	-	1	-	-	-	-	-
askos													
whole	-	-	-	-	-	-	-	-	-	-	-	1	-
other	-	-	-	-	-	-	-	-	-	1	-	-	-
lekanis lid	-	-	-	-	-	-	-	-	-	-	1	-	-
lekanis/pyxis													
rim	-	-	-	-	-	-	-	-	-	-	-	1	-
lekythos													
whole	-	-	-	-	-	-	-	-	-	1	-	-	-
other	-	1	-	-	-	-	1	-	-	-	-	-	-
lid													
rim	-	-	-	-	-	-	-	-	1	-	-	1	-
other	-	1	-	-	-	-	-	-	-	-	-	-	-
pyxis													
profile	-	-	-	-	-	-	-	-	-	-	-	1	-
Plain ware													
amphoriskos													
foot	-	-	-	-	-	-	-	-	-	-	-	-	1
lid													
rim	-	-	-	-	-	-	-	-	-	-	-	2	-
pyxis													
other	-	-	-	-	-	-	-	-	-	-	-	1	-
Coarse ware													
pyxis lid													
rim	-	-	-	-	-	-	-	-	-	1	-	-	-

Table 18. House E Northeast: Other Pottery Variables

	House 7 Floors	House 7 Negative features	House A Floors	House A Negative features	House C Floors	House C Negative features	House D Floors	House D Negative features	House E Floors	House E Negative features
Fine ware										
Food: serve / consume										
bowl	44	23	23	4	37	3	34	20	45	1
dish	-	1	1	-	-	-	-	-	-	-
plate	-	2	-	-	4	-	3	-	-	-
saltcellar	3	2	2	-	3	-	4	3	3	-
Drink: consume										
bolsal	11	7	6	1	20	-	29	2	16	2
cup	5	4	2	-	2	1	3	1	3	-
cup kantharos	-	2	1	-	1	-	2	2	6	-
cup skyphos	-	1	1	1	6	-	3	3	5	-
kalathos	-	-	1	-	-	-	1	-	-	-
kantharos	1	1	-	-	4	-	1	1	4	-
kylix	-	1	-	-	-	-	-	1	-	-
mug	20	1	8	2	11	-	7	5	13	-
skyphos	60	40	42	19	54	1	60	18	69	4
stemless cup	34	3	11	2	21	1	15	8	21	-
stemmed cup	-	-	-	-	-	-	-	-	4	-
Drink: serve / pour										
chous	1	-	-	-	-	-	-	-	-	-
jug	18	5	2	-	10	1	3	-	10	-
oinochoe	6	2	4	1	11	2	12	5	12	-
olpe	4	-	2	-	-	-	1	-	2	-
Drink: serve / contain										
amphora	3	1	-	-	1	-	-	-	1	-
hydria	1	-	-	-	-	-	-	-	-	-
krater	15	6	-	1	7	-	9	3	5	1
pelike	1	-	-	-	3	-	1	-	-	-
Other										
amphoriskos	-	-	1	-	1	-	-	-	-	-
askos	2	1	2	-	3	-	5	-	1	-
feeder	-	-	-	-	-	-	-	1	-	-
jar	1	-	-	-	-	-	-	-	-	-
lekanis / pyxis	3	2	3	-	1	-	1	2	1	-
lekythos	1	2	3	1	1	-	3	-	1	-
lid	-	1	-	-	3	-	5	-	4	-
pyxis	-	-	-	-	-	-	-	-	2	-
pyxis lid	-	-	1	-	1	-	1	-	1	-
storage bin	1	-	-	-	-	-	-	-	-	-
tray	-	-	-	-	1	-	-	-	-	-
Plain ware										
Food: prepare / serve										
basin	-	-	-	1	-	-	1	6	2	-
bowl	12	20	4	-	8	-	4	4	7	-
dish	-	-	-	-	2	-	-	-	-	-
lekane	28	10	5	-	4	12	13	4	12	-
mortar	3	2	-	-	2	-	5	-	2	-
plate	-	-	-	-	-	-	-	1	-	-
strainer	-	-	-	-	-	-	1	1	-	-

Table 19. Frequency of Vessel Types per House Based on Minimum Number of Vessels Represented from Level A Stratum

	House 7		House A		House C		House D		House E	
	Floors	Negative features	Floors	Negative features	Floors	Negative features	Floors	Negative features	Floors	Negative features
Drink: consume										
cup	-	-	-	-	-	-	-	-	1	-
Drink: serve/pour										
jug	32	28	28	1	33	5	31	7	64	1
Drink: serve/contain										
krater	-	-	-	-	-	-	1	-	2	-
Food/drink: store/contain										
amphora	38	15	16	-	65	19	49	5	62	1
hydria	1	-	-	-	-	-	1	-	3	-
jar	-	-	-	-	-	-	-	1	-	-
pithos	-	2	3	-	1	1+	-	-	2	-
storage bin	5	1	1	-	1	-	5	1	-	-
Other										
amphoriskos	-	-	-	-	-	-	-	-	1	-
aryballos	-	-	-	-	1	-	-	-	-	-
askos	1	-	-	-	-	-	-	-	-	-
lid	4	1	2	-	1	-	3	-	3	-
louterion	-	-	-	-	-	-	-	-	5	-
pyxis	-	-	-	-	-	-	2	-	-	-
thuribile	-	-	-	-	-	-	-	-	1	-
tray	-	-	-	-	-	-	-	1	-	-
tripod?	-	-	1	-	-	-	-	-	-	-
Coarse ware										
Food: prepare/serve										
basin	3	-	-	-	-	-	1	-	3	-
bowl	1	3	-	-	1	-	2	-	8	-
lekane	1	-	-	-	2	-	4	-	2	-
lid	1	-	-	-	-	-	-	1	-	-
mortar	3	-	1	-	1	-	1	-	2	-
plate	-	-	-	-	-	-	-	-	-	-
strainer	-	-	-	-	-	-	-	2	1	-
Food: cook										
chytra	29	4	10	11	6	-	8	14	31	1
eschara	-	-	-	-	-	-	-	-	2	-
griddle	3	-	2	-	-	-	5	1	4	-
lid	15	3	7	-	15	2	22	1	9	-
lopas	50	52	41	-	54	-	44	11	52	1
Drink: serve/pour										
jug	7	3	2	-	1	-	-	1	4	1
Food/drink: contain/store										
pithos	2	1	10	-	7	3	6	15	12	-
pithos lid	3	-	1	-	1	-	13	-	1	-
storage bin	-	-	1	-	1	-	2	1	9	-
Other										
askos	-	-	-	-	-	-	1	-	-	-
louterion	-	-	1	-	1	-	-	-	-	-
pyxis lid	-	-	-	-	-	-	-	-	1	-

Table 19 (continued). Frequency of Vessel Types per House Based on Minimum Number of Vessels Represented from Level A Stratum

Glossary and Abbreviations

ambitus — alleyway
andron — men's dining room
andronitis — men's residential area (including andron)
anta — pilaster or attached pillar, especially common in domestic architecture as framing elements of doorways
ashlar — cut stone masonry with squared edges
aule — courtyard
balaneion — bathing area
bothros — pit
dado — painted border at the base of a wall (baseboard)
dayroom — principle indoor room for family activities (especially women and children) beyond the kitchen
exedra — a rectangular recessed space opening off the courtyard
gynaikonitis — women's residential area also known as the "gynaikon"
histeon — loom room
horos — inscribed stone marker, often relating to property boundaries, terms of lease, sale, or mortgage
insula — rectangular to square block of constructions (e.g., houses) that share party walls, typically bounded on four sides by streets
ipnos — bathing area
isonomia — literally "equality under the law," a concept whereby societal balance is maintained through the harmonious ordering of physical, political, and religious spheres
kopron — pit used for collection of organic and inorganic household debris, the contents of which would periodically be carried out to gardens and fields as fertilizer
kylikion — cupboard
locus — a spatial designation applied to areas in the houses at Halieis and, in particular, the artifacts recovered from these areas that may correspond to a room, a part of a room, or even portions of more than one room
oecus — in Latin (from Greek "oikos"), a large room or hall; also applied to the tri-partite kitchen, bath, and flue arrangement in Olynthian houses
oikos — house, household; also a large room or hall in the house, referred to at Halieis as the "dayroom"
orthostate — the lowest course of a wall, typically of ashlar masonry, above the foundation
pastas — a rectangular porch opening off the northern side of the courtyard
pitheon — storage room
prostas — a square to rectangular porch opening off the northern side of the courtyard
prothyron — doorway, especially that between the house and the outside world
pyrgos — tower
sima — vertical line of tile protecting the edge of a roof

socle	the footing of a wall
sterculinum	in Latin, the equivalent of "kopron"
tamieion	storage room
thalamos	inner chamber, often a bedroom
transverse hall	designation adopted at Halieis for any porch opening off the northern side of a courtyard that typically leads to other rooms
zembili	basket used for collecting excavation finds, holding ca. one-third hectoliter or one bushel

AE	bronze (Latin "aes")
BF	black figure
BG	black gloss ("glaze")
CW	coarse ware
d.	depth
FE	iron (Latin "ferrum")
FW	fine ware
HC	Halieis clay (tiles, terracotta figurines, loom weights, etc.)
HL	Halieis lamps
HM	Halieis metal
HN	Halieis numismata (coins)
HP	Halieis pottery
HS	Halieis stone
HV	Halieis varia (bone, shell, glass, etc.)
m	meter/meters
masl	meters above sea level
mbsl	meters below sea level
MNV	minimum number of vessels represented
n.a.	"not available" (information not in trench notebooks)
PB	lead (Latin "plumbum")
PW	plain ware
RF	red figure
TR	trench
u.	unit/units

Literature Cited

ARV[2] J. D. Beazley. 1963. *Attic Red-figure Vase-Painters.* 2d ed. Oxford: Clarendon Press.

CVA *Corpus Vasorum Antiquorum*

IG *Inscriptiones Graecae*

SIG W. Dittenberger. 1915–24. 3d ed. *Sylloge Inscriptionum Graecarum.*

Acheson, Phoebe E. 1997. "Does the 'Economic Explanation' Work? Settlement, Agriculture, and Erosion in the Territory of Halieis in the Late Classical-Early Hellenistic Period." *Journal of Mediterranean Archaeology* 10: 165–90.

Adriani, Achille, Nicola Bonacasa, Carmela Angela Di Stefano, Elda Joly, Maria Teresa Manni Piraino, Giulo Schmiedt, and Aldina Tusa Cutroni. 1970. *Campagne di scavo, 1963–1965.* Himera, 1. Rome: "L'Erma" di Bretschneider.

Alcock, Susan E., John F. Cherry, and Jack L. Davis. 1994. "Intensive Survey, Agricultural Practice and the Classical Landscape of Greece." In Morris 1994c: 137–70.

Allegro, Nunzio, Oscar Belvedere, Nicola Bonacasa, Rosa Maria Bonacasa Carra, Carmela Angela Di Stefano, Elena Epifanio, Elda Joly, Maria Teresa Manni Piraino, Amedeo Tullio, and Aldina Tuso Cutroni. 1976. *Campagne di scavo, 1966-1973.* Himera, 2. Rome: "L'Erma" di Bretschneider.

Allinson, Francis G. 1930. *Menander, The Girl from Samos.* The Loeb Classical Library. New York: G. P. Putnam's Sons.

Allison, Penelope M., ed. 1999. *The Archaeology of Household Activities.* London: Routledge.

Ammerman, Rebecca Miller. 1990. "The Religious Context of Hellenistic Terracotta Figurines." In *The Coroplast's Art: Greek Terracottas of the Hellenistic World,* ed. Jaimee P. Uhlenbrock, 37–46. New Rochelle, N.Y.: A. D. Caratzas.

Amouretti, Marie-Claire. 1986. *Le pain et l'huile dans la Grèce antique: De l'araire au moulin.* Les Annales littéraires de l'Université de Besançon. Centre de recherche d'histoire ancienne, 328. Paris: Les Belles Lettres.

Amouretti, Marie-Claire, and Jean-Pierre Brun, eds. 1993. *La production du vin et de l'huile en Méditerranée. Bulletin de correspondance hellénique* Supplement 26. Paris: Diffusion de Boccard.

Amyx, Darrell A. 1958. "The Attic Stelai: Part III." *Hesperia* 27: 163–310.

Andel, Tjeerd H. van, and Curtis N. Runnels. 1987. *Beyond the Acropolis: A Rural Greek Past.* Stanford: Stanford University Press.

Anderson-Stojanović, Virginia. 1998. "Dye Works or Olive Press: A Reconsideration of Installations in the Rachi Settlement at Isthmia." Paper presented at the 99th Annual Meeting of the Archaeological Institute of America, Chicago, Illinois, 27–30 December 1997. Abstract in *American Journal of Archaeology* 102: 369.

———. 1997. Review of Bowkett 1995. *The Journal of Hellenic Studies* 117: 244–45.

———. 1996. "Excavations in the Rachi Settlement at Isthmia, 1989." *Hesperia* 65: 57–98.

Andronikos, Manolis. 1984. *Vergina: The Royal Tombs and the Ancient City.* Athens: Ekdotike Athenon.

Arnold, Philip J., III. 1990. "The Organization of Refuse Disposal and Ceramic Production within Contemporary Mexican Houselots." *American Anthropologist* 92: 915–32.

Aschenbrenner, Stanley E. 1976. "Archaeology and Ethnography in Messenia." In *Regional Variation in Modern Greece and Cyprus: Toward a Perspective on the Ethnography of Greece,* ed. Muriel Dimen and Ernestine Friedl, 158–67. Annals of the New York Academy of Sciences, 268. New York: New York Academy of Sciences.

Ault, Bradley A. 1999a. "Die klassische *Aule.* Höfe und Freiraum." In Hoepfner 1999c: 537–44.

———. 1999b. "Koprones and Oil Presses at Halieis: Interactions of Town and County and the Integration of Domestic and Regional Economies." *Hesperia* 68: 549–73.

———. 1994. "Classical Houses and Households: An Architectural and Artifactual Case Study from Halieis, Greece." Ph.D. diss., Indiana University, Bloomington. *Dissertation Abstracts International* 56-01, Section A, 0606; University Microfilms no. AAI9518532.

———. 1987. "The Spatial Distribution of Cooking Pottery at Ancient Halieis." Paper presented at the 88th General Meeting of the Archaeological Institute of America, San Antonio, Texas, 27–30 December 1986. Abstract in *American Journal of Archaeology* 91: 273.

Ault, Bradley A., and Lisa C. Nevett. 1999. "Digging Houses: Archaeologies of Classical Greek and Hellenistic Domestic Assemblages." In Allison 1999: 43–56.

Austin, M. M., and P. Vidal-Naquet. 1977. *Economic and Social History of Ancient Greece: An Introduction*. Berkeley: University of California Press.

Aylward, William. 1999. "Studies in Hellenistic Ilion: The Houses in the Lower City." *Studia Troica* 9: 159–86.

Bagnasco, Marcella B., ed. 1992. *Lo scavo di Marasà Sud: Il sacello tardo–arcaico e la "Casa dei Leoni."* Studi e materiali di archeologia, 4. Florence: Casa editrice le Lettere.

Barber, Elizabeth J. W. 1994. *Womens' Work: The First 20,000 Years. Women, Cloth, and Society in Early Times*. New York: W. W. Norton.

———. 1992. "The Peplos of Athena." In *Goddess and Polis: The Panathenaic Festival in Ancient Athens*, ed. Jennifer Neils, 103–17. Princeton: Princeton University Press.

———. 1991. *Prehistoric Textiles: The Development of Cloth in the Neolithic and Bronze Age*. Princeton: Princeton University Press.

Barnes, Jonathan, ed. 1984. *The Complete Works of Aristotle: The Revised Oxford Translation*. Bollingen Series, 71.2. Princeton: Princeton University Press.

Barr-Sharrar, Beryl. 1988. "The Hellenistic House." In *Hellenistic Art in the Walters Art Gallery*, ed. Ellen D. Reeder, 59–67. Baltimore: Trustees of the Walters Art Gallery.

Baumeister, August, ed. 1885–1889. *Denkmäler des klassischen Altertums: Zur erläuterung des Lebens der Griechen und Römerin Religion, Kunst und Sitte*. Munich and Leipzig: R. Oldenbourg.

Bérard, Claude, Christiane Bron, Jean-Louis Durand, Françoise Frontisi-Ducroux, François Lissarrague, Alain Schnapp, and Jean-Paul Vernant. 1989. *A City of Images: Iconography and Society in Ancient Greece*. Princeton: Princeton University Press.

Bergquist, Birgitta. 1990. "Sympotic Space: A Functional Aspect of Greek Dining Rooms." In Murray 1990: 37–65.

Binford, Louis R. 1962. "Archaeology as Anthropology." *American Antiquity* 28: 217–25.

Bintliff, John L., and Anthony M. Snodgrass. 1985. "The Cambridge/Bradford Boeotian Expedition: The First Four Years." *Journal of Field Archaeology* 12: 123–61.

Boardman, John. 1990. "*Symposion* Furniture." In Murray 1990: 122–31.

———. 1989. *Athenian Red Figure Vases: The Classical Period*. London: Thames and Hudson.

Boehlau, Johannes, and Karl Schefold. 1940. *Larissa am Hermos. Die Ergebnisse der Ausgrabungen, 1902–1934*. Vol. 1, *Die Bauten*. Berlin: W. de Gruyter.

Bölte, Felix. 1912. "Halieis." In Wissowa and Kroll 1893–. 7.2: 2246–52.

Bommelaer, Jean-Françoise. 1988. Review of Hoepfner and Schwandner 1994 (first ed., 1986). In *Revue archéologique* 1988: 395–97.

Bonacasa, Nicola. 1976. "Himera: A Greek City of Sicily." *Archaeology* 29.1: 42–51.

Bookidis, Nancy. 1993. "Ritual Dining at Corinth." In *Greek Sanctuaries: New Approaches*, ed. Nanno Marinatos and Robin Hägg, 45–61. London: Routledge.

———. 1990. "Ritual Dining in the Sanctuary of Demeter and Kore at Corinth: Some Questions." In Murray 1990: 86–94.

Bookidis, Nancy, and Ronald S. Stroud. 1997. *The Sanctuary of Demeter and Kore. Topography and Architecture*. Corinth, 18, pt. 3. Princeton: American School of Classical Studies at Athens.

Booth, Willam J. 1993. *Households: On the Moral Architecture of the Economy*. Ithaca: Cornell University Press.

Bosanquet, Robert C. 1901–1902. "Excavations at Praesos, 1." *Annual of the British School at Athens* 8: 231–70.

Bowkett, Laurence C. 1995. *The Hellenistic Dye-Works*. Well-Built Mycenae: The Helleno-British Excavations within the Citadel at Mycenae, 1959–1969, fasc. 36. Oxford: Oxbow Books.

Boyd, Thomas D. 1981. "Halieis: A Fourth Planned City in Classical Greece." *Town Planning Review* 52: 143–56.

Boyd, Thomas D., and Michael H. Jameson. 1981. "Urban and Rural Land Division in Ancient Greece." *Hesperia* 50: 327–42.

Boyd, Thomas D., and Wolf W. Rudolph. 1978. "Excavations at Porto Cheli and Vicinity, Preliminary Report IV: The Lower Town of Halieis, 1970–1977." *Hesperia* 47: 333–55.

Brumfield, Allaire. 1997. "Cakes in the Liknon. Votives from the Sanctuary of Demeter and Kore on Acrocorinth." *Hesperia* 66: 147–72.

Burford, Alison. 1993. *Land and Labor in the Greek World*. Baltimore: Johns Hopkins University Press.

Cahill, Nicholas D. 1991. "Olynthus: Social and Spatial Planning in a Greek City." Ph.D. diss., University of California, Berkley. *Dissertation Abstracts International* 53-05, Section A, 1564; University Microfilms no. AAI9228589.

———. 2002. *Household and City Organization at Olynthus*. New Haven: Yale University Press.

Camp, John McK., II. 1986. *The Athenian Agora: Excavations in the Heart of Classical Athens*. London: Thames and Hudson.

———. 1982. "Drought and Famine in the Fourth Century B.C." In *Studies in Athenian Architecture, Sculpture, and Topography Presented to Homer A. Thompson*, 9–17. *Hesperia* Supplement 20. Princeton: American School of Classical Studies at Athens.

———. 1977. "The Water Supply of Ancient Athens from 3000 to 86 B.C. Ph.D. diss., Princeton University. *Dissertation Abstracts International* 38-01, Section A, 0410; University Microfilms no. AAI7714245.

Carroll-Spillecke, Maureen. 1989. *ΚΗΠΟΣ. Der antike griechische Garten*. Wohnen in der klassischen Polis, 3. Munich: Deutscher Kunstverlag.

Cartledge, Paul, ed. 1998. *The Cambridge Illustrated History of Ancient Greece*. Cambridge: Cambridge University Press.

———. 1983. "'Trade and Politics' Revisited: Archaic Greece." In *Trade in the Ancient Economy*, ed. Peter Garnsey, Keith Hopkins, and C. R. Whittaker, 1–15. Berkeley: University of California Press.

Cook, Arthur B. 1964. *Zeus. A Study in Ancient Religion*. Vol. 1. New York: Biblio and Tannen (originally published 1914–1940, Cambridge: Cambridge University Press).

———. 1965. *Zeus. A Study in Ancient Religion*, Vol. 2. New York: Biblio and Tannen. (originally published 1914–1940, Cambridge: Cambridge University Press).

Cordsen, Anne. 1995. "The Pastas House in Archaic Greek Sicily." In Fischer-Hansen 1995: 103–21.

Cox, Cheryl A. 1998. *Household Interests: Property, Marriage Strategies, and Family Dynamics in Ancient Athens*. Princeton: Princeton University Press.

Crouch, Dora P. 1993. *Water Management in Ancient Greek Cities*. Oxford: Oxford University Press.

Dakaris, Sotirios I. 1989. *Kassope: Neoteres Anaskaphes (1977–1983)*. Ioannina: Ioannina University.

———. 1986. "To Orraon: To Spiti stin Archaia Epeiro." *Archaiologike Ephemeris*: 108–46.

Dalcher, Katharina. 1994. *Das Peristylhaus 1 von Iaitas: Architektur und Baugeschichte*. Studia Ietina, 6. Zurich: Archäologisches Institut der Universität Zürich.

D'Andria, Francesco, and Katia Mannino, eds. 1996. *Ricerche sulla casa in Magna Grecia e in Sicilia*. Università di Lecce Scuola di specializzazione in archeologia classica e medioevale, Archeologia e storia, 5. Galatina: Congedo Editore.

Daniel, Glyn. 1981. *A Short History of Archaeology*. London: Thames and Hudson.

Daremberg, Charles, and Edmond Saglio. 1877–1919. *Dictionnaire des antiquités grecques et romaines d'apres les textes et les monuments*. Paris: Hachette.

Daux, Georges. 1966. "Chronique des fouilles et découvertes archéologiques en Grèce en 1965: Porto Chéli, fouilles américanes." *Bulletin de correspondance hellénique* 90: 786–91.

Deal, Michael. 1985. "Household Pottery Disposal in the Maya Highlands: An Ethnoarchaeological Interpretation." *Journal of Anthropological Archaeology* 4: 243–91.

———. 1983. "Pottery Ethnoarchaeology among the Tzeltal Maya." Ph.D. diss., Simon Fraser University. *Dissertation Abstracts International* 46–02, Section A, 0457; University Microfilms no. AAI0555842.

Demand, Nancy H. 1990. *Urban Relocation in Archaic and Classical Greece: Flight and Consolidation*. Oklahoma Series in Classical Culture, 6. Norman: University of Oklahoma.

Dengate, Christina, James A. Dengate, Michael H. Jameson, Jane H. Leslie, David S. Reese, and Charles K. Williams II. n.d. *The Acropolis and Upper Town*. The Excavations at Ancient Halieis, 3. Bloomington: Indiana University Press, forthcoming.

Dohm, Karen M. 1996. "Rooftop Zuni: Extending Household Territory beyond Apartment Walls." In *People Who Lived in Big Houses: Archaeological Perspectives on Large Domestic Structures*, ed. Gary Coupland and E. B. Banning, 89–106. Monographs in World Archaeology, 27. Madison, Wisc.: Prehistory Press.

Drerup, Heinrich. 1967. "Prostashaus und Pastashaus: Zur Typologie des griechischen Hauses." *Marburger Winkelmannprogramm* 1967: 6–17.

Ducrey, Pierre, Ingrid R. Metzger, and Karl Reber. 1993. *Le Quartier de la Maison aux mosaïques*. Eretria: Fouilles et recherches, 8. Lausanne: Éditions Payot.

Dufkova, Marie, and Jan Pecirka. 1970. "Excavations of Farms and Farmhouses in the Chora of Chersonesos in the Crimea." *Eirene* 8: 123–74.

Dunbabin, Thomas J., and Alan A. A. Blakeway, eds. 1960. *Pottery, Ivories, Scarabs, and Other Objects from the Votive Deposits of Hera Limenia*. Perachora: The Sanctuaries of Hera Akraia and Limenia, 2. Oxford: Clarendon Press.

Dvorsky-Rohner, Dorothy. 1995. "Greek Domestic Architecture: An Ethnoarchaeological Model for the Interpretation of Space." *Archaeological News* 20: 1–10.

Dyson, Stephen L. 1999. "Brahmins and Bureaucrats: Some Reflections on the History of American Classical Archaeology." In *Assembling the Past: Studies in the Professionalization of Archaeology*, ed. Alice B. Kehoe and Mary Beth Emmerichs, 103–16. Albuquerque: University of New Mexico Press.

———. 1998. *Ancient Marbles to American Shores: Classical Archaeology in the United States*. Philadelphia: University of Pennsylvania Press.

———. 1993. "From New to New Age Archaeology: Archaeological Theory and Classical Archaeology—A 1990's Perspective." *American Journal of Archaeology* 97: 195–206.

———. 1989a. "Complacency and Crisis in Late Twentieth-Century Classical Archaeology." In *Classics: A Discipline and Profession in Crisis*, ed. Phyllis Culham and Lowell Edmunds, 211–20. Lanham, Md.: University Press of America.

———. 1989b. "The Role of Ideology and Institutions in Shaping Classical Archaeology in the Nineteenth and Twentieth Centuries." In *Tracing Archaeology's Past: The Historiography of Archaeology*, ed. Andrew L. Christenson, 127–35. Carbondale: Southern Illinois University Press.

———. 1981. "A Classical Archaeologist's Response to the 'New Archaeology.'" *Bulletin of the American Schools of Oriental Research* 242: 7–13.

Edmonds, John Maxwell, ed. and trans. 1957. *The Fragments of Attic Comedy*. Leiden: E. J. Brill.

Edwards, Charles M. 1984. "Aphrodite on a Ladder." *Hesperia* 53: 59–72.

Edwards, G. Roger. 1975. *Corinthian Hellenistic Pottery*. Corinth, 7, pt. 2. Princeton: American School of Classical Studies at Athens.

Eickstedt, Klaus-Valtin von. 1991. *Beiträge zur Topographie des antiken Piräus*. Bibliotheke tes en Athenais Archaiologikes Hetaireias, 118. Athens: Athenais Archaiologike Hetaireia.

Étienne, R. 1991. Review of Hoepfner and Schwandner 1994 (first ed., 1986); Schuller, Hoepfner, and Schwandner, 1989; and Carroll-Spillecke 1989; in *ΤΟΠΟΙ. Orient-Occident* 1: 39–47.

Fiedler, Manuel. 1999. "Leukas: Wohn- und Alltagskultur in einer nordwestgriechishen Stadt." In Hoepfner 1999c, 412–26.

Fine, John V. A. 1951. *Horoi: Studies in Mortgage, Real Security, and Land Tenure in Athens. Hesperia* Supplement 19. Princeton: American School of Classical Studies at Athens.

Finley, Moses I. 1973. *The Ancient Economy*. Sather Classical Lectures, 43. Berkeley: University of California Press.

———. 1952. *Studies in Land and Credit in Ancient Athens, 500–200 B.C. The Horos-Inscriptions*. New Brunswick, N.J.: Rutgers University Press.

Fischer-Hansen, Tobias, ed. 1995. *Ancient Sicily*. Acta Hyperborea, 6. Copenhagen: Museum Tusculanum Press.

Foley, Anne. 1988. *The Argolid 800–600 B.C.: An Archaeological Survey*. Studies in Mediterranean Archaeology, 80. Goteborg: Paul Åströms Förlag.

Forbes, Hamish A. 1993. "Ethnoarchaeology and the Place of the Olive in the Economy of the Southern Argolid, Greece." In Amouretti and Brun 1993: 213–26.

———. 1992. "The Ethnoarchaeological Approach to Ancient Greek Agriculture: Olive Cultivation as a Case Study." In Wells 1992: 87–101.

Forbes, Hamish A., and Lin Foxhall. 1978. "The Queen of All Trees: Preliminary Notes on the Archaeology of the Olive." *Expedition* 21.1: 37–47.

Foxhall, Lin. Forthcoming. *Olive Cultivation in Ancient Greece: Seeking the Ancient Economy*. Oxford: Oxford University Press.

———. 1997. "Appendix 1: Ancient Farmsteads, Other Agricultural Sites, and Equipment." In *A Rough and Rocky Place: The Landscape and Settlement History of the Methana Peninsula, Greece*, ed. Christopher Mee and Hamish Forbes, 257–68. Liverpool: Liverpool University Press.

———. 1993. "Oil Extraction and Processing Equipment in Classical Greece." In Amouretti and Brun 1993: 183–99.

Gallant, Thomas W. 1991. *Risk and Survival in Ancient Greece: Reconstructing the Rural Domestic Economy*. Stanford: Stanford University Press.

Garland, Robert. 1998. *Daily Life of the Ancient Greeks*. Westport, Conn.: Greenwood Press.

Garnsey, Peter. 1988. *Famine and Food Supply in the Graeco-Roman World: Responses to Risk and Crisis*. Cambridge: Cambridge University Press.

Gehrke, Hans-Joachim. 1989. "Bemerkungen zu Hippodamos von Milet." In Schuller, Hoepfner, and Schwandner 1989: 58–68 (with discussion).

Gies, Joseph, and Frances Gies. 1979. *Life in a Medieval Castle*. New York: Harper and Row.

Goldberg, Marilyn Y. 1999. "Spatial and Behavioural Negotiation in Classical Athenian City Houses." In Allison 1999: 142–61.

Graham, A. J. 1998. "The Woman at the Window: Observations on the 'Stele from the Harbour' of Thasos." *Journal of Hellenic Studies* 118: 22–40.

Graham, J. Walter. 1974. "Houses of Classical Athens." *Phoenix* 28: 45–54.

———. 1966. "Origins and Interrelations of the Greek House and the Roman House." *Phoenix* 20: 3–31.

———. 1954. "Olynthiaka, 5–6." *Hesperia* 23: 320–46.

Grandjean, Yves. 1988. *Recherches sur l'habitat thasien à l'époque grecque*. Études thasiennes, 12. Paris: Diffusion de Boccard.

Grant, Michael. 1990. *The Visible Past: Greek and Roman History from Archaeology, 1960-1990*. New York: Scribners.

Gulick, Charles B. 1930. *Athenaeus*, vol. 4. The Loeb Classical Library. New York: G. P. Putnam's Sons.

Haagsma, Margriet J. 1994. "Domestic Activities in Private and Public Spheres: A Case Study from New Halos." Paper presented at the 95th annual meeting of the Archaeological Institute of America, Washington, D.C., 27–30 December 1993. Abstract in *American Journal of Archaeology* 98: 336–37.

———. 1991. "Halos 1991: A Preliminary Report." *Newsletter of the Netherlands Institute at Athens* 4: 1–12.

———. 1990. "The Use of Space in Three Hellenistic Houses at Halos, Greece." M. Phil. thesis, Cambridge University.

Hadas, Moses, ed. 1962. *The Complete Plays of Aristophanes*. New York: Bantam.

Hadjisavvas, Sophocles. 1992. *Olive Oil Processing in Cyprus from the Bronze Age to the Byzantine Period.* Studies in Mediterranean Archaeology, 99. Nicosia: Paul Åströms Förlag.

Halstead, Paul, and John O'Shea, eds. 1989. *Bad Year Economics: Cultural Responses to Risk and Uncertainty.* Cambridge: Cambridge University Press.

Hanson, Victor D. 1998. *Warfare and Agriculture in Classical Greece.* Rev. ed. Berkeley: University of California Press.

Harper, David B. 1976. "Just Add Water . . ." *Expedition* 19.1: 40–49.

Harris, Edward C. 1989. *Principles of Archaeological Stratigraphy.* Rev. ed. London: Academic Press.

Harris, Edward C., Marley R. Brown III, and Gregory J. Brown, eds. 1993. *Practices of Archaeological Stratigraphy.* London: Academic Press.

Harward, Vernon Judson. 1982. "Greek Domestic Sculpture and the Origins of Private Art Patronage." Ph.D. diss., Harvard University. *Dissertation Abstracts International* 43-05, Section A, 1326; University Microfilms no. AAI8222641.

Hellmann, Marie-Christine. 1994. "La maison grecque: Les sources épigraphiques." *Topoi* 4: 131–46.

Hillier, Bill, and Julienne Hanson. 1984. *The Social Logic of Space.* Cambridge: Cambridge University Press.

Hodder, Ian. 1991. *Reading the Past: Current Approaches to Interpretation in Archaeology.* Rev. ed. Cambridge: Cambridge University Press.

———. 1990. *The Domestication of Europe: Structure and Contingency in Neolithic Societies.* Oxford: Blackwell.

Hodkinson, Stephen. 1988. "Animal Husbandry in the Greek Polis." In *Pastoral Economies in Classical Antiquity,* ed. C. R. Whittaker, 35–74. Proceedings of the Cambridge Philological Society Supplement 14. Cambridge: Cambridge Philological Society.

Hoepfner, Wolfram. 1999a. "Athen und Attika." In Hoepfner 1999c: 223–60.

———. 1999b. "Delos. Die Stadt der Kaufleute." In Hoepfner 1999c: 507–24.

———, ed. 1999c. *Geschichte des Wohnens. Band I: 500 v. Chr.–500 n. Chr. Vorgeschichte - Frühgeschichte - Antike.* Stuttgart: Deutsche Verlags-Anstalt (Wustenrot Stiftung, Deutscher Eigenheimvereine. V., Ludwigsburg).

———. 1999d. "Hausformen und ihr Wandel." In Hoepfner 1999c: 138–48.

———. 1989. "Die frühen Demokratien und die Architekturforschung." In Schuller, Hoepfner, and Schwandner 1989: 9–16 (with discussion).

———. 1986. *Architektur und Demokratie. Wohnen in der klassischen Polis.* Thyssen Vorträge. Auseinandersetzung mit der Antike 2, ed. H. Flashar. Bamberg: C. C. Buchners Verlag.

Hoepfner, Wolfram, and Gunnar Brands, eds. 1996. *Basileia: Die Paläste der hellenistischen Könige.* Mainz: von Zabern.

Hoepfner, Wolfram, Sotirios Dakaris, Konstantina Gravani, and Ernst-Ludwig Schwandner. 1999a. "Kassope: Eine spätklassische Streifenstadt in Nordwestgriechenland." In Hoepfner 1999c: 368–83.

———. 1999b. "Orraon: Einen geplante Kleinstadt in Epirus." In Hoepfner 1999c: 384–411.

Hoepfner, Wolfram, and Ernst-Wilhelm Osthues. 1999. "Kolophon." In Hoepfner 1999c: 280–91.

Hoepfner, Wolfram, and Ernst-Ludwig Schwandner. 1999. "Dystos: Eine Kleinstadt auf Euböa." In Hoepfner 1999c: 352–67.

———. 1994. *Haus und Stadt im klassischen Griechenland.* Wohnen in der klassischen Polis 1. Rev. ed. Munich: Deutscher Kunstverlag.

Holland, Leicester B. 1944. "Colophon." *Hesperia* 13: 91–171.

Hug, August. 1930. "Matta." In Wissowa and Kroll 1893–. 14.2: 2310.

Humphreys, Sally C. 1967. "Archaeology and the Social and Economic History of Classical Greece." *La parola del passato* 22: 374–400.

Isler, Hans Peter, and D. Käch, eds. 1997. *Wohnbauforschung in Zentral und Westsizilien.* Zurich: Archäologisches Institut der Universität Zurich.

Jameson, Michael H. 2001a. "A Hero Cult at Halieis." In ΙΘΑΚΗ. *Festschrift für Jörg Schäfer zum 75. Geburtstag am 25. April 2001,* ed. Stephanie Böhm und Klaus-Valtin von Eickstedt, 197–202. Würzburg: Ergon Verlag.

———. 2001b. "Oil Presses of the Late Classical/Hellenistic Period." In *Techniques et sociétés en Méditerranée. Hommage à Marie-Claire Amouretti,* ed. Jean-Pierre Brun and Philippe Jockey, 281–99. Paris.

———. 1996. "Houses, Greek." In *Oxford Classical Dictionary,* 730–31. 3d ed. Oxford: Oxford University Press.

———. 1992. "Agricultural Labor in Ancient Greece." In Wells 1992: 135–46.

———. 1990a. "Domestic Space in the Greek City-State." In Kent 1990: 92–113.

———. 1990b. "Private Space and the Greek City." In Murray and Price 1990: 171–95.

———. 1977/78. "Agriculture and Slavery in Classical Athens." *Classical Journal* 73: 122–45.

———. 1974. "The Excavation of a Drowned Greek Temple." *Scientific American* 231.4: 111–19.

———. 1969. "Excavations at Porto Cheli and Vicinity, Preliminary Report I: Halieis, 1962–1968." *Hesperia* 38: 311–42.

Jameson, Michael H., Curtis N. Runnels, and Tjeerd H. van Andel. 1994. *A Greek Countryside: The Southern Argolid from Prehistory to the Present Day.* Stanford: Stanford University Press.

Jardé, Auguste. 1925. *Les céréales dans l'antiquité grecque.* Paris: Éditions de Boccard.

Jenkins, Ian D. 1985. "The Ambiguity of Greek Textiles." *Arethusa* 18: 109–32.

Jerkich, Louis. 1974. "Some Corinthian Roof Tiles from Halieis. A Report on Some Roof Tiles Excavated in the Summer of 1974." Paper, Indiana University, Bloomington, 1974.

Jones, Glynis, Kenneth Wardle, Paul Halstead, and Diana Wardle. 1986. "Crop Storage at Assiros." *Scientific American* 254.3: 96–103.

Jones, John Ellis. 1975. "Town and Country Houses of Attica in Classical Times." In *Thorikos and the Laurion in Archaic and Classical Times*, ed. H. Mussche, Paule Spitaels, and F. Goemaere-De Poerck, 63–140. Miscellanea Graeca, 1. Ghent: Belgian Archaeological Mission in Greece.

Jones, John Ellis, A. J. Graham, and L. H. Sackett. 1973. "An Attic Country House below the Cave of Pan at Vari." *Annual of the British School at Athens* 68: 355–452.

Jones, John Ellis, L. H. Sackett, and A. J. Graham. 1962. "The Dema House in Attica." *Annual of the British School at Athens* 57: 75–114.

Jongman, Willem. 1988. *The Economy and Society of Pompeii*. Dutch Monographs on Ancient History and Archaeology, 4. Amsterdam: J. C. Gieben.

Kanowski, M. G. 1984. *Containers of Classical Greece: A Handbook of Shapes*. New York: University of Queensland Press.

Kent, Susan, ed. 1990. *Domestic Architecture and the Use of Space: An Interdisciplinary Cross-Cultural Study*. New Directions in Archaeology. Cambridge: Cambridge University Press.

Keuls, Eva C. 1985. *The Reign of the Phallus: Sexual Politics in Ancient Athens*. New York: Harper and Row.

———. 1983. "Attic Vase-Painting and the Home Textile Industry." In *Ancient Greek Art and Iconography*, ed. Warren G. Moon, 209–30. Madison: University of Wisconsin Press.

Kiderlen, Moritz. 1996. "Zum gesellschaftichen Kontext und zur schichtspezifischen Zuordnung grosser Stadthäuser des 4. und 3. Jhs. v. Chr." In Hoepfner and Brands 1996: 76–83.

———. 1995. *Megale Oikia: Untersuchungen zur Entwicklung aufwendiger griechischer Stadthausarchitektur von der Früharchaik bis ins 3 Jh. v. Chr.* Hürth: Verlag Martin Lange.

Klaffenbach, Günther. 1953. *Die Astynomeninscrift von Pergamon*. Abhandlungen der Deutschen Akademie der Wissenschaften zu Berlin, 6. Reprint, Akademie-Verlag, Berlin, 1977.

Klein, Anita E. 1932. *Child Life in Greek Art*. New York: Columbia University Press.

Koster, Joan B. 1976. "From Spindle to Loom: Weaving in the Southern Argolid." *Expedition* 19.1: 29–39.

Krause, Clemens. 1977. "Grundformen des griechischen Pastashauses." *Archäologischer Anzeiger* 1977: 164–79.

Kron, Uta. 1992. "Frauenfeste in Demeterheiligtümern: Das Thesmophorion von Bitalemi. Eine archäologische Fallstudie." *Archäologischer Anzeiger* 1992: 611–48.

Lamb, W. R. M. 1927. *Plato, Protagoras*. The Loeb Classical Library. Cambridge, Mass.: Harvard University Press.

Lang, Franziska. 1996. *Archaische Siedlungen in Griechenland: Struktur und Entwicklung*. Berlin: Akademie Verlag.

Lang, Mable. 1968. *Waterworks in the Athenian Agora*. Excavations of the Athenian Agora Picture Books, 11. Princeton: American School of Classical Studies at Athens.

Latte, Kurt. 1966. *Hesychii Alexandrini Lexikon*, vol. 2. Commission for the Corpus Lexicographorum Graecorum, Copenhagen. Copenhagen: Ejnar Munksgaard Editore.

Lissarrague, François. 1998. "Intrusions au gynécée." In *Les mystères du gynécée*, ed. Paul Veyne, Françoise Lissarrague, and Françoise Frontisi-Ducroux, 155–78. Paris: Gallimard.

Löhr, Christoph. 1990. "Griechische Häuser: Hof, Fenster, Türen nach 348 v. Chr." In *Licht und Architektur*, ed. Wolf-Dieter Heilmeyer and Wolfram Hoepfner, 10–19. Schriften des Seminars für klassische Archäologie der Freien Universität Berlin. Tübingen: E. Wasmuth.

McAllister, Marian H. 2005. *The Fortifications and Adjacent Structures*. Excavations at Ancient Halieis, 1. Bloomington: Indiana University Press.

———. 1973. "The Fortifications of Ancient Halieis." Ph.D. diss., Bryn Mawr College. *Dissertation Abstracts International* 36-12, Section A, 8143; University Microfilms no. AAI7613775.

McCredie, James R. 1971. "Hippodamos of Miletos." In *Studies Presented to G. M. A. Hanfmann*, ed. David G. Mitten, John G. Pedley, and Jane A. Scott, 95–100. Fogg Art Museum-Harvard University Monographs in Art and Archaeology, 2. Cambridge, Mass.: Harvard University Press.

McKay, Alexander G. 1988. "Houses." In *Civilization of the Ancient Mediterranean: Greece and Rome*, ed. Michael Grant and Rachel Kitzinger, 3: 1363–83. New York: Scribner's.

Marchant, E. C. 1938. *Xenophon, Memorabilia. Oeconomicus*. The Loeb Classical Library. Cambridge, Mass.: Harvard University Press.

Martin, Roland. 1973. "Rapports entre les structures urbaines et les modes de division et d'exploitation du territoire." In *Problèmes de la terre en Grèce ancienne*, ed. Moses I. Finley, 97–112. Civilisations et sociétés, 33. Paris: Mouton.

Mattingly, David J. 1996. "First Fruit? The Olive in the Roman World." In *Human Landscapes in Classical Antiquity: Environment and Culture*, ed. Graham Shipley and John Salmon, 213–53. London: Routledge.

Miller, Andrew M. 1996. *Greek Lyric: An Anthology in Translation*. Indianapolis: Hackett.

Miller, Stephen G. 1978. *The Prytaneion: Its Function and Architectural Form*. Berkeley: University of California Press.

Morgan, Gareth. 1982. "Euphiletos' House: Lysias I." *Transactions of the American Philological Association* 112: 115–23.

Morris, Ian. 1998a. "Archaeology and Archaic Greek History." In *Archaic Greece: New Approaches and New Evidence*, ed. Nick Fisher and Hans van Wees, 1–92. London: Duckworth.

———. 1998b. "Remaining Invisible: The Archaeology of the Excluded in Classical Athens." In *Women and Slaves in Greco-Roman Culture: Differential Equations*, ed. Sandra R. Joshel and Sheila Murnaghan, 193–220. London: Routledge.

———. 1994a. "Archaeologies of Greece." In Morris 1994c: 8–47.

———. 1994b. "The Athenian Economy Twenty Years after *The Ancient Economy*." *Classical Philology* 89: 351–66.

———, ed. 1994c. *Classical Greece: Ancient Histories and Modern Archaeologies*. Cambridge: Cambridge University Press.

Murray, Oswyn, ed. 1990. *Sympotika: A Symposium on the* Symposion. Oxford: Clarendon Press.

Murray, Oswyn, and Simon Price, eds. 1990. *The Greek City: From Homer to Alexander*. Oxford: Oxford University Press.

Mussche, Herman F., Jean Bingen, J. Ellis Jones, and Mark Waelkens. 1990. *Rapport préliminaire sur les 13ᵉ, 14ᵉ, 15ᵉ, et 16ᵉ campagnes de fouilles, 1977/1982*. Thorikos, 9. Ghent: Comité des fouilles belges en Grèce.

Neudecker, Richard. 1994. *Die Pracht der Latrine. Zum Wandel öffentlicher Bedürfnisanstalten in der kaiserzeitlichen Stadt*. Studien zur antiken Stadt, 1. Munich: Verlag Dr. Friedrich Pfeil.

Nevett, Lisa C. 1999. *House and Society in the Ancient Greek World*. New Studies in Archaeology. Cambridge: Cambridge University Press.

———. 1995a. "Gender Relations in the Classical Greek Household." *Annual of the British School at Athens* 90: 363–81.

———. 1995b. "The Organisation of Space in Classical and Hellenistic Houses from Mainland Greece and the Western Colonies." In Spencer 1995: 89–108.

———. 1994. "Separation or Seclusion? Towards an Archaeological Approach to Investigating Women in the Greek Household in the Fifth to Third Centuries B.C." In *Architecture and Order: Approaches to Social Space*, ed. Michael P. Pearson and Colin Richards, 98–112. Material Cultures. New York: Routledge.

———. 1992. "Variation in the Form and Use of Domestic Space in the Greek World in the Classical and Hellenistic Periods." Doctoral diss., Cambridge University.

Nilsson, Martin P. 1961. *Greek Folk Religion*. New York: Harper and Row (first published as *Greek Popular Religion*, New York: Columbia University Press, 1940).

———. 1960a. "Griechische Hausaltäre." *Opuscula Selecta*. Skrifter utgivna av Svenska Institutet I Athen, 80, II:3, 265–70. Lund: Glerup.

———. 1960b. "Roman and Greek Domestic Cult." *Opuscula Selecta*. Skrifter utgivna av Svenska Institutet I Athen, 80, II:3, 270–85. Lund: Glerup.

Nowicka, Maria. 1975. *Les maisons à tour dans le monde grec*. Academia Scientiarum Polona. Bibliotheca antiqua, 15. Warsaw: Wydawn. Polskiej Akademii Nauk.

Oldfather, W. A. 1926. *Epictetus*, vol. 1. The Loeb Classical Library. New York: G. P. Putnam's Sons.

Orlandini, Piero. 1966. "Lo scavo del Thesmophorion di Bitalemi e il culto delle divinità ctonie a Gela." *Kokalos* 12: 8–35.

Orton, Clive. 1989. "An Introduction to the Quantification of Assemblages of Pottery." *Journal of Roman Pottery Studies* 2: 94–97.

———. 1980. *Mathematics in Archaeology*. Cambridge: Cambridge University Press.

Osborne, Robin. 1985. "Buildings and Residence on the Land in Classical and Hellenistic Greece: The Contribution of Epigraphy." *Annual of the British School at Athens* 80: 119–28.

Owens, E. J. 1983. "The Koprologoi at Athens in the Fifth and Fourth Centuries B.C." *Classical Quarterly* n.s. 33: 44–50.

Paice, Patricia. 1991. "Extensions to the Harris Matrix System to Illustrate Stratigraphic Discussion of an Archaeological Site." *Journal of Field Archaeology* 19: 17–28.

Payne, Sebastian. 1985. "Zooarchaeology in Greece: A Reader's Guide." In *Contributions to Aegean Archaeology: Studies in Honor of W. A. McDonald*, ed. Nancy C. Wilkie and William D. E. Coulson, 211–44. Publications in Ancient Studies, 1. Minneapolis: Center for Ancient Studies, University of Minnesota.

Pemberton, Elizabeth G. 1989. *The Sanctuary of Demeter and Kore: The Greek Pottery*. Corinth, 18, pt. 1. Princeton: American School of Classical Studies at Athens.

Pesando, Fabrizio. 1989. *La casa dei greci*. Biblioteca di archeologia, 11. Milan: Longanesi.

———. 1987. *Oikos e Ktesis: La casa greca in età classica*. Pubblcazioni degli Istituti di Storia della Facoltà di Lettere e Filosofia. Perugia: Quasar.

Pinkwart, Doris, and Wolf Stammnitz. 1984. *Peristylhäuser westlich der unteren Agora*. Altertümer von Pergamon, 14. Berlin: de Gruyter.

Pomeroy, Sarah B. 1997. *Families in Classical and Hellenistic Greece: Representations and Realities*. New York: Clarendon Press.

———. 1995. "The Contribution of Women to the Greek Domestic Economy: Rereading Xenophon's *Oeconomicus*." In *Feminisms in the Academy*, ed. Domna C. Stanton and Abigail J. Stewart, 180–95. Ann Arbor: University of Michigan Press.

———. 1994. *Xenophon, Oeconomicus: A Social and Historical Commentary, with a New English Translation.* New York: Oxford University Press.

Pope, Maurice. 1976. *The Ancient Greeks. How They Lived and Worked.* Chester Springs, Penn.: Dufour Éditions.

Popham, M. R., P. G. Calligas, and L. H. Sackett. 1993. *The Protogeometric Building at Toumba.* Lefkandi, 2. Athens: British School of Archaeology.

Pottier, Edmond. 1904. "Matta." In Daremberg and Saglio. 1877–1919.

Pritchett, W. Kendrick. 1953. "The Attic Stelai. Part I." *Hesperia* 22: 225–99.

———. 1956. "The Attic Stelai. Part II." *Hesperia* 25: 178-328.

Quennell, Marjorie, and C. H. B. Quennell. 1931a. *Everyday Things in Archaic Greece.* London: Batsford.

———. 1931b. *Everyday Things in Classical Greece.* London: Batsford.

Raeder, Joachim. 1984. *Priene: Funde aus einer griechischen Stadt in Berliner Antikenmuseum.* Bilderheft der Staatlichen Museen Berlin Preussischer Kulturbesitz, 45/46. Berlin: Antikenmuseum.

Rapoport, Amos. 1969. *House Form and Culture.* Englewood Cliffs, N.J.: Prentice-Hall.

Reber, Karl. 1998. *Die klassischen und hellenistischen Wohnhäuser im Westquartier.* Eretria: Ausgrabungen und Forschungen, 10. Lausanne: Éditions Payot.

———. 1988. "Aedificia graecorum: Zu Vitruvs Beschreibung des griechischen Hauses." *Archäologischer Anzeiger* 1988: 653–66.

Reese, David S. 1989. "Iron Age Purple Dye-Production in Greece." Unpublished paper.

———. 1987. "Palaikastro Shells and Bronze Age Purple Dye-Production in the Mediterranean Basin." *Annual of the British School at Athens* 82: 201–6.

Reinders, H. Reinder. 1988. *New Halos: A Hellenistic Town in Thessalia, Greece.* Utrecht: HES Publishers.

Renfrew, Colin. 1980. "The Great Tradition versus the Great Divide: Archaeology as Anthropology?" *American Journal of Archaeology* 84: 287–98.

Rhodes, P. J., trans. 1984. *Aristotle, The Athenian Constitution.* New York: Penguin.

Rice, Prudence M. 1987. *Pottery Analysis: A Sourcebook.* Chicago: University of Chicago Press.

Richter, Gisela M. A. 1966. *The Furniture of the Greeks, Etruscans, and Romans.* London: Phaidon.

Richter, Gisela M. A., and Marjorie J. Milne. 1935. *Shapes and Names of Athenian Vases.* New York: Plantin Press.

Rider, Bertha C. 1915. *The Greek House: Its History and Development from the Neolithic Period to the Hellenistic Age.* Cambridge: Cambridge University Press.

Robinson, David M. 1946. *Domestic and Public Architecture.* Excavations at Olynthus, 12. The Johns Hopkins University Studies in Archaeology No. 36. Baltimore: The Johns Hopkins Press.

Robinson, David M., and J. Walter Graham. 1938. *The Hellenic House.* Excavations at Olynthus, 8. The Johns Hopkins University Studies in Archaeology No. 25. Baltimore: The Johns Hopkins Press.

Robinson, Eric W. 1997. *The First Democracies: Early Popular Government outside Athens.* Historia Einzelschriften, 107. Stuttgart: F. Steiner.

Rostovtzeff, Michael I., Alfred R. Bellinger, C. Hopkins, and C. B. Welles. 1936. *The Excavations at Dura-Europos: Preliminary Report of the Sixth Season of Work, October 1932–March 1933.* New Haven: Yale University Press.

Rowland, Ingrid D., and Thomas N. Howe, trans. 1999. *Vitruvius: Ten Books on Architecture.* New York: Cambridge University Press.

Rudolph, Wolf W. 1984. "Excavations at Porto Cheli and Vicinity, Preliminary Report VI: Halieis, the Stratigraphy of the Streets in the Northeast Quarter of the Lower Town." *Hesperia* 53: 123–70.

———. 1983. "Final Report: Halieis (1975)." *Archaiologikon Deltion* 30, 1975, B'1 [1983]: 64–73.

———. 1979a. "Excavations at Porto Cheli and Vicinity, Preliminary Report V: The Early Byzantine Remains." *Hesperia* 48: 294–320.

———. 1979b. "Final Report: Halieis (1974)." *Archaiologikon Deltion* 29, 1973–74, B'2 [1979]: 265–68.

———. 1974. "Excavations at Porto Cheli and Vicinity, Preliminary Report, III: Excavations at Metochi 1970." *Hesperia* 43: 105–31.

Runnels, Curtis N., Daniel J. Pullen, Susan Langdon, eds. 1995. *Artifact and Assemblage: The Finds from a Regional Survey of the Southern Argolid, Greece.* Vol. 1, *The Prehistoric and Early Iron Age Pottery and the Lithic Artifacts.* Stanford: Stanford University Press.

Runnels, Curtis N., and Tjeerd H. van Andel. 1987. "The Evolution of Settlement in the Southern Argolid, Greece: An Economic Explanation." *Hesperia* 56: 304–34.

Sallares, Robert. 1991. *The Ecology of the Ancient Greek World.* Ithaca: Cornell University Press.

Saprykin, Sergei J. 1994. *Ancient Farms and Land-Plots on the Khora of Khersonesos Taurike: Research in the Herakleian Peninsula, 1974–1990.* McGill University Monographs in Classical Archaeology and History, 16. Amsterdam: J. C. Gieben.

Schauenburg, Konrad. 1972. "Frauen im Fenster." *Mitteilungen des Deutschen Archäologischen Instituts* 79: 1–15.

Scheidel, Walter. 1995. "The Most Silent Women of Greece and Rome: Rural Labour and Women's Life in the Ancient World (I)." *Greece and Rome* 42: 202–17.

———. 1996. "The Most Silent Women of Greece and Rome: Rural Labour and Women's Life in the Ancient World (II)." *Greece and Rome* 43: 1–10.

Schiffer, Michael B. 1996. *Formation Processes of the Archaeological Record.* Salt Lake City: University of Utah Press (originally published 1987, Albuquerque: University of New Mexico Press).

Schmitt-Pantel, Pauline. 1992. *La cité au banquet: Histoire des repas publics dans les cités grecques*. Collection de l'École française de Rome, no. 157. Rome: Ecole française de Rome.

———. 1990. "Sacrificial Meal and *Symposion*: Two Models of Civic Institutions in the Archaic City?" In Murray 1990: 14–33.

Schuller, Wolfgang, Wolfram Hoepfner, and Ernst-Ludwig Schwandner, eds. 1989. *Demokratie und Architektur: Der hippodamische Städtebau und die Entstehung der Demokratie (Konstanzer Symposion vom 17. bis 19. Juli 1987)*. Wohnen in der klassischen Polis, 2. Munich: Deutscher Kunstverlag.

Schwandner, Ernst-Ludwig. 1999a. "Fussböden." In Hoepfner 1999c: 528–29.

———. 1999b. "Türen." In Hoepfner 1999c: 531–32.

———. 1999c. "Fenster." In Hoepfner 1999c: 532–34.

———. 1978. "Zu technischen und ökonomischen Problemen des griechischen Wohnungshaus in klassischer Zeit." In *Wohnungsbau im Altertum*, 105–13. Diskussion zur Archäologischen Bauforschung, 3. Berlin: Deutsches Archäologisches Institut.

Shanks, Michael. 1996. *Classical Archaeology of Greece: Experiences of the Discipline*. London: Routledge.

Sismanides, K. L. 1986. "Anaskaphe taphikou tumbou stin Ayia Parakesevi Thessalonikes. Enas neos makedonikos taphos." *Archaiologike Ephemeris* 1986: 60–98.

Sjövall, Harald. 1931. *Zeus im altgriechischen Hauskult*. Lund: H. Ohlsson.

Slater, William J., ed. 1991. *Dining in a Classical Context*. Ann Arbor: University of Michigan Press.

Small, Allister M., B. Roe, J. W. Hayes, C. J. Simpson, G. Guzzetta, M. MacKinnon, and S. G. Monckton. 1994. "A Pit Group of c. 80–70 B.C. from Gravina di Puglia." *Papers of the British School at Rome* 72: 197–260.

Smith, Michael E. 1992. "Braudel's Temporal Rhythms and Chronology Theory in Archaeology." In *Archaeology, Annales, and Ethnohistory*, ed. A. Bernard Knapp, 23–34. Cambridge: Cambridge University Press.

Smyth, Herbert W. 1938. *Aeschylus, Prometheus Bound*. The Loeb Classical Library. Cambridge, Mass.: Harvard University Press.

Snodgrass, Anthony M. 1988. *An Archaeology of Greece. The Present State and Future Scope of a Discipline*. Sather Classical Lectures, 53. Berkeley: University of California Press.

———. 1985. "The New Archaeology and the Classical Archaeologist." *American Journal of Archaeology* 89: 31–37.

Soren, David, and Jamie James. 1988. *Kourion: The Search for a Lost Roman City*. New York: Anchor Press.

Sparkes, Brian A. 1981. "Not Cooking, but Baking." *Greece and Rome* 28: 172–78.

———. 1965. "The Greek Kitchen: Addenda." *Journal of Hellenic Studies* 85: 162–63.

———. 1962. "The Greek Kitchen." *Journal of Hellenic Studies* 82: 121–37.

Sparkes, Brian A., and Lucy Talcott. 1970. *Black and Plain Pottery of the Sixth, Fifth, and Fourth Centuries B.C.* The Athenian Agora, 12. Princeton: American School of Classical Studies at Athens.

———. 1951. *Pots and Pans of Classical Athens*. Athenian Agora Picture Book, 1. Princeton: American School of Classical Studies at Athens.

Spencer, Nigel, ed. 1995. *Time, Tradition, and Society in Greek Archaeology: Bridging the "Great Divide."* London: Routledge.

Themelis, Petros. 1999. "Ausgrabungen in Kallipolis (Ost-Aetolien)." In Hoepfner 1999c: 427–40.

Thompson, Dorothy B. 1971. *An Ancient Shopping Center: The Athenian Agora*. Athenian Agora Picture Book, 12. Princeton: American School of Classical Studies at Athens.

Thompson, Homer A. 1959. "Activities in the Athenian Agora: 1958." *Hesperia* 28: 91–108.

Thür, Gerhard. 1989. "Wo wohnen die Metöken?" In Schuller, Hoepfner, and Schwandner 1989: 117–21.

Travlos, John. 1971. *Pictorial Dictionary of Ancient Athens*. New York: Praeger.

Trendall, Arthur D. 1989. *Red Figure Vases of South Italy and Sicily*. New York: Thames and Hudson.

Trümper, Monika. 1998. *Wohnen in Delos: Eine baugeschichtliche Untersuchung zum Wandel der Wohnkultur in hellenistischer Zeit*. Internationale Archäologie, 46. Rahden: Verlag Marie Leidorf GmbH.

Tsakirgis, Barbara. Forthcoming, a. *The Domestic Architecture of the Hellenistic and Roman Periods*. Morgantina Studies, 6. Princeton: Princeton University Press.

———. Forthcoming, b. "Fire and Smoke: Hearths, Braziers, and Chimneys in the Greek House." In *Building Communities: House, Settlement and Society in the Aegean and Beyond*, ed. Ruth Westgate, Nick Fisher, and James Whitley. British School at Athens Studies.

———. 1997. "Houses and Housing Districts Shed New Light on Life in Ancient Athens." *Newsletter: American School of Classical Studies at Athens* 39: 1, 13.

———. 1996. "Houses and Households (review article)." *American Journal of Archaeology* 100: 777–81.

———. 1995. "Morgantina: A Greek Town in Central Sicily." In Fischer-Hansen 1995: 123–47.

———. 1994. "'Lovely Mute Ghosts': The Greek Houses of Ancient Sicily." Paper presented at the 95th Annual Meeting of the Archaeological Institute of America, Washington, D.C., 27–30 December 1993. Abstract in *American Journal of Archaeology* 98: 298.

———. 1989. "The Universality of the Prostas House." Paper presented at the 90th General Meeting of the Archaeological Institute of America and the First Joint Archaeological Congress, Baltimore, Maryland, 5–9 January 1989. Abstract in *American Journal of Archaeology* 93: 278–79.

———. 1984. "The Domestic Architecture of Morgantina in the Hellenistic and Roman Periods." Ph.D. diss., Princeton University. *Dissertation Abstracts International* 44-12, Section A, 3733; University Microfilms no. AAI8405873.

Vatin, Claude. 1976. "Jardins et services de voirie." *Bulletin de correspondance hellénique* 100: 555–64.

Vickers, Michael. 1999. *Images on Textiles. The Weave of Fifth-Century Athenian Art and Society*. Xenia, 42. Constance: Universitätsverlag Konstanz.

Walker, Susan. 1983. "Women and Housing in Classical Greece: The Archaeological Evidence." In *Images of Women in Antiquity*, ed. Averil Cameron and Amélie Kuhrt, 81–91. London: Croom Helm.

Walter-Karydi, Elena. 1996. "Die Nobilitierung des griechischen Wohnhauses in der spätklassischen Zeit." In Hoepfner and Brands 1996: 56–61.

———. 1994. *Die Nobilitierung des Wohnhauses. Lebensform und Architektur in spätklassischen Griechenland*. Xenia, 35. Constance: Universitätsverlag Konstanz.

———. 1998. *The Greek House. The Rise of Noble Houses in Late Classical Times*. Athens: The Archaeological Society of Athens.

Watson, Patty Jo. 1979. *Archaeological Ethnography in Western Iran*. Viking Fund Publications in Anthropology, 57. Tuscon: University of Arizona Press.

Webster, T. B. L. 1969. *Everyday Life in Classical Athens*. London: Batsford.

Wells, Berit, ed. 1992. *Agriculture in Ancient Greece. Proceedings of the Seventh International Symposium at the Swedish Institute at Athens, 16-17 May 1990*. Skrifter utgivna av Svenska institutet i Athen 4°.42. Stockholm: Swedish Institute at Athens.

White, K. D. 1970. *Roman Farming*. London: Thames and Hudson.

Wiegand, Theodor, and Hans Schrader. 1904. *Priene. Ergebnisse der Ausgrabungen und Untersuchungen in den Jahren 1895–1898*. Berlin: G. Reimer.

Wiencke, Matthew I. 1947. "Greek Household Religion." Ph.D. diss., Johns Hopkins University.

Williams, Charles K., II. 1981. "The City of Corinth and Its Domestic Religion." *Hesperia* 50: 408–21.

Williams, Hector. 1996. "Excavations at Stymphalos, 1995." *Echos du Monde Classique / Classical News and Views* (n.s.) 15: 75–98.

Williams, Hector, Gerald Schaus, Susan Marie Cronkite Price, Ben Gourley, and Holly Lutomsky. 1997. "Excavations at Stymphalos, 1996." *Echos du Monde Classique / Classical News and Views* (n.s.) 16: 23–73.

Willey, Gordon R., and Philip Phillips. 1958. *Method and Theory in American Archaeology*. Chicago: University of Chicago Press.

Wilkinson, Tony J. 1982. "The Definition of Ancient Manured Zones by Means of Extensive Sherd Sampling Techniques." *Journal of Field Archaeology* 9: 323–33.

Wissowa, Georg, and Wilhelm Kroll, eds. 1893–. *Paulys Real-Encyclopädie der klassischen Altertumswissenschaft*. Stuttgart: Alfred Druckenmüller.

Wright, James C. 1982. "Excavations at Tsoungiza (Archaia Nemea): 1981." *Hesperia* 51: 375–97.

Wulf, Ulrike. 1999. *Die Stadtgrabung, 3: Die Hellenistischen und römischen Wohnhäuser von Pergamon*. Altertümer von Pergamon, 15. Berlin: Walter de Gruyter.

Wulf-Rheidt, Ulrike. 1998. "The Hellenistic and Roman Houses of Pergamon." In *Pergamon: Citadel of the Gods*, ed. Helmut Koester, 299–330. Harvard Theological Studies, 46. Harrisburg, Penn.: Trinity Press International.

Yavis, Constantine G. 1949. *Greek Altars: Origins and Typology, Including the Minoan-Mycenaean Offertory Apparatus. An Archaeological Study in the History of Religion*. St. Louis, Mo.: St. Louis University Press.

Young, John H. 1963. "A Migrant City in the Peloponnesus." *Expedition* 5.3: 2–11.

Young, Rodney S. 1951. "An Industrial District in Ancient Athens." *Hesperia* 20: 135–288.

Index

Bradley A. Ault received his Ph.D. in Classical archaeology from Indiana University and is Associate Professor of Classics at the State University of New York at Buffalo. He has been awarded Horstman and Fulbright Fellowships for research at the Freie Universität, Berlin, and the American School of Classical Studies at Athens respectively. He has also held the Blegen Research Fellowship at Vassar College. Ault has participated in archaeological research at Greek and Roman sites from Britain to Israel. One of his areas of specialization is the archaeology of the ancient Greek city and household. With Lisa C. Nevett, he has edited a collection of papers, *Ancient Greek Houses and Households* (2005). He is also the author of a number of articles on Greek domestic architecture and household matters that have appeared in the journals *Hesperia* and *Classical World,* as well as in several edited volumes.

Figures

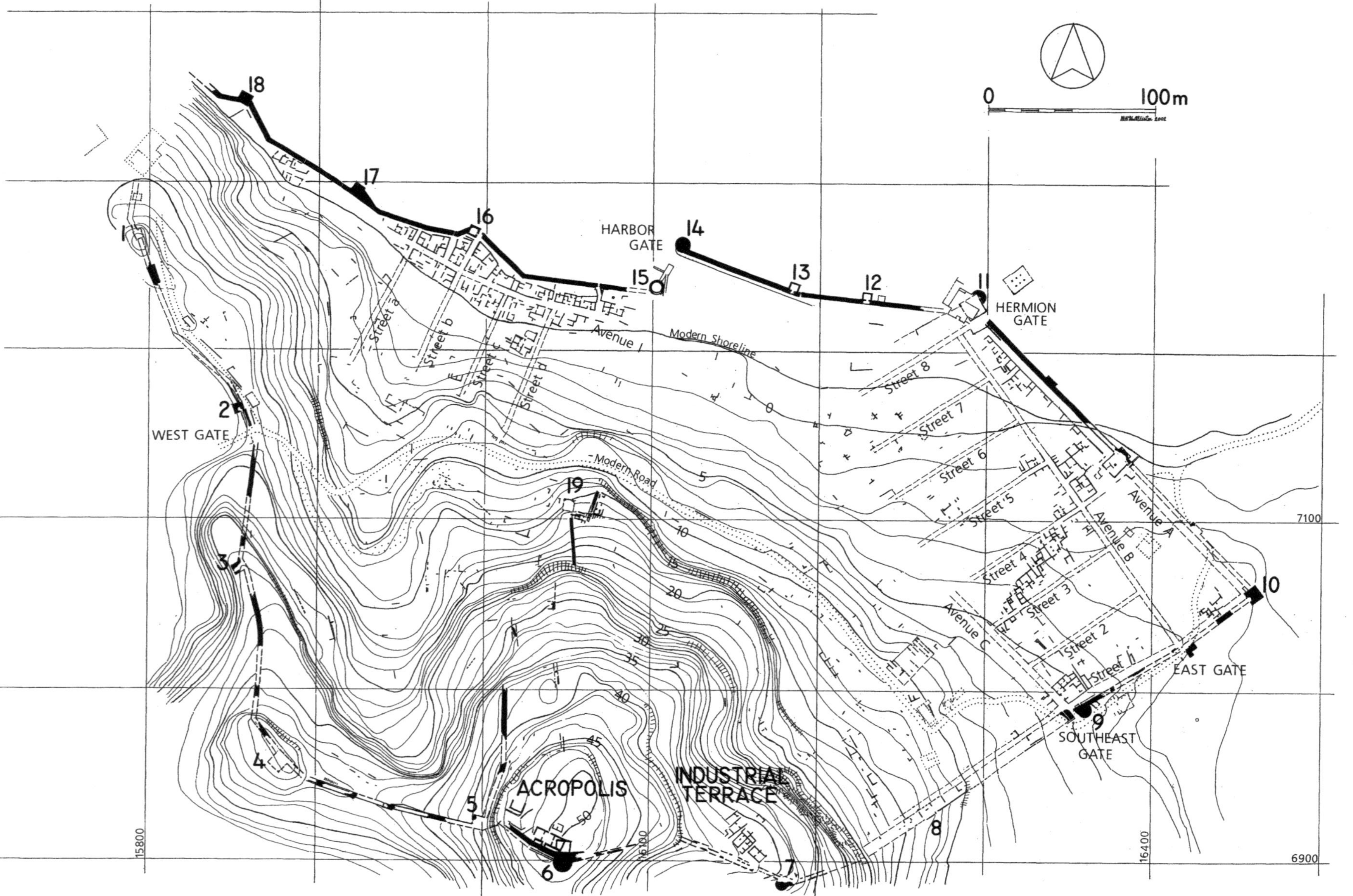

Figure 1. Overall site plan

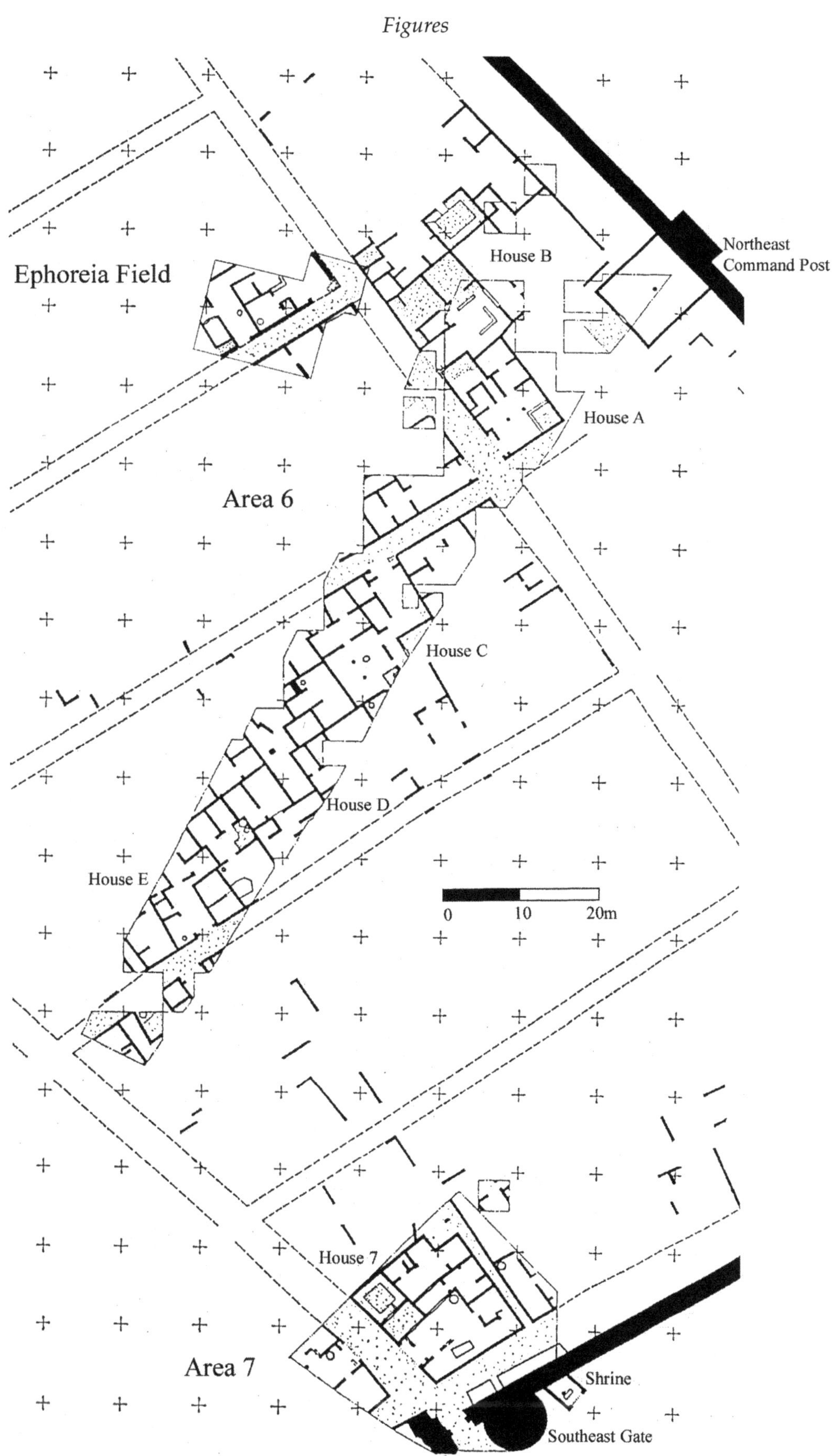

Figure 2. Areas 6 and 7

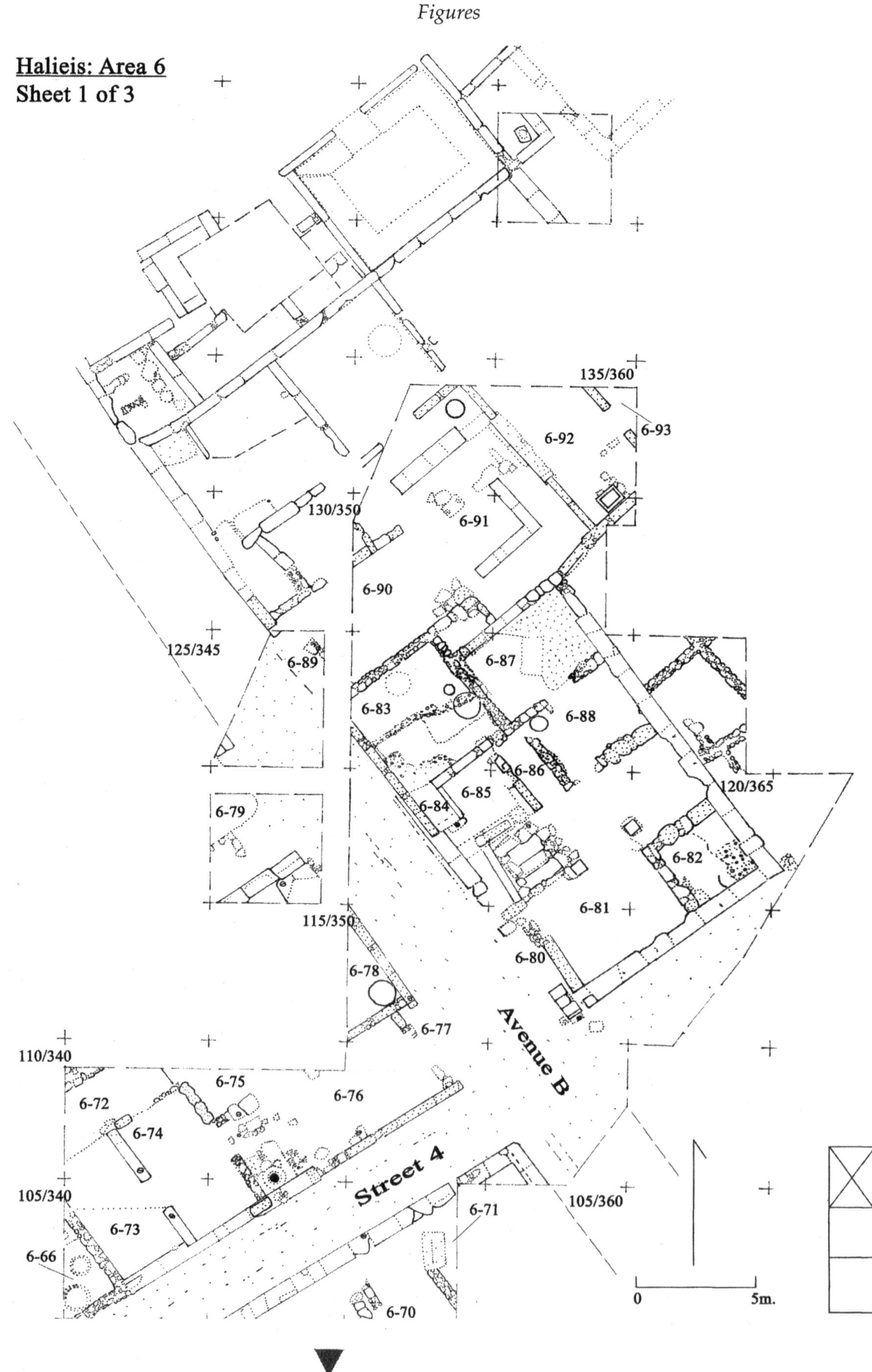

Figure 3. Area 6: northern third (actual state)

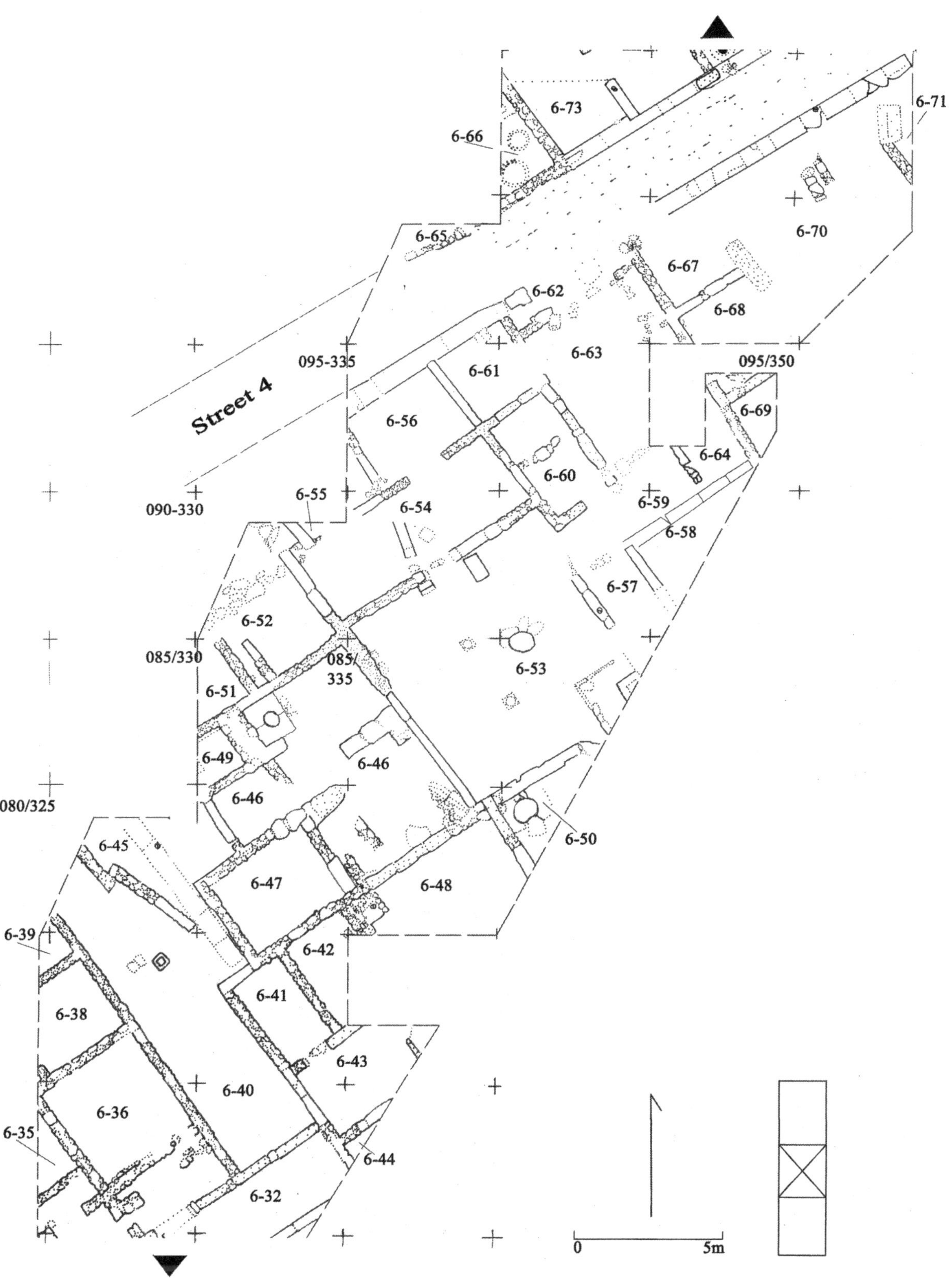

Figure 4. Area 6: central third (actual state)

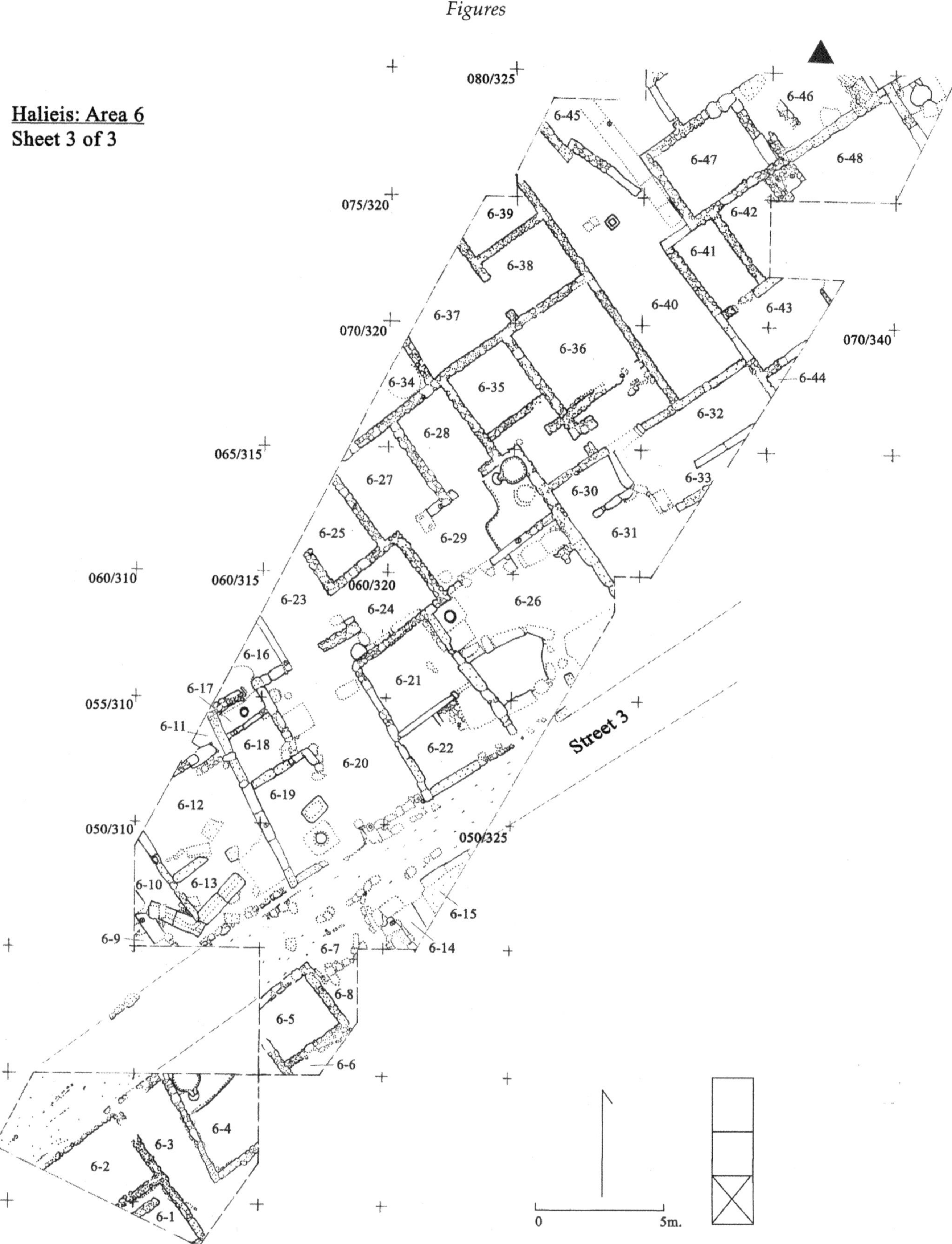

Figure 5. Area 6: southern third (actual state)

Halieis: Area 7

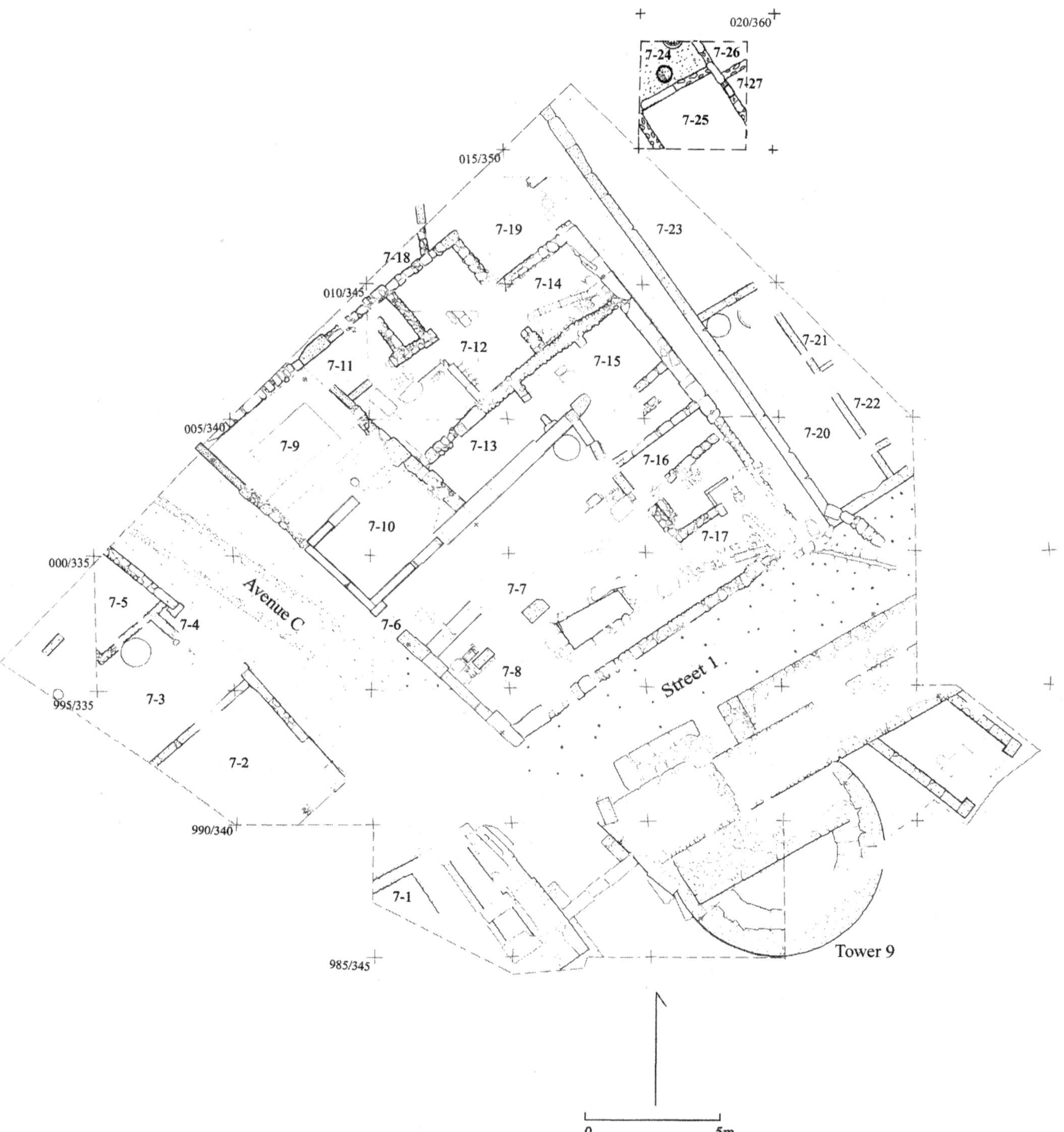

Figure 6. Area 7 (actual state)

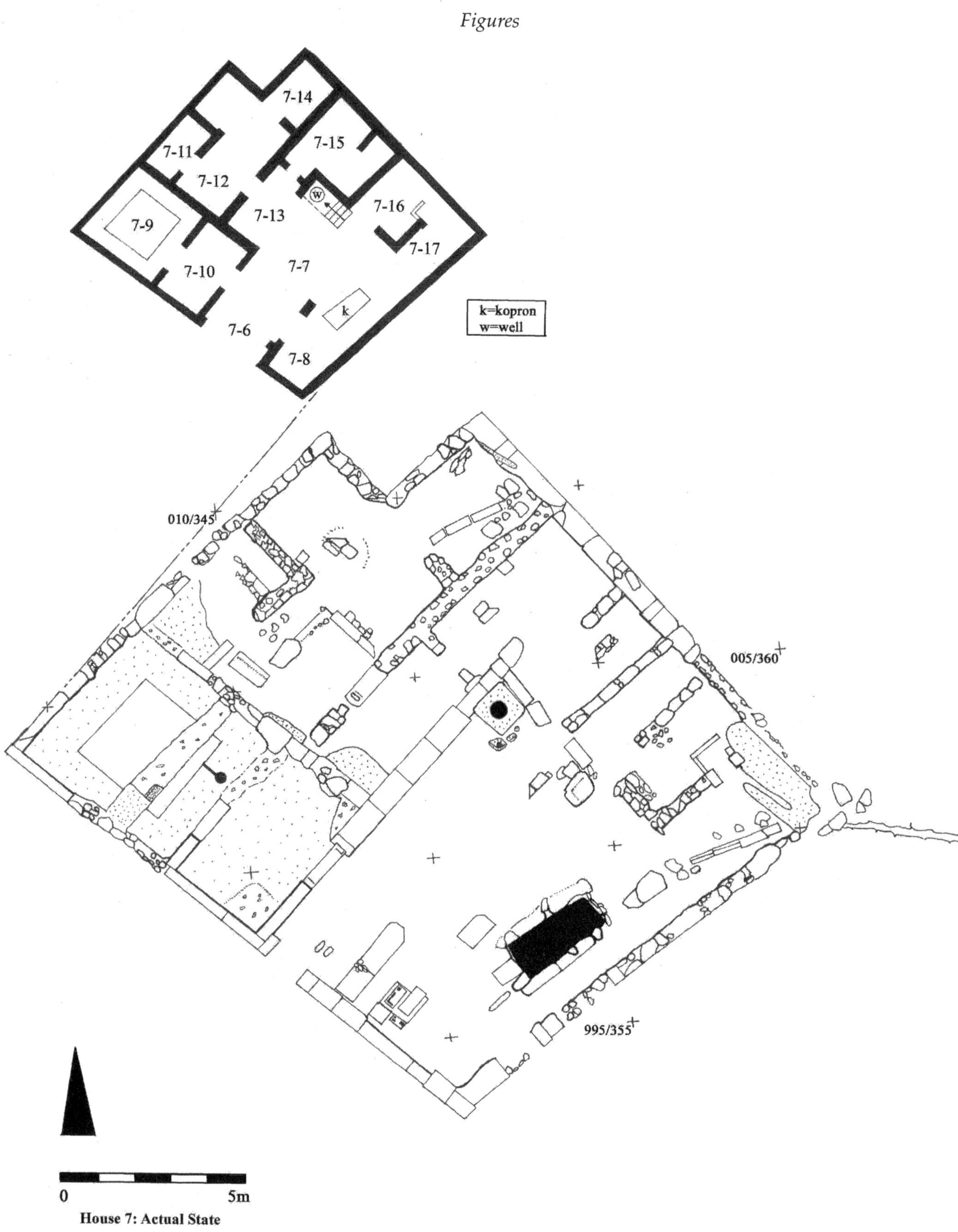

Figure 7. House 7: actual state and small schematic

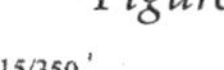

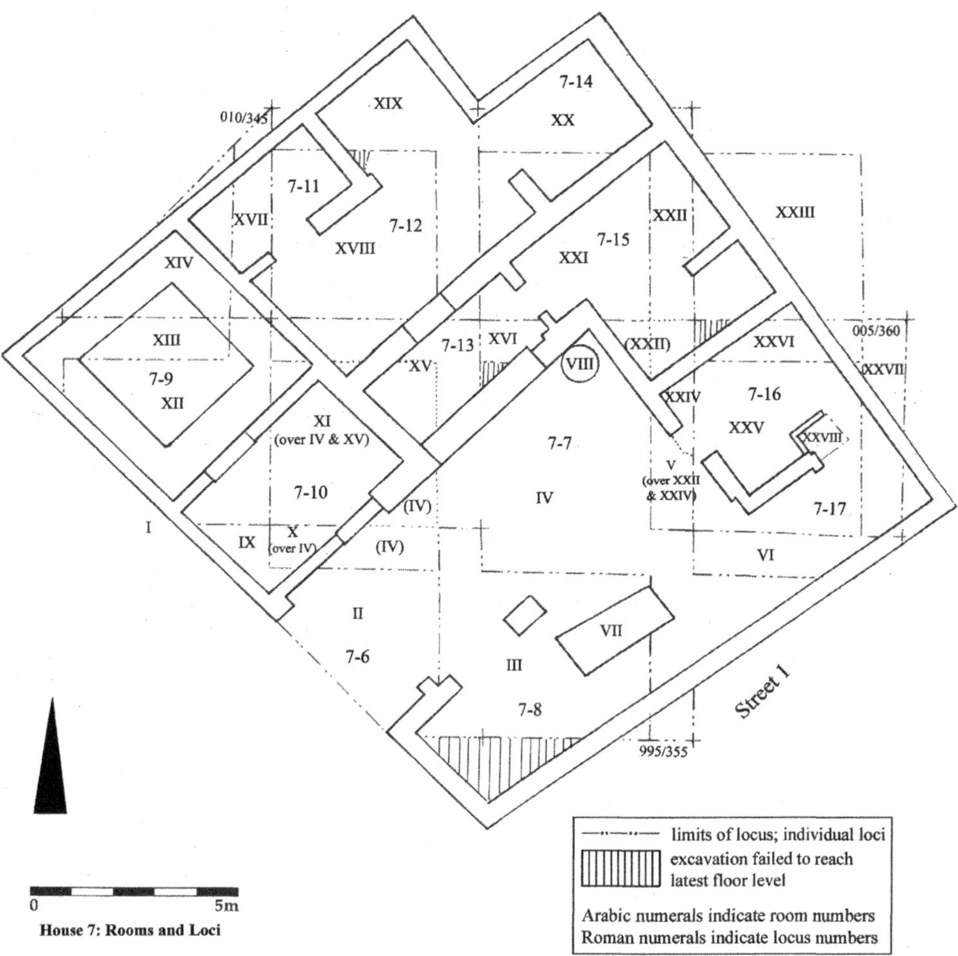

Figure 8. House 7: rooms and loci

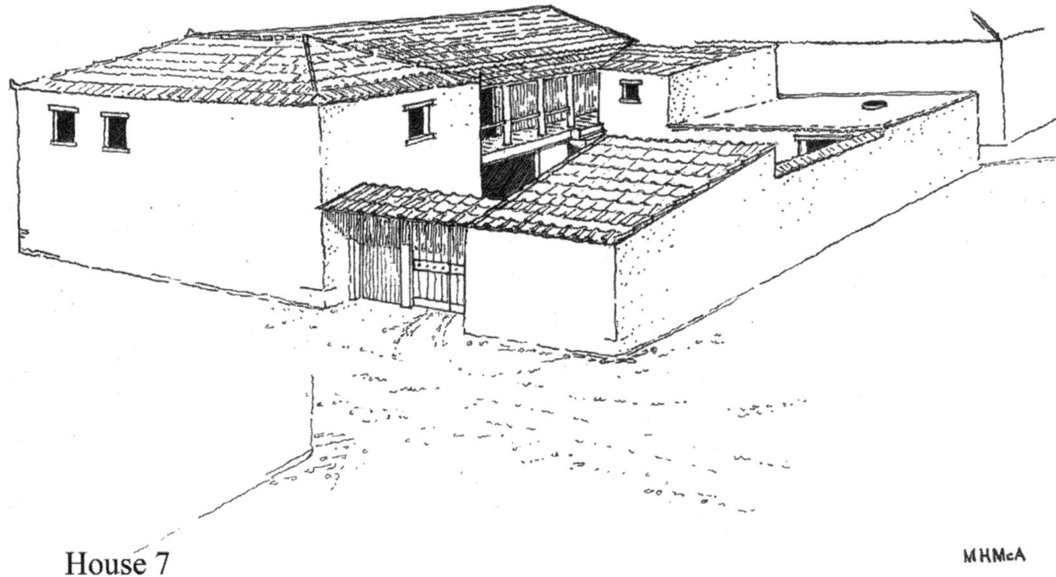

Figure 9. House 7: reconstruction

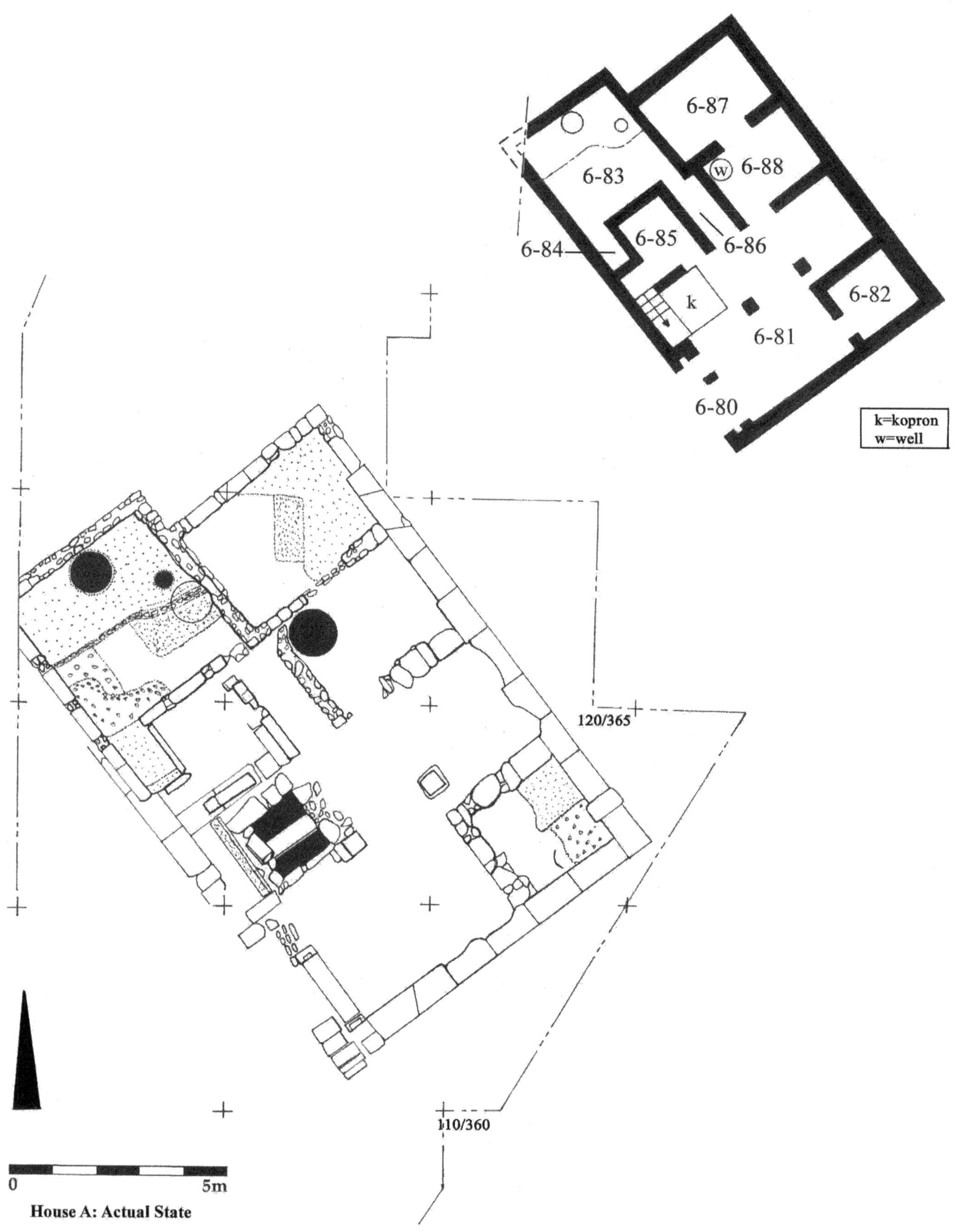

Figure 10. House A: actual state and small schematic

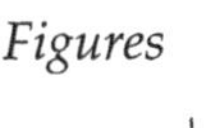

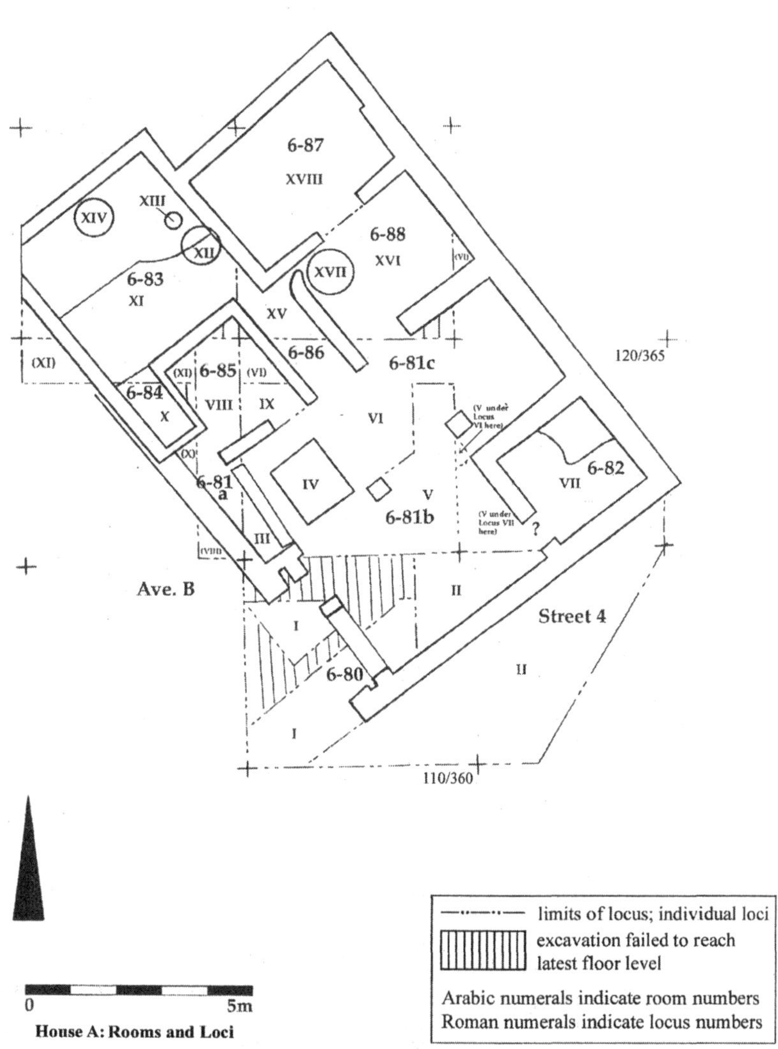

Figure 11. House A: rooms and loci

House A

Figure 12. House A: reconstruction

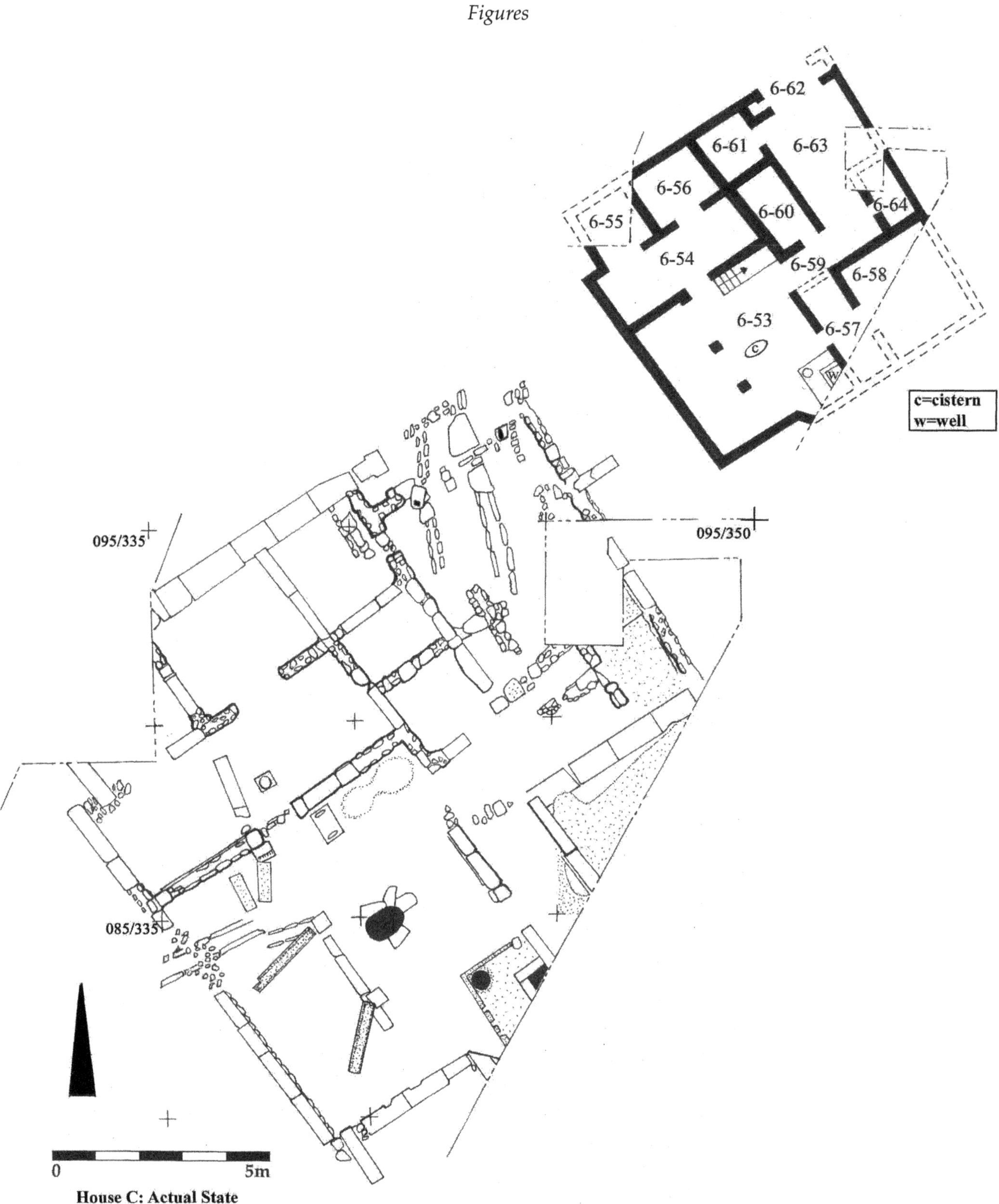

Figure 13. House C: actual state and small schematic

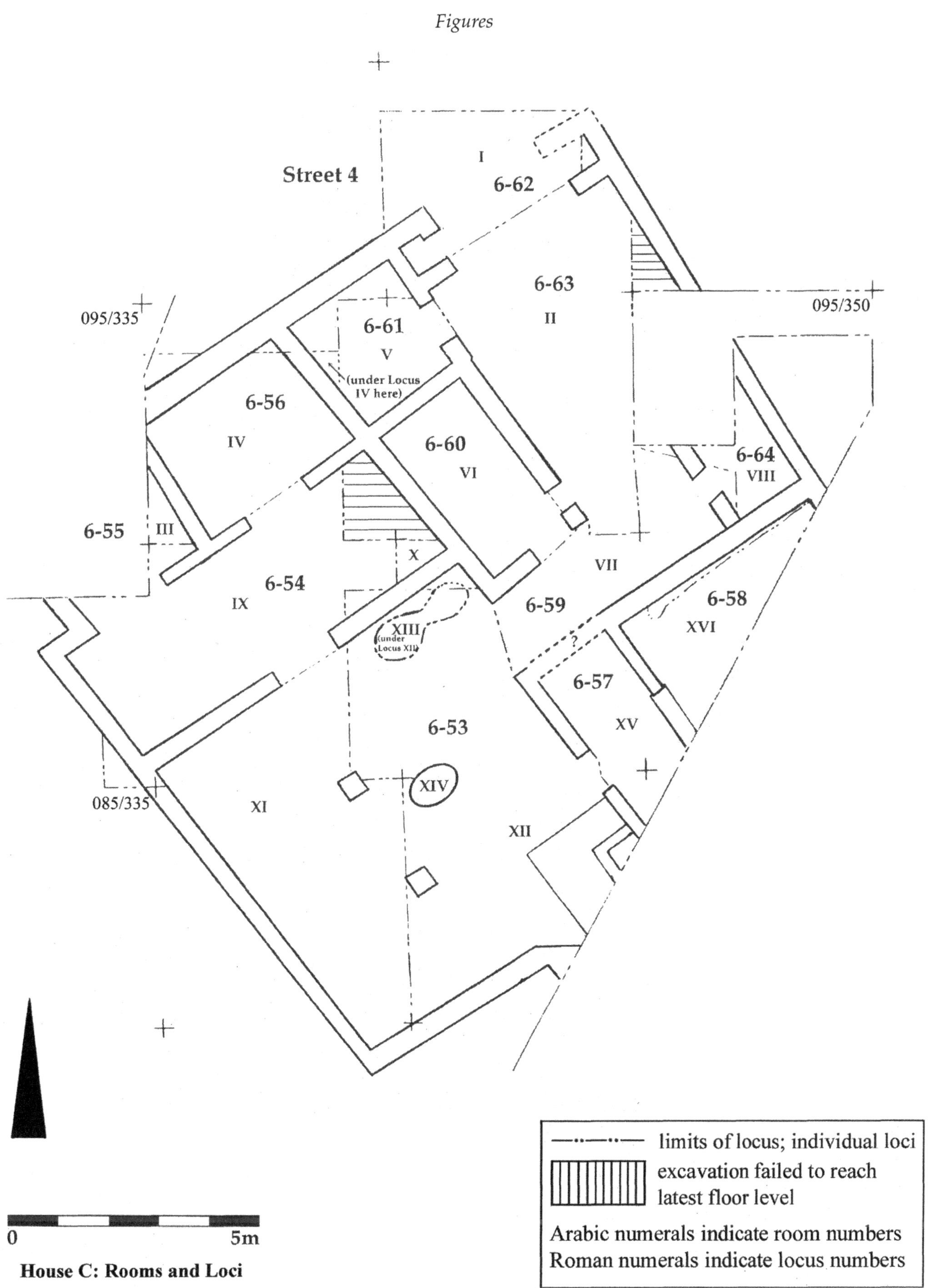

Figure 14. House C: rooms and loci

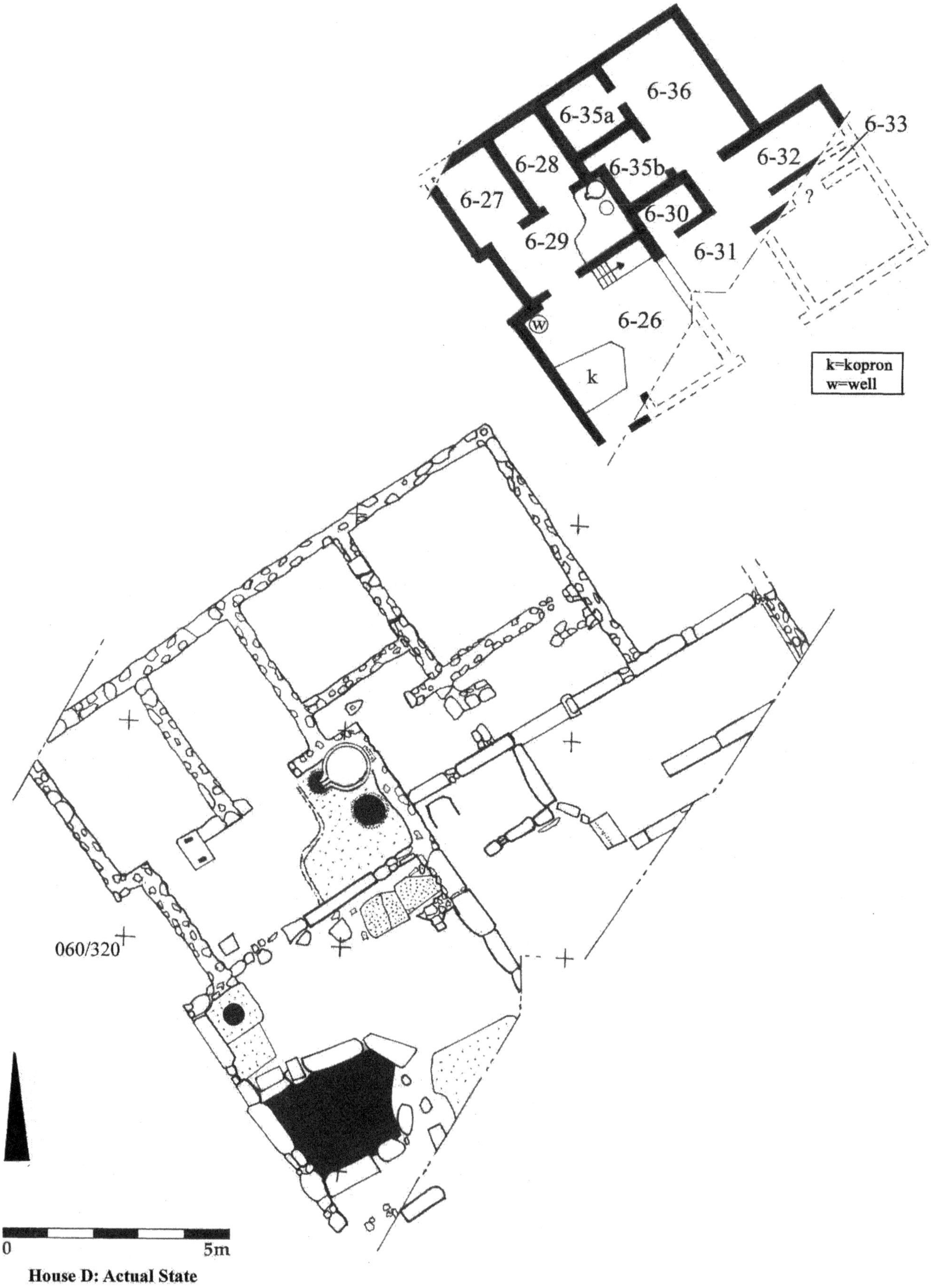

k=kopron
w=well

House D: Actual State

Figure 15. House D: actual state and small schematic

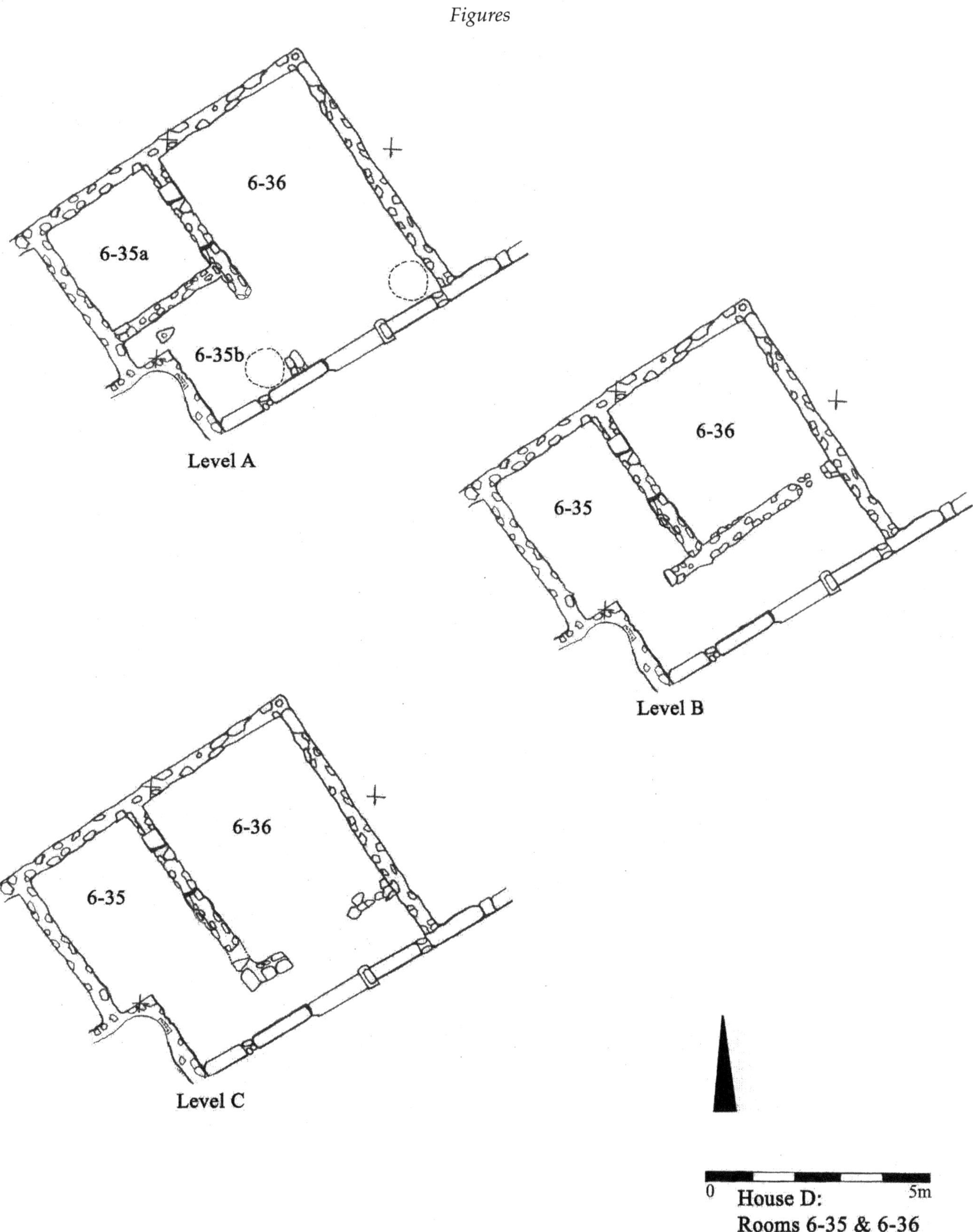

Figure 16. House D: Rooms 6-35 and 6-36 in Levels A–C

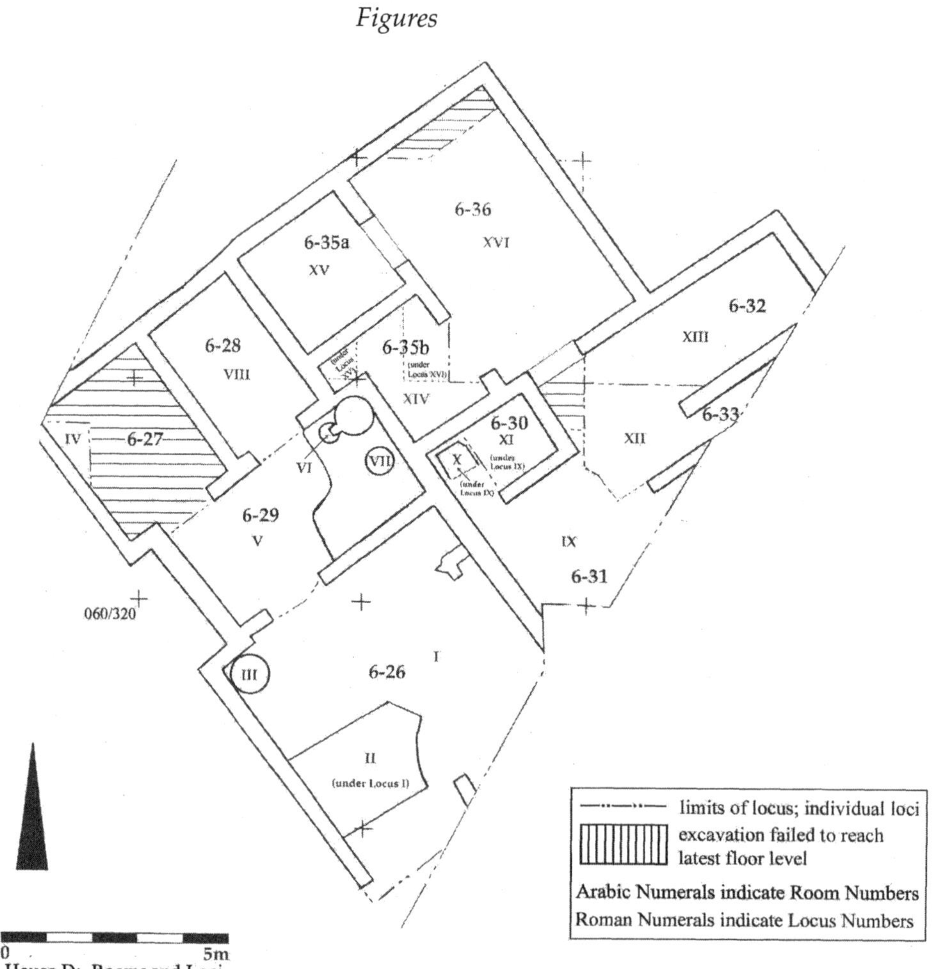

Figure 17. House D: rooms and loci

Houses E & D

Figure 18. Houses E and D: reconstruction

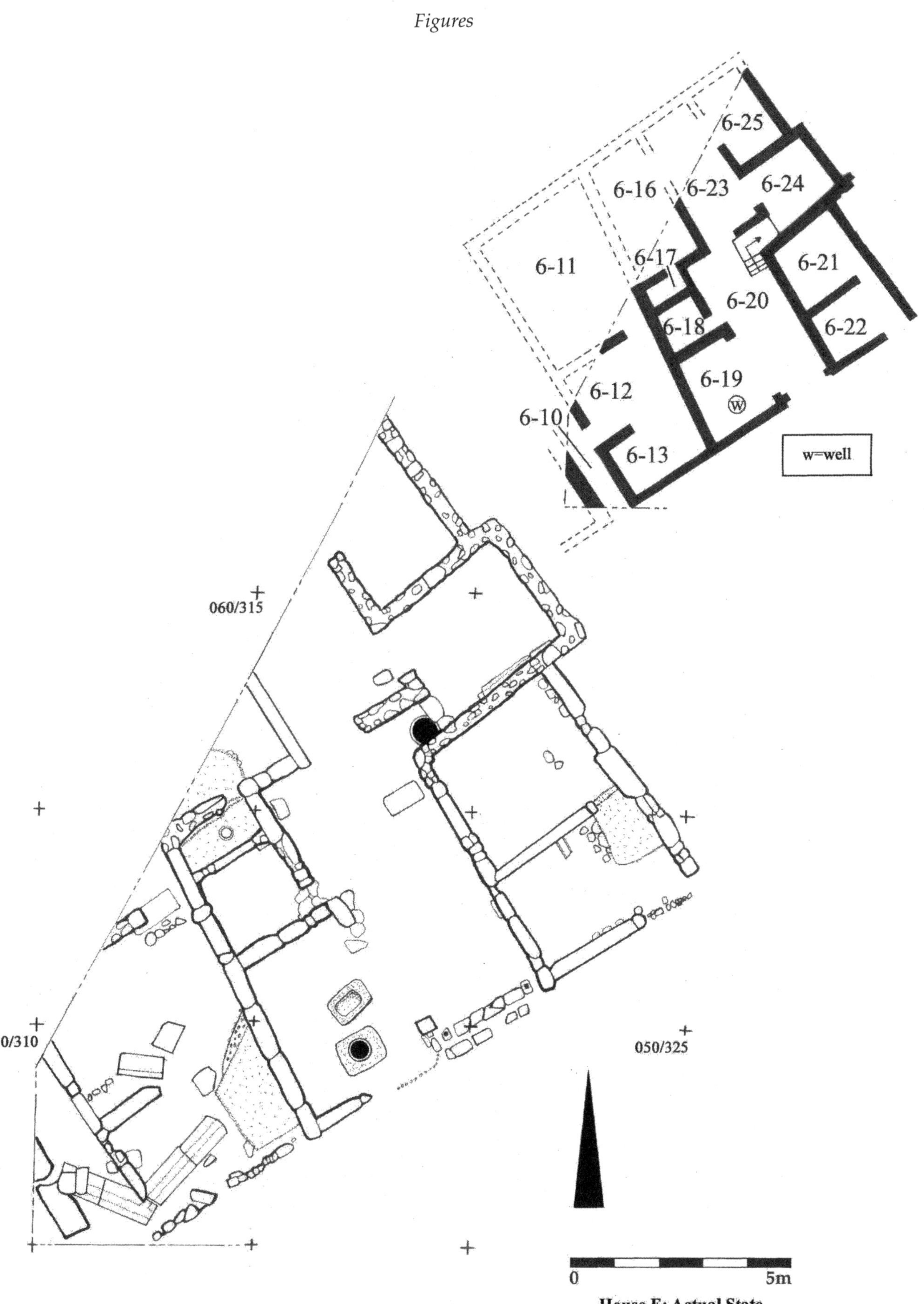

Figure 19. House E: actual state and small schematic

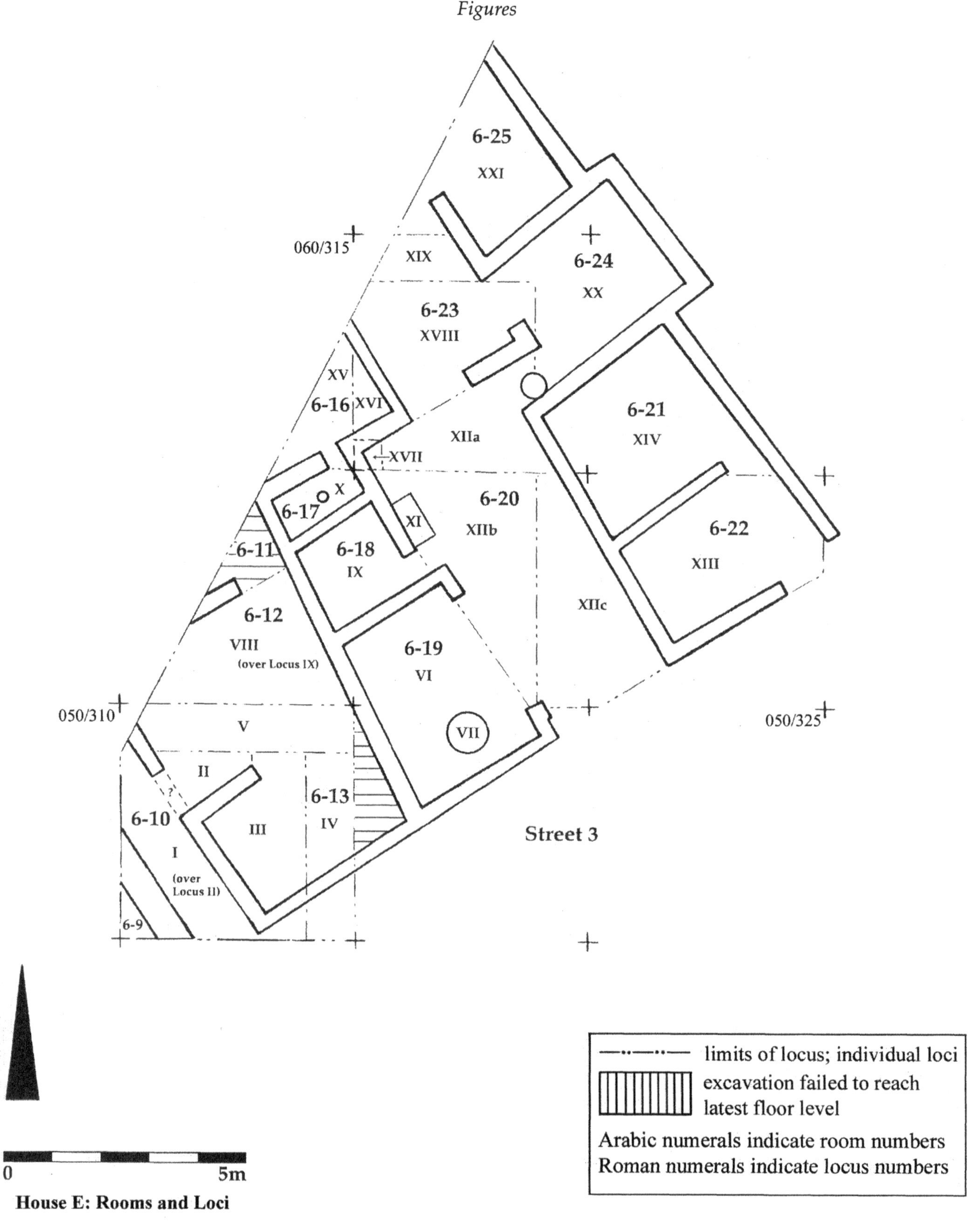

Figure 20. House E: rooms and loci

Plates

Plate 1. Areas 6 and 7: balloon photo

Plate 2. Area 7: balloon photo

Plate 3. General view of Area 7 before 1975 excavations, from west

Plate 4. Rooms 7-3, 7-4 (prothyron), and 7-5, from northeast (TR 000/340)

Plate 5. Room 7-20 (with press bed), ambitus, and Room 7-15, from northeast (TR 010/360)

Plate 6. Rooms 7-24–7-27, from northeast (TR 020/360)

Plate 7. Room 7-6 (prothyron), from southwest in Ave. C (TR 000/350)

Plate 8. Kopron (Room 7-7), from northeast side (TR 000/355)

Plate 9. Room 7-9: in situ pottery in basin of andron platform (TR 005/345)

Plate 10. Room 7-9: cut-away strip of andron floor, from northeast (TR 005/345)

Plate 11. Rooms 7–11 and 7–12, from northeast; stony built feature below latest floor surface of Room 7–12 (TR 010/350)

Plate 12. Room 7-16, from southwest (in Room 7-7), with Room 7-17 (and hearth) to right (TR 005/360)

Plate 13. View northwest up ambitus with Room 7-17 on left (TR 005/360)

Plate 14. Room 6-91 (courtyard) from north corner, with well in foreground, and Room 6-92 on left (TR 135/355)

Plate 15. View northeast from Room 6-91 (courtyard) to Rooms 6-92 and 6-93 (TR135/360)

Plate 16. Andron of House B, from northeast (Area T)

Plate 17. Andron and kitchen of House B, from south (Area T)

Plate 18. Kitchen in House B, from southeast (Area T)

Plate 19. Cement-paved bath off kitchen in House B, from southwest (Area T)

Plate 20. Cement-paved bath off kitchen in House B, from northwest (Area T)

Plate 21. Area 6: northern portion, view to southwest

Plate 22. Area 6: view southwest from TR 075/325 (Room 6-37 in right foreground)

Plate 23. Rooms 6-66 and 6-73, from northwest (TR105/345)

Plate 24. Room 6-76: pithos-headed well, from northwest (TR 110/350)

Plate 25. Room 6-74: red and white painted plaster in southwest corner (TR 105/345)

Plate 26. Room 6-40: view south with tile fall in north balk of TR 075/330; pillar and altar visible within debris

Plate 27. Room 6-40: view west over north balk of TR 075/330 with tile fall, pillar and altar

Plate 28. Room 6-40: view of pillar and altar, from southwest (TR 075/33)

Plate 29. View southeast to House D, Rooms 6-35a and 6-35b, with Room 6-34 in right foreground

Plate 30. Room 6-41, from northwest side (TR 105/345)

Plate 31. Room 6-4, with press bed, from east (TR 040/315)

Plate 32. House A: balloon photo

Plate 33. Rooms 6-80 and 6-81: view northeast across prothyron into court

Plate 34. House A: southern half from south corner (in Street 4)

Plate 35. House A: view southwest over central section, from northeast side of Room 6-81c

Plate 36. Kopron (Room 6-81) with tile fill, from southwest side

Plate 37. Kopron (Room 6-81) emptied of fill, from east; fallen door jamb on southwest side (TR 120/360)

Plate 38. Room 6-82 (andron?) from east corner

Plate 39. House A: view southeast along central axis; Room 6-86 in middle ground

Plate 40. House A: northwest quarter with kitchen/bath complex (Rooms 6-83 and 6-84), from southeast (in Room 6-85)

Plate 41. House A: northern half, from southwest side (from Avenue B, outside Room 6-83)

Plate 42. House A: northern half, from north corner, with Rooms 6-87 and 6-88 in foreground

Plate 43. Room 6-88, from west (TR125/360)

Plate 44. Area of House C: balloon photo

Plate 45. Street 4, Room 6-62 (prothyron), and northwest end of Room 6-63, from above (TR100/345)

Plate 46. Rooms 6-63 and 6-62: westernmost drain, from south (TR 095/345)

Plate 47. Room 6-60: view from north corner with hopper mill exposed and pithos in southwest corner (TR 095/345)

Plate 48. Room 6-53 (porticoed courtyard): view from east side with fallen columns and well platform (cistern mouth not yet exposed)

Plate 49. Rooms 6-54 (transverse hall) and 6-53 (porticoed courtyard), from northwest (TR 085/340, TR 085/345, TR 090/340, TR 090/345)

Plate 50. Fallen sandstone pilaster in Room 6-53 (courtyard) and Doric capital in Room 6-54 (transverse hall), from southeast (TR 090/340)

Plate 51. Room 6-53 (courtyard): well platform in southeast corner, from northwest (TR 085/345; tile fall showing in north scarp)

Plate 52. Room 6-53 (courtyard): northeast corner, with tile fall in western plaster-lined hollow and eastern plaster-lined hollow emptied out (TR 090/340, TR 090/345)

Plate 53. Room 6-54 (transverse hall) with wall plaster and Doric capital in situ (TR 090/340)

Plate 54. Area of House D: balloon photo

Plate 55. Kopron (Room 6-26) with fill intact, from northeast

Plate 56. Kopron (Room 6-26) emptied of fill, from northeast

Plate 57. Pan tiles from kopron in Room 6-26

Plate 58. Cover tiles from kopron in Room 6-26

Plate 59. Room 6-29 (with press) from northwest corner of Room 6-26 (court)

Plate 60. Rooms 6-35 and 6-36: view north from south corner of Room 6-35b showing early walls (TR 070/330)

Plate 61. Room 6-35b: pottery deposit in east corner (TR 065/330)

Plate 62. Area of House E: balloon photo

Plate 63. View southeast across Rooms 6-17 (bath) and 6-18, to Room 6-20 (court) and prothyron

Plate 64. Room 6-19: view from northwest corner showing fallen door jamb, trough, and wellhead (TR 050/320)

Plate 65. Room 6-19: detail of wellhead, from east (TR 050/320)

Plate 66. View southwest in Room 6-20 (courtyard) to negative feature, rubble spread, and Rooms 6-18 and 6-19

Plate 67. View west from Room 6-21 across Room 6-20 (courtyard; stair base and bothroi) to Rooms 6-16 and 6-17 (kitchen and bath unit), and Room 6-18

Plate 68. Room 6-17 (bath; TR 055/315), from Room 6-16 to north

Plate 69. Room 6-24: inscribed blocks HS 532 and HS 533 from southeast; miniature kotyle behind and bolsal to left (TR 060/320)

Plate 70. Room 6-24: inscribed blocks HS 532 and HS 533 from northeast; miniature kotyle behind (TR 060/320)

Plate 71. View west down Street 3 to Room 6-13 (TR 050/315–050/320)

Plate 72. Andron in Area T, from west

Plate 73. Andron in Area T, detail of plaster feature: "feet"

Plates

www.ingramcontent.com/pod-product-compliance
Lightning Source LLC
LaVergne TN
LVHW071148090826
844660LV00059B/291

* 9 7 8 0 2 5 3 3 4 7 0 9 1 *